D1177157

Managing Leviathan

Managing Leviathan

Environmental Politics
and the Administrative State

Second Edition
Revised

edited by
Robert Paehlke and Douglas Torgerson

broadview press

©2005 Robert Paehlke and Douglas Torgerson

All rights reserved. The use of any part of this publication reproduced, transmitted in any form or by any means, electronic, mechanical, photocopying, recording, or otherwise, or stored in a retrieval system, without prior written consent of the publisher — or in the case of photocopying, a licence from Access Copyright (Canadian Copyright Licensing Agency), One Yonge Street, Suite 1900, Toronto, Ontario M5E 1E5 — is an infringement of the copyright law.

Library and Archives Canada Cataloguing in Publication

Managing Leviathan : environmental politics and the administrative state / edited by Robert Paehlke and Douglas Torgerson.—2nd ed. rev.

Includes bibliographical references and index.
ISBN 1-55111-583-2

1. Environmental policy.   2. Bureaucracy.   I. Paehlke, Robert II. Torgerson, Douglas, 1948-

HC120.E5M36 2005   363.7'056   C2004-907184-X

Broadview Press Ltd. is an independent, international publishing house, incorporated in 1985. Broadview believes in shared ownership, both with its employees and with the general public; since the year 2000 Broadview shares have traded publicly on the Toronto Venture Exchange under the symbol BDP.

We welcome comments and suggestions regarding any aspect of our publications — please feel free to contact us at the addresses below or at broadview@broadviewpress.com / w ww.broadviewpress.com.

North America
Post Office Box 1243, Peterborough, Ontario, Canada K9J 7H5
3576 California Road, Orchard Park, NY, USA 14127
Tel: (705) 743-8990; Fax: (705) 743-8353;
e-mail: customerservice@broadviewpress.com

UK, Ireland, and continental Europe
NBN Plymbridge, Estover Road, Plymouth PL6 7PY UK
Tel: 44 (0) 1752 202301 Fax: 44 (0) 1752 202331
Fax Order Line: 44 (0) 1752 202333
Customer Service: cservs@nbnplymbridge.com Orders: orders@nbnplymbridge.com

Australia and New Zealand
UNIREPS, University of New South Wales
Sydney, NSW, 2052
Tel: 61 2 9664 0999; Fax: 61 2 9664 5420
email: info.press@unsw.edu.au

Broadview Press gratefully acknowledges the support of the Ministry of Canadian Heritage through the Book Publishing Industry Development Program.

Typesetting and assembly: True to Type Inc., Mississauga, Canada.

PRINTED IN CANADA

Contents

Acknowledgements / vii
Notes on Contributors / ix
Preface to the Second Edition / xi
Preface to the First Edition / xiii

PART I: THE ENVIRONMENT AS AN ADMINISTRATIVE PROBLEM

1 Environmental Administration: Revising the Agenda of Inquiry and Practice
Douglas Torgerson and Robert Paehlke / 3

2 Obsolescent Leviathan: Problems of Order in Administrative Thought
Douglas Torgerson / 11

3 Democracy and Environmentalism: Opening a Door to the Administrative State?
Robert Paehlke / 25

PART II: TECHNIQUES AND PROCESSES OF ENVIRONMENTAL ADMINISTRATION

4 Ecological Reason in Administration: Environmental Impact Assessment and Green Politics
Robert V. Bartlett / 47

5 Environmental Regulation and Risk-Benefit Analysis: From Technical to Deliberative Policy Making
Frank Fischer / 59

6 Designs for Environmental Discourse Revisited: A Greener Administrative State?
John S. Dryzek / 81

7 The Ambivalence of Discourse: Beyond the Administrative Mind?
Douglas Torgerson / 97

PART III: THE POLITICS OF ENVIRONMENTAL ADMINISTRATION

8 Class, Place, and Citizenship: The Changing Dynamics of Environmental Protection
Ted Schrecker / 125

9 We Just Don't Know: Lessons about Complexity and Uncertainty in
   Canadian Environmental Politics
   Robert B. Gibson / 145

10 Environmental Politics and Policy Professionalism: Agenda Setting,
    Problem Definition, and Epistemology
    Douglas Torgerson / 171

11 Depoliticizing Environmental Politics: Sustainable Development
    in Norway
    Ingerid S. Straume / 191

12 Democratic Deliberation and Environmental Policy: Opportunities
    and Barriers in Britain
    Graham Smith / 209

13 Outside the State: Australian Green Politics and the Public Inquiry
    into Uranium
    Timothy Doyle / 235

14 Participation and Agency: Hybrid Identities in the European Quest
    for Sustainable Development
    Andrew Jamison / 257

15 Responses to Environmental Threats in an Age of Globalization
    Jennifer Clapp / 271

16 Green Governance and the Green State: Capacity Building as a Political
    Project
    Peter Christoff / 289

CONCLUSION

17 Environmental Politics and the Administrative State
    Robert Paehlke and Douglas Torgerson / 313

Index / 327

Acknowledgements

For funding in support of parts of the work on this edition, the editors thank the Frost Centre, Trent University, and the Committee on Research, Trent University. Many of the chapters in this edition appear for the first time here (these are designated below as "new"). Others, with one exception, are drawn from material published in the first edition (extent of change is noted below in each case). Chapter numbers below refer to this edition. Page numbers refer to the first edition (except in one instance, as indicated, to a journal). Earlier sources for some of the material drawn from the first edition are listed in the Acknowledgements to that edition. All material is used here in accordance with copyright:

Preface to the First Edition (penultimate paragraph deleted), pp. 1–4; Torgerson and Paehlke, ch. 1 (minor corrections), pp. 7–16; Torgerson, ch. 2 (minor corrections), pp. 17–33; Paehlke, ch. 3 (revision), pp. 35–55; Bartlett, ch. 4 (revision), pp. 81–96; Fischer, ch. 5 (new); Dryzek, ch. 6 (revision), pp. 97–111; Torgerson, ch. 7 (substantial revision), pp. 115–61; Schrecker, ch. 8 (substantial revision), pp. 165–99; Gibson, ch. 9 (substantial revision), pp. 243–57; Torgerson, ch. 10 (revision), *Polity* 9, pp. 345–74; Straume, ch. 11 (new); Smith, ch. 12 (new); Doyle, ch. 13 (new); Jamieson, ch. 14 (new); Clapp, ch. 15 (new); Christoff, ch. 16 (new); Torgerson and Paehlke, ch. 17 (revision), pp. 285-301.

Notes on Contributors

Robert V. Bartlett of Purdue University was the visiting Frank Church Distinguished Professor of Public Policy at Boise State University in 2003–04. He has published many articles and book chapters and is the author, co-author, or editor of eight books or monographs on environmental politics, including *Deliberative Environmental Politics* (MIT, forthcoming).

Peter Christoff is coordinator of environmental studies in the School of Anthropology, Geography and Environmental Studies (SAGES) at the University of Melbourne. He is the author of numerous chapters and articles on Australian environmental policy and politics, as well as on ecological modernization and ecological citizenship. He is also vice-president of the Australian Conservation Foundation.

Jennifer Clapp is associate professor of international development studies and environmental and resource studies at Trent University. Her publications focus on the interface between the global economy and the environment, and include *Toxic Exports: The Transfer of Hazardous Wastes from Rich to Poor Countries* (Cornell, 2001) and *Paths to a Green World: The Political Economy of the Global Environment* (co-authored with Peter Dauvergne, MIT, 2005). She is also associate editor of the journal *Global Environmental Politics*.

Timothy Doyle is reader in the School of History and Politics at the University of Adelaide, where he teaches and researches politics and environmental studies. In his academic capacity, he has taught and contributed to university courses in the United Kingdom, the United States, Malaysia, India, and Australia. He has recently published *Environmental Movements in Majority and Minority Worlds* (Rutgers, 2005), *Environment and Politics* (co-author, Routledge, second edition, 2001), and *Green Power* (University of New South Wales, 2000).

John S. Dryzek is professor of political science and social and political theory, Research School of Social Sciences, Australian National University. His recent books include *Deliberative Democracy and Beyond* (Oxford, 2000), *Post-Communist Democratization* (co-author, Cambridge, 2002), and *Green States and Social Movements: Environmentalism in the United States, United Kingdom, Germany, and Norway* (co-author, Oxford, 2003).

Frank Fischer is professor of political science at Rutgers University and member of the Center for Global Change and Governance. His most recent books are

Citizens, Experts, and the Environment: The Politics of Local Knowledge (Duke, 2000) and *Reframing Public Policy: Discursive Politics and Deliberative Practices* (Oxford, 2003).

Robert B. Gibson is professor of environment and resource studies at the University of Waterloo. He specializes in environmental policy issues and the integration of broad sustainability considerations in urban growth management, corporate greening initiatives, and environmental assessments at the project and strategic levels. He has been co-editor and editor of *Alternatives Journal* since 1984.

Andrew Jamison is professor of technology and society in the Department of Development and Planning, Aalborg University. He has written on environmental politics for over 30 years, from his first book, *The Steam-Powered Automobile: An Answer to Air Pollution* (Indiana, 1970), to his most recent, *The Making of Green Knowledge: Environmental Politics and Cultural Transformation* (Cambridge, 2002).

Robert Paehlke is professor in the Environmental and Resource Studies Program at Trent University. His books include *Environmentalism and the Future of Progressive Politics* (Yale, 1989) and *Democracy's Dilemma: Environment, Social Equity and the Global Economy* (MIT, 2003). He is a founding editor (1971) of *Alternatives Journal* and editor of *Conservation and Environment: An Encyclopedia* (Taylor & Francis, 1995).

Ted Schrecker is a political scientist and a senior policy researcher at the Institute of Population Health, University of Ottawa. He is a co-author of *Fatal Indifference: The G8, Africa and Global Health* (University of Cape Town Press, 2004), the editor of *Surviving Globalism: The Social and Environmental Challenges* (Macmillan, 1997), and has published widely on environmental policy and law.

Graham Smith is a senior lecturer in politics and international relations at the University of Southampton. He is the author of *Deliberative Democracy and the Environment* (Routledge, 2003) and *Politics and the Environment: From Theory to Practice* (with James Connelly, Routledge, second edition, 2003) and has published a number of essays on democratic and green political theory.

Ingerid S. Straume is a doctoral candidate at the Institute for Educational Research at the University of Oslo, where she has lectured on democracy and the value of political life. She has completed a master's thesis and published articles on Local Agenda 21, environmentalism, and democracy. Her current doctoral thesis is in the philosophy of education with particular attention to the political thought of Cornelius Castoriadis.

Douglas Torgerson is professor of political studies, environmental and resource studies, and cultural studies at Trent University. There he is director of the Center for the Study of Theory, Culture, and Politics and was previously director of Administrative and Policy Studies. He is the author of *The Promise of Green Politics: Environmentalism and the Public* Sphere (Duke, 1999) and past editor of *Alternatives Journal* and *Policy Sciences.*

Preface to the Second Edition

Environmentalism emerged on the public scene in two great waves of activism and attention, the first coming in the late 1960s and early 1970s and the second following in the late 1980s and early 1990s. Published fifteen years ago in the midst of the second wave, the first edition of this book set out to advance a change in the agenda of inquiry and practice by proposing an alternative orientation to environmental administration. The formulation of that orientation remains essentially unaltered in this edition (stated without change in the preface to the first edition and in ch. 1, while being restated in a slightly revised manner in the conclusion, ch. 16).

The orientation of this book is now more well developed and established in the administrative and policy literature than it was fifteen years ago. This orientation now clearly intersects with widespread efforts to shape administration and policy along lines that coincide with deliberative—or discursive—approaches to democracy. That connection, intimated in the first edition, becomes emphatic in many new and revised chapters in this edition. Our main point remains, however, that we wish to promote work along these lines on the ground that such innovation appears to be more instrumentally effective in responding to environmental challenges than conventional approaches. Although we generally agree with the view that endorses deliberative approaches to democracy because of their greater democratic legitimacy, that is a separate point and not one on which we are especially concerned to focus attention with this book.

One thing that has clearly changed since the first edition is the context. Environmentalism obviously does not now have the salience that it had in the midst of the second wave, which culminated in the Earth Summit that was held in Rio de Janeiro under the auspices of the United Nations in 1992. In assessing the current status of environmentalism, however, we are not much interested in simply taking a snapshot. We prefer to consider things in a larger historical context. In that context, we believe that environmentalism continues to have its ups and downs. Environmentalism may not be at the crest of one of its waves, but neither is it going away any time soon. Environmental concerns are now firmly entrenched on an increasingly global scale, institutionalized in state and quasi-state agencies as well as in civil society. Moreover, the object of that concern—crisis tendencies in the environment—has, to say the least, hardly become any less significant.

What is most remarkable about the current context, in regard to the industrially advanced countries, is the emergence of American exceptionalism. Antienvironmentalism was already dramatically and scandalously obvious in the United States under the administration of Ronald Reagan. However, American exceptionalism on the global stage was first clearly prefigured by George H.W. Bush at the Rio Earth Summit and was later underscored by George W. Bush's rejection of the Kyoto climate change accord. Even when the American administration is not anti-environmentalist and, indeed, promises to embrace environmental causes, the tight tensions and balances of US federal politics make difficult any determined advance in this regard—as can be seen in the disappointing outcomes under Bill Clinton and Al Gore. This means that imaginative experimentation with environmental administration and policy is now more likely to come from elsewhere. To say that does not mean that there is no room in America for innovation, but it is likely to come only in spite of the federal government, perhaps regardless of which party holds the White House. Places where we find scope for environmental innovation in the US are at the municipal and state levels and even within the private sector. On the whole, nonetheless, there is vastly more innovation in Europe, and it is at times promoted at high governmental and administrative levels. For example, in Europe the idea of ecological modernization has emerged significantly over the past decade or so. This is obviously no magic wand, and there is undoubtedly much to criticize about this idea and its implementation, as well as other European developments. Still, in Europe there is at least a discursive context in which environmental issues are officially deemed important. Discourse in America, by contrast, involves intense struggle over the relevance and reality of environmental concerns that are taken for granted on the European scene. Substantial developments along the lines we endorse would thus seem more likely to emerge there, at least initially, than in the United States.

The case material in this edition is extensively revised. In the first edition, material was deliberately focused almost exclusively on the US and Canada, offering little attention to comparative or international issues. (The original preface noted this focus in its penultimate paragraph, which has been deleted in this new edition.) Now the focus has been changed to include not only the US and Canada, but also Europe and Australia, as well as to incorporate greater attention to global concerns.

—The Editors

Preface to the First Edition (1990)

The calm voice of the official assures the public that the proper administrative procedures are in place: all is under control, and environmental protection can be taken for granted. Yet just when the populace seems lulled again into a sense of security, another environmental crisis captures the focus of popular attention. One after another, an apparently unending series of household words enters the language: acid rain, dioxins, PCBs, sewage sludge, ozone depletion, nuclear meltdown. Also newly thrust into the everyday vocabulary are names of environmental trouble-spots: Love Canal, Three Mile Island, Bhopal, Chernobyl, Valdez. The official image of order is each time, at least momentarily, jostled aside by an image of a world running out of control.

Environmental politics is alive with these conflicting images. In political and economic life, administrative organizations want to define environmental troubles as manageable problems that can be subjected to rules and procedures consistent with established priorities. To see environmental problems otherwise is portrayed as irrational and socially irresponsible, as threatening disorder. Yet even as some environmental activists tone down their rhetoric and gain legitimacy in public debates governed by the administrative idiom, events often overtake everyone: official assurances and compromise proposals ring hollow whenever a new disaster becomes visible. And many environmental activists remain fully opposed to the administrative world, viewing state and economy—the present organization of public and private power—as requiring nothing less than a total and immediate transformation. The alternative is catastrophe. They will have nothing to do with Leviathan.

Although official imagery can become unsettled, there remains a certain reflex response which seems sure to restore popular faith in Leviathan—in the administrative state, or more broadly, the centralized, hierarchical administrative form that dominates advanced industrial society. For a prevailing bias sees this as the only possible administrative form, and the effective management of environmental problems thus appears to demand support for this order and its outwardly sincere and competent efforts. Democracy itself seems somehow at odds with proper environmental management.

While the conventional administrative viewpoint is comfortable with this latter conclusion, the idea has also been voiced by a type of environmentalism which has rather desperately reached out for an authoritarian solution. The opposite environmentalist position—the flat rejection of the prevailing administrative apparatus—has yet to offer more than a vague belief in principles of decentralization, participatory democracy, and natural harmony. This rejection of administration is easily ridiculed and dismissed because it has produced little as yet by way of a plausible approach to problems of environmental management. The hard-headed realism of the administrative mind seems to confront nothing more substantial than a naïve sentimentalism.

An exploration of environmental politics and administration, this book is designed to directly counter the conventional administrative bias of centralization and hierarchy by questioning the nature of administration and its relationship to democracy. This focus directs attention as well to the context and definition of environmental problems.*

Often, democracy and administration are thought to be necessarily at odds; the debate is over which of the two should be sacrificed. Any defense of democracy will, indeed, be feeble on these terms if humanity faces serious environmental problems requiring effective administration. The terms of debate may shift dramatically, however, if we consider the potential for democracy and effective administration to be mutually supportive: then principles of decentralization and participation themselves become relevant to managing Leviathan. If democracy were necessary for the successful resolution of environmental problems, the tables would indeed be turned on the conventional administrative bias.

Contemporary developments in administrative theory have already challenged this bias: the variability, complexity, and political character of administrative situations have all been recognized. Decentralization and participation are increasingly viewed as instrumentally—as well as morally—valuable. This volume builds upon this tendency with essays emphasizing the political character of environmental administration and probing the potential of decentralization and participation for defining and resolving environmental problems.

To counter a prevailing bias, one need not offer a completed conception to replace it. At issue is a matter of orientation, and the task is to show the limits of a particular focus while identifying forces and interests which make that focus rigid, rendering it resistant to alternatives. By drawing attention to the resistances that sustain a bias, this effort promotes a reorientation but does not pretend to offer a neat and clear alternative. The goal of this volume is rather to help revise the agenda of inquiry and practice in environmental decision making. This does not mean necessarily substituting one bias for another (as some might be eager to say): the point, rather, is to open up questions which have been closed or which have never been clearly posed and considered—to encourage a more flexible orientation, attentive to the context and the constraints that shape inquiry and practice.

While guided by both environmental and democratic concerns, this volume is deliberately designed to be exploratory—in a sense, inconclusive. For example,

---

* The editors assume sole responsibility for the design and purpose of the volume as a whole. The authors are individually responsible for their particular articles.

the full potential of decentralization, often a focus of environmentalists, has certainly been neglected in administrative thought and practice. To say this, however, is not to argue that centralization in environmental management should or could simply be replaced with decentralization. Within the general reorientation that we propose, it is indeed a key tenet that the definition and solution of problems must take account of the complexities of particular contexts. Further work along these lines is a task for ourselves and others.

Overall, in recognizing a complex array of environmental problems, the latter part of this century has come in for a considerable shock. Despite efforts to absorb this shock through administrative imagery and routine, the recognition of environmental problems has been unsettling to the expectations of order and progress that have guided industrialization and helped to construct the edifice of modern administration. It is at least questionable whether the outlook promoting this pattern of development is capable of grasping and effectively handling the incalculable environmental impact that the pattern inadvertently generates. A re-examination of the conventional approach to environmental administration is thus surely in order.

If the approach advanced here has any validity, then decentralization and participation have a potential to promote the effective handling of environmental problems. We do not know precisely what this potential is, but hope that it might serve to improve both environmental protection and the prospects of enhancing democracy. Moving in this direction would certainly affect the management of Leviathan. Whether it could ultimately mean moving beyond Leviathan is another intriguing question—one that requires first, however, a revision of the present agenda of inquiry and practice.

—The Editors

PART I

The Environment as an Administrative Problem

If there is a problem, better management is often assumed to be the solution. This assumption has deeply influenced the rise of advanced industrial societies and now guides much of the response to environmental problems. The environmental challenge demands effective administration, and some fear that this may force a sacrifice of democracy. The image of Leviathan thus reassures even as it threatens.

We find another way of looking at the situation, however, if we focus on the limits of administration as it is conventionally conceived and practiced. Administrative organizations have been especially effective in dealing with narrowly defined problems. By and large, conventional administration seems to work so long as there is no need to worry about side-effects. The difficulty, however, is that the environment has emerged as a major problem precisely *as* an accumulation and interaction of side-effects.

There are, of course, specific problems of the environment which current administrative activities help to mitigate. But, despite particular successes—and no matter how ingenious and dedicated individual administrators may be—it does nonetheless seem that conventional administration ultimately confronts insurmountable obstacles to effective environmental management. The chapters in Part I focus on the nature of these obstacles and explore the prospect that they might be overcome through a revised, more democratic approach to administrative inquiry and practice.

1

Environmental Administration: Revising the Agenda of Inquiry and Practice

Douglas Torgerson and Robert Paehlke

Concern has often been voiced about the undemocratic tendencies of the administrative state. However, it has usually been thought that these tendencies must, to a large extent, be tolerated because of the administrative exigencies of an advanced economy and society. Complex problems are deemed to require a concentration of knowledge and power in centralized hierarchies. This alignment of knowledge and power has been considered unavoidable, albeit regrettable from a democratic perspective—an administrative necessity in the emergence of industrial civilization.

Now, we are told, industrialization faces a range of problems greatly exceeding in complexity those earlier confronted. The advent of environmental problems, in particular, poses difficulties that can be handled only through professional expertise and specialized organization. Notions of decentralization and public participation may have appeal, but they should not be allowed to interfere with the really serious business of administration in an advanced industrial society.[1]

Continued orderly development would thus necessitate Leviathan in the form of the administrative state. Even if this is not precisely Hobbes's Leviathan, an order governed by a central power of absolute authority—even, that is, if the principle of popular sovereignty is maintained along with formal institutions of democracy—the administrative state still remains set in the basic order of centralization and hierarchy which Hobbes discerned and encouraged in the early emergence of the modern state. Hence the hard, if sad, truth is that operating the administrative state—managing Leviathan—necessarily extracts sacrifices from democracy.[2]

We question the view that undemocratic measures are necessary for effective administration[3]—particularly given the advent of environmental problems. Even though there is now much discussion of the so-called NIMBY (not-in-my-back-yard) Syndrome and of popular resistance to necessary measures of environmental management, it was indeed a popular upsurge and sense of environmental crisis over three decades ago which gave rise to administrative reforms for environmental protection.

A landmark event in this regard was the establishment of the *National Environmental Policy Act* of 1969 in the United States. Passed in the midst of a fervor of environmental concern, this legislation required agencies of the federal government to prepare environmental impact statements for activities "significantly affecting the quality of the human environment." Against the backdrop of a burgeoning environmental movement, the proposed Trans-Alaska Pipeline was the first major project to be affected by the new legislation. By demanding that the requirements of environmental impact statements be rigorously observed and by initiating court action, environmental groups sought to slow governmental approval. While action in the courts was eventually undercut by what amounted to a Congressional exemption of the pipeline from the requirements of the legislation, the opposition of environmentalists did focus attention on a clear need: as industrialization expands into new territory—in both the technological and geographical sense—large projects require careful scrutiny even to accord with the interests of their proponents. In the case of the pipeline, environmentalists were able to demonstrate that the engineering plans first proposed were unsuited to Alaskan conditions: subsequent changes avoided a fiasco.[4]

The chances for effective environmental protection were clearly enhanced by public involvement—by challenges to the ensemble of public and private bureaucracies that would otherwise have been left to themselves to design, construct, operate, and regulate the pipeline. Here and elsewhere, indeed, it would seem that tendencies toward the effective handling of environmental problems come not because of bureaucracy, but in spite of it.

Do some problems arising in the aftermath of industrialization require significantly greater public participation and decentralized initiative than is normally allowed in the realm of the administrative state? Much evidence suggests so, but our point is not to offer a final answer to the question. What we recommend, instead, is simply for this question to counter prevailing presuppositions in favor of centralized hierarchy. In the context of these presuppositions, many possible initiatives that might simultaneously advance both democracy and effective administration appear implausible. For the possible to be discovered and rendered plausible requires a reorientation of administrative inquiry and innovation. What this volume as a whole presents is no general theory, then, but evidence and ideas to encourage new hypotheses and a reframing of problems.

Conventional approaches to administration presuppose a central position of planning and control, a unified will privileged by superior knowledge. Politics presupposes differences in interests and perspectives along with a dispersion of power; and this is what conventional administration seeks to exclude in principle, or at least to keep to a minimum, collapsing a diversity of interests into a single, homogeneous interest.[5] Not only does this perspective miss the actual dynamics of organizational relationships: what is also overlooked is the way observations, insights, and ideas are influenced by interest and position. Knowledge is not something that can somewhere be insulated and enshrined, for, to be relevant, it depends always upon the context and dynamics of organizational activity. Those in a position to know (in significant part) are those involved in this activity who have an interest in inquiry—in clearly and continuously sorting out aspects of a developing process.

In practice, the positions and interests of central organizational actors screen out the perception of relevant features of situations and problems. Conventional orientations are thus limited, ironically, in the very realm that they take to be their own: knowledge. In particular, their sources of knowledge are inadequate to problems arising from new, complex, and dynamic situations; and these are the kinds of conditions that seem to arise with striking frequency now that much industrialization has run its course.

While our focus here is on environmental problems arising in this aftermath of industrialization,[6] limitations of the conventional administrative perspective have long been recognized in efforts to promote decentralization and participation in organizations. These efforts, of course, were typically contained within centralized hierarchies and served to reinforce the legitimacy of established administrative organizations; yet these same efforts also pointed to the potential effectiveness of alternative organizational forms. This potential, perceived even in the emergence of industrialization, now is often considered especially significant with the advent of post-industrial technologies that rely dramatically upon knowledgeable, committed, innovative, and flexible people in the organization. Beyond the context of manufacturing, moreover, public participation has been viewed as potentially important in the effective "co-production" and delivery of services.[7] Our approach to environmental policy and administration is intended to complement investigation and experimentation along these lines. We do not know how far this direction might fruitfully be explored, whether with regard to manufacturing, services, environmental problems, or other areas. That is to say, we do not predict in advance how helpful decentralization and participation may prove to be in administration generally. Nor, we would add, do we suggest that such measures should necessarily be pursued only to the extent that they can prove themselves administratively effective: interest in democratic government and society would give further cause to move in this direction. We are convinced, however, that an interest in democracy is not the only reason to do so—and that the supposed conflict between democracy and effective administration is typically overdrawn.

What is it that lends plausibility to the way this conflict is usually treated? The short answer to this question is the specter of disorder. The conventional bias in favor of centralized hierarchy has regarded alternative organizational forms not simply as potentially less effective, but as practically impossible—as illusions offering a short path to chaos and ruin. Since there can supposedly be no secure order without centralized hierarchy, the choice of organizational form is dictated by administrative necessity. We can see through this notion, however, if we recognize that we are never confronted with order as such, but always with a particular order—and that any particular order is bound up with particular interests. This recognition points to the hidden political dimension contained in claims that any particular order is administratively necessary.[8] Experiments with alternative organizational forms may well provoke disorder, but this is not necessarily because such forms are administratively impossible.

Different organizational forms bring to the fore different interests and thereby generate conflicts that are unsettling to the notion that administration must proceed from one legitimate will—a single, unified authority. Inasmuch as the agenda of administrative inquiry and practice presupposes this notion, changes allowing the entry of different legitimate interests into the decision process will threaten to provoke unpredictable changes to that agenda and the way it is set:[9] new issues can then be identified, and problems redefined in novel ways.

Resistance to such change can be expected even though innovations might contain features helpful to the interests of the established order. For the prevailing configuration of interests will both inhibit clear perception of potential advantages and promote considerable concern about an anticipated loss of control. The potential for a loss of control will be sensed as a definite threat to a particular order and its prevailing interests; and this loss will readily be both regarded and portrayed as the advent of chaos.

To protect a given order in the name of administrative necessity is thus to resist revisions to the agenda of inquiry and practice. But this resistance takes a toll: administrative capacity to learn is necessarily constrained as divergent interests and perspectives are excluded from serious consideration; ritual and routine tend to predominate in the definition and handling of problems. Indeed, it has been argued that administrative organizations should, in their own interests, recognize and deliberately allow the political processes that pervade them. Especially when organizations face complex and changing circumstances, explicit organizational politics serves to draw attention to the array of factors that need to be taken into account in defining and solving problems.[10] This argument, of course, challenges the conventional bias in favor of centralized hierarchy by raising the prospect of alternative forms of effective administration. In contrast, preoccupation with maintaining order rules out an open airing and resolution of the conflicts rooted in differing interests. Politics, rendered illegitimate, is thereby obscured and suppressed—though, of course, not eliminated. Administration conventionally proceeds with the idea that it is, or ought to be, entirely separate from politics.

Yet the idea that administration can be insulated from politics is no longer able to withstand scrutiny. The persistence of this idea is partly because of a general bias, but also partly because of particular interests and priorities. The conventional exclusion of politics from administration is, indeed, not strictly administrative, but broadly political; its *raison d'être* is to protect administrative organizations from the unwelcome change in established priorities that any questioning of the existing agenda threatens to create.

The organizations and procedures that the administrative state has developed for environmental protection often prove themselves to be dramatically ineffective. Of course, one does not have to look to the conventional bias of administrative thought and practice to find a reason for this ineffectiveness. Whether one's analysis is informed by pluralist, elite, or class models,[11] it is not difficult to conclude that environmental management has typically had a low priority, despite much rhetoric. Thus it could reasonably be argued that broad social and political forces, rather than administration, constitute the real problem in blocking effective environmental management. But we would maintain that the forms and practices of administration are interwoven with these social and political forces.

This complex of forces manifests itself differently in various socio-political contexts. For example, if we were to broadly compare capitalist and socialist societies, we would certainly find different patterns of socio-political forces. Generally speaking, however, we would also find a low priority placed upon effective environmental management compared to that placed upon effective industrial development.[12] The relatively low priority placed upon environmental protection, moreover, is not unrelated to the typical form of administration.

Bureaucracy, Weber maintained, is a reliable and effective instrument.[13] Yet Weber did not argue that bureaucracy is an instrument suitable for just any purpose. Indeed, in broad historical terms, he saw bureaucracy as an organizational form reflecting and reinforcing a particular pattern of development: the rationalization and industrialization of the world. Bureaucratization thus contains an agenda of historical development: the salience of this form of centralized hierarchy has as a purpose the promotion of particular interests. The order serves a certain conception of progress and the socio-political forces promoting it.

To question the prevailing administrative form is unavoidably also to question prevailing priorities, for the two are interwoven. Beyond the question of priorities, moreover, is the issue of whether centralized hierarchy—particularly bureaucratic organization—could ever be sufficient for, or appropriate to, the task of effective environmental management. Can bureaucracy, in other words, deal effectively with the unanticipated consequences of the pattern of development that it promotes and in which it participates? From a conventional administrative viewpoint, this question might well appear nonsensical. Yet in the contemporary development of administrative theory, the basic idea has become commonplace: the appropriateness of an organizational form depends upon the task at hand. By putting a twist on the "contingency" approach to administration,[14] we thus suggest that the advent of environmental problems tends to challenge, rather than reinforce, the conventional presuppositions of administration, particularly those favoring centralized hierarchy and a closed process of decision making.

The administrative state is often viewed through a focus that directs attention strictly to the organization of public government. However, the administrative state has emerged within a broader context; there has been a tendency for public and private bureaucracies—despite conflicts—to develop patterns of mutually supportive relationships that shut other potential participants out of the decision-making process. The context, more broadly considered, is one of rationalization, industrialization, and bureaucratization; and the administrative state thus plays a key part in a world largely dominated by an ensemble of great organizations.[15] Of course, the domination is by no means complete or perfectly coordinated: the task of managing Leviathan continually confronts and generates problems. Here a political dimension of this management becomes evident.

Environmental politics, in particular, holds up a mirror to the world of administration, showing its bias and limits. Concern for the efficient use of natural resources has, of course, long been expressed within the world of administrative organizations,[16] and the administrative state has considered resource management to be a province of its own. The emergence of environmental politics in the latter part of the twentieth century, however, is a token of the failings of the administrative state. Beyond pointing out shortcomings of the administrative state in its own terms, environmental politics at times also raises doubts about the fundamental thrust of industrialization, and—even more broadly—questions both the viability and morality of the human domination of nature.

The administrative state, of course, seldom seems moved by such critique, but rather—by virtue of organizational structures and priorities—seeks to absorb it, consistently reasserting the necessity of a conventional mode of administration. From this perspective, the advent of environmental politics is reduced to an expression of narrowly self-serving groups and individuals; hence the desire of people to keep environmental problems out of their own areas, out of their own backyards, is deemed a socially pathological response to a natural and necessary course of development—a response termed the NIMBY Syndrome. The task of administration is thus identified as one of containing and overcoming irrational resistance.

The not-in-my-backyard attitude was early identified as a problem by those involved in the emergence of environmental politics. Yet their definition of the problem varied dramatically from that promulgated from the conventional administrative perspective. For those attempting to mobilize environmental concern in society, NIMBY was typically seen as a necessary initial step in the development of an environmentally concerned and informed citizenry.[17] The development and participation of such a citizenry was regarded as necessary politically in giving salience to environmental concerns. Here environmental politics was to intervene in the management of Leviathan, promoting different priorities that the conventional perspective tended to ignore.

Yet such a change of political priorities anticipates a change of administrative structures: at a minimum, the task of managing Leviathan can be viewed as one requiring more active involvement by various segments of the population at large. This prospect is, to a large extent, in accord with the vision of self-management in a participatory society.[18] Moving to a world beyond Leviathan, however, is difficult to accept as an immediate goal. Indeed, the present concerns of environmental politics cannot avoid the continuing problem of managing Leviathan.

NOTES

1 This outlook represents a continuation of the early conservationist orientation, which accorded well with conventional administration and was challenged by the dramatic outburst of environmentalism in the 1970s. On this point, see Robert Paehlke, "Democracy and Environmentalism: Opening a Door to the Administrative State," in this volume. For an insightful discussion of democratic participation in the context of the administrative state, see R.W. Phidd, "The Administrative State and the Limits of Rationality," in O.P. Dwivedi, ed., *The Administrative State in Canada* (Toronto: University of Toronto Press, 1982). *Cf.* Emmette S. Redford, *Democracy in the Administrative State* (New York: Oxford University Press, 1969), ch. 8. Redford formulates a concept of "workable democracy" which takes as fixed the conditions which have produced the administrative state.

2 For further discussion and references to relevant literature, see Douglas Torgerson, "Obsolescent Leviathan: Problems of Order in Administrative Thought," in this volume.

3 Effectiveness and efficiency are sometimes clearly distinguished, sometimes implicitly conflated. Effectiveness here primarily means getting the job done—achieving a goal. Yet this notion of effectiveness cannot altogether exclude considerations of efficiency since some notion of reasonable or satisfactory cost is normally implicit in a goal. Efficiency also presupposes effectiveness since, obviously, a goal cannot be efficiently achieved without first actually being achieved. We acknowledge—though for purposes of the present discussion believe we need not discuss—the complex conceptual difficulties arising from problems of implementation. We also do not believe we need to discuss here the economic concept of efficiency, which seems (if strictly followed) to require administratively (if not humanly) impossible calculations of universal costs and benefits. *Cf.* Herbert A. Simon, *Administrative Behavior: A Study of Decision-Making Processes in Administrative Organization*, 3rd ed. (New York: The Free Press, 1976); Laurence H. Tribe, "Policy Science: Analysis or Ideology?" *Philosophy and Public Affairs* 2(1972): 66–110. Jeffrey Pressman and Aaron Wildavsky, *Implementation*, 3rd ed. (Berkeley: University of California Press, 1984); Clarence N. Stone, "Efficiency versus Social Learning: A Reconsideration of the Implementation Process," *Policy Studies Review* 4.3(1985): 484–96.

4 It was concluded that a hot oil pipeline should not be buried in permafrost; hence a section was built above ground. See Mary C. Berry, *The Alaska Pipeline: The Politics of Oil and Native Land Claims* (Bloomington: Indiana University Press, 1975), pp. 103–07. *Cf.* Martin Stuart Baker, "Implication of the National Environmental Policy Act," in Wolfgang F.E. Preiser, ed., *Environmental Design Research* (Stroudsburg, PA: Dowden, Hutchinson and Ross, 1973), vol. 2, pp. 89–92; Frederick R. Anderson, *NEPA in the Courts: A Legal Analysis of the National Environmental Policy Act* (Washington, DC: Resources for the Future, 1973), chs. 1, 8.

5 See Jeffrey Pfeffer, *Power in Organizations* (Boston: Pitman Publishing, 1981), esp. chs. 1, 3. *Cf.* Douglas Torgerson, "Limits of the Administrative Mind: The Problem of Defining Environmental Problems," in Robert Paehlke and Douglas Torgerson, eds., *Managing Leviathan: Environmental Politics and the Administrative State* (Peterborough, ON: Broadview Press, 1990).

6 Industrialization is not over, but neither is it new; and enough has passed to allow us to perceive previously unanticipated aspects of its aftermath. Indeed, the emergence and articulation of widespread environmental concern may be taken as an historical event which has rendered this aftermath visible. This event, moreover, has converged with the now common notion that social and economic developments are ushering in a "post-industrial" era. This notion is by itself significant if the shaping of the future is somehow bound up with its perception. We make no bold predictions, but inquiry cannot dispense with implicit or explicit judgments constituting a form of historical orientation. See Douglas Torgerson, "Contextual Orientation in Policy Analysis: The Contribution of Harold D. Lasswell," *Policy Sciences* 18(1985): 241–61. For discussion of some relevant issues, see Timothy W. Luke and Stephen K. White, "Critical Theory, the Informational Revolution, and an Ecological Path to Modernity," in John Forester, ed., *Critical Theory and Public Life* (Cambridge, MA: MIT Press, 1985).

7 See, e.g., Larry Hirschhorn, *Beyond Mechanization: Work and Technology in a Postindustrial Age* (Cambridge, MA: MIT Press, 1986); Richard Sundeen, "Coproduction and Communities: Implications for Local Administrators," *Administration and Society* 16.4(1985): 387–402. Mary Parker Follett, *Dynamic Administration: The Collected Papers of Mary Parker Follett*, 2nd ed. (New York: Hippocrene Books, 1977), remains striking as a contribution along these lines from the 1920s.

8 For a case in point, see David Dickson, *Alternative Technology and the Politics of Technical Change* (Glasgow: Fontana, 1974).

9 On agenda setting, see, e.g., Robert W. Cobb and Charles D. Elder, "The Politics of Agenda Building: An Alternative Perspective for Modern Democratic Theory," *Journal of Politics* 33.4(1971): 892–915.

10 See Pfeffer, ch. 9.

11 For a useful comparison of pluralist, elite, and class models, see Robert R. Alford, "Paradigms of Relations between State and Society," in Leon Lindberg *et al.*, eds., *Stress and Contradiction in Modern Capitalism: Public Policy and the Theory of the State* (Lexington, MA: Lexington Books, 1975).

12 *Cf.* Donald R. Kelley *et al.*, *The Economic Superpowers and the Environment* (San Francisco: W.H. Freeman, 1976).

13 For further discussion of Weber, see Torgerson, "Obsolescent Leviathan."

14 For a succinct discussion of this approach in relation to others, see Fred Luthans, "The Contingency Theory of Management," *Business Horizons* 16(1973): 63–72.

15 *Cf.* Torgerson, "Limits of the Administrative Mind."

16 *Cf.* Samuel P. Hays, *Conservation and the Gospel of Efficiency: The Progressive Conservation Movement, 1890–1920* (New York: Anteneum, 1968).

17 By the early 1970s, there were explicit discussions along these lines in environmentalist circles. On the loose identity of public-interest groups generally as a democratic social movement, see Michael W. McCann, "Public Interest Liberalism and the Modern Regulatory State," *Polity* 21.1(1988): 373–400. *Cf.* the concept of "new social movements" as discussed, e.g., in Luke and White, pp. 40ff, 53 n46.

18 *Cf.* Carole Pateman, *Participation and Democratic Theory* (Cambridge: Cambridge University Press, 1975); C. B. Macpherson, *The Life and Times of Liberal Democracy* (Oxford: Oxford University Press, 1977); Benjamin R. Barber, *Strong Democracy: Participatory Politics for a New Age* (Berkeley: University of California Press, 1984); Gar Alperovitz, "Towards a Decentralist Commonwealth," in Howard J. Ehrlich *et al.*, eds., *Reinventing Anarchy* (London: Routledge and Kegan Paul, 1979).

2

Obsolescent Leviathan: Problems of Order in Administrative Thought

Douglas Torgerson

Canst thou draw out leviathan with an hook?... Canst thou put an hook into his nose?... Will he make many supplications unto thee? will he speak soft words unto thee? Will he make a covenant with thee? wilt thou take him for a servant for ever? Job 41:1–4.

Upon ascending to power, a new regime expresses grave concern about the condition of the public treasury. The profligate ways of the past will, it is announced, now have to end. Officials receive their orders and set quietly to work while the populace is left in suspense about the import of the announcement. Later it is learned that—among other things—certain funds no longer will be available to help keep track of a spread of poisons in the earth, air, and water. Consternation and controversy follow among the public, and the decision even gives rise to complaints among officials, who say they were not properly consulted. A senior administrator meets with his staff and acknowledges their concerns: "A number of people have told me, 'if you had ... consulted us, we program managers—we people who really know what is going on and what we are doing—we could have given you a better way out and we would have given you some different ways of cutting back.'" The administrator points to his own problems, to imperatives of speed and discretion which left him no real option, but he agrees with a principle which underlies the complaints: "when you don't act democratically, when you act from the top, ... well you make mistakes." When these words mysteriously appear in the press, many members of the public express agreement; they say that they have thought much about the problem

11

of spreading poisons—and that the government should consult the citizenry when deciding what is important.

The senior administrator in this true story[1] implicitly recognized what has long been identified as a key question of administration—the problem of centralization versus decentralization.[2] Tight control at the center can undermine the pattern of communication needed to support decision making by leaving out of the process those who really grasp an issue and know how to deal with it. This problem, often evident within the framework of an administrative apparatus, also pertains to the relationship between an organization and those outside its formal boundaries. More broadly, in the context of contemporary concerns, the problem involves the relationship between the administrative state and the citizenry of an advanced industrial society.

Centralization seems to be almost a natural reflex of administration. Indeed, early in the twentieth century, the first attempt to develop a general theory of administration portrayed centralization as part of the "natural order."[3] Even then, it was clear that decentralization was a necessary counterpart to centralization, and much subsequent administrative thought has labored with the question of how these opposing pulls should be balanced. Nonetheless, a prejudice favoring centralization has remained as a permanent fixture in the universe of administration. Especially in the face of emergencies, pressing problems, crises, the standard reflex has been to look for a central authority to take charge, to maintain or restore order.

LEVIATHAN AND ENVIRONMENT

This reflex certainly sprang into operation with the emerging perception of an environmental crisis in the latter part of the twentieth century. Sometimes bluntly and simplistically stated as the need for an "environmental dictator," the appeal to a central authority was at times also carefully formulated to retain certain vestiges of democratic values. Nonetheless, the accent throughout clearly presupposed the effectiveness of centralized authority and reflected the traditional focus of administrative thought. In a sophisticated version of this approach, William Ophuls looked back to Hobbes and defined the problem as a question of "Leviathan or Oblivion?" Interpreting Hobbes as advocating "autocracy with power residing preferably in the hands of one man," Ophuls sought to preserve democratic values as much as possible, but he nonetheless concluded that solving the environmental crisis required submission to "a higher power": "the tragic necessity of Leviathan."[4]

Hobbes proposed his Leviathan as an order of absolute authority, sanctioned by reason. Fear of disorder, Hobbes maintained, was sufficient for all rational individuals to invest their natural powers in a sovereign individual or group capable of maintaining control. A striking portrayal of Hobbes's view is presented in the famous 1651 frontispiece to *Leviathan*, in which a colossal monarch rises above and surveys the city below. With sword and scepter in either hand, the monarch casts a gaze of serenity and benevolence; his body, upon inspection, appears moreover as a composite of the individual bodies of citizens, each distinct and all reverently facing him. Hobbes's Leviathan may seem, at first glance, itself to be the absolute ruler, but this is a misleading impression; for the sovereign is a distinct *part* of Leviathan—of this "mortal god"—and all citizens are, in turn, themselves distinct parts, incorporated into the whole. Yet the impression is only partially misleading; for the sovereign is the "soul" of Leviathan, the concentration of all powers and wills into a single power and will, the mainspring of action, so to speak. No power can approach the power of Leviathan because all powers constitute and participate in this being; its life depends not only upon the acquiesence of subjects to the sovereign, but also upon the active transfer of their powers to him, by which they all individually place themselves at his disposal and forsake any action not authorized by him. In this manner, the citizens both support the sovereign and enact Leviathan, which—although their own creation—now appears as a power distinct from and above them, in essence represented by the sovereign.[5] Once established, the distinct power of the sovereign becomes the single legitimate source of direction in society; neither wisdom nor tradition has any independent authority:

> Would you have every man to every other man alledge for Law his own particular Reason? There is not amongst Men a Universal Reason agreed upon in any Nation, besides the Reason of him that hath the Soveraign Power. Yet though his Reason be but the Reason of one Man, yet it is set up to supply the place of that Universal Reason, which is expounded to us by our Saviour in the Gospel; and consequently our King is to us the Legislator both of Statute-Law and of Common-Law.[6]

For Hobbes the main question is not whether the sovereign is wise, but whether he is obeyed, for it is obedience that ensures order.

The appeal of Leviathan is, indeed, the appeal of order; and the problem of order appears to become salient as one contemplates various scenarios of environmental crisis. To look to Hobbes for a solution, however, is to ignore the sense in which he is part of the problem—how the perception of environmental crisis may reflect the obsolescence of Leviathan. The organizational form contemplated in Hobbes is a rationally constructed artifice of centralized power, an instrument of order exercised through formal patterns of command and obedience. Historically, this is the form adopted in the emergence of the modern state as it arose from diverse, inconsistent patterns of medieval authority. By cutting through traditional bonds and entanglements, the modern state—in both absolutist and liberal versions—cleared an orderly, predictable space for increasingly abstract and standardized relationships in state, economy, and society. The formation and expression of public opinion fostered and guided these developments in a manner that Hobbes did not foresee, even though his own ideas exerted a seminal influence. As it happened, the main currents of public opinion were guided by notions of order and progress that reinforced trends of abstraction and standardization in state, economy, and society even while advancing the principle—anathema to Hobbes—of popular sovereignty. The culmination of these trends, moreover, was curiously in tune with Hobbes in the sense that it fostered an order of formalized and centralized authority while depriving public opinion of its vitality and independence—a world of great organizations, in which the modern state emerged as an administrative state.[7] This is the world that Max Weber witnessed developing in the early part of the last century. The future, he believed, would be cast in this mold. Although by no means personally enamored of this prospect, Weber provided a striking account of what we have come to know as the traditional approach to administration.

It is possible to discern a "problem of order" in Hobbes, but this is not simply because the presuppositions of his theory point to an essentially fragmented social universe. In the seventeenth century, he perceives a society that can be held together only if individuals, forsaking the thrust of their passions, rationally relinquish their personal powers and subjugate themselves to a single, overarching authority. Hobbes's presuppositions also serve to articulate salient characteristics of his age.[8] For Weber, in contrast, what impends in the early twentieth century is the "iron cage" of an economy and society cut to fit bureaucratic organization. The autonomy of the individual does not threaten to undo the prevailing order; indeed, the readiness of the individual to submit rationally to authority is so evident that it becomes possible to identify a source of authority typical of this age—one beyond either charisma or tradition, one that would have pleased Hobbes: the ground of authority that Weber called "rational." An order based upon such authority was one that Hobbes could identify as something in need of construction. For Weber, this order was one to be grimly acknowledged.[9]

The image of Hobbes's Leviathan is the image of an overarching authority enforcing order upon a naturally recalcitrant subject-matter. Fear of the implications of environmental crisis provides a motive to reassert this order by resurrecting Leviathan. Here the diagnosis takes the source of the crisis to be the "possessive individualism" that Hobbes attributed to human nature and which, in any case, has emerged as a distinguishing feature of human beings in the modern age.[10] Reliance upon Hobbes thus takes the possessive individual as given and tends to reinforce the notion that rationality demands quiescence and unquestioning obedience to a superior authority. What is thereby ruled out is the idea of a vital and informed public opinion capable of criticizing, shaping, and participating in authority. Indeed, the notion of resurrecting Leviathan ignores the extent to which Leviathan is alive and well, represented in the institutions that Weber saw emerging with the rationalization, bureaucratization, and industrialization of the world. For even though a culture of possessive individualism certainly contains a frightening potential, a mere reassertion of authority over individuals misses the mark, which we need to recognize as Leviathan itself.

That is to say, a largely centralized mode of administration in state, economy, and society has performed key functions both in advancing industrialization and in generating those very problems that have elicited a perception of environmental crisis. If Leviathan, in this sense, has been a key tool in shaping the modern world, then the problems of that world lead us to ask whether the tool is not now obsolescent. For the very source of order now appears as a source of impending disorder.

ADMINISTRATION RE-EXAMINED

The traditional approach to administration endures today despite challenges in both theory and practice. Images of centralized hierarchy—such as Weber's bureaucracy or Hobbes's Leviathan—continue to profoundly influence organizational structure and conduct, together with the way problems are identified and handled. Yet this approach persistently encounters difficulties, and it has become apparent that these difficulties are themselves often generated by this very approach. While centralized hierarchy has demonstrated its effectiveness for certain purposes, this organizational form also often shows itself to be inept, or at least not as effective as possible alternatives.

The consideration of alternatives for industrial organization has been an important focus in the development of management thought at least since the late 1920s.[11] The intense focus on such alternatives today could well be viewed—as earlier interest in them has, indeed, rightly been seen—as part of a quest for more subtle means of manipulating the human factor in production. This interpretation cannot be dismissed, but the current focus is also informed by a recognition that new technologies are rendering the traditional approach to administration increasingly less effective.[12] Similarly, in such areas as service delivery, occupational safety, health care, rural projects, community planning, and urban development, decentralized initiative has been identified as often a vital component of effective administration. Moreover, a key point arising from the literature, implicitly and explicitly, is that the potentials of decentralization and participation are contingent, i.e., context-dependent. Indeed, consistency on this point is not surprising because, as a counter to traditional presuppositions, the focus on decentralization and participation is necessarily at odds with a centralizing orientation typically insensitive to what is local and particular: the centralizing approach generally seeks to render its subject-matter homogeneous, hence manageable.[13]

Environmental problems are our particular concern here, and it is evident that they have largely been generated or magnified by centralized hierarchies. It thus seems at least questionable whether these problems can be identified and resolved through an extension of this organizational form. Indeed, the present situation provides grounds for a critical examination of the traditional prejudices of administration—and for an exploration of alternative approaches. Here Weber offers a point of departure.

The rise of the administrative state may, indeed, be considered in terms of Weber's description of the rationalization of the modern world. The essence of rationalization, for Weber, was a central "belief" of modern culture that "there are no mysterious incalculable forces ... that one can, in principle, master all things by calculation." This belief both promoted and appeared to be validated by the emergence of industrialization, that "tremendous cosmos of the modern economic order." Central to these developments, moreover, was the advent of bureaucratization: the rising significance of formal organization in both the state and the economy. In both public and private organizations, the administrative apparatus was designed for calculability and efficiency through formal hierarchies of personnel with strictly delimited functions. The anonymity and formalization of relationships in bureaucracy made the organization a reliable instrument for those who controlled it and a predictable mechanism for those who dealt with it. Even resistance to bureaucratic control would fall prey to the logic of bureaucratic organization. "The whole pattern of everyday life," Weber said, "is cut to fit this framework."[14]

What makes bureaucratic administration "rational," according to Weber, is that it exercises control through knowledge. This is mainly the knowledge of "the personally detached and strictly objective *expert*," who discharges responsibilities according to rules and calculations "without regard to persons." Exerted thus primarily through technical knowledge, bureaucratic control is also enhanced through "official secrets." Each organization typically reinforces its power by hiding "its knowledge and intentions" and excluding "the public."[15]

Bureaucratization would, in Weber's view, be a common feature of both planned and market economies, although he did allow for a difference. The "single hierarchy" of the planned economy would create a monolithic structure, in contrast to the parallel operations—with some potential conflict—typical of public and private bureaucracies in a market economy.[16] In either case, however, the welfare of the mass of the population would remain dependent upon an overarching "bureaucratic apparatus"—"upon the continuous and correct functioning" (in the case of the market economy) both of state administration and of the increasingly "bureaucratic organizations of private capitalism."[17]

It was long after Weber that the term "administrative state" came into use.[18] Yet Weber was early to perceive a concentration of power in the enclaves of administration: "In the modern state the actual ruler is necessarily and unavoidably the bureaucracy...." While Weber was concerned to identify ways of mitigating state bureaucratic power—keeping it in check primarily through the instrument of parliamentary review—he resigned himself to the extraordinary effectiveness of the organizational machine: "The future," Weber wrote in 1918, "belongs to bureaucratization...."[19]

In light of Weber, the rise of the administrative state appears as a necessary concomitant of the rationalization and industrialization of the world. What we witness is not, then, simply a change in the locus of state power, but the emergence of a more or less cohesive administrative sphere upon which all social life is now largely dependent. The relatively recent concept of "bureaucratic symbiosis" seems simply an extension of Weber's thesis: "Organization ... relates effectively to organization. The various specialists of the private bureaucracy work readily with their opposite numbers in the public bureaucracy pooling information for a jointly achieved decision."[20] Despite apparent conflict, according to this conception, a largely closed administrative world now promotes, monitors, and regulates the industrial economy. This formulation may be a substantial exaggeration, but the advance of industrialization has certainly reinforced a tendency toward a closed process of administrative decision making. The rapid technological development of industrial society has been accompanied by an increased reliance upon the administrative sphere and its experts, deemed necessary to perform the calculations required to master an increasing range of complex, technical problems.

Here a conflictual relationship becomes collaborative; a mutual accommodation of interests and perspectives tends, in effect, to bring public and private organizations together in what becomes a largely cohesive administrative apparatus. Of course, there remain counter tendencies. Nothing said here is meant to deny the obvious fragmentation both within and among public and private administrative structures.[21] No monolith is being conjured up. What is doubtful, nonetheless, is whether this administrative sphere, this partly coherent, partly fragmented pattern of bureaucratic organizations, has the collective capacity to identify and regulate effectively the range of environmental problems it generates. Can everything really be mastered by calculation?

An affirmative answer to this question is no longer generally taken for granted. Indeed, inasmuch as administrative thought has reflected the exigencies of administrative practice, significant doubts have been posed concerning the traditional presupposition of a detached mind capable of rationally governing a centralized hierarchy.[22] Even Hobbes, we may recall, did not hold that the sovereign reason should necessarily be wise, only that it should maintain order. For what both Hobbes and Weber knew was that order was a precondition for predictability; human affairs were not necessarily calculable—they were potentially chaotic—but they could be made calculable through the enforcement of order. A key problem increasingly recognized now in administrative thought is that of order generating disorder; here the presuppositions of hierarchy, centralization, and calculability are drawn into question.

In the technocratic orientation to administration, these presuppositions are retained in a modified form. While the centralized hierarchy is attenuated in favor of a systems approach capable of a more deliberate balancing of centralization and decentralization, this technocratic approach remains wedded typically to a single point of reference: an abstract "decision-maker" or a "controlling group" as the ultimate source of direction. Abstraction and formality remain central features of a style focused upon defining and treating administrative problems as matters suitable for calculation. Yet the problems must be cut down to manageable size.[23] Indeed, in what has been called the "neo-Weberian model,"[24] we find the world of administration inhabited by "administrative man," one who deals not with the full complexity of things, but who (as described by Herbert Simon) remains "content" to follow a greatly simplified map, since "he believes that the real world is mostly empty—that most of the facts of the real world have no great relevance to the particular situation he is facing and that most significant chains of causes and consequences are short and simple."[25] If Weber envisioned an administrative complex towering over an increasingly calculable world, the neo-Weberian model portrays a world that is at least manageable—that is, calculable enough for most administrative purposes. In either case, those within the administrative structure remain narrowly focused on what is directly relevant to their own particular functions. The final guarantee of both the traditional and technocratic approaches, moreover, remains a faith in the secure order of Leviathan. It can be taken for granted that no radical decentralization or expansion of participation has any place in the administrative sphere—that such moves could only pose a threat to order.

Yet the presuppositions of traditional and technocratic orientations have been challenged by the argument of Emery and Trist in the latter part of the twentieth century that a "gross increase in ... *relevant uncertainty*"[26] has made environmental complexity a necessary focus of concern. The environment is now a problem that the traditional and technocratic approaches to administration themselves persistently exacerbate:

> The very success of the technocratic bureaucracy ... has led to dysfunctional effects. For these immense organizations go it alone without regard to what others are doing, while interdependencies ... are increasing.... Concentrated largely on their own short-term specific objectives, they have given only marginal attention to the longer-term, more general effects of their actions on wider systems. These effects have not been supposed to be their business. As a result, unintended consequences pile up....[27]

The upshot of this line of argument is that, far from becoming more calculable or unproblematic, the organizational environment has become so troublesome that the bureaucratic form itself is moribund and needs to be replaced by another organizational form. In the early twentieth century, according to Eric Trist, Weber had unveiled "bureaucracy as a newly perfected organizational monument ...," but later conditions in the century taught the need for "identifying and becoming skilled in practising, an alternative organizational principle."[28]

This conclusion is a culmination of various developments in administrative thought that converged to question reliance upon centralized hierarchy as the "one best way" to approach organization and administration. Here the focus on the salience and complexity of the "human factor" has combined with the recognition that different approaches to administration differ in their effectiveness depending upon the situation—i.e., upon differences in contingencies such as the task at hand, the mechanical apparatus, the type of people involved, the material resources available, and the environment external to the organization.[29] The systems approach, moreover, has emerged as necessary in establishing a conceptual grasp of this multitude of variables. Even though such conceptualization has generally been sought as a means of reasserting order and control in a domain that threatened to become too complex and dynamic to manage, the systems approach does not in principle maintain the privileged position that the centralized hierarchy had traditionally been assigned. Indeed, in focusing upon the organizational environment, Trist and others have pressed the systems approach in a manner that explodes the typical technocratic framework.[30]

The concept of organizational environment here refers primarily to organizations interacting through the broader ensemble of social and economic conditions. It is a short step, however, to include the conditions of the natural environment. Indeed, this step has been taken in a systems-theoretic argument by Hooker and van Hulst, who maintain that "massive, narrowly focused bureaucracies of 'experts'"—both public and private—exhibit "an incompetence to deal with the key holistic features of reality." There is, in other words, a mis-match between the prevailing form of human organizations and the systemic properties of the natural environment. With each organization oriented to the efficient performance of specific functions, the ensemble of public and private bureaucracies persistently generates a vast, complex array of unintended, unanticipated consequences that often eludes effective monitoring and control. Narrowly conceived organizational goals combine with highly restricted patterns of information flow to obscure the connection between particular organizational operations and the relevant totality of direct and indirect outcomes. Effective monitoring and control of environmental problems would thus require the information flows and "complex feedback patterns" that are obtainable only by matching the internal arrangement of organizational relationships to "the external system structure." "Meaningful public control," it is concluded, "... calls for decentralization and democratization." The exigencies of the administrative task themselves thus call for a "radical decentralization" of institutions[31]—a change which is, of course, political as well as administrative.

CONCLUSION

Once we recognize the prevailing form of order as generating disorder, the issue of centralization and decentralization can be recast. However, the pronounced centralizing bias typical of administrative thought continues to reassert itself in the very terminology that allows us to formulate the issue: decentralization remains a variant upon the natural and normal. We have no easy way of expressing the notion of a pattern of organization that is at once radically decentralized and coherent—except, perhaps, the term "anarchy" (which, of course, carries the strong popular connotation of chaos).[32]

Hobbes formulated the modern conception of organization as an artifice, severed from tradition, which could be rationally designed upon the basis of calculable criteria. By the terms of Hobbes's argument, what was to be achieved was order as such: the sole secure order possible in light of human nature—a centralized hierarchy subordinated to a single, ultimate authority. Leviathan, for Hobbes the only reliable order which reason could construct from nature, was modified at the hands of his liberal successors—from Locke to Bentham—and acquired a clear historical purpose: progress in the subordination of nature to human goals.[33] Here Weber remains illuminating because he portrays the apotheosis of centralized hierarchy—bureaucratization—as part of the wider processes of industrialization and rationalization. He describes bureaucracy as an effective instrument in the hands of those who control it. Yet his analysis shows bureaucratic organization to be effective for certain purposes, not necessarily for all. (Indeed, Weber could imagine the eventual collapse of the modern industrial cosmos from a constraint of energy resources.)[34] Bureaucracy has been effective in promoting industrialization, in both capitalist and socialist economies. Yet we have not generally witnessed bureaucracy handling effectively the serious problems generated by industrialization. Indeed, the administrative sphere has—in either economic form—remained oriented toward industrialization.[35]

In the present historical context, a recourse to Leviathan would merely tend to reinforce the very order that has generated the problem. Yet it is at least plausible to suggest that the prevailing administrative form needs to be challenged, not strengthened—that the sphere of administration should, indeed, be radically transformed. The point is not to advocate further reliance upon the economic "invisible hand" that the administrative sphere employs to a greater or lesser extent in different countries. Such a move would not necessarily alter the basic form or diminish the extent of the prevailing administrative apparatus.[36] Instead, to press the question as one of administrative form is to focus upon the distinctly political character of the issue. A radically decentralized and democratic alternative would necessarily open up the administrative world to the influence of interests that have generally been excluded or marginalized. To say this is also to suggest, of course, that the prevailing administrative form is not maintained simply because of some supposed "administrative" necessity; the administrative sphere resists even the serious consideration of alternatives because of the conjunction of ideological presuppositions, particular interests, and shared purposes constituting that domain.[37]

Yet as the limitations of this administrative form become apparent in particular cases, there will be various pressures and piecemeal initiatives that will at least seem to anticipate broader innovations and a more sweeping redefinition of the problem. Already, the voice of marginal and local interests has been clearly significant both in warning the administrative sphere of major environmental dangers and in taking the initiative to mitigate environmental damages. The question now is the extent to which such interests will participate in, and perhaps transform, the management of Leviathan. At once administrative and political, the question is also historical—whether, in the aftermath of much industrialization, an alternative pattern of administration and development will emerge.

As one of the architects of modernity, Hobbes both reaffirmed and—despite himself—placed at risk the principle of absolute authority. For this authority was to be legitimated no longer by an unquestioned tradition, but by reason alone—as exercised by a multitude of possessive individuals all fearfully calculating and planning for their security. For Hobbes, reason demanded obedience by all to the dictates of a single authority—in effect, the abdication of the sovereign reason of each in favor of one sovereign reason representing all. In the emergence of modernity, political and administrative thought has repeated Hobbes's disposition by generally recognizing the "necessity" of centralized hierarchy, even while affirming the principle of popular sovereignty.[38] Since Hobbes, nonetheless, this disposition has expressly been founded upon argument. Even though both traditional and technocratic approaches to administration have taken the argument to be closed, current signs of the obsolescence of Leviathan provide an opportunity to re-open the question. The point is not simply to substitute a decentralizing bias for a centralizing bias; the balancing of the two remains an issue to be addressed. To re-open the question, however, means that traditional and technocratic fixations are to be challenged by a diversity of interests and perspectives previously excluded from serious consideration. Already in this questioning, then, we anticipate broader participation in inquiry and discussion: an institutionalization of discourse at odds with centralized hierarchy.

NOTES

1   The story is that of the Conservative government that came to power in Canada in 1984. Considerable controversy arose over the budget cuts that the new government required of Environment Canada, especially those concerning the elimination of research programs to monitor levels of toxic chemicals in herring gulls in the Great Lakes region. In the midst of this controversy, a tape recording of a meeting between the Deputy Minister, Jacques Gérin, and his staff was leaked to the press. See Michael Keating, "More Environment Cuts Hinted," *The Globe and Mail* 12 Dec. 1984, p. 5. On the reaction of citizens' groups, see Robert Gibson, "The Government Shows Its Colours," *Alternatives* 12.2(1985): 49–52.

2   See, e.g., Herbert A. Simon, *Administrative Behavior: A Study of Decision-Making Processes in Administrative Organization*, 3rd ed. (New York: The Free Press, 1976), pp. 234ff.

3   Henri Fayol, *General and Industrial Management* (London: Pitman Publishing, 1967 [1916]), p. 33.

4   William Ophuls, "Leviathan or Oblivion?" in Herman E. Daly, ed., *Toward a Steady-State Economy* (San Francisco: W.H. Freeman, 1973), pp. 219, 229. *Cf.* William Ophuls, *Ecology and the Politics of Scarcity* (San Francisco: W.H. Freeman, 1976); "Technological Limits to Growth Revisited," *Alternatives* 4.2(1975): 4–11; "The Politics of Transformation," *Alternatives* 6.2(1977): 4–8. The idea of an "environmental dictator" was explicitly discussed during the 1970s in some environmental organizations as an approach to the perceived environmental crisis. There is a significant literature on the "neo-Hobbesian" approach of Ophuls and others. See, e.g., K.J. Walker, "The Environmental Crisis: A Critique of Neo-Hobbesian Responses," *Polity* 21.1(1988): 67–81.

5   Thomas Hobbes, *Leviathan* (Harmondsworth: Penguin Books, 1968 [1651]). For passages especially relevant to these points, see pp. 81–82, 150–51, 189–91, 289–90,

312–13, 375, 376ff. The frontispiece contains an explicit reference to *Job*. For Hobbes's discussion of this text, see p. 362. For an important discussion of Hobbes which draws attention to the frontispiece, see Sheldon S. Wolin, *Politics and Vision: Continuity and Innovation in Western Political Thought* (Boston: Little, Brown, 1960), ch. 8. My view of Hobbes has been significantly influenced by C.B. Macpherson, *The Political Theory of Possessive Individualism: Hobbes to Locke* (Oxford: Oxford University Press, 1964).

6   Thomas Hobbes, *A Dialogue between a Philosopher and a Student of the Common Laws of England* (Chicago: University of Chicago Press, 1971 [1681]), p. 67. The speech is by the "Philosopher."

7   *Cf.* Gianfranco Poggi, *The Development of the Modern State* (Stanford: Stanford University Press, 1978); Karl Polanyi, *The Great Transformation: The Political and Economic Origins of our Time* (Boston: Beacon Press, 1957). Also *cf.* J.B. Bury, *The Idea of Progress* (New York: Dover Publications, 1955 [1932]), esp. p. 76.

8   See Macpherson, *Possessive Individualism*, Ch. 2. The Hobbesian "problem of order" is a well-known theme in Parsons. For a discussion which draws upon unpublished sources, see William Buxton, *Talcott Parsons and the Capitalist Nation-State: Political Sociology as a Strategic Vocation* (Toronto: University of Toronto Press, 1985), pp. 20ff, 256ff.

9   Max Weber, *The Protestant Ethic and the Spirit of Capitalism* (New York: Charles Scribner's Sons, 1958), p. 181; Max Weber, *Economy and Society*, 2 vols. (Berkeley: University of California Press, 1978), vol. 1, p. 215; J.P. Mayer, *Max Weber and German Politics*, 2nd ed. (London: Faber and Faber, 1956).

10 Macpherson, *Possessive Individualism*; *cf.* C.B. Macpherson, "Hobbes' Bourgeois Man," in his *Democratic Theory* (Oxford: Clarendon Press, 1973). Remarkably, the neo-Hobbesian literature presents an historically abstract concept of the "tragedy of the commons," ignoring the way in which the enclosures movement historically relied upon state intervention to end the regulation of common lands by tradition. See Garrett Hardin, "The Tragedy of the Commons," *Science* 162 (1968): 1243–48, and Garrett Hardin and John Baden, eds., *Managing the Commons* (San Francisco: W.H. Freeman, 1977) in contrast to Polanyi, *The Great Transformation*. This irony deserves greater attention.

11 Especially remarkable in this regard was Follett's work on management during the 1920s. See Mary Parker Follett, *Dynamic Administration: The Collected Papers of Mary Parker Follett*, 2nd ed. (New York: Hippocrene Books, 1977). Also see, e.g., Elton Mayo, *The Human Problems of an Industrial Civilization* (New York: Viking Press, 1960 [1933]); Joan Woodward, *Industrial Organization: Theory and Practice*, 2nd ed. (London: Oxford University Press, 1980 [1965]).

12 *Cf.*, e.g., Larry Hirschhorn, *Beyond Mechanization: Work and Technology in a Postindustrial Age* (Cambridge, MA: MIT Press, 1986). Also *cf.* Reinhard Bendix, *Work and Authority in Industry: Ideologies of Management in the Course of Industrialization* (New York: Harper and Row, 1963); Frank Fischer, "Ideology and Organization Theory," in Frank Fischer and Carmen Sirianni, eds., *Critical Studies in Organization and Bureaucracy* (Philadelphia: Temple University Press, 1984).

13 See Adam W. Herbert, "Management under Conditions of Decentralization and Citizen Participation," *Public Administration Review* 32 (1972): 622–37. John D. Montgomery, "When Local Participation Helps," *Journal of Policy Analysis and Management* 3.1(1983): 90–105, stresses the importance of differences in types of administrative activity; and Richard A. Sundeen, "Coproduction and Communities: Implications for Local Administrators," *Administration and Society* 16.4(1985): 387–402, emphasizes the importance of differences in types of locality. Both conventional administration and an approach reliant upon decentralization and participation, of course, involve difficulties. Curtis Ventriss and Robert Pecorella, "Community Participation and Modernization: A Reexamination of Political Choices," *Public Administration Review* 44 (1984), pp. 224–31, shows how the choice of difficulties—and potentials—is political: the perception that

the current course of modernization is inevitable fosters the notion that following the conventional approach is somehow neutral, purely administrative. Also see, on some particular issues, David W. Orr, "U.S. Energy Policy and the Political Economy of Participation," *Journal of Politics* 41.4(1979): 1027–56; on energy and health systems, C.A. Hooker and R. Van Hulst, "The Meaning of Environmental Problems for Public Political Institutions," in William Leiss, ed., *Ecology versus Politics in Canada* (Toronto: University of Toronto Press, 1979); and, for complementary discussions of health problems in the workplace, Robert Sass, "The Underdevelopment of Occupational Health and Safety in Canada," and Robert Paehlke, "Occupational Health Policy in Canada," both in the Leiss volume. *Cf.* Timothy W. Luke and Stephen K. White, "Critical Theory, the Informational Revolution, and an Ecological Path to Modernity," in John Forester, ed., *Critical Theory and Public Life* (Cambridge, MA: MIT Press, 1985); Gar Alperovitz, "Towards a Decentralist Commonwealth," in Howard J. Ehrlich *et al.*, eds., *Reinventing Anarchy* (London: Routledge and Kegan Paul, 1979).

14 Max Weber, "Science as a Vocation," in *From Max Weber: Essays in Sociology* (New York: Oxford University Press, 1958), p. 139; Weber, *Protestant Ethic*, p. 181; Weber, *Economy and Society*, vol. 1, pp. 223–24; vol. 2, pp. 874–975. *Cf.* Alfred Schutz, "The Problem of Rationality in the Social World," in his *Collected Papers*, vol. 2 (The Hague: Martinus Nijhoff, 1964), p. 71.

15 Weber, *Economy and Society*, vol. 1, p. 225; vol. 2, pp. 975, 992. The knowledge of the public bureaucracy is exceeded only by that of the private bureaucracy since commercial enterprises are ever mindful of the costs of miscalculation and since secrets are "more safely hidden in the books of an enterprise than ... in the files of public authorities" (vol. 2, p. 994). Consequently, public administration often finds itself in a constrained and disadvantaged position when dealing with private business management.

16 Weber, *Economy and Society*, vol. 2, p. 1402; *cf.* vol. 1, pp. 224–25.

17 Weber, *Economy and Society*, vol. 2, p. 988.

18 See Dwight Waldo, *The Administrative State* (New York: The Ronald Press, 1948).

19 Weber, *Economy and Society*, vol. 2, pp. 1393, 1401. *Cf.* p. 1418: "There is no substitute for the systematic cross-examination (under oath) of experts before a parliamentary commission in the presence of the respective departmental officials." Also *cf.* pp. 992–93, 997–98, 1403, 1419–31.

20 John Kenneth Galbraith, *Economics and the Public Purpose* (New York: Mentor Books, 1975), pp. 155–56.

21 For a penetrating analysis of a case of fragmentation in public bureaucracy, see Edgar J. Dosman, *The National Interest: The Politics of Northern Development 1968–75* (Toronto: McClelland and Stewart, 1975). However, for a neo-Marxian effort to demonstrate a wider systemic logic to this fragmentation, see Rianne Mahon, "Canadian Public Policy: The Unequal Structure of Representation," in Leo Panitch, ed., *The Canadian State: Political Economy and Political Power* (Toronto: University of Toronto Press, 1979). *Cf.* Jürgen Habermas, *Legitimation Crisis* (Boston: Beacon Press, 1975), pt. 2, chs. 4–5.

22 On this and related points, see Douglas Torgerson, "Limits of the Administrative Mind: The Problem of Defining Environmental Problems," in Robert Paehlke and Douglas Torgerson, eds., *Managing Leviathan: Environmental Politics and the Administrative State* (Peterborough, ON: Broadview Press, 1990).

23 *Cf.* Herbert A. Simon, "The Structure of Ill-structured Problems" (1973), in his *Models of Discovery* (Dordrecht, Holland: D. Reidel Publishing, 1977).

24 Charles Perrow, *Complex Organizations: A Critical Essay*, 2nd ed. (Glenview, IL: Scott, Foresman, and Company, 1979), ch. 4.

25 Simon, *Administrative Behavior*, pp. xxix–xxx.

26 F.E. Emery and E.L. Trist, "The Causal Texture of Organizational Environments" (1965), in F.E. Emery, ed., *Systems Thinking*, 2 vols., rev. ed. (Harmondsworth: Penguin Books, 1981), vol. 1, p. 254 (original emphasis).

27 Eric Trist, "A Concept of Organizational Ecology," *Australian Journal of Management* 2.2(1977): 166.

28 Trist, "A Concept of Organizational Ecology," p.167.

29 See, e.g., T. Burns, "Mechanistic and Organismic Structures" (1963), in D.S. Pugh, ed., *Organization Theory*, 2nd ed. (Harmondsworth: Penguin Books, 1984); Paul R. Lawrence and Jay W. Lorsch, *Organization and Environment: Managing Differentiation and Integration* (Boston: Harvard University, 1967); P.G. Herbst, *Alternatives to Hierarchies* (Leiden: Martinus Nijhoff, 1976).

30 See, e.g., C. West Churchman, *The Systems Approach*, rev. ed. (New York: Dell Publishing, 1979); John D. McEwan, "The Cybernetics of Self-organizing Systems" (1963), in C. George Benello and Dimitrios Roussopoulos, eds., *The Case for Participatory Democracy* (New York: The Viking Press, 1972).

31 Hooker and Van Hulst, "The Meaning of Environmental Problems," pp. 131–34.

32 On the achievement of "harmony" under anarchy, see Peter Kropotkin's 1905 *Encyclopedia Britannica* article "Anarchism," in Peter Kropotkin, *Kropotkin's Revolutionary Pamphlets* (New York: Dover Publications, 1970), esp. p. 284. Also see Howard J. Ehrlich, "Anarchism and Formal Organizations: Some Notes on the Sociological Study of Organizations from an Anarchist Perspective," in Ehrlich *et al.*, eds., *Reinventing Anarchy*.

33 "The experience of what the royal authority could achieve encouraged men to imagine that one enlightened will, with a centralised administration at its command, might accomplish endless improvements in civilisation." Bury, *The Idea of Progress*, p. 76. *Cf.* Macpherson, *Possessive Individualism*, chs. 2, 5–6; C.B. Macpherson, *The Life and Times of Liberal Democracy* (Oxford: Oxford University Press, 1977), chs. 1–2. Also *cf.* Elie Halévy, *The Growth of Philosophic Radicalism* (Boston: Beacon Press, 1955). The role of Locke as an apostle of "progress" is emphasized in Victor Ferkiss, *The Future of Technological Civilization* (New York: George Braziller, 1974).

34 Weber, *Protestant Ethic*, p. 181.

35 *Cf.* Donald R. Kelley, *et al.*, *The Economic Superpowers and the Environment* (San Francisco: W.H. Freeman, 1976).

36 *Cf.* Torgerson, "Limits of the Administrative Mind."

37 *Cf.* David Dickson, "Limiting Democracy: Technocrats and the Liberal State," *Democracy* 1 (1981): 61–79; T.J. Schrecker, *Political Economy of Environmental Hazards* (Ottawa: Law Reform Commission of Canada, 1984).

38 *Cf.* Jean-Jacques Rousseau, "A Discourse on Political Economy" (1758), in *The Social Contract and Discourses* (London: Everyman's Library, 1966), esp. pp. 236–42.

3

Democracy and Environmentalism: Opening a Door to the Administrative State?

Robert Paehlke

In the 1970s, the early days of environmentalism, bleak political and economic conclusions were frequently drawn regarding the impact of environmental realities on democratic practice. Some lamented the possible demise of democratic practice on the shoals of coming economic scarcity of "environmental" origin.[1] The suspicion was also voiced that environmentalism itself, whatever its merits, might harbor a threat to democratic institutions.[2] While these concerns were made in a theoretically cogent manner, the day-to-day practice of environmental politics and policy throughout the 1970s and 1980s had an opposite effect: democratic processes were generally enhanced. Moreover, the environmental movement itself has been at odds with the technocratic administrative state, environmentalists characteristically distrusting bureaucratic—and even some scientific—expertise.[3] Environmentalist organizations have all along favored openness and participation in environmental administration, thereby reflecting deeply democratic impulses. Arguably, especially perhaps in today's era of global-scale environmental decision making, the successful resolution of environmental problems is more likely in a context that is more rather than less democratic.

ENVIRONMENTALISM AND THE END OF DEMOCRACY: THE THEORY

William Ophuls and Robert Heilbroner made the pessimistic case regarding democracy in an age of environmental limits. Ophuls, a political theorist, wrote in a Hobbesian spirit; Heilbroner, an economist, offered a modern update of the Malthusian dilemma. Unlike Malthus, however, both Ophuls and Heilbroner understood many of the complexities of resource scarcity. They did not characterize the problem as simply the product of excessive population growth. Unlike Hobbes, neither unambiguously welcomed increased authority as a necessary protector of commodious living; indeed, they expressed profound regret regarding the undemocratic future they concluded was likely and necessary. Each came to gloomy economic and political conclusions after a quite careful review of future resource availability, food-growing capabilities, likely population growth, pollution, and the general environmental impacts of human economic activities, and, most important perhaps, future energy options.

As Ophuls put it,

> Once relative abundance and wealth of opportunity are no longer available to mitigate the harsh political dynamics of scarcity, the pressures favoring greater inequality, oppression, and conflict will build up, so that the return of scarcity portends the revival of age-old political evils, for our descendants if not for ourselves. In short, the golden age of individualism, liberty and democracy is all but over.[4]

Similarly, Heilbroner drew this conclusion:

> ... given these mighty pressures and constraints we must think of alternatives to the present order in terms of social systems that offer a necessary degree of regimentation as well as a different set of motives and objectives. I must confess I can picture only one such system. This is a social order that will blend a "religious" orientation and a "military" discipline. Such a monastic organization of society may be repugnant to us, but I suspect it offers the greatest promise for bringing about the profound and painful adaptations that the coming generations must make.[5]

In keeping with the view of many 1970s environmentalists, both anticipated a coming era of resource scarcity and environmental limits. From this followed the need for severe political control, economic restraint, and enforced discipline uncharacteristic of liberal-democratic societies and capitalist economies.

Writing at about the same time as Heilbroner and Ophuls, but without being explicitly familiar with their particular arguments, John Passmore presents the following in seeming reply:

> The view that ecological problems are more likely to be solved in an authoritarian than in ... a liberal democratic society rests on the implausible assumption that the authoritarian state would be ruled by ecologist-kings. In practice there is more hope of action in democratic societies. In the United States, particularly, the habit of local action, the capacity of individuals to

initiate legal proceedings, and the tradition of public disclosure are powerful weapons in the fight against ecological destruction.[6]

But elsewhere in his argument Passmore fears that the expansion of governmental responsibilities virtually implies the "gradual emergence of a bureaucratic police state."[7] Further, at several points Passmore characterizes environmentalists as possessing an enthusiasm for coercion, generally without granting the existence of a stronger tendency within the movement to precisely the opposite: popular empowerment with enhanced participation and openness.[8]

Like those of Ophuls and Heilbroner, Passmore's argument has provided considerable fuel to those who would prefer virtually any form of economic growth to even a modicum of environmental protection, if forced to choose. These critics and editorial writers have continuously told the public that environmentalists are anti-democratic elitists. A particular point of criticism is that environmentalists are themselves usually economically comfortable and thus for the most part unconcerned about the loss of jobs implicit in the policies they espouse; and this point has been effectively countered elsewhere.[9] However, the general allegation that environmentalism is anti-democratic has not been clearly rebutted from an environmentalist perspective. Here I offer one response to this charge.

One might claim that Ophuls and Heilbroner simply over-reacted to the implications of exponential population growth, the 1970s energy crisis, and the seemingly sudden visibility of environmental degradation. Such a conclusion may well be valid in hindsight, but is far too easy. For example, while there are now signs that global population stabilization may be possible, it remains a very long way from achievement, and we still face coming declines in fossil fuel availability largely unprepared and unmindful of the extent of the challenge before us.[10] It is clear as well that grain-producing capabilities can be, and indeed have been, radically expanded in most of the Third World.[11] However, this latter achievement rests in turn on radical increases in the use of water and fertilizer, and therefore fossil fuel, inputs. These increases may be unsustainable in the long run.[12] Whether or not this change is temporary, it is not obvious that population stabilization will be achieved before we reach the limits of ecologically sound and sustainable food-production capabilities.

Finally here, though there are now signs that the economic and political systems of many developed nations can stop growth in total energy demand, there is limited evidence that the political will can be mustered to oversee any long-term reduction in that demand, however gradual.[13] Indeed, a more convincing case can be made that the future holds a long series of economic lurches created by energy supply problems dwarfing those of 1979–1983. Overall one might conclude, again with the advantage of hindsight, that the economic and resource arguments lying behind the frightening political visions of the 1970s were overstated, but nonetheless may yet prove an important dimension of our long-term future.

The more serious error of Ophuls, Heilbroner, and others is their underestimation of the capabilities of democratic political institutions. At least some nations may find an answer to future economic, environmental, and resource problems in *more* rather than *less* democracy. Democracy, participation, and open administration carry not only a danger of division and conflict, but as well perhaps the best means of mobilizing educated and prosperous populations in difficult times. Indeed, the environmental issues of the 1970s have, in practice, often led to the revitalization and expansion of participatory opportunities.

ENVIRONMENTALISM AND DEMOCRATIC PRACTICE: OPENING A DOOR

Several important analysts of the environmental movement have noted a reasoned and principled inclination of many environmental organizations to the open administration of environmental and resource policies. To some extent this emphasis contrasts with the perspective of earlier conservationists, particularly with the faith they placed on expert administration and governmental bureaucracies as protectors of the public interest.[14] Richard Andrews noted that conservationists assumed that there was a "single public interest" that "could be discovered or determined by experts."[15] In practice, however, it was found that the very private interests that were to be controlled by public servants (acting in the public interest) came themselves to dominate the resource-management agencies. Those private interests in effect came to determine the public interest jointly with those employed by the public bureaucracies. In response to this pattern, "[t]he solution demanded by environmentalists was open access to administrative decision processes for all interested persons."[16] Thus, with this experience and perception, environmentalists typically urged greater openness and greater public involvement in administrative decision making.

One can link this distinctive emphasis to some important academic perceptions of the 1950s and 1960s. In the 1950s, Grant McConnell and others linked the concept of the "captured" administrative agency to conservation issues. McConnell argued that administrative decisions regarding valuable resources are never exclusively technical in nature; they are political and value-laden. As he put it in a study of the US Forest Service: "Any decision that will in fact be made will be in terms of the particular set of values held by the administrator, or perhaps, by the particular set of pressures that are brought to bear on him."[17] Similarly Lynton Caldwell, writing in 1963, observed that

Scientists may one day tell us what kinds of environment are best for our physical and mental health, but it seems doubtful if scientists alone will be able to determine the environmental conditions that people will seek. There will surely remain an element of personal judgment that cannot be relegated to the computer.[18]

In short, expertise is necessary to achieving effective environmental decision making, but it is not sufficient. Effective decision making, from an environmentalist viewpoint, involves both expertise and the views of those who are most affected by the decisions at hand. All views, environmentalists have consistently argued, must be aired openly. Again, as Andrews put it, it has been the view of environmentalists that "in closed or low visibility arenas the power of highly organized private interests is maximized."[19] Among environmentalists there has always been a very strong sense of the public's right to know and to be involved in the decisions that affect their lives. Rachel Carson, whom many have called the founder of environmentalism, wrote in *Silent Spring* in 1960,

> It is not my contention that chemical insecticides must never be used. I do contend that we have put poisonous and biologically potent chemicals indiscriminately into the hands of persons largely or wholly ignorant of their potentials for harm. We have subjected enormous numbers of people to contact with these poisons, *without their consent, and often without their knowledge.*[20]

The early statements of McConnell, Caldwell, and Carson and early analyses of the environmental movement by Andrews, Hays, Schnaiberg, and others suggest that there is a strong link between environmentalism and enhanced democratic openness and participation.[21] This link in principle, as we shall see, was generally carried through into the early practice of environmental administration in the 1970s.

The development of participatory opportunities at the national level began in the United States with the Administrative Procedures Act of 1946. The anti-pollution bills of the 1960s revived this initial effort, and a significant leap, in the view of some analysts, was made with the National Environmental Policy Act (NEPA) of 1969. NEPA, as is well known, required the preparation of environmental impact statements and open agency consideration of alternatives. Executive Order 11514, which followed, required timely public information and ("whenever appropriate") public hearings. The NEPA process also created an additional basis for litigation by environmental interest groups and citizens, and such activity increased considerably, especially in the early years of the bill.[22] More than a decade after its passage Lynton Caldwell wrote the following by way of a summary evaluation:

> The genius of NEPA lies in its linkage of mandatory procedure to substantive policy criteria and in the pressure it brings on administrative agencies to consider scientific evidence in their planning and decision-making. NEPA is importantly, even though secondarily, a full disclosure or public participation law. Other statutes provide more explicitly for this procedural reform, although NEPA adds to their strength.[23]

Not all analysts of NEPA, however, have been so favorably disposed to its effectiveness, especially as a means of enhancing public involvement. Sally

Fairfax, writing in *Science* in 1978, argued that NEPA locks environmental activists into an unduly formal set of procedures and reduces the effectiveness of their participation in a sea of paperwork: "While it cannot be conclusively demonstrated, the public involvement that NEPA has induced is so formal, so predictable, and so proposal-oriented that it seems to have stifled meaningful dialogue between citizens and agencies."[24] Indeed, in Fairfax's view, NEPA may well have stifled public participation in environmental decision making which was developing well in any case prior to 1969.[25] In expressing her doubts about NEPA, Fairfax makes clear that public participation regarding environmental protection was increasing in a variety of ways prior to NEPA and continued to expand after NEPA in ways Fairfax contends were unrelated to that particular bill. As an example of this, Fairfax carefully documented the ways in which "standing" before the US courts on environmental matters broadened independently from the provisions of NEPA. Although formally providing participatory procedures, she thereby suggested, the new administrative mechanism served to contain rather than expand the impulses of popular participation.

For our purposes here we do not need to resolve the debate regarding the strengths and weaknesses of this particular bill. The reality doubtless lies between Fairfax's skepticism and Caldwell's general comfort. But no one questions that citizen participation was an important part of the early stages of the environmental era. More than that, environmentalists—Fairfax among them— have consistently pressed at every opportunity for more and more effective means of involving the public in decision-making processes.

It is hardly surprising that agencies have sought to structure, and in effect control, public involvement. As Fairfax noted, they naturally want to promote the expansion of their attentive publics, their clientele. But bureaucracies, almost by definition, seek silence, and if open to participation, prefer managed participation. Max Weber observed this early in the century when he described what we have come to call the administrative state:

> Every bureaucracy seeks to increase the superiority of the professionally informed by keeping their knowledge and intentions secret. Bureaucratic administration always tends to be an administration of "secret sessions": insofar as it can, it hides its knowledge and action from criticism.[26]

In effect, environmental organizations have sought to counter this tendency; indeed, the whole body of early US environmental legislation was, in part, a means of opening a door to the administrative state. The expansion of democratic practice was sometimes consciously intended and sometimes simply the outcome of the fact of participation—of attempts to reverse or modify existing environmental policies by legal, democratic means. In general the participatory dimensions of environmental legislation both promote and place orderly bounds on participation. In so doing, such legislation limits, but at the same time legitimizes, such participation. Limitation is particularly important to some in decision-

making agencies; similarly, legitimation can prove to be very important to environmentalists, especially in political contexts where environmentalism is less favored
by the political leadership of the day, or of lesser interest to the public at large.

Throughout the 1970s, new environmental legislation in the United States and
elsewhere contained provisions assuring public participation.[27] Indeed, every
major piece of US environmental legislation in the 1970s allowed for public participation in environmental decision making. Environmental legislation that did
not add new channels for public involvement was rarely, if ever, proposed and
never enacted in this period.

THE 1980S AND SINCE: CLOSING THE OPEN DOOR?

The Reagan years in the United States showed how easily public sentiment can
become tentative about environmental concerns. In such a context a political
leadership hostile to environmental protection can roll back earlier gains very
rapidly, even if majority, but more subdued, public support still exists. But public participation provisions built into legislation can be very important within a
climate of relative indifference. Knowledge of what is going on and vehicles for
comment and action can help to check a hostile bureaucracy. Such supports are
also essential as particular issues jump into and then fade from the headlines, as
the issue attention cycle continues its seemingly inevitable rhythms.[28] The Reagan administration sought to close the open door in environmental administration, but in eight years was never fully able to do so. During those years the environmental movement grew in strength rather than faded, in part because there
were windows into the administrative world and in part because those put in
place to close the doors were either unappealing or dishonest, or both.

In Canada, where the tradition of cabinet government has normally led to a
more closed administrative process, environmental decision making has also led
to a perceived need for enhanced public involvement. However, greater governmental caution regarding openness has led, for example, to an environmental
assessment process, both federal and provincial, which is generally more limited.
Nonetheless, Canadian environmentalists have also consistently sought more
open and participatory administrative procedures.[29] For example, while decision
making regarding pesticides in Canada was historically a closed and cautious
process (cautious in the sense that there has been a general absence of significant
challenges to the preferences of farmers or the agricultural chemical industry),
environmentalists sought to open the process to greater public scrutiny. For
decades the process most often simply followed the environmental challenges to
pesticide use that were previously sustained in the United States. However, in the
wake of the US Industrial Biotest (IBT) scandals, Agriculture Canada, the
responsible ministry, was pushed to revise decision procedures significantly and
to increase openness and opportunities for public inputs significantly.[30] More
recently, citizen activism at the municipal level has blocked the cosmetic use of
pesticides on lawns in several cities, including Toronto.

In general, though, the hesitation to encourage and promote ongoing public involvement in administrative and legal decision making in Canada stands in contrast to the extent to which normal ad hoc participatory policy instruments have been applied to environmental issues. Specifically in Canada, as in Britain and Australia, Royal Commissions were frequently appointed to deal with environmental matters. It has seemed at times, especially when environmental issues were highly prominent, that this device of long-standing general use has been tailor-made for controversies of an environmental nature. There was a general lull in the use of this instrument through the 1990s, but a commission of inquiry was struck yet again following the events at Walkerton, Ontario (discussed below).

Even today, by far the single most important use of environmental Royal Commissions in Canada was the federal government's Mackenzie Valley Pipeline Inquiry headed by Mr. Justice Thomas R. Berger.[31] The Berger Commission (1974–1977) was highly innovative with respect to public involvement. Berger spent days and even weeks in each of very many, very small native villages in the remote and distant northern reaches of Canada. Hearings were as informal as necessary to make participants comfortable, and television and media coverage of some of these meetings was extensive. Berger's more recent efforts in Alaska showed a similar approach and have elicited this comment:

> In the inquiry process Tom Berger has created what may well become the most important invention of the Twentieth Century. We could call it a "Cross-Cultural Hearing Aid." In his second northern inquiry, Berger journeyed to 62 villages all over Alaska to listen to Eskimos, Indians, and Aleuts. The "hearing aid" quality of both efforts derived primarily from the media coverage (which differed considerably in the two cases), the provision of interpreters in Native languages, and, in the case of the MVP Inquiry, the concurrent organizing work undertaken by Dene Nation field workers.[32]

The first Berger Commission set an example of effective public participation noted worldwide. It also, to some extent, reinforced the sense of caution in Canadian governmental circles about the political risks associated with the public inquiry process. Nonetheless, numerous other inquiries followed the Berger inquiry, mostly within provincial rather than federal jurisdiction and including most notably, in Ontario, the Royal Commission on Electric Power Planning, the Royal Commission on the Northern Environment, and the Royal Commission on Matters of Health and Safety Arising from the Use of Asbestos. All of these inquiries utilized an extensive public hearing process. In addition, at least three other provinces held inquiries regarding the environmental and/or occupational health effects of uranium mining when the health effects associated with that occupation gained wide public attention and concern. In each of these cases, and many others, there has been extensive public involvement, often encouraged by intervener funding and generally involving participation from a wide variety of social groups.[33]

Until economic factors rendered concern about the expansion of nuclear energy at least temporarily moot, public involvement in environmental decision making was probably most extensive in the case of nuclear power plants, uranium mining, and nuclear fuel processing. This was true in Canada, the United States, Australia, and most Western European countries. In Canada the environmental impact assessment process has been extensively used, as have Royal Commissions. Regular Canadian channels for decision making regarding nuclear safety have, however, been very closed indeed.[34] In the United States, the public has been far more involved in the regular decision channels regarding nuclear power. In Britain and Australia, large-scale special inquiries have been used. In continental Europe, large-scale public reviews, extra-parliamentary dissent, and referenda have been commonplace in France, the former West Germany, Sweden, Austria, the Netherlands, Switzerland, and elsewhere. In Sweden, for example, a long process of special public discussions led, in 1979, to a halt to new reactor construction and a possible phasing out of nuclear power by 2010. Sweden previously was relatively heavily dependent on nuclear electricity.

As Nelkin and Pollack wrote, following an extended study of participation in nuclear decision making in several European jurisdictions,

... the participatory ideology has been "contagious." Demands for increased public involvement have spread from one sector to another; the experiments in the area of nuclear policy were but a natural extension of political reforms directed to democratization in the workplace ... [and elsewhere].[35]

They continue:

The experiments to date surely represent more an effort to convince the public about the acceptability of government decisions than any real sharing of power. Yet even the limited increase in public discussion has influenced nuclear policies, at the very least encouraged greater caution. In the long run, the implementation of public policies concerning technology and the very legitimacy of the responsible authorities may depend on the politics of participation.[36]

These words take on new meaning in the realization that the inquiries in question in this case preceded both Chernobyl and Three Mile Island. These events suggest that the doubts of a skeptical public may have been at least as reliable as the views of the "objective" experts in the employ of governments and the nuclear industry. Following these events both public and private authorities were more wary of proceeding with nuclear or other high-risk technologies without some process of public involvement. Indeed, the whole process of risk assessment, when seen as a technical (non-participatory) exercise, has faced heavy criticism within and outside the environmental movement as fundamentally anti-democratic.

The recent trend in the use of public inquiries in Canada has been much more mixed. Despite considerable public concern over the use of genetically modified (GM) crops and a widespread desire for labeling, there has been no public inquiry on this question. However, in Europe, as Andrew Jamison discusses in his chapter in this volume, there have been innovative public participation processes on this and other issues. The reason for this is plain: in Europe, the level of active public concern about the environment, and GM crops in particular, has been higher than in North America.[37] This suggests that there is a public involvement tipping point at which the use of inquiry processes cannot be avoided.

One might even hypothesize that when the public is openly alarmed, public inquiries should be used. Even governments hostile to both public participation and environmental protection will still respond if they fear for their futures. That was the case with the extreme, neo-conservative Harris government in Ontario in May 2000. Seven people died and thousands were made sick by contaminated tap water in Walkerton, shortly after the privatization of water testing and other related budgetary cutbacks and changes in regulatory procedures. A thorough public inquiry with widespread public participation, conducted by Judge Dennis O'Connor, laid explicit blame on both the provincial government and on malfeasant local water officials. Shortly thereafter Premier Harris resigned, and in 2003 the Conservative government was defeated, suggesting that their fears were well founded.

Innovative public participation in the environmental policy arena has taken other forms as well. These forms include such diverse initiatives as community right-to-know legislation, internal responsibility systems regarding occupational health and safety, the use of referenda in environmental matters, and direct participatory interaction between environmental citizen organizations and corporations.

Community right-to-know and, as in New Jersey, for example, state right-to-know legislation became increasingly popular during the 1980s.[38] These laws, by-laws, and ordinances require the disclosure of all sites where certain hazardous chemicals are manufactured or stored and the routes on which they are transported. In some cases these disclosures complement requirements on manufacturers and industrial users to inform their employees about chemicals to which those workers may be exposed. Community right-to-know can be important to residential and commercial property owners and to firefighters, for obvious reasons. A right-to-know approach has also been included on at least one occasion at the federal level, in Title 3 of the superfund amendments. This basic right to know the risks to which citizens are being subjected has been established reasonably widely, but it took a quarter of a century from the time that Rachel Carson argued, with regard to pesticides, that such a right existed.[39]

An occupational health and safety internal responsibility system had been established by the 1980s in several Canadian provinces, most notably Ontario, Quebec, Saskatchewan, Alberta, and British Columbia.[40] The system involves three basic rights: the right to know, the right to a union-management (or worker-management) health and safety review committee, and the right to refuse unsafe work. Here again is a legislated requirement of openness and participation, this time throughout the private sector with respect to employer-employee relations in the health and safety field. The internal responsibility system provides a means whereby individuals can, in principle, achieve workplace safety without the need to resort to actions so drastic as plant-wide strikes. Katherine Swinton has noted that many believe that this system is superior to a system wholly dependent on either management initiatives or government inspection, or both:

> Prevention is more likely to occur through an effective internal responsibility system and worker participation. Worker input into occupational health and safety regulation, whether in establishing programs to improve health in the workplace or in carrying out inspections utilizes the workers' experience and knowledge of the workplace. Those on the shop floor are likely to be aware of the unused machine guard or the clogged ventilation system....[41]

She goes on to argue that especially those managers who feel that more responsibility for health and safety must ultimately rest with workers appreciate the educative and peer-pressure aspects of the system. But Swinton also makes clear that many workers and union leaders

> see participation in regulating the workplace as a basic right. It is a worker's health and bodily integrity which are threatened by hazardous conditions, and he should be given sufficient information to evaluate the risks, opportunity for questioning the existence of such hazards, and a voice in their control.[42]

An internal responsibility system has considerable potential as a device for mobilizing industrial workers to a greater participatory role in workplace decision making. This is a prospect that has not been lost on pro-union observers in the United States. Charles Noble concluded for this very reason that a system of this sort would be preferable to the existing practice of the Occupational Safety and Health Administration.[43] But one must be clear that either instrument of protection is less effective within the climate created by global economic integration in a form that systematically exports industrial employment.

The third in our list of techniques, the referendum, though less widely noted, has been used in many US states, at one point especially for initiatives concerning refillable containers and nuclear issues.[44] In the 1980s, for example, there were referenda on nuclear power, toxic chemicals, urban growth, radioactive waste dumps, and toxic waste treatment facilities in various states.[45] A wide variety of environmental referenda have been conducted in California since, with mixed results. We might recall as well the important use of the referendum on nuclear power in Sweden in the 1970s. Since about 1990 this instrument has been used less frequently with regard to environmental initiatives.

In this period there has, however, been an increase in direct interaction between corporations and citizen organizations on environmental matters. This shift reflects the rising power of corporations in the era of global economic integration and the corresponding widespread decline in the willingness on the part of governments to challenge industries. Perhaps the first notable example of this was the 1990–91 joint Waste Reduction Task Force struck by the Environmental Defense Fund and the McDonald's Corporation that led to the demise of the clamshell packaging for hamburgers. The early 1990s saw, especially in Canada, the wide use of so-called multi-stakeholder sustainable development committees. And most recently, the World Resources Institute has worked with utilities and business schools and has directly challenged the business strategy of the US auto industry as overly dependant on large vehicles that are uneconomic outside the United States and losing their market share within. All of these initiatives involve considerable public participation through environmental non-governmental organizations (NGOs), but they find government either uninvolved or just one participant among many.

The forms of public involvement discussed here are ones that intervene in the decision making processes of administrative organizations. As we review the current scene of public participation in environmental administration, one final matter should be considered. Weber pointed out that those who sought to challenge an administrative apparatus were typically forced to adopt a similar administrative form. As mechanisms for the articulation of interests, political parties in particular have tended to follow the path of bureaucratization. The issue that arises here, then, is the organizational form adopted by environmentalists for the mobilization of environmental opinion.

What we find among environmental organizations is ambivalence and diversity: there is at times some amount of bureaucratization, but there is also strong resistance to this tendency. This resistance has become especially clear when environmentalists have organized political parties. Here we might note in particular the matter of party organization in the early days of the German Green Party. The German Greens made several notable participatory innovations. The party's federal assembly met annually, half of the membership of the party's federal board of directors was newly elected each year, and only one re-election to the same position was permitted. There were even efforts to rotate holders of elected office within their terms, but the party backed off from this as too destabilizing.

Nonetheless, it was expected in those early days that few if any officeholders would seek re-election to avoid the entrenchment of particular individuals in power. As the party came nearer to a share of power (and then entered government) this rule went by the board, but efforts remain to decentralize control of the party and to actively involve a maximum proportion of the membership involved in party governance. In power as part of a national coalition government and governing outright on the municipal level, German Greens have worked to enhance public participation in the wider society.[46] Other Green parties are structured in a more participatory fashion than are other political parties or, for that matter, many environmental NGOs. Notably, as well, the Green electoral breakthrough in San Francisco in 2003 was rooted in one of the most highly participatory electoral efforts in recent US history, especially at the municipal level.

CONCLUSION

In sharp contrast to the theoretical views noted at the outset, environmentalism has in practice widely and consistently led to (or at least sought) an expansion of democratic opportunities and an opening of administrative decision making to public participation. Environmentalists have highly valued both the protection and the further development of democratic institutions. Even the emphasis on potential threats to democracy in the writings of Ophuls and Heilbroner can be interpreted as further evidence of such concern, however pessimistic their overall conclusions. With the advantage of hindsight, we might now conclude that both Ophuls and Heilbroner were looking too widely, and perhaps too early, to see the consistency of the pattern set out in this essay. It does not necessarily follow, of course, that the potential next wave of resource limitations on economic prosperity will not seriously weaken the democratic hopes and efforts of today's environmentalists.[47] What needs rethinking is the character of the relationship between the quality of democratic institutions and processes and the actuality of resource and environmental limitations.

One important dimension of this rethinking is the relationship between elites, masses, and economic growth. Volkmar Lauber and Mark E. Kann, without apparently being aware of each other's work, argued that it is elites—particularly economic elites in the case of Kann and political elites in the case of Lauber—that pursue economic growth to the detriment of the environment.[48] The general public, both maintain, would be relatively more open to accepting restraints on such forms of economic growth. As Kann put it: "There are no guarantees that people will make wise decisions, but they have an incentive to do so: they must live with the consequences."[49] This is, of course, too simple: some populations can export some of the environmental costs of their economic gains to other jurisdictions or impose them on future generations. Nonetheless, Kann's central assertion may remain valid: "My thesis is that to the extent that the environment has been influenced in the United States it has mainly been influenced by elites who exercise concentrated power on their own behalf."[50] Lauber's suggested cure, moreover, is one with which both Kann and I would be comfortable: "power today is too closely linked with growth. Under those circumstances it seems more promising to restrain and limit power. For that purpose, liberal democracy is rather well fitted; it is one of the problems for which it was designed."[51]

Lauber, Kann, Ophuls, and Heilbroner could not have imagined in detail the world in which we have arrived in the early part of this new millennium. However, they anticipated the spirit of what we are seeing: an administration in Washington that not only does not hold public hearings on energy policy but that is prepared to go to the Supreme Court to protect its perceived right not even to disclose the names of those attending such meetings. That policy, it turns out, all but ignores the possibility of taking energy conservation seriously. The Bush administration is also prepared to throw fiscal caution to the winds to assure short-term economic growth and to go to war to assure, or attempt to assure, a dominant position in the oil-producing regions of the world. This is elite-driven economic growth with a vengeance.

In the future, environmental protection may well mandate economic restraint. What sorts of economic restraints are likely to arise in a world where, for example, conventional energy resources are more limited than they are today? Will adequate environmental protection require economic restraints that a democratic majority could not be persuaded to actively insist upon? That is perhaps the heart of the dilemma that all societies may well soon face. This problem cannot be solved here, but it is important to recognize it sooner rather than later.[52]

What can be ventured are some limited observations. First, democracy may be the best political tool humankind has developed for mobilizing populations, especially educated and at least moderately prosperous ones.[53] Environmentalists have, at least implicitly, sensed this. Since they often call for significant changes in socio-economic organization, and even socio-economic goals, innovative democratic means may be the best, if not the only, means of achieving their goals. This may be particularly true as global economic integration advances. In this context, democratic innovation must be carried through to the international level lest all nations be forced to compete with ever-lower taxation and ever less stringent social and environmental standards.

One understanding of the relationship between resource limitations, environmentalism, and democracy different from and more suited to an age of globalization than that of Ophuls, Heilbroner, and Passmore, is that of Richard J. Barnet. Barnet reviewed the same range of issues that Ophuls and Heilbroner considered. He came to similarly pessimistic conclusions regarding future resource prospects typical of the late 1970s, but he explicitly rejected both their neo-Malthusian and neo-Hobbesian conclusions: "In today's world," he first noted, "the heirs of Malthus preach what they call 'lifeboat ethics,' claiming the same monopoly on realism that fortified the dismal preacher when he pronounced his death sentence for the poor."[54] And he went on to add this: "Despairing of human altruism to subordinate the quest for personal enrichment to the common good, the heirs of Hobbes have seized upon the dangers of ecological catastrophe to legitimate the modern-day Leviathan."[55] In stark contrast to both these views, Barnet noted the importance of democracy as an educational and mobilizing tool:

Democracy is under severe attack at the moment when gathering evidence suggests that popular participation is a survival value. Major structural changes cannot take place in any country without the mobilization of the whole people. The solution to the energy crisis in the U.S., for example, requires a degree of public understanding and participation which our political institutions do not know how to achieve.[56]

This conclusion is even more apt now twenty-five years after it was written. Even Barnet, however, may have underestimated to some extent the potential power of effective democratic institutions. Goldrich's analysis of the process that followed the Northwest Power Act of 1980 is a case in point, as are many of the examples already noted above. Both the Northwest Power Planning Council, an official planning body, and the Northwest Conservation Act Coalition, a citizen body, sought "to integrate the values of environmental enhancement, citizen participation in government decision-making, and economic development."[57] The point is that all things environmental do not necessarily involve bleak economic and political scenarios.

A wide variety of environmental measures, including recycling and sustainability-oriented industrial redesign, household energy conservation, the separation of household wastes, sustainable agriculture and forestry, and enhanced use of public transportation require active public involvement, but also generally produce more rather than fewer employment opportunities. However, most such measures may involve economic dislocations, economic costs for someone to bear, and, in some cases, induced inconveniences. But the general public, polls suggest, is not unwilling to make sacrifices to achieve environmental protection. Political participation can help make the necessary effort as well as the attendant redistribution of costs and benefits fairer and more widely understood. Democratic mobilization is essential to the achievement of such policies in the face of the opposition of vested interests that such policies frequently engender.

In conclusion, I would stress what I think is obvious: environmental politics, especially in North America, must be a centrist and democratic politics. To achieve this environmentalists must be constantly mindful of the socio-economic impacts of whatever measures they propose and must counter those that claim that environmental rollbacks, or access to other nations' resources, is somehow essential to our "way of life." Environmentalists should continue to emphasize the positive side of their program—sustainable and decentralized economic development and employment opportunities.[58] Finally, environmentalism cannot be successful in the long run without a continuous enhancement of opportunities for democratic participation.

NOTES

1 William Ophuls, *Ecology and the Politics of Scarcity* (San Francisco: W.H. Freeman, 1977); Robert L. Heilbroner, *An Inquiry into the Human Prospect* (New York: W.W. Norton, 1974). A thoughtful response to this literature from a perspective similar to that in this chapter is David W. Orr and Stuart Hill, "Leviathan, the Open Society and the Crisis of Ecology," in David W. Orr and Marvin S. Soroos, eds., *The Global Predicament:*

Ecological Perspectives on World Order (Chapel Hill: University of North Carolina Press, 1979). I came upon this excellent article shortly after the original publication of an earlier version of this essay in *Environmental Ethics* 10(Winter, 1988): 291–308.

2 John Passmore, *Man's Responsibility for Nature* (London: Duckworth, 1974). Passmore's case was made against what he saw as dangerous tendencies within environmentalism; the arguments of Ophuls and Heilbroner focused on the political implications of environmental and resource scarcity. Passmore might well regard Ophuls and Heilbroner as examples of that which he feared. Passmore's work has, of course, been seen as problematic in several regards. See, e.g., Robin Attfield, *The Ethics of Environmental Concern* (Oxford: Basil Blackwell, 1983); Val Routley, "Critical Notice of John Passmore, *Man's Responsibility for Nature*," *Australasian Journal of Philosophy* 53(1975): 171–85.

3 It is this environmentalist distrust of "established" science that seems to disconcert Passmore. Passmore concentrated perhaps too much on extreme statements of this distrust and did not appreciate that such doubts, rather than being a threat to democratic values, could support more participatory forms of decision making. Further, one might add that the recognition that in some contexts science and values become inextricably linked can also result in better science.

4 Ophuls, *Ecology and the Politics of Scarcity*, p. 145.

5 Heilbroner, *An Inquiry into the Human Prospect*, p. 161.

6 Passmore, *Man's Responsibility for Nature*, p. 183.

7 Passmore, *Man's Responsibility for Nature*, pp.193–94.

8 Passmore, *Man's Responsibility for Nature*, pp. 60–61, 96, and 99. To his credit Passmore does allow the possibility that environmentalism may turn out to be an "anti-bureaucratic" force (see p. 183n.).

9 Regarding the net positive effect on employment opportunities associated with pro-environmental policies see, for example, the numerous studies cited in Frederick H. Buttel, Charles C. Geisler, and Irving W. Wiswall, eds., *Labor and the Environment* (Westport, CT: Greenwood Press, 1984) and in David B. Brooks and Robert Paehlke, "Canada: A Soft Path in a Hard Country," *Canadian Public Policy* 6(1980): 444–53 and Robert Paehlke, "Work in a Sustainable Society," in Roger Keil, et al., eds, *Political Ecology: Global and Local* (London: Routledge, 1998), pp. 272–91.

10 The United Nations now projects that global population stability will be achieved over the next century at perhaps a total of ten billion souls, roughly twice the present population. However, given the fact that until the 1970s population growth had done little but accelerate for centuries this new projection is as much hope as certainty.

11 For an overinterpretation of this new reality see Peter Drucker, "The Changed World Economy," *Foreign Affairs* 64(1986): 768–91.

12 That is, not only will it be difficult to achieve further increases, but those that have occurred may be at least in part temporary. Obviously we cannot count on long-term supplies of those fertilizers that are obtained from fossil fuels. Some irrigation water as well is drawn from non-replenishing sources and most irrigation affects soil salinity. Biotechnology may find ways around some of these limits, but gains without costs can hardly be assumed.

13 That is, the early 1980s saw a halt to energy demand growth, but the mid-1980s have witnessed a considerable and unwarranted relaxation of attention to this issue.

14 I discuss this theme more extensively in "Participation in Environmental Administration: Closing the Open Door?" *Alternatives* 14.2(1987): 43–48. Indeed the conservation movement often seemed to assume that public bureaucracies could somehow objectively determine the "public interest."

15 Richard N.L. Andrews, "Class Politics or Democratic Reform: Environmentalism and American Political Institutions," *Natural Resources Journal* 20(1980): 228.

16 Andrews, "Class Politics or Democratic Reform," p. 237.

17 Grant McConnell, "The Conservation Movement—Past and Present," *Western Political Quarterly* 7(1954): 471.

18 Lynton K. Caldwell, "Environment: A New Focus for Public Policy?" *Public Administration Review* 23(1963), p. 139.

19 Andrews, "Class Politics or Democratic Reform," p. 237.

20 Rachel Carson, *Silent Spring* (Greenwich, CT: Fawcett Publications, 1962), p. 22. Emphasis added.

21 Sources not thus far cited are Samuel Hays, "From Conservation to Environment: Environmental Politics in the United States Since World War Two," *Environmental Review* 6.2(1982): 14–41; and Allan Schnaiberg, *The Environment: From Surplus to Scarcity* (New York: Oxford University Press, 1980).

22 Lettie McSpadden Wenner, "The Misuse and Abuse of NEPA," *Environmental Review* 7(1983): 229–54; on this point see esp. pp. 229–31.

23 Lynton K. Caldwell, *Science and the National Environmental Policy Act* (Tuscaloosa: University of Alabama Press, 1982), p. 74. A quite effective, pro-NEPA argument is also made by Serge Taylor in *Making Bureaucracies Think: The Environmental Impact Assessment Strategy of Administrative Reform* (Stanford: Stanford University Press, 1984).

24 Sally K. Fairfax, "A Disaster in the Environmental Movement," *Science* 199(1978): 746.

25 For example, Fairfax dates the origins of greater participatory involvement in administration to the Administrative Procedures Act of 1946.

26 Max Weber, "Bureaucracy," in *From Max Weber: Essays in Sociology* (New York: Oxford University Press, 1946), p. 233.

27 This generalization holds for the Clean Air Acts of 1970 and 1977, the 1972 amendments to the Federal Water Pollution Control Act, the Toxic Substances Control Act (TSCA) of 1976, the Resource Conservation and Recovery Act (RCRA) of 1976, and the Comprehensive Environmental Response, Compensation, and Liability Act of 1980, the so-called "superfund" legislation.

28 *Cf.* Robert Paehlke and Douglas Torgerson, "Toxic Waste and the Administrative State: NIMBY or Participatory Management," in Robert Paehlke and Douglas Torgerson, eds., *Managing Leviathan: Environmental Politics and the Administrative State* (Peterborough: Broadview Press, 1990); and Walter A. Rosenbaum, "The Politics of Public Participation in Hazardous Waste Management," in James P. Lester and Ann O'M. Bowman, eds., *The Politics of Hazardous Waste Management* (Durham, NC: Duke University Press, 1983).

29 Regarding both the cautiousness and the call for reform see Robert B. Gibson and Beth Savan, *Environmental Assessment in Ontario* (Toronto: Canadian Environmental Law Research Foundation, 1986); G.E. Beanlands and P.N. Duinker, *An Ecological Framework for Environmental Impact Assessment in Canada* (Halifax: Dalhousie University Institute for Resource and Environmental Studies, 1983); Evangeline S. Case *et al.*, eds., *Fairness in Environmental and Social Impact Assessment Processes* (Calgary: University of Calgary Law School, 1983); and J.B.R. Whitney and V.W. Maclaren, eds., *Environmental Impact Assessment: The Canadian Experience* (Toronto: Institute for Environmental Studies, University of Toronto, 1985).

30 See *National Workshop on Risk-Benefit Analysis* (Ottawa: Pesticides Directorate, Environment Canada, 1985); and William Leiss, *The Risk Management Process* (Ottawa: Pesticides Directorate, Agriculture Canada, October 1985). Regarding IBT see Samuel Epstein, *The Politics of Cancer* (San Francisco: Sierra Club Books, 1978).

31 See the final report of this commission, *Northern Frontier/Northern Homeland*, 2 vols. (Ottawa: Supply and Services Canada, 1977); for a lucid commentary see Douglas Torgerson, "Between Knowledge and Politics: Three Faces of Policy Analysis," *Policy Sciences* 19(1986): 33–59.

32 Walt Taylor and Peggy Taylor, review of Thomas R. Berger's *Village Journey: The Report of the Alaska Native Review Commission*, *Alternatives* 14(1987): 35.

33   For a good overview of the use of the inquiry process see Liora Salter and Debra Slaco, *Public Inquiries in Canada* (Ottawa: Science Council of Canada, 1981).

34   See G. Bruce Doern, "The Atomic Energy Control Board," in G. Bruce Doern, ed., *The Regulatory Process in Canada* (Toronto: Macmillan Company of Canada, 1978).

35   Dorothy Nelkin and Michael Pollack, "The Politics of Participation and the Nuclear Debate in Sweden, the Netherlands, and Austria," *Public Policy* 25(1977): 333–57.

36   Nelkin and Pollack, "The Politics of Participation," pp. 356–57. See also Dorothy Nelkin and Michael Pollack, *The Atom Besieged* (Cambridge, MA: MIT Press, 1981).

37   See Christopher Rootes, ed., *Environmental Process in Western Europe* (Oxford: Oxford University Press, 2003).

38   Mary Louise Adams, "Right to Know: A Summary," *Alternatives* 11.3/4(1983): 29–36. For a discussion of the extent to which recent federal initiatives in this area have been an attempt to pre-empt state and local efforts see P.R. Tyson, "The Preemptive Effect of the OSHA Hazard Communication Standard on State and Community Right to Know Laws," *Notre Dame Law Review* 62(1987): 1010–23; and Albert R. Matheny and Bruce A. Williams, "The Crisis of Administrative Legitimacy: Regulatory Politics and The Right-to-Know," in Robert Paehlke and Douglas Torgerson, eds., *Managing Leviathan: Environmental Politics and the Administrative State* (Peterborough: Broadview Press, 1990), pp. 229–41.

39   See 14 above. In that statement Carson went on to say, "If the Bill of Rights contains no guarantee that a citizen shall be secure against lethal poisons distributed by either private individuals or by public officials, it is surely only because our forefathers, despite their considerable wisdom and foresight, could conceive of no such problem."

40   See, e.g., G.B. Reshenthaler, *Occupational Health and Safety in Canada* (Montreal: Institute for Research on Public Policy, 1979); Katherine E. Swinton, "Enforcement of Occupational Health and Safety Legislation: The Role of the Internal Responsibility System," in Kenneth Swan and Katherine E. Swinton, eds., "Studies in Labour Law" (Toronto: Butterworths, 1982); and T.F. Schrecker, *Workplace Pollution* (Ottawa: Law Reform Commission of Canada, 1986). The term *internal responsibility system* was first used by Dr. James Ham, head of the Ontario Royal Commission on the Health and Safety of Workers in Mines (1976).

41   Swinton, "Enforcement," p. 146.

42   Swinton, "Enforcement," pp. 146–47.

43   Charles Noble, *Liberalism at Work* (Philadelphia: Temple University Press, 1986).

44   See, e.g., William U. Chandler, *Materials Recycling: The Virtue of Necessity* (Washington, DC: Worldwatch Institute, 1983).

45   See *Environmental Action* 18.4(1987): 6.

46   Gerd Langguth, *The Green Factor in German Politics* (Boulder, CO: Westview Press, 1986), pp. 47–49.

47   That is, how solid are the participatory structures that have been established? Would they withstand, for example, another wave of oil-price shocks? Would we not see environmental impact analysis by-passed in any future "crisis" mentality? Or indeed will environmental protection stand up in the face of the economic fall-out that may yet result from the last price shock?

48   Mark E. Kann, "Environmental Democracy in the United States," in Sheldon Kamieniecki, Robert O'Brien, and Michael Clarke, eds., *Controversies in Environmental Policy* (Albany: SUNY Press, 1986), pp. 252–74; and Volkmar Lauber, "Ecology, Politics, and Liberal Democracy," *Government and Opposition* 13(1978): 199–217.

49   Kann, "Environmental Democracy in the United States," p. 253.

50   Kann, "Environmental Democracy in the United States," p. 253.

51   Lauber, "Ecology, Politics, and Liberal Democracy," p. 217.

52   For further discussion, see Robert Paehlke, *Environmentalism and the Future of Progressive Politics* (New Haven: Yale University Press, 1989) and *Democracy's Dilemma:*

Environment, Social Equity and the Global Economy (Cambridge, MA: MIT Press, 2003).

53 There has been an extensive literature regarding the relationship between democracy, socio-economic development, and political mobilization—particularly work in the 1960s by J.P. Nettl, Karl Deutsch, Phillips Cutright, S.M. Lipset, Karl de Schweinitz, Jr., Lyle W. Shannon, and Deane Neubauer.

54 Richard J. Barnet, *The Lean Years: Politics in the Age of Scarcity* (New York: Simon and Schuster, 1980), pp. 297–98.

55 Barnet, *The Lean Years*, p. 302.

56 Barnet, *The Lean Years*, p. 313.

57 Daniel Goldrich, "Democracy and Energy Planning: The Pacific Northwest as Prototype," *Environmental Review* 10(1986): 211.

58 By decentralization I do not mean to suggest that the geographic dispersion of populations is environmentally appropriate. On the contrary, environmentalists, in my view, have significantly underestimated the technical and political links between environmental protection and urbanism. See Robert Paehlke, *Bucolic Myths: Towards a More Urbanist Environmentalism* (Toronto: Institute for Urban and Community Studies, University of Toronto, 1986).

PART II

Techniques and Processes
of
Environmental Administration

The administrative response to environmental problems has been ambivalent. Much of the response has been conventional, involving modest reforms to the established procedures and structures of an administrative apparatus historically dedicated to the advance of industrialization. Still, there have been innovations which do at least point toward a form of environmental administration that would entail a significant departure from this conventional orientation. But even as innovative techniques and processes raise the prospect of something radically new, they are simultaneously drawn back toward the sphere of standard operating procedures. This ambivalence draws attention to the inevitable interweaving of politics and administration and suggests that the future of environmental administration depends very much upon that of environmental politics.

The articles in Part 11 explore the nature and potential of environmental administration. Although the authors strike different and, at times, conflicting notes, they are all concerned with the potential for a mode of administration which would break through conventional boundaries. Questioning the nature of reason and examining the role of expanded public discussion, the chapters may also be viewed as part of a larger methodological ferment which rejects the technocratic posture of a once-dominant positivism while seeking a fundamental reorientation of administrative and policy studies.

4

Ecological Reason in Administration: Environmental Impact Assessment and Green Politics

Robert V. Bartlett

All thinking worthy of the name must now be ecological, in the sense of appreciating and utilizing organic complexity, and in adapting every kind of change to the requirements not of man alone, or of any single generation, but of all his organic partners and every part of his habitat.[1]

ADMINISTRATIVE THEORY AND THE ENVIRONMENTAL PROBLEMATIQUE

Current administrative institutions are in no way adequate to the challenge presented by the modern environmental predicament. Accepting the administrative state as a permanent feature of the political landscape means accepting that, if environmental problems are to be solved, they must be solved in major part administratively—through more, different, somehow better administration. This is the point of departure for a majority of environmental reformers and policy analysts, who worry little about the fundamental structure of their political world. Yet deeper analysis of the capabilities of bureaucratic organizations and administratively dominated systems, both governmental and non-governmental, leads other theorists to raise troubling questions about the real possibilities of effective environmental administration.

These concerns arise less from the myths of the tyranny or the incompetence of the bureaucrat than from a realization of the significance of a partial congruence between the underlying causes of environmental degradation and the underlying imperatives of large, modern, administrative organizations. The impracticality of many of the prescriptions offered by ecofeminists, deep ecologists, green anarchists, and bioregionalists does not diminish the validity of their critiques of centralized hierarchical authority, instrumental rationality, and organizational power "in the service of anthropocentric arrogance."[2] The environmental problematique has, without question, given rise to an institutional crisis. And the converse is true as well: every identifiable primary and proximate cause of contemporary environmental degradation can be linked in myriad ways to the seemingly inherent ecological deficiencies, or pathologies, of the administrative state.[3]

Thus the administrative state presents an unhappy conundrum for theorists of environmental politics. To accept the administrative state largely as it is is to accept severe limits on the structuring of the environmental problematique for analysis—limits so severe as possibly to exclude any truly attractive solutions. The risk always is one of treating symptoms, a strategy that may complicate and even prevent timely diagnosis and treatment of causes. Energies may be focused instead on critiques of the administrative state itself, analyses of improbable alternatives, and normative arguments for wholesale social and political restructuring—"making the administrative state disappear" or "assume that the administrative state has withered away." The risk here is that of irrelevancy, in both the action world of politics and the theoretical world of scholarship.

Indeed, the dilemma may have no satisfactory escape, although few would be willing to admit as much. Perhaps, then, more attention ought to focus on possible strategies that neither accept the administrative state for what it is nor require its dismantling before a replacement is erected. The "creative third alternatives" that may hold the most promise, for both action and analysis, are what might be called subversive or "worm in the brain" strategies.[4] Such strategies involve dismantling or transmogrifying the administrative state from within—gradually and not entirely predictably—while remaking individual values and patterns of thinking and acting and, perhaps, while promoting "the preconditions for more substantial institutional innovation."[5] One example of a policy strategy of this kind is mandatory environmental impact assessment.

Although impact assessment was one of the major innovations in policy making and administration of the twentieth century, it yet has received little attention from political or policy theorists, who have tended to underestimate and misread its power, complexity, and subtlety.[6] As "feedforward" mechanisms, several variants of impact assessment such as technology assessment and social impact assessment are significant for environmental politics.[7] As a way of forcing explicit consideration to environmental concern, of course, the impact assessment approach that is of most interest is environmental impact assessment (EIA).

EIA is centrally important, not only because of its obvious relevance to environmental politics and the administrative state, but also because, unlike other forms of impact assessment, its underlying logic is in principle anchored in a distinctive rationality, namely, ecological rationality.[8] On the surface, EIA, like other forms of impact assessment, appears as a straightforward strategy that seeks to mitigate the destructive potential of industrial society, to ameliorate impact by basing action on greater and more widespread knowledge, and, thus, to enhance the ordinary rationality of policy and decision.[9] But by requiring, fostering, and reinforcing ecological rationality, both inside and outside of government, environmental impact assessment is subversive of the traditional administrative state. As such, it may have a far greater significance for environmental politics than has yet been recognized.

ECOLOGICAL RATIONALITY
AND THE ADMINISTRATIVE STATE

Ecological rationality is a rationality "of living systems, an order of relationships among living systems and their environments."[10] As such, it is a form of practical reason that can be distinguished from other prominent forms, such as technical, economic, social, legal, and political rationality.[11] According to Paul Diesing, technical rationality seeks efficient achievement of a single goal.[12] Economic rationality entails the maximum achievement of a plurality of goals. Underlying technical and economic rationality is the principle of efficiency; both are based on an order of measurement, comparison of values, and production. Social rationality seeks integration in social relations and social systems, an ordered social interdependence that makes social action possible and meaningful. Legal rationality refers to the reason inherent in any clear, consistent, and detailed system of formal rules for preventing disputes and providing solutions. Political rationality is a rationality of decisionmaking structures, of a practical intelligence capability for solving problems facing a society. Its principle of order is that of facilitating arrival at effective collective decisions.

All of these forms of reason are relevant to an analysis of politics in the administrative state. The narrowly instrumental character of administration and administrative organizations makes technical and economic rationalities dominant; indeed, the dominance of these rationalities is the defining feature of modern industrial societies.[13] The concept of rationality itself in such societies is often identified exclusively as technological and economic rationality. Max Weber was only the first to argue that the growth and spread of bureaucracy is explained by its inherent instrumental rationality—in other words, its peculiar legal and political rationality enhances its technical and economic rationality. Many post-Weberian critiques of bureaucracy focus on the pathologies or dysfunctions deriving from its flawed social rationality.[14] And the administrative state exists in and must make use of a non-social environment with which it must be at least minimally compatible. The ecological rationality of any social system, over the long run, must substantially coincide with the ecological rationality of its supporting physical environment.

The various forms of rationality are at least partly incompatible, and they may fundamentally conflict.[15] Nor are they of all the same order of importance. Diesing (who does not explicitly consider ecological rationality) argues that political rationality has precedence over other forms "because the solution of political problems makes possible an attack on any other problem while a serious political deficiency can prevent or undo all other problem solving."[16] John Dryzek argues persuasively that ecological rationality is a still more fundamental kind of reason: "The preservation and promotion of the integrity of the ecological and material underpinning of society—ecological rationality—should take priority over competing forms of reason in collective choices with an impact upon that integrity."[17] The priority of ecological rationality, according to Dryzek, is lexical. That is, it has absolute priority over other forms of reason because long-term, serious conflict between ecological rationality and other forms of rationality will result in the elimination of the other forms. This notwithstanding, ecological rationality does not fully pre-empt or supplant other forms of rationality: rarely is it completely determinative and it has little relevance to many dimensions of human activity.[18]

Each of these forms of reason can be reflected at three different levels of rationality: functional, substantive, and procedural. Functional rationality is the rationality inherent in the functioning of systems, societies, or organizations. The functional rationality of a system is the degree to which system behavior is organized according to particular principles and can be understood by reference to principles of order.[19] Functional rationality does not necessarily imply that a system is engaged in the process of thinking or reasoning. Nor does it imply that the principles underlying a given functional rationality must be known by any individual person—only that they be knowable.

Substantive rationality applies to individual decisions or actions.[20] It is an attribute of the behavior itself and refers to whether behavior is "appropriate to the achievement of given goals within the limits imposed by given conditions and constraints."[21] Substantive rationality is a standard for judging and labeling behavior—a behavior is substantively rational if it is appropriate or correct (if it *appears* to be rational).

Procedural rationality, in turn, refers to the actual processes of reasoning, the cognitive procedures used to choose actions.[22] It describes an intelligent system's ability to discover appropriate adaptive behavior.[23] Rationality in this sense is not an attribute of an action or behavior but an attribute of a deliberative, intellective process—synonymous with the common sense use of the term "reasoning."

The relationships among functional, substantive, and procedural rationality are problematic. Some individual actions may be non-rational (substantively) in the context of a society or organization that is highly rational (functionally). That is, even though some behaviors of some individuals cannot be labeled rational—they are not appropriate to the achievement of the individual's goals within the limits of conditions and constraints—the social system of which these individuals are a part may still exhibit a high degree of functional rationality. A functionally rational economy, for example, may be based in large part on predictable non-rational behavior by individuals. Likewise, individual behaviors may be rational (substantively) even though no reasoning (procedural rationality) was employed by the individual in choosing the behaviors. And, as mentioned earlier, a system may be rational (functionally) without any person understanding (procedural rationality) its principles of order.

Linkages among these levels of rationality can be found, although they are not all fixed and they seem to be in one direction only. Functional ecological rationality does not require substantive ecological rationality, but substantive ecological rationality across all individual behaviors should result in functional ecological rationality.[24] Likewise, substantive ecological rationality does not require procedural ecological rationality, but the probability that behaviors will be substantively rational is greater to the extent that humans and human systems reason ecologically before acting.

Linkages among functional, substantive, and procedural rationality are especially important in relating ecological rationality to the environmental predicament of the administrative state. The ultimate concern, of course, is with functional ecological rationality. Does a social system or organization, or do such systems collectively, exhibit ecological rationality? That is, is behavior organized according to ecological principles of order?

It is not *necessary* that ecological principles be understood, or even that reasoning occur, to achieve functional ecological rationality. Ecosystems completely devoid of humans have somehow managed. The only known examples of whole human societies exhibiting ecological rationality are certain traditional cultures lacking formal scientific understanding of ecological relationships. Many traditional cultures and earlier great civilizations have not been ecologically rational and collapses of these cultures can be explained in ecological terms.[25] Each and every action or behavior need not be ecologically rational— the functional ecological significance of individual behaviors depends on the homeostatic and adaptive capabilities of particular ecosystems and the consequences of exceeding those capabilities (both of which may vary, evolve, or shift, gradually or abruptly). Many traditional human societies may have tended to exhibit functional ecological rationality because those societies that failed to do so did not long survive—the punishment for ecological unreasonableness imposed by an indifferent universe.

Thus functional ecological rationality may provide an indispensable standard for evaluating human systems, but alone it provides rather weak guidance for action. For humans, trial and error is a less-than-desirable approach to design of social institutions when choices are irreversible and errors are extraordinarily costly. The only other routes to functional ecological rationality may be through substantive and procedural rationality.

The problem is one of meta-design and meta-policy. Dryzek analyzes and evaluates major existing social choice mechanisms—markets, administered systems, law, moral persuasion, polyarchy, bargaining, and armed conflict—according to a functional ecological rationality standard comprising five criteria: negative feedback, coordination, flexibility, robustness, and resilience.[26] His assessment of these major social choice mechanisms is at best mixed: "Any 'winner' among the seven types of social choice would, then, be little more than the best of a poor bunch."[27]

The design problems Dryzek spells out are ones of identifying means of social choice that (1) will perform better than existing institutions with respect to the functional ecological rationality standard and (2) will facilitate their own critical examination and, if necessary, modification and supersession. Dryzek finds only a very limited number of alternatives that meet these conditions. His agenda for institutional reconstruction includes local autonomy, self-sufficiency, and radically reducing or eliminating hierarchy, thereby facilitating collective decision making through limited bargaining and the practical reason of deliberative democracy.[28]

Dryzek acknowledges the problem of how to get from here to there. The difficulty is that existing, ecologically irrational social choice mechanisms will not just fade away:

> Any piecemeal introduction of innovative forms of social choice into a world of ecologically irrational mechanisms is perilous. For example, markets "imprison" governmental social choice; a legal system formalizes social interactions beyond its bounds; and the existence of administrative prerogatives and polyarchical imperatives can undermine discursive innovations.... Systems have a remarkable capacity to frustrate structural change.... [They] therefore compound their ecological irrationality by securing their own perpetuation.[29]

If the necessary preconditions for institutional redesign do not reside in existing social choice mechanisms, how can a process of institutional innovation ever be initiated, and what hope is there that it would be allowed to proceed to fruition, inasmuch as "the liberal bureaucratic state ... imperils such institutional innovations"? For Dryzek and most political theorists who have considered the question, the "preferred location for discursively democratic institutions, discursive designs, and new social movements in particular is a public space where individuals can congregate and confront the state." Incipient discursive designs or experiments (such as public inquiries, environmental mediation, regulatory negotiation, or alternative dispute resolution) need to remain autonomous from the state, because "flirtation with the state ... raises the possibility that discursive designs will be co-opted and henceforth used as instruments of state power."[30] An autonomous public sphere would need to confront and challenge the administrative state while being benignly neglected by it, an unlikely prospect in the face of any significant success. "The prospects might seem quite dim." [31]

Moreover, there is nothing in the establishment of this kind of public sphere that would guarantee the abolition of the administrative state, which leaves little room for either optimism or hope except in maintaining the challenge offered by a marginal public sphere, which might inspire widespread reconsideration of the ordering of collective life.[32] Dryzek editorializes that, while waiting and hoping, both "proponents of and participants in discursive designs should be careful to avoid complicity in the complex *status quo*." The quandary is seemingly intractable—engagement with the administrative state leads to fatal contamination and the co-optation of any incipient alternatives to it, but assuming the disintegration and fading away of the administrative state is implausible in the extreme and a prescription for irrelevance.

The way out of this apparent dilemma is to shrug off the sometimes utopian tendencies of democratic theorizing, which can become an excuse for avoiding messy, inconvenient realities, and to consider instead how experimentation with social choice mechanisms might undermine the administrative state and set it on a desirable path of evolution. In short, we should heed Robert Paehlke's counsel to avoid "an overly theoretical approach to the problem of environment and democracy."[33] The potential for productive experimentation with existing mechanisms increases as our understanding of them increases. Experimentation and evaluation need not be limited to particular combinations but might entail creatively tinkering with the imperatives of a given mechanism or grafting onto it entirely new but compatible mechanisms. In addition to enhancing functional ecological rationality, such tinkering might also promote "the preconditions for more substantial institutional innovation," thus complying with Dryzek's two major design criteria.

The design and evaluation of alternative mechanisms need not be haphazard and unguided. As noted earlier, there are two routes to achieving functional ecological rationality: trial and error, or the institutionalization of substantive and procedural rationality. If the kinds of decentralized and discursive social choice structures that Dryzek recommends are ever to prevail, it will not only be because they are informed by deliberative democratic theories, but because they turn out to be the kinds of social structures that best institutionalize substantive and procedural ecological rationality. And it will be because predecessor mechanisms paved the way, transforming (subverting) older established structures and mechanisms through earlier efforts to institutionalize ecological rationality. An autonomous public sphere might indeed be a fertile space for cultivating alternatives to the administrative state (as well as markets and capitalism), but just as crucial to success in taming currently dominant institutional forms are deliberative institutional innovations that undercut and subvert the administrative state while advancing state-associated democratization.

We now have, in fact, an instructive inventory of wide-reaching institutionalizations of deliberative environmental democracy, innovations that might also be understood as capacity building for ecological rationality in modern society. These range from practical measures for better realizing participatory liberalism to grassroots ecosystem management, from environmental right-to-know requirements to normative precommitments to certain environmental values such as preservation of endangered species or the ozone layer.[34] Perhaps the most significant example of such tinkering with the basic structures of the administrative state and liberal capitalism is environmental impact assessment. It represents a beachhead of ecological rationality that opens the way to further evolution. It certainly is not the only way of importing ecological rationality into the administrative state, but it may be one of the most insidious. There is reason to think it may be a particularly virulent kind of "worm in the brain."

ECOLOGICAL RATIONALITY
THROUGH IMPACT ASSESSMENT

Environmental impact assessment does not establish ecological rationality by technique. The impact of EIA on behaviors and processes is not automatic, nor is it simple. EIA originated as an experiment in institutionalizing ecological rationality in government and the wider society.[35] It can do this in several ways. The logic of EIA is more sophisticated than merely that of making government more like science, or of naively attempting rational comprehensive decision making, or of enhancing rationality in policy making through systematic generation and dissemination of knowledge.[36] Simple models of how EIA works or is supposed to work are common not only among the critics of EIA but among many of its advocates as well. In fact, many EIA systems at initiation have been superficially imitative programs, "based on a misreading of how the EIS [environmental impact statement] process works."[37] But the history of EIA is sprinkled with stories of intendedly ineffectual EIA systems that unexpectedly turned out to be consequential. Moreover, there is a tendency for EIA to export its imperatives into other social choice mechanisms—for example, EIA is now widely required by lending institutions to protect mortgaged assets from possible future environmental liability.

In thirty-some years, we have only begun to understand with some depth how and why EIA works. Serious analyses of EIA as a policy-making strategy or as a mechanism for social choice have been amazingly few, even as EIA has developed, evolved, and spread to every part of the globe. There have been some impressive theoretical advances and penetrating analyses even though, as Geoffrey Wandesforde-Smith argues, "new questions about the meaning of the EIA process have always run ahead of the availability of definitive answers to earlier questions about how the process works and why it works the way it does."[38]

We know that EIA certainly can exist merely as symbolic window dressing, with little or no real influence on choice processes. It can be "frozen out" from any real policy or institutional effectiveness—completely co-opted by the administrative state—if it is not sufficiently linked, formally and informally, to the ways problems are defined, structured, and addressed. Because of its own limited applicability and capacity, EIA does not have the capacity to replace wholly other social choice mechanisms. But EIA can be appended to, and integrated with, most other social choice mechanisms, to some effect. The dynamics of markets can be altered, the coordinative capabilities of bargaining and mutual adjustment can be enhanced, the rigidity of law can be lessened. In spite of some tensions between the democratic and rational imperatives of EIA, for the most part they are compatible and mutually reinforcing.[39] The many possible variations of EIA systems or strategies are (and must be) tailored to particular political and cultural contexts, and as such will have differing consequences.

Some researchers of EIA find special significance in the ways that "formal structures can tap the powerful, informal incentives that operate inside every administrative agency, and which link it to the external world, so as to produce agencies that continuously and progressively think about environmental values."[40] Serge Taylor attributes successful EIA institutionalization to a virtually self-sustaining and self-regulating interplay of variables internal and external to an administrative agency.[41] EIA thus functions as a mechanism for social discovery of viable new political arrangements and for learning new ways of thinking about problems.

EIA can be adapted to a changing political and economic climate, and can be an active agent in changing that climate. A key engine driving EIA as an adaptive, learning process is "individual entrepreneurial and strategic responses to a changing world," which creates a capacity for evolutionary policy change in the politics of EIA.[42] An EIA system offers opportunities and incentives for political individuals to "put their imprint on policy change by inventing and building coalitions, by making the case for change on the merits, and, above all,.... by developing and affirming in EIA their environmental values."[43] Thus, EIA can be a very powerful mechanism for influencing social choice, but not through coercion. Rather, EIA is a "catalytic" control: "Catalytic controls require the bureaucracy to act and direct the bureaucracy towards certain goals but do not rob it of the capacity for creative problem-solving.... They prod, stimulate, and provoke bureaucrats but also allow them to be both innovative and efficient."[44]

The theorist or analyst who looks only for dramatic impacts or only for obvious direct effects is likely to be unimpressed. Comprehending the significance and potential of EIA requires appreciation for the complexity of ways in which choices are shaped, channeled, learned, reasoned, and structured before they are "officially" made. When EIA succeeds in making far-reaching modifications in the substantive outcomes of social activities, it does so by changing, formally and informally, the premises and rules for arriving at legitimate decisions.

By requiring and encouraging political actors, as individuals and as organizations, to think ecologically and to consider environmental values, EIA imbeds procedural ecological rationality in political institutions. By establishing, continuously reaffirming, and progressively legitimating environmental values and ecological criteria as standards by which individual actions are to be structured, chosen, and evaluated, EIA institutionalizes substantive ecological rationality. Although certainly not without weaknesses even as a strategy complementing other social choice mechanisms, EIA receives a positive evaluation with regard to all five of Dryzek's criteria of functional ecological rationality. It exhibits considerable potential as a device for negative feedback (as well as for "feedforward"). Its coordinative capabilities are substantial. It is modestly robust, flexible, and resilient. Unlike other social choice mechanisms, EIA does not tend to displace rather than to confront ecological problems.

Successful EIA changes the criteria by which choices may be shaped and made. It requires consideration of particular sets of factual premises and otherwise precarious values, and it demands the kinds of reasoning associated with those values and factual premises. It changes patterns of relationships among organizations and among individuals inside and outside of organizations. It creates powerful incentives, formal and informal, that thereafter force a great deal of learning and self-regulation upon individual and organizational actors. And it provides opportunities for individuals to develop and affirm environmental values and to press for innovative adaptation of structures and processes to a changing world.

ECOLOGICAL RATIONALITY
AND ENVIRONMENTAL DEMOCRACY

Options for extending and restructuring fundamentally the roles of EIA in various social choice arenas will remain available, and may even be adopted in foreseeable circumstances, paving the way for even more substantial, probably not yet imagined, institutional innovation. The co-evolution of politics and policy through EIA and other political processes will continue—restructuring environmental politics in the administrative state informally, subtly, and profoundly by promoting procedural and substantive ecological rationality. EIA systems and other deliberative innovations will continue to work to subvert and constrain the administrative state and its capitalist and market context, "softening" the constraints and imperatives the state imposes on its relations with the arena of green civic politics, further recasting the complicated relationships the nascent green public sphere has with the administrative state. This continued "eating away" effect by EIA and other "worms" is necessary if we ever are to get from here to there—in Douglas Torgerson's phrase, for "the creation of we for public discourse."[45] EIA systems at their best are attempts to institutionalize public deliberation focused on ecological rationality, an important first and even second step toward a time and place where liberal capitalism and the administrative state might benignly give way to the establishment and development of an environmental democracy informed by an autonomous public sphere.

NOTES

1 Lewis Mumford, *The Myth of the Machine: The Pentagon of Power* (New York: Harcourt Brace Jovanovich, 1970), p. 393.

2 John S. Dryzek, *The Politics of the Earth: Environmental Discourses* (New York: Oxford University Press, 1997), p. 172.

3 Douglas Torgerson, *The Promise of Green Politics* (Durham, NC: Duke University Press, 1999).

4   Ecology is a subversive science. Paul B. Sears, "Ecology—A Subversive Subject," Bio-
Science 14(1964): 11–13; Paul Shepard and Daniel McKinley, eds., *The Subversive Science: Essays Toward an Ecology of Man* (Boston: Houghton Mifflin, 1969). The worm
in the brain metaphor is suggested by Richard Mitchell: "Quite literally, the *thing* creeps
into your brain.... There it settles in and nibbles a bit here and a bit there.... The very way
you consider the world ... is subtly altered." *Less Than Words Can Say* (Boston: Little,
Brown, 1979), p. 10.

5   John S. Dryzek, *Rational Ecology: Environment and Political Ecology* (New York: Basil
Blackwell, 1987), p. 247. See also William T. Gormley, "Institutional Policy Analysis: A
Critical Review," *Journal of Policy Analysis and Management* 6(1987): 153–69.

6   Robert V. Bartlett and Priya A. Kurian, "The Theory of Environmental Impact Assessment: Implicit Models of Policy Making," *Policy and Politics* 27(1999): 415–33.

7   Herbert A. Simon, *The Sciences of the Artificial*, 2nd ed. (Cambridge, MA: MIT Press,
1981), p. 44; Robert V. Bartlett, ed., *Policy Through Impact Assessment: Institutionalized
Analysis as a Policy Strategy* (Westport, CT: Greenwood Press, 1989) and "Rationality
and the Logic of the National Environmental Policy Act," in John Dryzek and David
Schlosberg, eds., *Debating the Earth: The Environmental Politics Reader* (New York:
Oxford University Press, 1998), pp. 85–95.

8   Dryzek, *Rational Ecology*, and "Ecological Rationality," International Journal of Environmental Studies 21(1983): 5–10; Robert V. Bartlett, "Ecological Rationality: Reason
and Environmental Policy," *Environmental Ethics* 8(Fall 1986): 221–39; Val Plumwood,
"Inequality, Ecojustice and Ecological Rationality," in Dryzek and Schlosberg, eds.,
Debating the Earth: The Environmental Politics Reader, pp. 559–83; Robert V. Bartlett
and Walter F. Baber, "From Rationality to Reasonableness in Environmental Administration: Moving Beyond Proverbs," *Journal of Management History* 5(1999): 55–67.

9   See, e.g., Dryzek, *Rational Ecology*, p. 189.

10   Bartlett, "Ecological Rationality," p. 229.

11   Paul Diesing, *Reason in Society: Five Types of Decision and Their Social Conditions*
(Urbana: University of Illinois Press, 1962); see also Dryzek, "Ecological Rationality";
Dryzek, *Rational Ecology*, pp. 55–58; Bartlett, "Ecological Rationality."

12   Diesing, *Reason in Society*.

13   Dryzek, *Rational Ecology*, p. 55; Mumford, *The Myth of the Machine*; and Jacques Ellul,
The Technological Society (New York: Alfred A. Knopf, 1964).

14   Robert K. Merton, *Social Theory and Social Structure* (Glencoe, IL: The Free Press,
1957); Walter F. Baber, *Managing the Future: Matrix Models for the Postindustrial
Polity* (University, AL: University of Alabama Press, 1983).

15   Bartlett and Baber, "From Rationality to Reasonableness"; Bartlett, "Ecological Rationality"; Dryzek, "Ecological Rationality"; Dryzek, *Rational Ecology*, pp. 55–58; Diesing,
Reason in Society.

16   Diesing, *Reason in Society*, pp. 231–232. Diesing does, however, anticipate ecological
rationality as a prerequisite of social rationality: "Characteristic of a rational social system is its compatibility with the nonsocial environment..., to which it must be adapted if
it is to continue in existence" (p. 88).

17   Dryzek, *Rational Ecology*, pp. 58–59.

18   Bartlett, "Ecological Rationality," pp. 235–36; Dryzek, *Rational Ecology*, pp. 59–60.

19   According to Mannheim, functional rationality exists when "a series of actions is organized in such a way that it leads to a previously defined goal, every element in this series
of actions receiving a functional position and role. Such a functional organization of a
series of actions will, moreover, be at its best when, in order to attain the given goal, it
coordinates the means most efficiently. It is by no means characteristic, however, of
functional organization in our sense that this optimum be attained or even that the goal
itself be considered rational as measured by a certain standard...." Karl Mannheim, *Man
and Society in an Age of Reconstruction: Studies in Modern Social Structure* (New York:

Harcourt, Brace, 1948), pp. 52–53. Max Weber referred to a similar concept as formal rationality.

20 Also called substantial rationality by Mannheim and Diesing.

21 Herbert A. Simon, "From Substantive to Procedural Rationality," in Spiro J. Latsis, ed., *Method and Appraisal in Economics* (Cambridge: Cambridge University Press, 1976), pp. 130–31.

22 Herbert A. Simon, "Rationality as Process and as Product of Thought," *American Economic Review* 68.2(1978): 9.

23 Bartlett, "Ecological Rationality," p. 224.

24 This is not to say that functional ecological rationality is ever a logical necessity or inevitable; it is always possible (and in the long run, highly likely) for something beyond controllable human behavior to intervene and vitiate the existing functional rationality of a relevant ecosystem.

25 Clive Ponting, *A Green History of the World: The Environment and the Collapse of Great Civilizations* (New York: St. Martin's, 1992).

26 Dryzek, *Rational Ecology*, especially pp. 25–54.

27 Dryzek, *Rational Ecology*, p. 181.

28 John S. Dryzek, *Discursive Democracy: Politics, Policy, and Political Science* (New York: Cambridge University Press, 1990) and *Deliberative Democracy and Beyond: Liberals, Critics, Constestations* (New York: Oxford University Press, 2000).

29 Dryzek, *Rational Ecology*, p. 245.

30 Dryzek, *Discursive Democracy*, pp. 89, 220.

31 John S. Dryzek, "Designs for Environmental Discourse: The Greening of the Administrative State," in Robert Paehlke and Douglas Torgerson, eds., *Managing Leviathan: Environmental Politics and the Administrative State* (Peterborough, ON: Broadview Press, 1990), p. 106.

32 Dryzek, "Designs for Environmental Discourse," pp. 107–08.

33 Robert Paehlke, "Environmental Challenges to Democratic Practice," in William M. Lafferty and James Meadowcroft, eds., *Democracy and the Environment* (Brookfield, VT: Edward Elgar, 1996), p. 20.

34 Walter F. Baber and Robert V. Bartlett, "Toward Environmental Democracy: Rationality, Reason, and Deliberation," *Kansas Journal of Law and Public Policy* 11(2001): 35–64.

35 Bartlett, "Rationality and the Logic of the National Environmental Policy Act."

36 Bartlett and Kurian, "Theory of Environmental Impact Assessment."

37 Serge Taylor, *Making Bureaucracies Think: The Environmental Impact Statement Strategy of Administrative Reform* (Stanford, CA: Stanford University Press, 1984), p. 7.

38 Geoffrey Wandesforde-Smith, "EIA, Entrepreneurship, and Policy Change," in Bartlett, ed., *Policy Through Impact Assessment*, pp. 155–66.

39 Baber and Bartlett, "Toward Environmental Democracy"; Bartlett and Baber, "From Rationality to Reasonableness"; Walter F. Baber, "Impact Assessment and Democratic Politics," *Policy Studies Review* 8(1988): 172–78.

40 Wandesforde-Smith, "EIA, Entrepreneurship, and Policy Change," p. 156.

41 Taylor, *Making Bureaucracies Think.*

42 Geoffrey Wandesforde-Smith and J. Kerbavaz, "The Co-Evolution of Politics and Policy: Elections, Entrepreneurship and EIA in the United States," in Peter Wathern, ed., *Environmental Impact Assessment: Theory and Practice* (London: Unwin Hyman, 1988), pp. 161–91.

43 Wandesforde-Smith, "EIA, Entrepreneurship, and Policy Change."

44 Gormley, "Institutional Policy Analysis," p. 160.

45 Torgerson, *The Promise of Green Politics*, p. 157.

5

Environmental Regulation and Risk-Benefit Analysis: From Technical to Deliberative Policy Making

Frank Fischer

Conflicts between scientific expertise and politics have been part of environmental struggles from their beginning in the late 1960s. Not only are science and technology closely associated with the major causes of environmental degradation, but environmental science has also played a primary role in both detecting environmental problems and searching for workable solutions. Although the environmental movement began with the use of traditional political tactics (from street protests to lobbying) to organize for protection against the risk technologies, nuclear power being the most important case in point, the focus on risk has tended to shift the terms of political struggle. Over time the technical questions have largely replaced political questions at the center of the environmental debate. In the process, the primary focus shifted from the public arena of protest to the institutional arenas of expertise, in particular to governmental administrative arenas.[1] With this new phase of environmentalism, scientists, including "movement scientists," increasingly took center stage. As the technical dimensions of environmental problems increasingly involved sophisticated levels of physical and biological expertise, a technocratic form of environmentalism took shape, especially in the corridors of governmental decision making. In the 1970s and 1980s, environmental policy making was discussed more and more in the technical language of environmental management.

Throughout advanced industrial countries such as the United States, Canada, and Great Britain, environmental decision making became increasingly embedded in the languages of science-based techniques such as environmental impact statements, risk assessment, technology assessment, cost-benefit analysis, and risk-benefit analysis. Here scientific and technological determinations are pre-scribed as the primary way to set standards for protecting air, water, wildlife, and forests, among others, against the harmful effects of industrialization. In the United States, for example, most federal environmental programs mandate the implementing agencies to specify empirical standards for water and air quality, to spell out the appropriate control technologies for pollution sources, to iden-tify acceptable risks from exposure to toxic substances, and to make a multitude of other environmentally relevant technical judgments. Federal statutes, in effect, thrust upon governmental agencies the burden of scientifically defining acceptable levels of pollution, pollution abatement, and risk of exposure to envi-ronmental pollutants. For this purpose, federal and state environmental protec-tion agencies have developed extensive procedures for generating scientific information, from the development of internal expertise to external advisory boards.[2]

Basic to this development has been the conviction that good science can show us the way. This emphasis—if not faith—in scientific analysis was perhaps most clearly expressed by William Ruckelshaus, former director of the Environmental Protection Agency (EPA), when he wrote,

We are now in a troubled and emotional period for pollution control; many communities are gripped by something approaching panic, and the public discussion is dominated by personalities rather than substance. I believe that part of the solution to our distress lies with the idea that disciplined minds can grapple with ignorance and sometimes win: the idea of science. We will not recover our equilibrium without a concerted effort to more effectively engage the scientific community.... I need the help of scientists.[3]

In the 1980s the EPA established the technique of "risk-benefit analysis" as the basic scientific tool for agency decision making.[4] The reduction of risk, as a major EPA document flatly declared, was the fundamental mission of the agency. All agencies were subsequently required to rigorously calculate the monetarized costs of achieving a particular level of risk protection against the expected dollar benefits associated with each proposed regulatory rule.[5] Each new proposal has to pass such a risk-benefit analysis test before it can be con-sidered and adopted as law. As formally introduced—if not always practiced—the decisive test of any new environmental regulation is the ability of risk-ben-efit analysts to show that it efficiently offers a net benefit to society. As Andrews explained, by the end of the 1980s this "vocabulary of risk" had literally become the "primary language of environmental policy analysis and management" at the EPA.[6]

There is an extensive managerial literature that celebrates the use of these techniques as a way to bring greater objectivity and rationality to the decision process. Underlying these techniques is the utilitarian idea that empirically mea-sured consequences rather than social preferences provide the appropriate standards for policy making. Such methodologies, it is argued, are value-free and permit decision makers to focus on the issues independently of competing political ideologies. They are introduced on the conviction that science provides the foundation of rational decision making.

But this faith in scientific analysis proved to be much more precarious than Ruckelshaus and other such enthusiasts have recognized. In fact, science has very often only intensified the very politics that those who turned to it sought to circumvent. How this could happen is the central question I explore below. Because the experience with risk-benefit analysis clearly reflects the conflict between science and politics, it deserves more detailed examination. Before turning directly to questions of methodology, however, I first begin by considering the issue of environmental risk more generally.

ENVIRONMENTAL RISK

Since the 1980s risk has become the central category of environmental politics, with the politics of risk divided into two opposing camps. On one side of the issue have been the environmentalists. Calling attention to risks has been a central component of the environmental movement's activities. Environmentalists approach this by arguing that we live in the riskiest of times. The world, as they often contend, is on the brink of ecological disaster. Modern technology is seen constantly to generate new threats to the earth's life-support systems and thus, in turn, to the stability of social systems. Especially important to the argument is the synergistic effect of the mounting hazards. It is not just the appearance of new problems that is at issue, but the emergence of so many at the same time: toxic wastes, the ozone hole, the greenhouse effect, nuclear radiation, polluted air and water, the loss of diversity, and so on. Even though people are seldom exposed to one risk in isolation from the others, there exists little empirical information on the interactive effects of these dangers. For such reasons, those who see a dramatic increase in risks call for tighter control of technology, including the abandonment of technologies considered to be particularly risky (such as nuclear power and genetic engineering) and the need for the development and introduction of more environmentally benign technologies.

This view is, in fact, manifested in a very important contemporary political phenomenon, the so-called NIMBY phenomenon (not-in-my-backyard). In face of the risks associated with such industries as nuclear power, chemical manufacturing, and hazardous waste management, more and more environmentally concerned groups have blocked the siting of these facilities in their own communities. Many have described the politics of NIMBY as a serious threat to the future of such hazard-prone industries.[7]

Such worries about the riskiness of advanced technologies, coupled with the political gridlock often created by NIMBY, have elevated the "search for safety" to the top of the political agenda.[8] Indeed, the quest for safety has emerged as one of the paramount political issues of our time, both as a major public concern and a leading topic in intellectual discourse. In Germany, for example, it has led sociologist Ulrich Beck to define contemporary postindustrial society as the "risk society."[9] Whether or not advanced industrial society is adequately characterized as a risk society, the very nature of the polemic indicates the degree to which technological risk and its implications have emerged as fundamental societal concerns.

On the other side of the issue, the proponents of large-scale technological progress take grave exception to the environmentalist view. For corporate and governmental leaders in particular, risk and safety issues are greatly exaggerated. In their view, we actually live in the safest of times, although they concede the need to pay greater attention to the regulatory process. For them, risk is an essential component of modern society that must always be examined in relative terms. Risk, they argue, has to be seen as a mixed phenomenon, always producing opportunities as well as dangers. Most often, they contend, the debates about risks revolve only around *potential* dangers, all too frequently centering on high-impact accidents with low probabilities, such as nuclear meltdowns or runaway genetic mutations. Risk taking, in contrast, must be seen as necessary for successful technological change and economic growth, as well as the overall resilience and health of modern society.

This approach is grounded in the view that technological dangers have been grossly exaggerated by the "Luddites" in the environmental movement. The result, it is argued, is a high degree of exaggeration and ignorance among the public about the risks of modern technologies.[10] In this view, many of the contemporary hazards have decreased overall risk by replacing more dangerous ones.[11] People are seen to become more and more worried about less significant risks. The layperson, the argument goes, worries about living next to a hazardous waste incinerator, but thinks nothing about smoking cigarettes, which are said to be statistically much more dangerous to human health. Because this uncontrolled expansion of "irrational" beliefs is quite threatening to technological progress, managerial elites have seen the need to counter this anti-technology trend. Basic to their strategy has been the turn of "acceptable risk" and the methodology of risk-benefit analysis.[12] Risk-benefit analysis is the way to sort out the real dangers from the inflated rhetoric of the environmental movement.

The future of many new technologies is thought to depend upon the ability of regulatory institutions to relieve the public of its irrational fears. In taking up the challenge, the primary response of techno-industrial leaders has been to attempt to shift the focus of the risk debate to quantifiable technical factors derived from risk-benefit analysis. By supplying the public with more objective technical information about the levels of risks, the "irrationality" of contemporary political arguments can be countered with rationally demonstrable scientific data. The solution is to provide more information—standardized scientific information—to offset the irrationalities plaguing the uninformed. Providing this information is the task of "risk communication," which seeks to effectively disseminate the results of risk-benefit analysis to the public.

Scientific Indeterminacy
and Risk-Benefit Analysis

The turn to science as a firm basis for making and justifying reliable environmental decisions has proved to be much less promising for environmental policy than expected. One source of the problem is the claim to value-free objectivity. As experience has shown, the application of decision methods as risk-benefit analysis is often as much the reflection of technocratic ideology as a pursuit of science. Indeed, the adoption of decision technologies "is more often a response to powerful political interests than the product of an intellectual search for the best policy solution."[13] For many environmentalists this technocratic form of regulation is as much a part of the problem as the technologies that generate the pollution it is designed to control.

What its proponents did not realize was how "underdetermined" risk-benefit analysis would prove to be, to use the phrase of Collingsridge and Reeves.[14] Those who turned to science and scientific decision-making methods assumed an "overdetermined" model, expecting science to resolve questions in a way that would eliminate—or at least significantly reduce—political conflict among affected parties. However, the actual experience was quite different. Environmental politics was to entail a series of confrontations between scientific risk assessment and society that raised questions about science itself, questions about both the direction of scientific work and the assessment of its results.

The problem was straightforward. In dealing with policy decisions, the scientific community discovered that it could not answer the environmental questions with enough precision to be decisive. Indeed, scientific risk analysis often tended to raise new questions that it could not answer. And it was precisely this uncertainty that opened up—however unintendedly—the space for a politicization of analysis itself. In short, the outcome was the very opposite of what was hoped.

This politicization of risk-benefit analysis was possible because of its indeterminacy. Environmental issues pushed science into realms where the evidence was either limited or mixed. This indeterminate nature of the relevant scientific questions led to strong scientific and political disagreements. The fact that scientists could not settle such complex questions opened the door to competing interpretations of the same phenomena. Disputes over the health effects of radiation, dioxin, and lead revealed that something besides "objectivity" had come into play. This was especially the case in terms of the long-term, chronic effects of low-level exposures that required more sensitive measurements than had yet been perfected. The myriad of complex relationships entailed in the assessment of such risks was often subject to competing interpretations. At the same time, whereas knowledge was extensive about some subjects—for example, cancer—there was less about others, such as sperm defects. Or knowledge might be relatively extensive about some people (such as healthy, adult male workers), but less so about others (such as younger and older people). In short, scientific work had expanded the realm of what was *unknown* far more rapidly than it had the realm of the known.[15]

The nature of this indeterminacy gave rise to a model of regulatory policy making in the US that Jasanoff has labeled the "science policy paradigm."[16] Given the inability of the various environmental science advisory boards to establish conclusive findings upon which policy making could be based, a model for decision making emerged that brought together a mix of scientific and administrative-legal considerations. Evolving through Congressional legislation and agency practices, the paradigm evolved around three interrelated elements, each of which deeply influenced both agency procedures for evaluating science and the structure of scientific advisory processes. The first is the notion that agencies should be permitted to make regulatory decisions about risks on the basis of imperfect knowledge (that is, suggestive rather than conclusive evidence). The second element, a corollary of the first, is that science policy determination may be regarded as valid even if the scientific community does not universally accept it as such. And third, when risk experts disagree about the validity or interpretation of relevant data, the administrative agency should have the authority to resolve the dispute in a manner consistent with its legal mandate.

The model evolved in response to an unavoidable circumstance: decisions about risk have to be made. When science alone is incapable of providing decisive answers to questions of risk, the choice among conflicting assessments still has to be made. In light of this fact, according to the model, the decision should be made by the politically accountable agency in accordance with its lawful regulatory mission. Given their unique combination of technical and policy skills, the new environmental administrative agencies appeared, in principle, well qualified to make science policy determinations.

The full implications of agency authority in this area began to emerge only gradually as the courts advanced new interpretations of statutory language aimed at protection against health, safety, and environmental risks. The science policy paradigm assumed that high administrative discretion on the part of agencies in resolving scientific disputes would be coupled with equally high judicial deference to the agency's expert judgments. But as the courts began to exercise their obligation to monitor the agencies' substantive evidence and rationales for regulatory decisions, the expectation of judicial deference to administration gave way to a widespread practice of judicial review of technical decisions.[17] As the number of science-based regulatory decisions rose in the 1970s, this practice became extremely problematic for the science policy paradigm.

The courts can overrule decisions judged either to be insufficiently supported by the given evidence or to be an arbitrary or capricious abuse of discretion. In view of this mandate, the courts, especially in the early years of environmental decision making, began to take a close look at the technical evidence before them. While courts expressed no desire to make scientific findings on their own, they insisted on holding agencies accountable for a full and reasonable explanation of their technical determinations. In order to ensure that an agency acted "reasonably," the reviewing judge was entitled by this standard to probe into the administrators' scientific thought processes.

To simplify a complicated story, the consequence of the behavior of the courts was to make public the general inadequacy of the available knowledge about hazardous risks. Clearly revealed were the interpretive dimensions of decisions involved in scientific practices under conditions of uncertainty.[18] For the EPA this revelation was especially problematic because the agency was specifically given the task of making decisions in the face of scientific uncertainty.[19] Indeed, the science policy paradigm was established to facilitate such decisions. Agency officials were to collect the best expert judgments and then assemble them into reasonable rules fitting within the parameters of the ageny's legal mandate. But now the courts were criticizing the agency for playing the very role it had been assigned.

The result of these court opinions was to open a large hole through which the opponents of environmental regulation could introduce a politics of expertise. Since little could be "proven" in the conventional understanding of the term, all one had to do was find fault with a particular dimension of a risk analysis, a strategy most easily pursued through criticisms of experimental and statistical methods. Later the courts were to retreat from this position, permitting the agency to balance technical findings with more interpretive social and political considerations, as specified by Congress. By this time, however, the cat was out of the bag. As Jasanoff writes, "Inconsistent decisions and wavering judicial support underscored the political fragility of the science policy paradigm…."[20]

Although this message—"leave science to the scientists"—was superficially appealing, it failed to address the underlying problem of defining what counts as "science" in areas of methodological uncertainty and political conflict. The combination of indeterminacy and political pressure gave rise to the politics of expertise (and counter-expertise) that became rampant in environmental politics, involving both industry and the environmental movement. Those who were unhappy with particular outcomes could easily find or employ different experts to present the other side of the issue. If one wished to discredit a given risk analysis, it was easy to question its experimental or statistical methodology. Regardless of the merits of the study, one could argue with little difficulty that it failed to take into account other possible causes of a given effect. The intervening or confounding variable was of special interest to those who sought to draw attention away from a potential cause of contamination and direct it toward another. As Jasanoff observes, "the struggle for control over regulatory policy was thus played out in part on the fields of discourse, as terms like 'science,' 'policy' and even 'peer review' were redefined to fit different conceptions of the relationship between science and power."[21]

Given the unavoidable limitations of data about risks, protagonists in the politics of expertise can either demand higher levels of proof or draw conclusions on the basis of lower levels of certainty. Industry leaders and their experts pressed for more proof while environmentally oriented advisors usually argued that there was enough evidence to justify a conclusion, given the seriousness of potential consequences. Industry thus supported experts who argued that there was not yet enough solid evidence to justify the economic costs of a regulatory rule. In legislative, administrative, and court hearings these experts insisted on high levels of proof of harm. They criticized environmentalists' safety demands as unreasonable, as requiring degrees of protection that were unjustified because their need was unproven. Indeed, it was this industry argument that took the driver's seat in the 1980s with the arrival of the Reagan administration. Taking its lead from industry, this administration put strong pressure on the Environmental Protection Agency to adjust its public regulatory decision-making standards accordingly. By executive order, the Reagan administration mandated that all regulatory decisions be judged by a cost-benefit analysis, which in the case of environmental regulations was translated into risk-benefit analysis.

Disputes in this conflict were often played out in intensely emotional terms between two scientific camps. The more conventional scientists, on the one hand, argued that there was "absolutely no proof" that a given pollutant was harmful and derided dissenting scientists as tainted by non-scientific and emotional tendencies. The dissenting scientists, on the other hand, argued that those who demanded high levels of proof had their own unscientific commitments, whether in their predispositions or in their loyalties to the industries for which they worked or from which they received financial support.

Although the process was politically complex, it was heavily influenced by money.[22] Without great difficulty, one could trace respective positions to those who funded the risk-benefit research. The identification of problems for research, the selection of scientists to conduct it, and the construction of research designs stemmed all too often from choices made by those in private industry and government who supplied the research funds. Scientific research and advice were thus frequently shaped or influenced rather directly by the financial stake scientists had in its acceptance. In recognition of this relationship, major advisory boards took steps to exclude from their review committees scientists who were stockholders in either the companies for which they worked or those that financed activities the committee was asked to review. Later this exclusion was extended to include employees of a company or agency with a stake in the decision.

Environmentalists also came to recognize that members of the scientific community were generally quite critical toward public intervention in their affairs. Public involvement in the scientific aspects of environmental affairs, argued scientists, interferes with matters best left to experts. They tended to draw a distinction between informed and rational science, on the one hand, and far less informed and often emotional public debate on the other. In this respect, scientists have stood behind the customary understanding of science's role in public affairs—that of disinterested and objective investigators gathering knowledge for the public benefit. As public issues were often technical, scientists were called on to determine the facts on the grounds that scientists were disinterested parties, unbiased with regard to the particular outcome of inquiry and hence would be above controversy. Because science is "objective," as argued by Ruckelshaus and many others, it is seen to hold out the possibility of unifying contending sectors of society and politics.

In professional field after field, experts have argued that their role in environmental issues was—and should be—one of neutrality rather than advocacy. Indeed, if environmental experts had anything to offer, so they argued, it was their ability to substitute concrete facts for an uninformed emotional response to the problems at hand. But, as we have seen here, professional expertise has scarcely played this impartial role. Under the guise of scientific neutrality, policy experts have more often than not taken sides. We now come to a further aspect of the critique of regulatory science, namely the normative assumptions embedded in its methodologies.

"ACCEPTABLE RISK" AS TECHNO-INDUSTRIAL IDEOLOGY

Not only have the mountains of quantitative data amassed in risk-benefit analysis failed to reassure the public, but in many ways the approach has worsened the public's fears and anxieties. Environmentalists have managed to gain political advantage here. The use of technically based methods of risk-benefit analysis, they argue, represents little more than a example of the technocrat's inability or unwillingness to comprehend the underlying socio-political nature of the environmental crisis. While there are a number of variations to this argument, including a deep-seated critique of industrial society itself, let us consider the argument most central to the environmental rejection of risk-benefit analysis *per se*: the argument, namely, that such a technical framing of risk fundamentally distorts the socio-institutional nature of environmental problems.

According to the critical environmentalist, the troubles of risk-benefit analysis are rooted in the normative assumptions of a technocratic worldview that is itself the fundamental problem. Greens charge the proponents of risk-benefit analysis with—wittingly or unwittingly—introducing a way of understanding and treating technology that implicitly biases risk decision processes in favor of the dominant techno-industrial system and its managerial values. Through tacit assumptions that support the industrial status quo, the methodology undermines the very kinds of normative and moral discourses about environmental problems that greens seek to promote. Some, in fact, see risk-benefit analysis to be a strategy designed to do just that while deflecting the environmental movement's ability to rally political support against hazardous risks.

Consider, for example, the argument advanced by Langdon Winner, a leading critic of technological society.[23] Winner argues that an analytical emphasis on risk functions to shift inquiry away from traditional concepts such as "danger" and "hazards" to a more subtle and sophisticated exploration of statistical probabilities. What otherwise appears to be a fairly obvious link between technological causes and dangerous effects—for instance, the relationship between hazardous chemicals and cancer—tends to be transformed into a question fraught with scientific uncertainties. Whereas a hazard is easily recognized as a danger to health and safety—and thus reasonable people readily agree that something should be done about it—conceptual transformation of a hazard into a question of risk works to soften the appearance of the threat. By introducing a calculus of risks and benefits—that is, by asking people to balance the risk against the relative benefits that society more generally might derive from a techno-industrial process—the question of whether or not something should be done about the hazard becomes less clear. In fact, it might be decided that the benefit derived from learning to live with the danger outweighs a decision to take remedial action. For those like Winner who believe in the right of a safe environment, such compromises are unacceptable.

Take the case of a hazardous waste landfill. Without question, such toxic landfills are a threat to their neighbors. From the perspective of risk-benefit analysis, however, this threat can only be part of the story. The toxic threat must be balanced against the larger benefits to be derived from the chemical industry. Typically, the inclusion of the benefits favors the chemical industry, as well as the industrial system generally. But the threat will almost never be attractive to the community neighboring on the disposal site. In this way, risk assessment serves as a sophisticated technocratic tool designed to subordinate, if not altogether block, community interests and values. Any attempt to quantify such risks, critics argue, must be uncompromisingly rejected. The threatened community groups should just say "no."

Equally deceptive, according to critics of risk-benefit analysis, is its subtle emphasis on expert decision making. Once the participants in an environmental decision agree to shift deliberations about technological hazards to the weighting and comparing of the costs and benefits associated with different levels of risks, they enter into a realm of enormous uncertainties over which there is little chance of a relatively straightforward consensus. Not only are the commonsense assumptions underlying the concerns about hazards and dangers abruptly suspended, but any confidence people might have in their own ability to deal with such hazards yields to the rigors of excruciatingly detailed inquiries. Furthermore, because the exact nature of this (technological) cause and (environmental) effect relationship is very difficult to "prove" in the scientific sense of the term, the question of risk always remains open to interpretation. That is to say, the interpretation remains open to the judgments of those who purport to have expertise in the matter.

The consequence of this reliance on experts is thus an intellectual barrier to popular participation in the affected communities. Besides merely underplaying certain kinds of interests and values, the methodology functions in a way that that impedes the very participatory processes that make the advancement of community interests and values possible. In the place of public discourse about what ought to be done, the decision process is de facto dominated by the opinions of experts. Experts, rather than the citizens themselves, decide whether or not people will live next to a hazardous waste site. Many environmentalists describe this as a deliberate technocratic strategy of limiting the public's role in issues basic to the advance of techno-industrial society.

The risk debate is one that environmental groups can easily lose by the very act of entering it.[24] From the outset, those who might wish to propose limits upon any particular industrial or technological application are placed at a disadvantage. By accepting risk as a legitimate concept, environmentalists have to judge the harmful technological practices in terms of standards that they are likely to find alien. The standards themselves rest on techno-industrial value assumptions that environmentalists might otherwise wish to reflect upon, if not flatly reject. In this regard, as Winner puts it, environmentalists, "who enter the risk debate will resemble … the green horn enticed into a poker game in which the cards are stacked against him."[25]

The alternative, according to the greens, is to deny the legitimacy of risk and risk-benefit analysis's utilitarianism language altogether in environmental discourse. To circumvent the often mystifying effects of such language, greens counsel a retreat to more direct and emotive concepts such as danger, hazard, or peril. Ordinary citizens, they point out, have had a very long history of orienting themselves to dangers and have little trouble participating in decisions about the technological hazards that encroach directly upon their own lives. Even more importantly, the greens insist on a wider discussion of the value and acceptability of the standards of benefit against which risks are measured. Beyond the procedural biases of risk-benefit methodology—the balancing of risks and benefits and the turn to expert opinions—greens seek to engage the public in a broader discourse about the meaning of progress itself. Such a discussion raises basic questions about the techno-industrial society and brings the technocratic worldview into question.

While experts present their judgments as value-neutral scientific findings, greens contend that risk-benefit analysis's emphasis on potential benefits rests on basic value assumptions of a techno-industrial society. They point in particular to its commitment to the quantitative expansion of material production, higher levels of consumption, and a largely uncritical acceptance of new technological innovations, understood to be the basic engines driving production and consumption. For many greens, this claim about technology and progress is the deeper source of contention. In their view, the techno-industrial concept of progress is anything but an unqualified force of the "good society." Technocratic assumptions, they argue, have led to a materialist conception of the good life that is not only wasteful but ultimately alienating in human terms. It contributes to an "overconsumptive" society in which people increasingly attach more importance to unnecessary possession than to their neighbors. This is a "throwaway" society in which people are increasingly threatened by their own garbage, a society that all too casually toys with dangerous technological processes, from nuclear power to genetic bioengineering.[26]

According to the greens, the techno-industrial concept of progress rests on an antiquated—if not misbegotten—assumption about nature and natural resources, namely the view of nature as an object to be tamed and controlled by science and technology. Rather than being something with its own intrinsic value, a natural resource exists solely for expropriation by humankind; it is simply a raw mater-ial for the techno-industrial machine.[27] What is at issue is nothing less than a his-torical challenge to the techno-industrial worldview and its positivist mode of reason that have dominated the last two or three hundred years of Western soci-ety. The green critique of risk-benefit analysis can be adequately understood only in the context of this larger critique of the technocratic world.

In another sense, however, the problem is more than just a way of thinking. What makes such change so difficult is that the positivist mode of thinking in particular is deeply embedded in the design of our societal institutions and prac-tices, in particular bureaucratic government and the corporate marketplace. On the one hand, to be sure, this institutional dimension of the problems holds out some promising possibilities. Our institutions are our own creations, so we can eliminate such practices as risk-benefit analysis. On the other, such changes prove much more difficult than they first appear; they involve uprooting prac-tices basic to our way of life. As one aspect of a way of life generally proves to be interrelated with other aspects of the same way of life, such change proves to be no simple task.

THE ENVIRONMENTAL WORLDVIEW
AS SOCIO-CULTURAL KNOWLEDGE

While the majority of the public does not share the environmental worldview and the critique of industrial capitalism, the green perspective nonetheless has a res-onance with a wide segment of the population. Given that risk-benefit analysis cannot empirically answer the basic questions about risk confronting the public with a degree of confidence that provides the basis for political consensus, citi-zens have to rely on their own judgment. And for this they rely on their own socio-cultural knowledge about the society in which they live. Whereas risk-ben-efit analysis emphasizes scientific methods, empirical evidence, and expert judg-ments in making regulatory decisions, the citizens' socio-cultural mode of ratio-nality gives weight to personal and familiar experiences rather than depersonalized technical calculations.[28] Focusing on the opinions of traditional social and peer groups, socio-cultural rationality (or "cultural rationality" for simplicity) takes unanticipated consequences to be fully relevant to near-term decision making and trusts process over outcomes. Beyond statistical probabili-ties and risk-benefit ratios, public risk perception is understood through a dis-tinctive form of rationality, one that is shaped by the circumstances under which the risk is identified and publicized, the standing or place of the individual in his or her community, and the social values of the community as a whole. Such a cul-tural rationality is concerned with the impacts, intrusions, or implications of a particular event or phenomenon on the social world. And it is just such concerns on which the environmental worldview is built.

The turn to cultural rationality and its emphasis on social process is most apparent in the case of uncertain data. Uncertainty opens the door for competing interests to emphasize different interpretations of the findings. "Wicked" problems like NIMBY, moreover, raise normative as well as empirical uncertainty. The question of how to define the situation is as problematic as the question of what to do about it. Competing definitions emerge from multiple, often conflicting perspectives. In such cases politicians and activists advance counter-arguments about the nature or definition of the problem itself. Moreover, each side engages in what I have previously called the politics of expertise, employing the same or similar data to suit their own purposes.

And where does this leave the public? If two experts stand before an audience of citizens and argue over a given set of statistics, what basis does the citizen have for judging the competing claims? In this situation, citizens are forced to rely more on a socio-cultural assessment of the factors surrounding a decision.[29] And not without good reason. Although scientific experts continue to maintain that their research is value-neutral, the limits of such neutrality become apparent once the experts introduce their technical findings into the sociopolitical world of competing interests. In the absence of empirical agreement, there is every reason to believe that interested parties will strongly assert themselves, endorsing the findings that best suit their interests. In such cases, at least in the immediate situation, there is nothing science can do to mediate between conflicting claims. One can call for more research but, as experience shows, there is little likelihood that further research will resolve anything.

Cultural rationality is especially relevant when there is reason to believe in the possibility of deception or manipulation, as has often been the case in environmental politics. In a world of large industrial giants with vastly disproportionate power and influence compared to that of local communities, it comes as no surprise to learn that citizens tend to be wary of the kinds of distorted communications to which such asymmetrical relations typically give rise. When citizens have compelling reasons to suspect that a risk analysis is superficial or false, they can only turn to their own socio-cultural knowledge and examine the results in terms of previous social experiences. Turning away from expert views, they ask questions like these: What are our previous experiences with these people? Is there reason to believe we can trust them? Why are they telling us this? (Perhaps even, why don't they look us in the eye when they talk to us?) Such questions are especially pertinent when crucial decisions are made by distant, anonymous, and hierarchical organizations. Citizens want to know how conclusions were reached, whose interests are at stake, if the process reflects a hidden agenda, who is responsible, what protection they have if something goes wrong, and so on. If they believe the project engineers and managers either do not know what they are talking about, or are willing to lie to serve the purposes of their company, workers or citizens will obviously reject the risk assessment statistics put forth by the company. For example, if they have experiences that suggest they should be highly distrustful of particular plant company representatives or plant managers, such information will tend to override the data itself. From the perspective of cultural rationality, to act otherwise would itself be irrational.

Most fundamentally, socio-cultural knowledge, deduced in large part from past social experiences, tells citizens who they can trust and who they can't. Citizens' and workers' understandings of large-scale technologies are rooted in the socio-historical context in which they are embedded and experienced.[30] Technology itself is encountered as more than an assemblage of physical properties; it is experienced as an interplay between physical properties and institutional characteristics. As such, the ordinary social perceptions and assessments of technological risks by workers and citizens are rooted in their direct social experiences with the techno-managerial decision structures as well as social memory, interpreted and passed along by members of their own groups and communities. When the social relations of the workers and managers are pervaded by mistrust and hostility, the uncertainties of physical risks are amplified.[31]

In a society where the level of trust is low, cultural rationality will most likely caution citizens to be skeptical or resistant. Our socio-cultural experiences are, in this way, factored into our interpretations of the experts' technical data on risk. Such data, after all, are not only a statement about the degree of danger we face, but also a statement about the degree of danger that another group has placed us in. On this aspect of risk, the technical findings themselves are silent.

At this point, we can recognize that the critics who argue that the environmental movement is grounded more in social critique or political ideology than in good science are not entirely wrong.[32] Insofar as citizens interpret risks from the perspective of socio-cultural experiences, they do it within a belief system that supplies them with guidelines for action based on past experiences. Thus, in situations that are unclear, uncertain, or anxiety-provoking, citizens are especially open or amenable to such appeals, and the environmental movement stands ready to assist with a critique of technocratic ideology.

What the critics fail to recognize or acknowledge, however, is that such socio-cultural knowledge is inherent to the nature of the decision process. That is, in such situations there is no alternative but to seek out the guidance of common knowledge. Interpretations of how the social system works are precisely the kind of information that citizens need to help them link together their own knowledge and experiences into meaningful understandings of a particular situation. Since the turn to basic cultural orientations is in significant part a response to the fact that science cannot supply the needed answers, it is anything but irrational. Although critics portray the movement as merely appealing to the base instincts of the citizenry, their own call for more emphasis on science fails to grasp the point that this very call, wittingly or unwittingly, reinforces a technocratic ideology that obscures the socio-cultural dimensions of actual situations.

The critics of environmentalism fail to appreciate something else. Rather than just political rhetoric designed to change societies that "greens" dislike, environmentalism also provides citizens with interpretive knowledge about how the basic institutions of society work while offering tactics for change. Environmentalism helps to orient many citizens to a problematic situation facing them—in particular, to the question of who they should believe and trust? Missing is the recognition that people are often in need of just such orientation.

When confronted with risky circumstances, people look for help in understanding how such circumstances came about, how the system that created them really works—not just how officials say it works—and thus who or what they should worry about. Reliance on critical perspectives offers quick, shorthand guidance. Much more than half-truths distributed to defend a particular set of interests, such perspectives represent the interpretive synopsis of a long history of experiences with social phenomena. In a complex world they serve to translate basic messages down to a few manageable premises that can serve as guidelines for thought and action. This is not to say that people should not or do not reflect on the content of these perspectives, at least over time. But in uncertain situations that require action without the luxury of time, they help to give people a basic orientation.

Given the limits of science in questions of public policy, coupled with citizens' reliance on socio-cultural knowledge, how should we approach deliberation about environmental risk? Is there a "greener" alternative to risk-benefit analysis? Although the critics of environmentalism continue to argue for more and better science, they fail to see the necessity of socio-cultural discourse in the face of uncertainty. The solution is not to be found in greater scientific clarification *per se*, but rather in answers to questions about social institutions and the ways of life they produce. Whereas technocrats may dismiss such discussion as idealist, significant numbers of people are worried about the society they live in and believe that it does not work the way its leaders tell them it does. For this reason, any attempt to rule out socio-cultural knowledge can only miss a crucial part of the problem. The challenge ahead is not just to promote science, but rather how to better understand the interactions between science and ideology and, most importantly, how to systematically integrate facts and values in a more comprehensive analysis. For progressive environmentalists, the answer is to be found in a democratization of the regulatory process. This means replacing technocratic decision making with a more participatory form of interaction among policy analysts, decision makers, and citizens. Toward this end, critical social scientists have begun to offer an alternative mode of deliberative policy decision making and analysis.

The Deliberative Alternative

The turn to a deliberative approach is based on both empirical and methodological considerations. The first has to do with the problem of scientific indeterminacy. As we saw earlier in regard to the problem of scientific indeterminacy, the techno-empirical approach has proven unable to supply the kind of definitive answers needed to resolve policy disputes in ways that can facilitate regulatory decision making. For those versed in the post-empiricist and social constructionist approaches to science and technology studies, this comes as no surprise. Such scholars have shown how science itself is always a matter of forging consensus in an indeterminate world. Rather than a matter of objectively "proving" an empirical reality—as the neo-positivist understanding of scientific activity would have it—the work of the scientific community involves interpreting specific findings in particular social contexts. Science, it is shown, is always underdetermined and, for this reason, scientific judgment is as much a matter of a persuasive argument as it is of a hard and once-and-for-all tested fact. The point is especially important for an applied method such as risk-benefit analysis, as there can be no "one size fits all" regulations. Regulations are always applied to different socio-political circumstances in different empirical and normative contexts. But the crucial issue here is to see that this is not just a matter pertaining to an especially difficult problem such as environmental risk. Indeterminacy is inherent to science itself.

Despite the rhetoric of positivism, the scientific community is itself a deliberative community. Whereas proof under the neo-positivist or empiricist conceptions of science is inductively anchored in the reproduction of objective tests and statistical confirmation, post-empiricist constructionism relies on the discursive construction and synthesis of competing views.[33] Indeed, for constructionists the empirical data of a neo-positivist "proof" can be turned into knowledge only through interpretive interaction with the other perspectives. Meaning is conferred in examination of the data through conflicting frameworks or standpoints that can uncover or expose unrecognized and hidden suppositions. From this perspective, the crucial debate is often over the underlying assumptions that organize the data rather than the data *per se*. The scientists' deliberations produce new understandings in a process better framed as a "learned conversation" than the pursuit of empirical proof.[34] In this view, scientific theory is itself better understood as a conversation than as a set of established proofs.[35]

Knowledge, in this evolving conversation, is understood more accurately as consensually "accepted belief" than in terms of proof or demonstration. Such beliefs emerge through an interpretive forging of theoretical assumptions, analytical criteria, and empirical tests warranted by scholarly communities.[36] Instead of understanding these beliefs as the empirical outcomes of inter-subjectively reliable tests, the post-empiricist sees them as the product of a chain of interpretive judgments, both social and technical, arrived at by researchers in particular times and places. From this perspective, social scientific theories can be understood as assemblages of theoretical presuppositions, empirical data, research practices, interpretive judgments, voices, and social strategies.[37] One of the primary strengths of a theory, in this respect, is its ability to establish discursive connections and contrive equivalences among otherwise disparate elements, as well to incorporate new components.

The emphasis thus shifts from the narrow concerns of empirical theory to a multi-methodological orientation and the development of "a rich perspective" on human affairs.[38] In many ways, the adoption of a multi-methodological approach opens the door to a more subtle and complex form of analytical rigor. Instead of narrowly concentrating on the rules of research design, combined with statistical analysis (which usually passes for empirical rigor), the post-empiricist approach brings into play a multi-methodological range of intellectual skills, both qualitative and quantitative. Basic is the recognition that an epistemology that defines rationality in terms of one technique, be it logical deduction or empirical falsification, is too narrow to encompass the multiple forms of rationality manifested in scientific practices. The empirical-deductive logic employed in risk-benefit analysis is, in short, too confining for a methodology that needs to meaningfully combine quantitative and qualitative orientations. For this reason, post-empiricism seeks a new methodological configuration through an informal deliberative framework of practical reason.[39]

But empirical indeterminacy is not the only problem. Especially in the case of public policy issues, there is also the problem of normative indeterminacy. When a proposed environmental regulation is evaluated in the real world of public policy, much more than its efficiency or effectiveness is involved. Public policy is an instrument of the political world, where the normative question of what ought to be done is as central and important as the matters of technical efficiency in achieving prescribed goals. As the logic of practical reason makes clear, normative questions pertaining to the particular situation to which the rule or findings are to be applied—that is, the empirical and normative context of application—are as relevant to the stakeholders and other participants as the efficacy of a general rule. And beyond the pertinent situation, there are questions about both the nature and function of the particular social system, including its normative principles. In the conflictive world of politics, where both relative advantage and political ideology are basic to struggles for power and control, there is no escape from such debates. No matter how efficient a rule might be in technical terms, if it works to functionally support a set of social arrangements that are rejected by the participants, no amount of empirical evidence will be persuasive. In short, a method such as risk-benefit analysis contributes to only part of the debate about risky technologies and cannot answer the question in any conclusive fashion.

From these basic indeterminacies, it becomes clear that the purview of risk decisions has to go beyond the realm of science. For one thing, the scientific community itself is unable to agree on its own interpretations. Hence we witness the politics of expertise versus counter-expertise as manifest in confrontations between industry-supported scientists and environmental scientists. Here the public is left to choose on the basis of ideological and extra-scientific criteria because research by itself cannot answer the question. People ask, for example, who paid for the research, why someone is so hostile when we ask questions, and so on.

From the normative realm we further discover that included in such decisions are social and political questions that risk experts have no special ability or privilege to answer. These matters require judgments that should be left to the citizens themselves. Questions about how members of the local community want to live or which social ideals should take preference over others are issues for democratic citizens to decide themselves. In these matters experts are themselves only citizens.

Failure to face up to this wider spectrum of issues has led to public distrust about official risk assessments. The only way to deal with this problem is to extend the boundaries of the decision process. The main question is how to extend the boundaries to include a wider range of relevant participants. Here the deliberative approach comes into play. This approach seeks a broader under-standing of the relevant harms, losses, or consequences to the interested and affected parties, including what the affected parties believe the risks to be. It thus becomes necessary to bring these particular perspectives and knowledges onto the same level as those of the experts.

DELIBERATION AS REFORM PROPOSAL

Turning to the deliberative model is more than just an idle notion of the critical social theorists. Acknowledging the failure of an overly empiricist approach to risk analysis, the National Research Council in the US has called for an "ana-lytic-deliberative approach" to environmental and technological risk analysis. Organizations involved in dealing with risk-related issues, according to the Council, should make a special effort to ensure that the interested and affected parties have input into the decision process. Significantly, the Council empha-sizes the need to consider the basic analytic assumptions about risk-generating processes as well as the specific risk estimates. The challenges "of asking the right questions, making the appropriate assumptions, and finding the right ways to summarise information can only be met by designing processes that pay appropriate attention to each of these judgments, informing them with the best available knowledge and the perspectives of the spectrum of decision partici-pants."[40] Even though potentially more cumbersome and time-consuming in the short run, asserts the Council, it is better to err on the side of too much rather than too little deliberative participation at each step of the process. Only through such processes, it is argued, can organizations make choices and decisions that affected groups will accept and trust.

Toward this end, the Council advances an "analytic-deliberative method" as being capable of bringing together citizens and experts. Such a deliberative method is required to guide a participatory process that can more comprehen-sively formulate the decision problem, guide the analytical process to increase the understanding of decisions, uncover the meaning of findings and uncertain-ties, and enhance the ability of affected and interested groups to effectively par-ticipate in risk decision-making processes. This participation, it is argued, needs to begin in the early stages of the decision processes.

An analytic-deliberative approach is presented as a method for gaining knowl-edge about risky situations, forming understanding of the risks, and reaching agreement among participants. The approach recognizes that the effort to reduce the many dimensions of risk to a single metric, as in the case of risk-benefit analysis, leaves out the normative dimensions of such judgments. Because such methods necessarily oversimplify real-world situations, value judgments, and other normative judgments remain implicit and overlooked. For this reason, successful use of the proposed technique depends on methods that help to bring out these normative dimensions in the very design of the process, including the determination of the particular methods to be employed and the interpretation of findings.

Although the process of deliberation needs to be broader and more extensive for some hazardous situations than others, explains the Council, such discourse is necessary for all risk assessments. The Council suggests a number of guidelines for organizing a deliberative process. Perhaps most interesting is that organizations should take the extra initiative to reach out with technical assistance to unorganized or inexperienced groups in matters of risk analysis and regulatory policy. In the Council's words, "If some parties that are unorganized, inexperienced in regulatory policy, or unfamiliar with risk-related science are particularly at risk and may have critical information about the risk situation, it is worth while for the responsible organizations to arrange for technical assistance to be provided to them from sources that they trust."[41] The Council thus suggests that experts must at times assume the role of facilitators.

Moreover, the convenor of such analytic-deliberative processes should explicitly and clearly notify participants from the beginning about budgetary, legal, or other external factors likely to affect the nature and duration of the deliberations, as well as how their contributions to the deliberative process will be dealt with and used. The deliberative process, in this respect, must aim for fairness in choosing participants and in supplying them with access to the kinds of information and expertise that participants need to effectively engage in the deliberative process. Last but not least, flexibility should be built into the deliberative arrangements, including procedures for dealing with requests to re-examine or reconsider previous decisions, rules about time limits, or the availability of resources.

Deliberation, from this perspective, cannot be expected to end all controversy. It cannot, the Council explains (1987), ensure that decision makers and managers will pay heed to deliberation's outcomes, prevent dissatisfied groups from attempting to override or delay the process, or correct situations in which legal rules mandate considerations based on decision outcomes differing substantially from those that participants believe to be appropriate.[42] Controversies, in this regard, are constructive in helping to identify weak points from which science can profit rather than merely as barriers in the path of expert decision making. Opposing perspectives encourage in-depth analysis to identify and explicate a technology's risks and benefits and their social implications. Conflicting assessments of new technologies or of the environmental impacts of proposed projects can thus help to identify and evaluate potential problems.

Given that the Council has been a leading voice in the advance of risk analysis in its various forms, including the earlier development of the technocratic model, its call for an analytic-deliberative proposal can be seen as an important step forward. Although the technocratic approach still remains dominant, the fact that many of the contemporary modes were initially promoted and influenced by the Council offers some hope for change, even if slow and reluctant. Recognition of the importance of deliberation and participation by this prestigious body should not be underestimated; it represents a significant step toward reform. However, the importance of the Council's latest contribution will not be realized through intellectual innovation alone.

CONCLUSION

Environmental politics, as we have seen, took a technocratic turn as it reached the governmental agenda and the regulatory process. Risk-benefit analysis became the embodiment of this technocratic strategy. Problematically, though, the kind of empirical evidence offered by risk-benefit analysis was discovered to be unable to supply an acceptable basis for regulatory rule making. With the indeterminacy of scientific analysis and a neglect of the underlying normative issues, risk-benefit analysis has come under increasing criticism from a range of perspectives, including environmentalists, concerned citizens, and the prestigious National Research Council. The search for an alternative has centered on the need for a broader discussion of a wider range of interconnected issues, giving rise to calls for a deliberative approach to regulatory decision making.

A deliberative approach will not be introduced simply because it is a better idea. Reform in politics never comes from ideas alone, but is invariably the outcome of a convergence of a problem situation, the availability of an acceptable alternative, and politicians in search of a solution. While such convergence always comes about as a result of particular social and historical circumstances, it is never possible to predict its emergence. But change is possible, and here at least two of the elements are at hand. One is the intractable problem of risky technologies, which is inherent to the industrial system and badly in need of solution. The second is a good sense of what a solution could be. Indeed, the deliberative alternative has been endorsed by one of the most prestigious of scientific institutions. Missing is the politics to bring the change about, and the barriers to such a politics are not simple.

The deliberative approach ultimately involves a move toward a participatory democracy. Although deliberation is often restricted to expert and managerial circles, effectiveness in addressing the problem of the risk depends on its being extended to include the broader public. Insofar as the existing institutional system is techno-bureaucratic rather than participatory, there will be considerable resistance to the idea, even in the face of reform rhetoric about the need for citizen participation. Ultimately, the creation of political will rests with the environmental movement and its struggle with the prevailing forces of industrial society.

Notes

1 Samuel P. Hays, *Beauty, Health, and Permanence: Environmental Politics in the United States, 1955–1985* (Cambridge: Cambridge University Press, 1987).

2 Sheila Jasanoff, *The Fifth Branch: Science Advisors as Policymakers* (Cambridge, MA: Harvard University Press, 1990).

3 William D. Ruckelshaus, "Science, Risk, and Public Policy," in T.D. Goldfarb, ed., *Taking Sides: Clashing Views on Controversial Issues* (Guilford, CT: Duskin, 1991).

4 The methodology of risk-benefit analysis is fundamentally an integration of two methodologies: risk assessment and cost-benefit analysis. *Cf.* E. Crouch and R. Wilson, *Risk-Benefit Analysis* (Cambridge, MA: Ballinger, 1982).

5 The first step in a risk-benefit analysis is a risk assessment. The method of risk assessment is employed to evaluate risks resulting from both hazardous technologies and toxic health threats. Although the principles are the same, the assessment procedures are applied somewhat differently, depending on whether the focus is technology or health. *Cf.* Vincent T. Covello, *Risk Assessment Methods* (New York: Plenum Press, 1993), pp. 59–79. The goal is to accurately predict the health implications of a hazard before or after it exists and to establish valid safety standards to protect the exposed population. In the second phase, the objective is an explicit comparison of the benefits derived from a hazardous activity and the risks involved in that activity. The costs are defined in terms of specific levels of risk (rather than monetary value as would normally be the case in a standard cost-benefit analysis). The method thus involves calculating the benefits of a project (adjusted against regular costs, such as plant construction and maintenance costs), comparing the ratios of the risks to the benefits, and multiplying the resulting figure by the total number of people affected.

6 Richard Andrews, "Risk Assessment: Regulation and Beyond," in Norman J. Vig and Michael Kraft, eds., *Environmental Policy in the 1990s* (Washington, DC: Congressional Quarterly Press, 1990).

7 Charles Piller, *The Fail-Safe Society: Community Defiance and the End of American Technological Optimism* (New York: Basic Books, 1991).

8 Aaron Wildavsky, *The Search for Safety* (New Brunswick, NJ: Rutgers University Press, 1988).

9 Ulrich Beck, *The Risk Society* (Newbury Park, CA: Sage Publications, 1993).

10 National Research Council, *Understanding Risk: Informing Decisions in a Democratic Society* (Washington, DC: National Academy Press, 1989); Brian Wynne, *Risk Management and Hazardous Waste: Implementation and the Dialectics of Credibility* (Berlin: Springer, 1987).

11 Taking life expectancy to be the best overall measure of risk to health and safety, they point to substantial increases in this measure and show that these increases over time parallel the growing use of risky chemicals and dangerous technologies.

12 National Research Council, *Understanding Risk.*

13 Douglas Amy, "Decision Techniques for Environmental Policy: A Critique," in Robert Paehlke and Douglas Torgerson, eds, *Managing Leviathan: Environmental Politics and the Administrative State* (Peterborough, ON: Broadview Press, 1990), pp. 59–79.

14 David Collingsridge and C. Reeves, *Science Speaks to Power: The Role of Experts in Policymaking* (New York: St. Martin's Press, 1986).

15 Scientific conflicts over environmental issues have also resulted from the diverging perspectives of the different disciplines. As professional specialization increasingly led to more fragmented scientific disciplines, each group of specialists came to know more and more about less and less. Hence each specialization features its own distinctive outlook, giving rise to different conceptualizations of "reality."

16 Jasanoff, *The Fifth Branch*; Sheila Jasanoff, *Science at the Bar: Law, Science, and Technology in America* (Cambridge: Harvard University Press, 1995).

17 Jasanoff, *Science at the Bar*.

18 Jasanoff, *Science at the Bar*.

19 C.F. Cranor, *Regulating Toxic Substances: A Philosophy of Science and Law* (New York: Oxford University Press, 1993).

20 Jasanoff, *The Fifth Branch*.

21 Jasanoff, *The Fifth Branch*, pp. 59–60.

22 Hays, *Beauty, Health, and Permanence*; Jasanoff, *The Fifth Branch*; *Science at the Bar*.

23 Langdon Winner, *The Whale and the Reactor: The Search for Limits in an Age of High Technology* (Chicago: University of Chicago Press, 1986), pp. 138–54.

24 Winner, *The Whale and the Reactor*, pp. 138-54.

25 Winner, *The Whale and the Reactor*, p. 151.

26 Jonathon Porritt, *Seeing Green: The Politics of Ecology Explained* (Oxford: Basil Blackwell, 1986).

27 William Leiss, *The Domination of Nature* (Boston: Beacon Press, 1974).

28 Alfonso Plough and Sheldon Krimsky, "The Emergence of Risk Communications Studies: Social and Political Context," *Science, Technology, and Human Values* 12(1987): 3–4, 4–10; Frank Fischer, *Citizens, Experts, and the Environment: The Politics of Local Knowledge* (Durham, NC: Duke University Press, 2000).

29 Fischer, *Citizens, Experts, and the Environment*.

30 Frank Fischer, "Risk Assessment and Environmental Crisis: Toward an Integration of Science and Participation," in Susan Fainstein and Scott Campbell, eds., *Readings in Planning Theory* (London: Blackwell, 1999), p. 493.

31 Fischer, "Risk Assessment and Environmental Crisis," p. 493.

32 Charles T. Rubin, *The Green Crusade: Rethinking the Roots of Environmentalism* (New York: Macmillan, 1994); Mary Douglas and Aaron Wildavsky, *Risk and Culture* (Berkeley: University of California Press, 1982).

33 Marie Danziger, "Policy Analysis Postmodernized: Some Political and Pedagogical Ramifications," *Policy Studies Journal* 23(1995): 435–50.

34 Michael Oakeshott. *Rationalism in Politics and Other Essays* (Indianapolis: Library Press, 1959), pp. 488–541; Barbara Czarniawska, *A Narrative Approach to Organizational Studies* (Thousand Oaks, CA: Sage, 1998).

35 Deidre N. McCloskey, *The Rhetoric of Economics* (Madison: University of Wisconsin Press, 1985).

36 Larry Laudan, *Progress and Its Problems* (Berkeley: University of California Press, 1977); Harry Collins, *Changing Order: Replication and Induction in Scientific Practice* (Chicago: University of Chicago Press, 1992).

37 G. Deleuze and F. Guatani, *A Thousand Plateaus* (London: Athlone Press, 1987).

38 Stephen Toulmin, *Cosmopolis: The Hidden Agenda of Modernity* (Chicago: University of Chicago Press, 1990).

39 Frank Fischer, *Evaluating Public Policy* (Belmont, CA: Wadsworth, 1995).

40 National Research Council, *Understanding Risk*.

41 National Research Council, *Understanding Risk*.

42 National Research Council, *Understanding Risk*.

6

Designs for Environmental Discourse Revisited: A Greener Administrative State?

John S. Dryzek

The administrative state is not what it used to be, in environmental affairs no less than elsewhere. There is still plenty of administration around, even if we think of it in classic Weberian terms: hierarchical and pyramid-shaped, with a clear division of labor between sub-units in the hierarchy. However, many governments have been affected by reform waves as well as by the press of structural forces that complicate the picture by introducing other forms of collective choice into administration. One popular set of reforms at least in the Anglo-American liberal democracies is the marketization inspired by market liberalism and its associated public choice theory. Here the idea is to make government more like the market, not just through privatization of service delivery, but also through the introduction of competition within government structures (such as internal markets) and the establishment of consumer sovereignty in the operation of government. Paradoxically, such reform also requires a stronger state center to coerce the system into being more like a market.[1] Another set of reforms occurs with the "new governance" that shares some of the decentralist ideology of market liberalism on service delivery, but also sees government in forms of networks of partnership transcending traditional private-public boundaries and involving voluntary associations and corporations as well as government departments. Structurally, the rise of "transgovernmentalism" means that problem solving cuts across traditional boundaries, including national boundaries.[2] A more powerful structural force emanates from the transnational political economy—though, paradoxically, this may actually function to consolidate the hold of the administrative center because of the demands it makes for states to abide by the dictates of international competitiveness. The ideology of economic globalization reinforces this structural force, as governments everywhere come to believe they must sustain investor confidence and open their markets.

The administrative state has also come in for an intellectual battering from green political theory, an enterprise that blossomed in the 1990s. The majority view among green theorists is now clearly democratic. Moreover, the democracy in question is not a mere representative one that takes on green parties and green programs, otherwise engaging in business as usual (but see Goodin's rearguard action on behalf of a more conventional green politics).[3] Though the details vary, proposals for green democracy generally involve more participatory and discursive invigoration in the context of decision making that is not simply left to the relevant department of government.[4] While this theoretical program has had nothing like the impact of market liberalism and public choice, it does resonate with a range of real-world deliberative and democratic reforms that have been adopted, generally without much input from theorists. Paehlke pointed out in 1988 that the environmental area has led all others in democratic reforms such as right-to-know legislation, public inquiries, impact assessment with mandatory public comment, and the like.[5] This momentum continued in the 1990s, with various sorts of policy dialogues, citizens' juries, planning cells, consensus conferences, deliberative opinion polls, and community-organized popular epidemiology joining more established practices such as mediation and regulatory negotiation. These reforms and exercises often reached into the territory once described as administration. Although Habermas sketches a "two track" deliberative democracy with deliberation occurring in the public sphere and more formally in the legislature,[6] the intertwining of deliberation and administration suggests a "three track" model, with administration itself a deliberative democratic site.

This chapter does not, however, constitute a wholehearted celebration of the encroachment of deliberative democracy onto the territory of the administrative state. For this encounter does not necessarily produce happy outcomes. Seemingly democratic exercises might provide legitimating cover for business as usual—especially problematic when that business is itself being pulled in a particular anti-democratic direction by market liberalism and associated structural economic forces. Co-optation and deradicalization of environmentalist and citizen participants in these exercises are also possible. Overall, these sorts of developments might contribute to reduction in vitality of the green public sphere, whose importance has been established by Torgerson.[7] What needs to be done, then, is to sort out the most productive kind of relationship between the administrative state and deliberative democracy. There may turn out to be synergies, but there may also be irreducible conflict. We might even think about the displacement of the administrative state by discursive democracy. And we should also be open to the possibility that discursive democracy in the public sphere can actually benefit from a relatively obtuse administrative state, one that does *not* open itself up along the lines I have sketched.

In this chapter I will try to navigate a path through these thickets. I will begin by setting out the administrative state and a discursive democratic alternative in ideal-type terms, and examine their strengths and weaknesses in a way that is comparative but static. This comparison will come down in favor of discursive democracy as being intrinsically more likely to promote ecological values. However, diagnosis of the faults of the administrative state can be instructive, not just by pointing to the qualities that any institutional alternatives should seek, but also in identifying traps into which these alternatives might themselves fall. I then move to a more nuanced and analysis of the relationship between the administrative state and democracy, showing that green democratization of the administrative state is a worthwhile project—but exactly how and when it can take place depends crucially on the political-economic context.

THE CASE AGAINST ADMINISTRATION AS SUCH

The fact that the Western world's environment is in certain ways somewhat safer, cleaner, and more securely protected today than it was thirty years ago owes much to the efforts of the administrative state. But despite any such accomplishments, the effects of the administrative state in environmental affairs today seem problematical. What, then, is wrong with the administrative state when it comes to environmental protection? At least three shortcomings may be identified. First, in terms of the basic criterion of environmental quality, administration is less than it once was. That is, despite any past achievements, the administrative state is running out of steam. While the early years of administrative regulation may be credited with some fairly obvious improvements in environmental quality, further achievements are hard to come by. A comprehensive survey of the evidence on this score is beyond the scope of this chapter—and in any case, many of the sources that one might cite are highly partisan, producing conflicting evidence. This much, it seems, is apparent: in the United States and elsewhere, the early years of environmental concern around 1970 led to the adoption and implementation of policies with clear and obvious positive effects on environmental quality. Come the 1980s, the question of whether further policy efforts do or would produce benefits sufficient to justify their costs (irrespective of the metrics one applies) became controversial. Later, new approaches to environmental improvement involving integration of economic and environmental concerns were pioneered, especially in Northern European countries. But these approaches did not involve management of the economy-environment interface by administrative agencies. Instead, they saw a politics that engaged industry, government, and (moderate) environmentalists in complex relationships, sometimes adversarial, sometimes cooperative.

Administration in the environmental arena thus confronted a problem also found in other areas of administration: diminishing marginal returns to effort. For example, the Soviet experience shows that central economic planning is an excellent device for rapid transformation of a static agrarian society into an industrial power—but thoroughly inept after that initial transition has been secured. In education, it is fairly easy for an administrative state quickly to convert an illiterate population to a literate one—but very hard thereafter to equalize educational opportunity, eradicate pockets of illiteracy, or otherwise promote educational achievement. Turning to social welfare, it is easy to virtually eliminate malnutrition, or provide a decent standard of public health—but hard to maintain and refine a system of welfare and health care that does not produce perverse and conflicting incentives, or generate attitudes of helplessness and dependency in clients. In short, as Charles Lindblom puts it, administrative systems have "strong thumbs, no fingers."[8]

A second shortcoming is that any achievements that can be credited to the administrative state may have been purchased at the cost of advancing bureaucratization and the instrumental rationalization or control of society more generally. This is Max Weber's scenario: *zweckrationalität* triumphs precisely because it copes well with complex problems, but attendant upon this triumph is the demise of the more congenial features of human existence and association. Weber's fears are today echoed by everyone from conservative free marketeers to critical theorists and feminists.[9]

A third set of issues stems from the fact that the state as a whole has priorities that have little to do with environmental quality, which may be overridden when they clash with these other priorities. The precise content of state priorities is a matter of some dispute. But at a minimum, all states face the need to establish domestic order, secure themselves in a potentially hostile international order, and raise the funds to finance these activities.[10] Democratic states in particular are also faced with the need to legitimate the political economy in the eyes of their citizens most likely to suffer from the inequality and instability that the capitalist political economy can produce. The main legitimating device is the welfare state. Finally, problems of both finance and legitimacy point to states' continuing need to maintain business confidence in their activities, for otherwise they will be punished by economic downturn. While inexpensive environmental programs producing clear and substantial benefits will have little impact here, environmental policy may be a candidate for such punishment if and when diminishing returns of the sort discussed earlier set in. However, this scenario assumes a conflict between environmental values and economic goals. As we will see, discourses of sustainable development and ecological modernization seek to dissolve this conflict.

The roots of these three defects of the administrative state lie in its epistemology and in its context. The *epistemology* of administration—its implicit theory of knowledge—is an instrumental-analytic one. That is, administration implicitly regards rationality as the capacity to devise, select, and effect good means to clarified and consistent ends. In the context of complex problems, this capacity also requires breaking such problems down into simpler components. As Weber pointed out long ago, bureaucracy is a device for the task decomposition and allocation that are necessary whenever problems overwhelm the information-processing capabilities of a single individual (or small group of individuals). For all their protestations about matrix organization (which has been espoused, for example, by the United States Environmental Protection Agency), task forces, organic structures, mosaics, and the like, and despite the best efforts of organization theorists over the years, most large organizations are still bureaucratic in the Weberian sense—that is, hierarchical and pyramid-shaped—with both authority and (implicitly) knowledge concentrated at the apex of the pyramid. The apex is assumed to know better than the lower levels, at least to the extent it is assigning and coordinating tasks among them, thereby ensuring that overall solutions to problems will be constructed in a coordinated and effective fashion. Market-oriented reforms inspired by public choice theory often reinforce this model, even as they are justified in opposition to it. Such reforms generally involve a strengthened coordinating role for the administrative center, which organizes and oversees contract and competition in service delivery.

Now, Weber himself regarded this instrumental-analytic epistemology as an effective one, at least in terms of a capacity to resolve complex problems, if not in terms of the unfortunate byproduct of a loss of meaning in human existence. But it is now abundantly clear that there are limits to the capacity of bureaucratic forms of organization—and to the instrumental-analytic notion of rationality undergirding them—when it comes to truly complex problems. The reason is this: effective problem decomposition must be intelligent rather than arbitrary. And intelligent decomposition in turn requires that the sets and subsets into which a complex problem is divided should be relatively autonomous—that is, with a minimum of interactions across their boundaries. As complexity grows, then so will the number and variety of such interactions, until at some point the analytical intelligence at the center of the decision system is overwhelmed. The result is that time produces not a convergence on less problematical conditions, but endless displacement across the boundaries of sets and subsets.[11]

To what extent does this kind of administrative incapacity apply to environmental affairs? Ecological systems are indeed highly complex; as Barry Commoner puts it in crude but effective fashion, the first law of ecology is that "everything is connected to everything else."[12] One consequence is that attempts to resolve one environmental problem (for example, by building tall smokestacks to reduce local pollution) often simply create or exacerbate another kind of problem (for example, long-distance pollution such as acid rain).[13] The fact that most environmental agencies operate under the authority of a series of single-medium statutes (for example, the US *Clean Air Act, Clean Water Act,* and *Resource Conservation and Recovery Act*) further exacerbates this situation, given that none of these statutes recognizes the possibility of cross-medium displacement.

The *context* of environmental administration can be as debilitating as its epistemology. As I have already noted, states in market systems are constrained by their need to maintain the confidence of potential investors. Any state actions that threaten the profitability of industry and commerce are automatically punished by reduced investment followed by economic downturn.[14] If indeed there are diminishing returns to state effort on the environment, then it becomes increasingly likely that potentially effective environmental policies will be vetoed by the anticipation of market punishment. This perhaps explains the inaction on climate change by all governments, including those nominally committed to the cutbacks on greenhouse gas emissions specified in the 1997 Kyoto Protocol. Any significant amelioration of the problem will require action that is very costly not just to energy-using industry and consumers, but also to national economies. The potential economic impact may explain why real action on this issue has been very slow in coming. Paradoxically, apologists for polluting industry of all sorts are well aware of the high financial and economic costs associated with limiting greenhouse gas emissions, which is why they have an interest in keeping this issue on the political agenda. Attention may be deflected from other environmental issues where the cost-benefit ratio may be less favorable to inaction.

There are, then, a number of automatic constraints upon any state that operates in a market economy. These constraints apply irrespective of the degree to which the state features democratic as opposed to administrative control. However, the presence of these constraints can increase the relative weight of administration, because executive government is less subject to the indeterminacy in the production of public policies that democracy connotes.[15]

When the competitive market and its constraints are weakened in oligarchic or monopoly capitalist economies, some less automatic, but no less effective, constraints upon the administrative state come into play. Corporations in such circumstances become very powerful political players. Their influence can be exercised directly upon administrative agencies, as well as in legislative politics. Thus agencies purposely insulated from legislative oversight (in the US, the "New Deal" type, such as the Securities and Exchange Commission, or Nuclear Regulatory Commission) prove vulnerable to capture by the very interests they are supposed to regulate or control. To prevent this kind of capture, the US Environmental Protection Agency was established under the "action-forcing" authority of Congress.[16] But the events of the early 1980s, when President Reagan handed the EPA to individuals hostile to the very idea of environmental regulation, demonstrated that this kind of deliberately politicized agency too can be deflected from its mission by determined businesses conspiring with zealots in the upper reaches of the executive branch. And despite some undeniable achievements, the earlier history of the EPA shows that politicization of an agency can lead to strange bedfellows and peculiar compromises. Along these lines, Bruce Ackerman and William Hassler chronicle the life and times of a coalition between Western environmentalists and Eastern coal producers which pressed for a policy of forced scrubbing for emissions from all coal-fired power stations.[17] This policy effectively discriminated against Western producers of relatively clean, low-sulphur coal, thus keeping the West pristine and the East polluted.

This last example shows that environmental interests are not without influence in the administrative state, especially, perhaps, when they can ally with non-environmentalists, such as the Eastern coal producers just mentioned, or fiscal conservatives opposed to government subsidy of nuclear power. But when all is said and done the struggle is not an equal one. Business starts from a "privileged" position in interest group policies.[18] Business has more (financially) at stake; it has more to spend on lobbying, litigation, and campaign contributions; and it has more with which to threaten administrators and politicians (including withdrawal of the cooperation necessary to implement many public policies).

INSTITUTIONAL ALTERNATIVES: DISCURSIVE DESIGNS

An agenda for institutional change can be constructed by starting with the epistemological shortcomings of the administrative state. In direct contrast to the Weberian argument, let me suggest that institutions can be expected to resolve complex problems to the extent they embody principles of free discourse among equals. Institutions of this sort will have the added advantage of undermining the instrumental rationalization and domination attendant upon administration and the like. Later I shall suggest that such discursive institutions are themselves prone to subversion by some of the more insidious aspects of the very same context that constrains the existing efforts of the administrative state, but for the moment a focus on the positive is in order.

The principles of free discourse I have in mind are those elaborated by critical theorists and others who have attended closely to the linguistic aspect of political life. One of the better-known of such statements is associated with Jürgen Habermas's exposition of the idea of communicative rationality.[19] To Habermas, an interaction is communicatively rational to the extent that it proceeds among equally competent individuals under conditions free from domination, deception, self-deception, and strategizing. All that remains is the "forceless force of the better argument," which can relate to both normative judgments and empirical conditions and relationships. Habermas himself treats the details of social problem solving as the domain of "administrative power." It is subject to the deliberative democracy of the legislature (and, at one remove, the public sphere), but once laws are made, administration is just a matter of execution.[20] Thus administration is for Habermas a domain of instrumental-analytic rather than communicative rationality. However, let me suggest, first, that the principles of communicative rationality also give us the conditions for effectiveness in the resolution of complex social problems (including environmental ones), and second, that intimations of these principles can already be found in environmental politics.

To begin with my first contention (and here I summarize a more intricate argument),[21] communicative rationality is conducive to social problem solving inasmuch as it enables the individuals concerned with different facets of a complex problem to pool their understandings and harmonize their actions in the light of reciprocal understanding of the various normative issues at stake. This process proceeds in non-hierarchical fashion, and so no cognitive burden is imposed on any decision center. The interaction between different facets of a problem that constitute complexity is matched by communicative interaction among the individuals who care about each facet. And of course, the conditions of these communicative interactions are crucial if they are to ameliorate rather than exacerbate complexity, which is why they must be regulated by the canons of communicative rationality. Ideally, the product would then be agreement on actions. Agreement need not take the form of consensus on the reasons for actions, though understanding of the reasons held by other participants is important. People can often agree on what should be done without agreeing on an underlying normative framework.[22]

If my argument here holds, then one might anticipate institutional intimations of principles of free discourse—discursive designs—in the vicinity of complex social problems. Three such manifestations are worth noting in the environmental arena. In moving from the first to the third, one finds increasingly less in the way of communicative purity, but more in the way of a problem-solving orientation.

The first category is celebrated by critical theorists and other radical philosophers: new social movements (usually defined in terms of their egalitarian style, lack of ambition to share in governmental authority, concern with identity issues, and lack of connection to the working class). These movements include feminists, peace groups, radical environmentalists, and anti-nuclear activists. All are committed to relatively free and open interaction in their internal workings, and sometimes in the larger political relationships which they engage. One might argue that this relative communicative purity is purchased at the expense of effectiveness. However, social movements take effect in the realm of culture, not just public policy. Consider, for example, the effects of both feminism and environmentalism over the past 35 years. Moreover, social movements can influence the state from a distance. German governments in the 1980s cancelled nuclear power projects and adopted increasingly progressive environmental policies while anti-nuclear forces were denied direct access to policy-making venues.

A more explicit problem orientation may be found in the second and smallest but (arguably) most significant of my three categories, discursively designed public inquiries. This category is exemplified by the efforts in both Canada and the US of Thomas Berger, who has conducted a number of public inquiries on policy issues. Two of these have some connection with environmental issues: his inquiry into proposals to construct pipelines to bring oil and gas from the Canadian Arctic to southern markets,[23] and his investigation of the condition of Alaska's Native peoples in the light of the 1971 *Alaska Native Claims Settlement Act*.[24] These inquiries could be loosely styled as social and environmental impact assessment inasmuch as they involve scrutiny of the effects of past actions and contemplation of the consequences of alternative development strategies for a region and a people. In both these cases Berger created a forum in which concerned and affected individuals could state, create, and develop their positions (especially through their participation in community hearings). Both consisted of prolonged interaction between Berger himself, relevant experts (at least in the pipelines case), and community members. Berger's reports contained recommendations for policy actions built upon these interactions. In the pipelines case, he recommended that no pipelines be constructed before the settlement of Native lands claims and the strengthening of the Northern renewable resource economy. In the Alaska case, he suggested dismantling the regional corporations established by the 1971 Act and the transfer of their assets to revitalized tribal governments, which would also exercise political control in Native Alaska. But in both cases he was summarizing a consensus reached through discourse among participants who attained a degree of communicative competence made possible by the kind of forum Berger established.[25]

My third category covers discursive exercises more closely tied to the state than new social movements or discursively designed public inquiries. (Berger's pipelines inquiry was commissioned by the Canadian government, but the way he conducted it surprised and dismayed his sponsors.) This category consists of procedures such as environmental mediation, regulatory negotiation, and alternative dispute resolution. These procedures have in common the idea that parties to a dispute can reason through their differences in pursuit of an action-oriented consensus under the auspices of a neutral third party. They are often proposed and undertaken as alternatives to more established forms of conflict resolution, such as litigation or even violence. In the case of environmental mediation, participants might include environmentalists, developers, polluters, community groups, and government officials. Many of the cases of environmental mediation carried out in the 25 years since the technique was introduced have concerned domestic US disputes.[26] Conflicts over local air pollution, mining, water supply system construction, highway siting, hazardous waste treatment and disposal, and land use have been mediated. In most cases a determinate outcome has been reached and eventually—though this is not guaranteed—embodied in public policy. The rise of mediation parallels and reflects an explosion of interest in informal dispute resolution in a variety of domains, international as well as domestic.

The kinds of exercises discussed in the previous paragraph involve stakeholders and partisans, and as such are prone to the continued strategic pursuit of self-interest. An alternative kind of design involves deliberation by randomly selected citizens with no prior partisanship (except by chance). In the 1990s, this principle informed citizens' juries (which began in Minnesota but have flourished in the United Kingdom), planning cells (in Germany), consensus conferences (invented in Denmark), and deliberative opinion polls (invented by James Fishkin in the United States and carried out in several countries). Representatives of interest groups may appear as witnesses but are banished from actual deliberations. Such designs are intended to ascertain informed and considered public opinion. Normally they have an advisory rather than decision-making role. However, their recommendations can sometimes be adopted in public policy; for example, a deliberative poll recommending greater stress on conservation helped to change electrical supply policy in Texas, and a citizens' jury has been decisive on at least one occasion in health policy in the United Kingdom.

Discursive Designs in Context

The most glaring shortcomings of the agenda for institutional reconstruction intimated in the preceding section is its inattention to the more or less automatic constraints upon collective decisions discussed earlier in terms of context. In other words, to the extent they become involved in actual policy making, discursive designs might fall victim to exactly the same kinds of constraints and imperatives as the administrative state.

The extensive critique of environmental mediation developed by Douglas Amy merits attention here.[27] Amy argues that the fate and function of mediation is to co-opt potential troublemakers by extending to them the illusion of participation. Thus placated with symbolic rewards, environmentalists and others will acquiesce in "responsible" development or pollution, and capital will get its way no less than under more conventional political arrangements. Environmentalists and community activists will be seduced into becoming mere agents of the state and corporations, perhaps even of the Weberian process of instrumental rationalization. More insidiously, the very fact of sitting down on equal and reasonable terms with capitalists implies devaluation of *moral* concerns (for example, on behalf of ecological integrity as a basic value) to the status of mere particular interests, fit for tradeoff against the profits of polluters and developers. At best, one can expect little more than the conspiratorial externalization of the costs of an agreement, which may benefit the parties at the table but impose high costs on others (for example, consumers or distant ecosystems). The coalition between Western environmentalists and Eastern coal producers mentioned earlier is indicative of this last possibility (though it should be stressed that this coalition had nothing to do with mediation or any similar procedure).

At present, environmental mediation and regulatory negotiation exist on the margins of environmental policy making. If they were to become more central, then additional hazards in the form of the automatic constraint exercised by the market would loom larger. Policy-making discursive designs could not afford to upset market confidence any more than the administrative state could. How, then, may discursive designs be rescued from the state, capital, and market?

The critics of environmental mediation and alternative dispute resolution more generally are no help here, for all they ever recommend is a return to administration, litigation, or legislation.[28] In other words, they offer only a dubious conservatism in the form of a return to a discredited, costly, arbitrary, and ineffective *status quo*. If industry is advantaged in mediation, then it is no less advantaged in the courts.[29] Is there any alternative to this reactionary counsel?

The answer, it seems to me, is that discursive designs should seek a degree of distance from the state—and its economic imperatives. Such distance may of course be found in complete withdrawal from practical, problem-solving concerns, and sometimes new social movements adopt such a stance.[30] But there is an alternative to such withdrawal. Discursive designs could be located within and help constitute an autonomous public sphere, separate from but confronting and pressuring the state.[31] A public space of this sort is created whenever individuals congregate to scrutinize their relationships with one another and with the wider relations of power in which they are located. The subject of the public sphere is, as the name implies, *public* affairs. Perhaps the best historical example of a public sphere occurs in connection with the early bourgeois challenge to the feudal state, which disintegrated as the bourgeoisie itself sought and gained state power.[32] Later, socialist parties and unions based in the working class confronted the state from which they were at first excluded. The working-class public sphere diminished (but did not completely vanish) with the inclusion of its leadership in the emerging welfare state.

Today, an autonomous public sphere faces the task of discursively constructing challenges to the state. What, then, are the prospects for the development of such a public sphere free from domination by the agendas of corporations and/or the state? There are many obstacles, not least the ease with which some environmental leaders now access the state. Moderate environmentalists prize this access and influence over, but also complicity in, the process and content of public policy. More radical environmentalists such as Earth First!, Greenpeace, and anti-globalization protestors often reject both conventional strategic politics and the more discursive possibilities intimated here in favor of guerrilla theatre.[33]

Some cause of optimism may be found in the efforts of Thomas Berger alluded to earlier. His Alaskan inquiry in particular constitutes an exemplary instance of the creation and sustenance of a public sphere in and through which a coherent challenge to the state is constructed and a community is reconstituted. This inquiry was concerned with public affairs in two senses. First, its target was public policy (especially that of the US federal government). Second, and perhaps more significant, its subject was the self-determination of the collective future of a particular public: Alaskan Natives. The inquiry excluded government officials (except for local governments, which the inquiry was not challenging). It was constituted under the auspices of the Inuit Circumpolar Conference, a transnational organization of Inuit from Alaska, Canada, and Greenland, and financed by churches, foundations, local government, and Native Regional Corporations. The result was a forum in which ordinary Natives could testify, and to this end hearings were held in cities, villages, and fish camps throughout Alaska, at which 1,450 individuals spoke. These individuals presented viewpoints, debated them, and argued with one another and with Berger, all in a context rendered meaningful by the existence and prior deliberations of the inquiry. Thus the commission did not just collect and collate individuals' positions; it also constructed a community position on land, economy, and governance, transforming sporadic protests by individuals and groups into a coherent challenge on behalf of a community and its way of life.

The establishment of a public sphere of this sort does not, of course, bring with it the abolition or even attenuation of the administrative state. However, this establishment does mean that the pressures upon the state from its capitalist and/or market context would be counterbalanced by the challenge from the public sphere. A cynical observer might claim that, no less than before, the interests of capital and market would always prevail in this unequal struggle. If so, then the public sphere would prove but a minor irritant, irrelevant in the larger political-economic structure. But other outcomes are conceivable. Berger's pipelines inquiry, though sponsored by government, focused a challenge from the public sphere which eventually contributed to a state decision to overrule the interests of corporations, though the relative importance of this contribution compared to other influences on the decision (for example, a competing corporate proposal) remains unclear. And the public sphere created by new social movements does occasionally exert some influence (as my previous example of Germany in the 1980s makes clear).

Despite the possibilities associated with the idea of a public sphere, one should not underestimate the obduracy of the market, capitalism, and the administrative state itself. Moreover, it is hard to undermine these three obstacles to freely discursive public life simultaneously. Eliminating the *free* market is conceivable, and indeed is done quite often—but all such elimination usually produces is either monopoly capitalism and corporatism, with a concomitant enhanced capacity to exert direct pressure on the state, or an old-fashioned command economy that exacerbates the epistemological problems of administration discussed earlier. Abolishing capitalism, now hardly conceivable, might give us market socialism of some sort, which is as capable as a capitalist market of inflicting automatic punishment on government actions that threaten profitability, or, again, an economic system administered by state bureaucrats. Limiting the administrative state might produce only more of the market or monopoly capitalism (as in Chinese and Russian economic reforms).

As things stand, then, discursive designs are not in and of themselves blueprints for an alternative political-economic system. What they do offer is a challenge to dominant institutional forms, which might contribute to a reconsideration of the way we order collective life. But in maintaining this challenge, proponents of and participants in discursive designs should be careful to avoid complicity in the complex *status quo* to which discursive designs offer the hope of an alternative.

RECENT TRANSFORMATIONS

Any more extensive and consequential role for environmental discursive designs in transforming the character of the administrative state could be achieved only if state imperatives were less ineluctably stacked against both environmental values and the indeterminacy that democratic control connotes. There are in fact two ways in which state transformation may be occurring in just these terms, though they turn out not to be available to all states equally.

The first transformation comes with the increasing salience of issues relating to environmental risk. It is the thesis of Ulrich Beck that industrial society is undergoing transformation into risk society, whose defining feature is that the public no longer accepts risks as inevitably side effects of "progress," but instead regards them as undermining the basic ideas of technological progress and economic growth.[34] The resultant "reflexive modernity" therefore involves society's confrontation with its own economic foundations, opening up new possibilities for what Beck calls "subpolitics," which would cover a lot of the institutional innovations that I have styled discursive designs. If Beck is right, then risk issues present a legitimation crisis of the state—and given that legitimation is a core state imperative, it enables environmentalists to attach their defining interests to a core state imperative more securely than before. However, it is a big "if." Beck can support his case with a few examples from Germany in particular; but even there, politics is still mostly dominated by the old distributional conflicts and economic management issues of industrial society.

The second transformation is also most well developed in Northern Europe, in the form of an increasingly consequential discourse of ecological modernization. The basic idea of ecological modernization is that economic and environmental values can be mutually reinforcing. The reason is that pollution reduction equals efficiency in material usage and so production more generally. A clean environment means happy and healthy workers and high-quality inputs into economic processes (for example, clean water). There is money to be made in abatement technology.[35] To the extent this scenario holds, then the conflict between the state's economic imperative and environmental values is weakened, and indeed environmentalists can try to attach their interests to the economic imperative.

These two transformations do not, however, dispense with the need for more radical action in and through the green public sphere. Ecological modernization as a merely technocratic project does not need discursive democratization, and the technical changes to production processes that it entails do not constitute substantial transition to a greener political economy. For example, producing ever more fuel-efficient and less polluting cars is no use if the benefits are outpaced by growing numbers of cars and increases in miles per car per year traveled.[36] A stronger version of ecological modernization would involve putting more basic questions about the structure of the political economy on the table[37]—and the table itself would have to be a more discursively democratic one in order for these questions to be raised. Turning to risk-induced legitimation crisis, that crisis takes effect only because of the presence of powerful oppositional forces in the green public sphere. The discursive subpolitics of which Beck speaks somehow has to involve these forces, without blunting their critical edge. In sketching discursive designs at various degrees of distance from the state, I believe the requirements of such a vital, critical, and yet productive (in public policy terms) subpolitics can be met. This kind of subpolitics would be exactly what is required to push ecological modernization in a stronger direction.

Both ecological modernization and the risk society scenario have in recent years played themselves out much more strongly in Northern Europe—specifically, Scandinavia, the Netherlands, and Germany—than elsewhere. This explains why these countries are now environmental policy leaders, and why the United States, once a leader, is now a laggard.[38] Ecological modernization is hardly on the horizon in the United States, still stuck in an old-fashioned standoff between supporters and opponents of the environmental policy regime established around 1970, and barely updated since. The existence of the environmental justice movement in the United States shows that issues of environmental risk and an associated discursive subpolitics do exist there.[39] But absent any ecological modernization discourse, the conflict with the state's core economic imperative is just too intense, and economics normally prevails to frustrate both further discursive democratization and any more serious pursuit of ecological values.

Still, the conclusion is more positive than it could be a decade or so ago. The progress may be glacial, but at least now there are glimmers of what a green and discursively democratic—or, rather, greener and more discursively democratic state—might look like. But such a state cannot be envisaged without a green and discursively democratic public sphere at a critical distance.

NOTES

1 Andrew Gamble, *The Free Economy and the Strong State* (Basingstoke: Macmillan, 1988).

2 Anne-Marie Slaughter, "The Real New World Order," *Foreign Affairs* 76(1997).

3 Robert E. Goodin, *Green Political Theory* (Cambridge: Polity Press, 1992).

4 See, most recently, Graham Smith, *Deliberative Democracy and the Environment* (London: Routledge, 2003).

5 Robert Paehlke, "Democracy, Bureaucracy, and Environmentalism," *Environmental Ethics* 10(1988): 291–308.

6 Jürgen Habermas, *Between Facts and Norms: Contributions to a Discourse Theory of Law and Democracy* (Cambridge, MA: MIT Press, 1996).

7 Douglas Torgerson, *The Promise of Green Politics: Environmentalism and the Public Sphere* (Durham, NC: Duke University Press, 1999).

8 Charles E. Lindblom, *Politics and Markets: The World's Political-Economic Systems* (New York: Basic Books, 1977).

9 For a free-marketeer critique along these lines, see Milton Friedman and Rose Friedman, *Free to Choose* (New York: Harcourt Brace Jovanovich, 1979); for a critical theorist's account, see Ralph Hummel, *The Bureaucratic Experience*, 3rd ed. (New York: St. Martin's Press, 1985); for a feminist angle, see Kathy E. Ferguson, *The Feminist Case against Bureaucracy* (Philadelphia: Temple University Press, 1984).

10 See Theda Skocpol, *States and Social Revolutions* (New York: Cambridge University Press, 1979), pp. 24–33.

11 For details on this general argument, see Christopher Alexander, "A City is not a Tree," *Architectural Forum* 122.1(1965): 58–61 and 122.2(1965): 58–62; Todd R. La Porte, ed., *Organized Social Complexity: Challenge to Politics and Policy* (Princeton: Princeton University Press, 1975); John S. Dryzek, "Complexity and Rationality in Public Life," *Political Studies* 35(1987): 424–42.

12 Barry Commoner, *The Closing Circle* (New York: Bantam Books, 1972), p. 29.

13 For details on this argument as applied to ecological problems, see John S. Dryzek, *Rational Ecology: Environment and Political Economy* (New York: Basil Blackwell, 1987), pp. 16–20.

14 See Fred Block, "The Ruling Class Does Not Rule: Notes on the Marxist Theory of the State," *Socialist Revolution* 7.3(1977): 6–28; Charles E. Lindblom, "The Market as Prison," *Journal of Politics* 44(1982): 324–36.

15 See John S. Dryzek, *Democracy in Capitalist Times: Ideals, Limits, and Struggles* (Oxford: Oxford University Press, 1996), p. 80.

16 See Bruce A. Ackerman and William T. Hassler, *Clean Coal/Dirty Air* (New Haven, CT: Yale University Press, 1981), pp. 7–12.

17 Ackerman and Hassler, *Clean Coal*, pp. 7–12.

18 Lindblom, *Politics and Markets*, pp. 170–88.

19 See, for example, Jürgen Habermas, *The Theory of Communicative Action*, Vol. 1, *Reason and the Rationalization of Society* (Boston: Beacon Press, 1984).

20 Habermas, *Between Facts and Norms*.

21 For greater detail, see John S. Dryzek, *Discursive Democracy: Politics, Policy, and Political Science* (New York: Cambridge University Press, 1990), chs. 2 and 3.

22 See Alasdair Macintyre, "Does Applied Ethics Rest on a Mistake?," *The Monist* 67(1984): 498–513.

23 Thomas R. Berger, *Northern Frontier, Northern Homeland: The Report of the MacKenzie Valley Pipeline Inquiry* (Toronto: James Lorimer, 1977).

24 Thomas R. Berger, *Village Journey: The Report of the Alaska Native Review Commission* (New York: Hill and Wang, 1985).

25 For further approval of Berger's efforts on this score, see John Dryzek, "Policy Analysis as a Hermeneutic Activity," *Policy Sciences* 14(1982): 324–25; Douglas Torgerson, "Between Knowledge and Politics: Three Faces of Policy Analysis," *Policy Sciences* 19(1986): 46–51.

26 For an early survey, see Gail Bingham, *Resolving Environmental Disputes: A Decade of Experience* (Washington, DC: The Conservation Foundation, 1986).

27 Douglas Amy, *The Politics of Environmental Mediation* (New York: Columbia University Press, 1987).

28 See, e.g., David Schoenbrod, "Limits and Dangers of Environmental Mediation: A Review Essay," *New York University Law Review* 58(1983).

29 See Samuel P. Hays, *Beauty, Health, and Permanence: Environmental Politics in the United States, 1955–1985* (New York: Cambridge University Press, 1987), p. 483.

30 Such withdrawal is advocated for somewhat different reasons by Hannah Arendt, who believes authentic discursive politics can be found only in domains divorced from social problem solving. See Hannah Arendt, *The Human Condition* (Chicago: University of Chicago Press, 1958).

31 See Torgerson, *The Promise of Green Politics*.

32 See Jürgen Habermas, *The Structural Transformation of the Public Sphere: An Inquiry into a Category of Bourgeois Society* (Cambridge, MA: MIT Press, 1989 [1962]).

33 A specific problem that arises in applying the idea of a public sphere to ecological matters should be mentioned. The concept of a public sphere—and its communicative rationality—is rooted in a philosophical tradition that claims there should be a radical discontinuity between human dealings with one another and human dealings with nature. This tradition encompasses Aristotle, latter-day Aristotelians such as Hannah Arendt, and the Frankfurt School of critical theory. Its members argue that collective human life should be so structured as to prevent it becoming like human interaction with the natural world, which can only be instrumental and manipulative. Today, this judgment is based on a fear that the scientific and technical attitudes that have proven effective in controlling nature are increasingly being turned to the control of people. An ecological critique of

this tradition would argue two points. First, these scientific and technical attitudes are not as fruitful as they might seem, as contemporary environmental crises demonstrate. Second, there is a sense in which the natural world contains not just brute matter for human manipulation, but also *agency*. Recognition of this agency undermines the legitimacy of an instrumental, manipulative attitude to the natural world, just as a recognition of human agency undermines the legitimacy of social control. Acceptance of agency in nature does not imply a regressive commitment to nature's re-enchantment. It finds echoes in the works of some contemporary natural scientists; see, e.g., James Lovelock, *Gaia: A New Look at Life on Earth* (New York: Oxford University Press, 1979), and Evelyn Fox Keller, *A Feeling for the Organism: The Life and Work of Barbara McLintock* (San Francisco: W. H. Freeman, 1983). Thus there may be a sense in which natural entities can indeed participate in communicative practice. For a preliminary discussion of the implications of this recognition, see John S. Dryzek, "Green Reason: Communicative Ethics for the Biosphere," *Environmental Ethics* 12(1990): 195–210.

34 Ulrich Beck, *Risk Society: Towards a New Modernity* (London: Sage, 1992).

35 There is now an extensive literature on ecological modernization. See, for example, Peter Christoff, "Ecological Modernisation, Ecological Modernities," *Environmental Politics* 5(1996): 476-500; and the special issue of *Environmental Politics,* 9(1), Spring 2000.

36 George A. Gonzalez, "Democratic Ethics and Ecological Modernization: The Formulation of California's Automobile Emission Standards," *Public Integrity* 3(2001): 325–44.

37 Christoff, "Ecological Modernisation."

38 John S. Dryzek, David Downes, Christian Hunold, David Schlosberg, with Hans-Kristian Hernes, *Green States and Social Movements: Environmentalism in the United States, United Kingdom, Germany, and Norway* (Oxford: Oxford University Press, 2003).

39 David Schlosberg, *Environmental Justice and the New Pluralism: The Challenge of Difference for Environmentalism* (Oxford: Oxford University Press, 1999).

7

The Ambivalence of Discourse: Beyond the Administrative Mind?

Douglas Torgerson

To see the environment as an administrative problem means cutting the environment down to size and making it manageable. However, this approach quickly runs into trouble, and conventional administration betrays distinct inadequacies in grappling with the environment. These shortcomings suggest the need for new techniques and processes that will deal more sensitively and comprehensively with environmental complexities. This essay treats the limitations of conventional approaches in terms of a critique of the *administrative mind*—an image that, although often only implicit, pervades the discourse of the administrative world and constrains the handling of environmental problems. At least to the extent that it labors under the image of the administrative mind, conventional administration is itself an environmental problem.

Even efforts to escape conventional limitations in dealing with environmental problems will, if framed from the rationalistic vantage point of the administrative mind, remain fixated by the notion that problem solving is ideally a task of pure analysis that should exclude such irritants as interaction, discussion, and disagreement. The administrative mind would close the door on such troubles. Problem-solving innovations have, however, now emerged that stress the importance of openings for discourse, of spaces where problems may be openly discussed on roughly equal terms from diverse perspectives, including ones that directly challenge the presuppositions of the administrative mind.

Such discursive innovations are by no means a panacea, but neither do they necessarily merit a cynical reaction. Discourse is ambivalent. Discursive openings, that is, offer an ambivalent potential either to reinforce or to transform the boundaries of administration—a potential that can be assessed only in terms of political and historical contexts. A significant feature of the contemporary context is the emergence in civil society of critical public spheres—or "counterpublics"—including a green public sphere that throws into question conventional presuppositions about how environmental problems should be approached.[1]

The complex of administrative organizations that directs contemporary society gathers its legitimacy from its central role in propelling a seemingly natural and necessary course of industrial progress—planning, anticipating problems, and overcoming obstacles that arise. In the process, the conventional distinction between public and private sectors, while ritually reaffirmed and celebrated, becomes less functionally significant. The concept of a functionally interconnected *administrative sphere* becomes increasingly suitable in the context of a "whole society" viewed "as a firm intent on maximizing or optimizing the ratio of its outputs to inputs."[2] The concept of the state remains relevant, but not the state alone. The public spheres of civil society, that is, confront an administrative sphere that contains concentrations of both public and private power, notably those of both the state and the great capitalist corporations. Even the administrative sphere remains insufficient as a concept unless it is conceived beyond the boundaries of any single society and in the context of such features of globalization as internationally state-based agencies and transnational corporations.

For some time now, a striking emergence of unanticipated difficulties—in the form, particularly, of environmental problems—has been challenging the administrative sphere. Its aura of certitude and stability has been unsettled not only by apparent shortcomings in responding to these problems, but also by a troubling sense that the administrative sphere has itself been a prime agent in generating the problems in the first place. The administrative sphere particularly runs into trouble in trying to solve environmental problems because of the way its prevailing orientation, its allegiance to the administrative mind, leads it to *define* environmental problems. This is not to suggest, however, that it would be a simple matter for the administrative sphere to define these problems otherwise.

The image of the administrative mind is one of an impartial reason exercising unquestionable authority for universal well being; it is an image that projects an aura of certain knowledge and benign power. The administrative mind presents itself as detached from mundane troubles, able in principle to master all things through calculation. In the traditional version, administrative rationality depends upon unity under a single head with the authority to plan, organize, command, coordinate, and control. This notion, clearly stated in the first effort to formulate a comprehensive theory of administration, reaches back to the early part of the twentieth century but reflects as well the influence of early modern philosophy and medieval theology. Even as administrative theory sought to distance itself from crude administrative hierarchies through notions of cooperation and systemic functioning, a theological connection remained clear: "Out of the void comes the spirit that shapes the ends of men."[3] With the emergence of the more recent technocratic version, indeed, a clear locus of rational authority seems to vanish. The administrative mind here is diffused through a management information system that works according to self-evident axioms and uncontroversial postulates.[4]

What is self-evident and uncontroversial in this context is established by presuppositions of order and progress so that the administrative mind seems to operate on the basis of a broad, self-evident goal while establishing relatively narrow, short-term objectives and strategies. Even though opposed in principle, the traditional and technocratic versions of the administrative mind coexist in practice and can even complement each other in administrative discourse. Faith in "order and progress" tends, in any case, to pre-empt questions. Even though guided by reason and methodical discipline in seeking solutions to problems, the solemn and authoritative administrative mind coexists with its apparent opposite. The administrative mind peculiarly becomes associated with the mind of the magus, which penetrates the mysteries of being and performs incredible wonders. However incongruous, this association seems to cast a potent spell by joining the lure of the mysterious to the authority of an austere reason. The relationship also recalls the historical pattern whereby the attempt of modern technology and organization to master things through calculation emerges from and replaces the effort to gain mastery through magical enchantment.[5] What remains of old is not a method, but an aura, one that envelops the image of rationality and obscures the limits of the administrative mind.

UNEXPECTED PROBLEMS: THE ADMINISTRATIVE SPHERE AND THE ADMINISTRATIVE STATE

The administrative sphere prides itself on order, but it cannot control the consequences it generates. Coherence in this sphere is accompanied by persistent tendencies toward fragmentation and disorder, and the administrative mind is itself limited, particularly by its focus on promoting the modern vision of order and progress. Various disorders arose early with industrialization, indicating the need for a central authority to regulate and promote the steady course of progress. Profound disagreements over the nature and scope of this need did not alter the fact that, whenever problems threatened to thwart the realization of the modern vision, hope was generally placed in the agency of a competent and detached administration—in what has emerged as the administrative state.[6]

Anticipated in a sense throughout the rise of the industrialization, the administrative state was clearly recognized in the twentieth century when rationalization began to permeate economy and society with both industrial technology and bureaucratic organization. The formalized relationships impressed upon social life fell far short of producing overall coherence, and consequent problems of coordination—as they were viewed—placed demands upon the administrative capacity of the state. Problems were generally defined in terms of finding and pursuing the most efficient use of human and natural resources. The corresponding tasks of calculation, organization, and technological development called for a state administrative apparatus capable of functioning as regulator and promoter of an increasingly rationalized economy and society. These tasks necessitated a rationalized state able to formulate and implement policies based upon a sound assessment of what was required by the developing industrial order. In effect, this meant not only enhancing the administrative apparatus of the state, but also fostering and coordinating linkages throughout the administrative sphere as a whole.[7] Yet, while the administrative state can thus be regarded as a response to advancing industrialization and the spread of administrative organizations in society, the path for these latter developments had been cleared earlier by state policies that already involved a centralization and expansion of state administrative capacity.

The administrative state thus gives particular shape to the generally centralized form of the modern state. In contrast to the diverse and multifaceted patterns of authority characteristic of the feudal era, the modern state arose as a single, central authority. It achieved the clear subordination of other social interests, typically with monarchial dominance over the landed aristocracy, the clergy, and the towns.[8] A key policy thrust of the emerging modern state, and one often in conflict with traditional interests, was to expand national wealth by fostering the development of markets. Initially, this was done through the mercantilist integration of insulated, particularistic trading patterns into a comprehensive yet controlled market; later, it was achieved through the effort to erect the necessary framework for the market to stand more or less by itself—to operate as a self-regulating mechanism through a *laissez-faire* regime. The deliberate design and institutionalization of this market mechanism was conceived as a harmonization of society with the natural order and proceeded through the removal of state and traditional restrictions on the production and exchange of commodities.[9]

Still, the removal of restrictions on commodity production and exchange meant not the diminution of the state, but its refocusing and expansion. The project was conceived under the image of the cosmos as a mechanism—one, indeed, rationally designed by the mind of the Deity. By aligning economic life with the eternal natural laws of this design, the state would perform its ordained function and allow the market mechanism to operate freely in the generation of wealth. Yet *laissez-faire*, as a rationalistic scheme, required a sweeping transformation of society and involved the division of social life into distinct public and private sectors.[10] A major administrative effort by the state was required in establishing this division, removing restrictions on market activities and maintaining the conditions necessary for the operation of the market: "The road to the free market was opened and kept open by an enormous increase in continuous, centrally organized, and controlled interventionism.... Administrators had to be constantly on the watch to ensure the free working of the system."[11] In particular, major attention had to be given to three interrelated areas corresponding to the factors of production that were now to circulate freely as part of the exchange of commodities: land (i.e., enclosing, or privatizing, the commons), labor (i.e., promoting a mobile and disciplined workforce), and money (i.e., maintaining a currency standard).[12] These tasks involved an extensive reform, standardization, and rationalization of law, together with a centralization and transformation of traditionally dispersed and inchoate activities into functions of an ordered whole. Further expansion of state administrative capacity was prompted both by the social problems and disturbances of early industrialization and by the need for an infrastructure to promote continuing development. The market mechanism thus appears as a social instrument deliberately devised, produced, regulated, and maintained through the administrative apparatus of the state. The *laissez-faire* ideology provided a general prescription for harmonizing economy and society with the natural order; yet the implementation of corresponding policies generated social pressures and encountered exigencies not contemplated by the creed. The establishment of the market mechanism and the emergence of the administrative state constituted complementary, mutually reinforcing aspects of the same pattern of development—of a rationalized world increasingly under the influence of the administrative mind.

The administrative state should thus emphatically *not* be viewed as a vast apparatus of public administration, standing by itself. Rather, the administrative state should be seen as a distinctive historical phenomenon, coming into its own precisely when the state loses its stature as a single, overarching administrative structure. An historical dynamic of the market mechanism, still largely unacknowledged from a *laissez-faire* perspective, was for that mechanism to undermine itself by promoting a concentration of enterprise and an enormous expansion of bureaucratic administration in the great private corporations. The administrative state constitutes a key feature, then, of the more comprehensive administrative sphere, in which the position of the state as a clearly distinct and independent apparatus becomes significantly attenuated.[13] As part of this administrative sphere, indeed, the state proved far less effective in its *laissez-faire* mandate of maintaining competition than in such tasks as facilitating industrial coordination and helping to assess and harness the dormant resources of the earth for efficient use.[14] The orderly appearance of the administrative sphere accords with the expectations of the administrative mind and depends upon the calculable characteristics of both formal organization and commodity exchange. Yet, if fixated upon its own orderly aspects, the administrative sphere insulates itself from awareness of the disorders that it generates.

Not long after the administrative state had been formed and named—in the mid-twentieth century—the seemingly inevitable advance of rationalization began to encounter unanticipated obstacles. The burgeoning of industrial technology and bureaucratic organization began to generate problems that had been unintended and indeed unimaginable. As certain flaws in technology and bureaucracy became widely apparent, the rationalization of the world became increasingly vulnerable to questions that before could—to the extent they were even possible to ask—be readily deflected. This unsettling development did not, of course, occasion the collapse of the administrative state; the result, if anything, was intensified reliance upon it as a coordinating mechanism to solve the new problems. The reflex was to expand the scope of measurement and calculation, to devise a comprehensive system of planning and control—a mode of accounting, in short, that would monitor, anticipate, and internalize the diseconomies of industrial expansion.[15] The emergence of environmental problems has not yet substantially altered this orientation. On the fringes of administrative practice and in the domain of civil society, nonetheless, the monuments of administration have been called into question; and the array of environmental problems thus appears to contain a significant potential—that of promoting challenges both to the established pattern of development and to the conventional view of administration.

The emergence of the early modern state as the central, ascendant organizational structure in society was accompanied by the advent of public opinion from a "public sphere."[16] This arena of intellectual culture and political discourse, supported by the increasing availability of books and newspapers and by the associations encouraged by urban life, constituted a communicative space of civil society in which the appropriate role and particular policies of the state could be debated and criticized. Such criticism did not, however, entail fundamental opposition. Indeed, for the Enlightenment *philosophes* under absolutism, monarchial authority appeared necessary for the rationalization of the world as they envisioned it: the task was essentially one for an "omnipotent" despot who could be "enlightened" by ideas generated in the public sphere—who, in other words, would listen to advice, would recognize the "natural laws" of political economy, and would accept the "rationalist conclusions" applicable to state policy.[17] Although the potential of enlightened despotism also fascinated key intellectual figures under constitutionally limited monarchy, parliament there emerged as a significant forum for debating and shaping state policy.[18] A basic homogeneity of viewpoint was, nonetheless, ensured by strict limitations of the franchise to propertied men; the bourgeois class interest, in particular, provided determined support for policies aligned with the doctrines of early political economy. With the decline of absolutism and with the late nineteenth century expansion of the franchise, public opinion both expanded to incorporate more fully the articulation of socially subordinate interests and, paradoxically, tended to decline in significance.

Confronted by an administrative sphere that could readily lay claim to the knowledge and expertise required for rational policy making and implementation in a complex society, the public sphere during the twentieth century found itself increasingly marginalized. Indeed, the formation of public opinion itself came to be identified as an administrative problem to be accomplished through propaganda techniques that rely upon centralized media of communication.[19] Although the public sphere came at times in the twentieth century to be viewed as thoroughly homogenized and manipulated, there have been opposing signs of independence and vitality.[20] These signs have become especially salient with the advent of problems generated but unanticipated by the administrative apparatus of advanced industrial society.

Within civil society, the emergence of new social movements constitutes an institutional base for critical public spheres able to challenge the administrative sphere. Environmentalism, in particular, has fostered a green public sphere that underscores the limits of the administrative mind while challenging the presuppositions and priorities of industrialist discourse. The spectacular failure to anticipate the advent of environmental problems and to cope adequately with them indicates that, instead of being the solution to complexity, the administrative sphere is part of the problem. Administrative claims to a monopoly on relevant knowledge and expertise no longer go unchallenged, but are often challenged by knowledgeable and expert critics in the green public sphere.[21]

PROBLEMS OF DEFINING PROBLEMS

The sacred canopy of the administrative mind protects the world from chaos; it is a serious mind, relentless in demanding order in its domain.[22] Yet, as a discursive image that constrains problem definition in the administrative sphere of advanced industrial society, the administrative mind serves to generate disorders, especially with a complex of environmental problems that cannot be comprehended, much less controlled, through conventional devices. To this mind, pressures from an emerging public sphere are troublesome, risky, and unsettling; they are intrusions, likely to generate chaos. This mind cannot grasp the irony of the disorders it creates through the operations of its own apparatus—that is, through administrative techniques and processes that are implicitly guided by faith in the administrative mind.

The world of administration responds by reflex to its emerging problems—and this, perhaps, is its most pressing problem. The celebrated lack of imagination characteristic of the bureaucratic mentality is no doubt part of the difficulty. Indeed, schooled in routines, their attention fixed by rules and conventions, administrative officials are (we are told by proponents of rationalized organization) at best predictable. For if deviations from normal procedures are regarded as irresponsible, then little innovation is to be encouraged or expected in the solution or definition of problems.[23] Yet such clichés about bureaucracy do not adequately portray the administrative predicament: a paradox of this tedious institutional form is that it is invested with exalted imagery, the grand vision of order and progress ordained by the administrative mind—a vision that remains potent, even as present problems dramatically violate the expectations it fosters.

Far from resting in calm certitude, indeed, actual administration is notoriously uncertain and fallible. The imposing image of an administrative mind competes with a less exalted, distinctly mundane, process. Still, the notion of administrative problem solving as the exclusive domain of a detached and impersonal mind helps to orient a form of life characteristic of the administrative sphere. Although in everyday practice no one may fully and explicitly express faith in the administrative mind, the image is nonetheless potent, shaping perceptions, expectations, and viewpoints while limiting the way problems are defined. For problem solving to be a mere matter of calculation, all issues of problem definition would have to be thoroughly resolved, along with the identification of goals. However, a collision and coalescence of particular interests, coming from outside and within, is of course a salient feature of the administrative sphere. Actual administrative practice thus violates the conventional imagery of unity under an administrative mind where all are committed to a common goal.

To the extent that problem solving is influenced by the image of the administrative mind, whether overt or tacit, the effect is to obscure the actual process. Even when a fundamental consensus upon goals can be taken for granted, the search for means generates oppositions and tensions that can provoke a revision of goals. The definition of problems, that is to say, is not simply a matter of choosing goals; there is a complex interplay of means and goals as new difficulties or opportunities become apparent. The definition of a problem turns upon what concept gains prominence in focusing attention; as long as one concept fixes attention, perhaps because its influence is not noticed, the nature of the problem appears obvious. With an interplay among alternative concepts, however, the definition of the problem is thrown into question. Significant even in contexts of fairly routine administrative matters, such questioning may involve the issue, for example, of whether an organization faces a problem of transportation or of inventory, of attitudes or of structure, of machinery or of people. Similarly, questions may arise concerning the fundamental identity and direction of an organization. Here the emergence and clarification of a leading concept appears as the key breakthrough to a solution—in effect, it appears that the essential step in solving a problem lies in defining it. To say this is to say that problem solving is decisively involved with how attention is focused.[24] To reveal an organizing concept that has gone unnoticed serves to refocus attention and to open up the possibility of play and flexibility among concepts.

Much recent innovation in management thought may be interpreted as an attempt—usually remaining marginal in practice—to break free of that fascination with the administrative mind that has guided the understanding of problem solving in administrative organizations. Particularly in attempts to address the problem of problem definition, the accent has shifted from the remote operations of an austere mind to a communicative domain of multiple participants.[25] Indeed, it now becomes apparent that the judgments necessary in defining and redefining problems involves an inescapable interplay of opposing ideas and perspectives—of difference, divergence, and conflict. Even in the case of a single individual, this process of positing positions and oppositions is not eluded but internalized. Nonetheless, both for individuals and collectivities, the image of the administrative mind can still obscure and inhibit this process.

Concern with the problem of problem definition points to an opening, to a play and flexibility in conceptualization. By drawing attention, in particular, to the administrative mind as a guiding focus of conventional problem definition in administrative organizations, we can render explicit what is often implicit; we can draw to the forefront a typically ignored background. Such a move directs attention to context; orientation to context thus becomes something not passively received, but consciously developed and refined. As we probe constraints on attention, moreover, we pass beyond the administrative mind to its fundamental rationale: the vision of order and progress. By focusing upon this vision and questioning it, we advance a deliberate project of contextual orientation to the point of a conscious revision of past and future.[26]

DEFINING ENVIRONMENTAL PROBLEMS

Even to speak of environmental problems reflects some influence of the administrative mind. For the dramatic and widespread expressions of environmental concern, first voiced some three or so decades ago, were animated by an idea that the administrative mind was not prepared to contemplate: that there was a fundamental flaw in the whole pattern of industrial development. Progress, as a quest to dominate nature, was seen to be itself a source of disorder, disrupting the natural systems upon which civilization and human life depended. The concern being voiced was one focused not only on separate problems, but on a whole pattern of problems—the collective consequence of which, it was feared, could be to throw humanity out of the balance of nature. The concern was not just with problems, but with a crisis.

Environmental Crisis and the Administrative Sphere

Although environmental concern achieved considerable acceptance and even popularity, the perception of crisis was resisted and rejected by the administrative sphere; indeed, to perceive a fundamental flaw in the whole project of industrialization would be to question the *raison d'être* of this institutional complex. Accordingly, those articulating this sense of crisis were ridiculed—and ridiculed fairly easily since the rationalistic imagery of order and progress was at hand to help in portraying as emotional and irrational those who perceived a crisis. An anomaly in the universe of discourse, the perception of crisis was to be explained as an abnormality, as deviance stemming from social or psychological peculiarities, from some corruption of mental faculties. Those who spoke of crisis were the victims and purveyors of irrationalism because—it was charged with no hint of irony—they lacked *faith* in technology and progress.[27] The exuberant industrial growth and rapid technological innovation of the postwar period encouraged an optimistic atmosphere and gave credence to the notion that the management of government and industry was safely in the hands of experts.

The perception of an environmental crisis involved seeing various impacts of postwar expansion as an interrelated, emerging whole.[28] Ironically, this very perception gained support not only from the systems-theoretic focus of ecology, but also from systems-modeling techniques drawn from the new repertoire of technocratic management itself. With this appeal to rationalistic imagery, the perception of environmental crisis demanded a more measured response than name calling.[29] Still, the challenge that the perception of crisis posed to the administrative sphere was too fundamental to be faced directly. The administrative apparatus had been structured to promote industrialization, not to deal with the aftermath. With a comprehensive vision of order and progress taken for granted, the apparatus was structured so that its various parts would attend to specific, strictly delimited problems one at a time. Even rather routine difficulties were, of course, often complex enough to generate problems of coordination requiring policy adjustments and structural adaptations.[30] However, the structure had no capacity to respond to the perception of a crisis so pervasive and complex as potentially to strike at the foundations of the entire edifice—and to expose it as a house of cards. To be dealt with, the "crisis" had to be viewed and treated not comprehensively, as the product of a basic flaw in the whole project of industrialization, but in a manner that identified *manageable* problems. Although the problems could be regarded as somehow commonly "environmental," they had to be defined, in operational terms, as primarily separate, capable of being solved in a manner that matched the functional differentiation of the administrative apparatus.[31] This approach accorded not only with the established structure of administration, but also with a "commonplace" of the technocratic orientation: "that there is a high measure of certainty that problems have solutions before there is knowledge of how they are to be solved."[32] With this confidence and with environmental concern translated into discrete problems, faith in the established pattern of development could be reaffirmed.

An Alternative Future?

The perception of environmental crisis and continuing confidence in the path of industrialization arose from competing notions of an emerging whole, each necessarily based upon fragmentary evidence. Each notion, in other words, was part of a contextual orientation that contained a particular view of the pattern of historical development, a view which—again in each case—was expressed vigorously and lent a sense of future inevitability. Against the dream of an efficient and orderly future, the perception of environmental crisis posed the nightmare of an apocalypse in which nature would gain retribution for the violations of an arrogant humanity.[33] Although continuing confidence in the path of industrialization was reinforced by prevailing cultural norms, the perception of crisis could also draw upon elements of the culture with imagery reviving the romantic reaction against modernity, recalling bucolic myths and old doubts about progress, appealing to populist sentiment, and reverently picturing nature as something essentially harmonious.[34] Humanity, as a matter of both ethics and survival, should seek to live in harmony rather than in conflict with nature. This, it was suggested, was a lesson of ecology. Since this lesson was unlikely to be learned well or quickly enough, catastrophe was in the offing. This accent of environmentalist thought conveyed the idea that nothing short of a total and immediate transformation of the established path would do. Futile gestures or withdrawal were thus the typical consequences.

Nonetheless, there were significant environmentalist efforts to formulate a possible path of future development that would pose a distinct alternative to the established pattern—one accentuating ecological sensitivity, decentralized initiative, small-scale projects, "appropriate" technology, and community cooperation. This idea of an alternative pattern of development represented, in effect, an effort to promote a contextual reorientation by deliberately elaborating an image of past and future in sharp contrast to the received view. Although promoted as necessary for continued human well-being, an alternative pattern of development was by no means presented as inevitable; at most, it was a desirable possibility, one that could conceivably be pursued through concerted effort. Since it directly challenged the established administrative artifice and its expectations of order and progress, however, such an alternative could readily be rejected and ridiculed, portrayed as thoroughly unrealistic. Still, by addressing significant, concrete issues of administration and policy within the context of a comprehensively conceived alternative, this approach to development could at least unsettle the complacency of the conventional outlook and provide, by way of dramatic contrast, an intellectual space for questioning a prevailing conceptual framework.[35]

Administrative Responses

Such questioning could not really be taken seriously by the administrative mind. Having defined environmental concern in terms of manageable problems, the administrative sphere responded in a piecemeal fashion—in effect, seeking initially to "clean up" specific problems generated by industrialization. The chief strategy was state promulgation and enforcement of environmental standards that were designed with the announced purpose of keeping specific kinds of "pollution" within tolerable limits, while at the same time achieving a balance with established economic interests. These initiatives sometimes involved the revival or revision of existing regulations, sometimes the development of new ones. Even when effective on its own terms, however, this approach typically employed what—in retrospect—appear obviously to have been expedients and stopgaps: narrowly focused techniques that were insensitive to their own consequences, changing the location and character of emissions and wastes without eliminating the source of the problem.[36]

It was not necessary to admit to a pervasive environmental crisis for the administrative sphere to recognize, however reluctantly, that emerging patterns of technological innovation and economic expansion were bound to generate new problems. A concerted effort to advance an alternative pattern of development, however, would have taken as its central focus the purpose and design of new projects, both individually and collectively; indeed, a chief element of this approach would have been to draw explicit attention to the *pattern* of development and to foster an alternative to it that would anticipate and avoid formerly unanticipated problems. The response of the administrative sphere did not countenance such a decisive change in the existing pattern of development; nonetheless, attempts were made to design more sensitive anticipatory mechanisms while promoting the continuation of the established course. These mechanisms took the shape of innovations in planning techniques—in particular, technology assessment, environmental impact assessment, and social impact assessment. Although generally advanced from a technocratic posture accentuating the readily calculable and neglecting context, these planning innovations nonetheless implicitly acknowledged that difficulties had arisen with conventional expectations informed by the vision of order and progress. The application of these techniques was generally unenthusiastic; indeed, resistance by particular administrative organizations was often effective in preventing, curtailing, or circumventing anticipatory assessments. Still, this resistance itself suggests that the employment of these new techniques—however technocratically constrained—was worrisome for major interests involved in promoting the established pattern of development. For no matter how marginal the use of these techniques generally has been in the policy processes of the state and of corporations, their application nonetheless created a new factor that somehow had to be reckoned with and that, at important points, could affect the flow of decision making. Indeed, if not tightly controlled, such assessments not only could direct attention to fundamental problems about specific projects, but could also lead to a questioning of the whole pattern of industrial development—of order and progress itself.[37]

The agencies responsible for environmental management—regulation, impact assessment, and related procedures—were at times developed from already established units with different primary mandates; at other times, new units were created, yet typically with a marginal position within the administrative sphere as a whole. These organizational realignments were in keeping with what would seem a measured response of treating environmental concern in terms of manageable problems.[38] In contrast, many who perceived the advent of a pervasive environmental crisis demanded a far more dramatic response—one that would effectively subordinate the entire administrative sphere and society as a whole under a single head devoted to environmental management.[39] Of course, this proposal was a futile reflex: one that sought simply to change the goal orientation of the administrative mind while ignoring the historical and political processes that, in shaping the apparatus of the administrative sphere, have also promoted ends suited to its form. In any event, both of these approaches shared a view of environmental management as a discrete function, something added on somewhere to an administrative edifice whose basic form was to be taken for granted.

The industrial cosmos has so far been fashioned with abiding confidence in the administrative mind; and the administrative definition of environmental problems remains marked by this confidence. Taking for granted the structure and exigencies of the existing administrative sphere, together with assumptions of order and progress, the administrative mind defines manageable problems and develops manageable solutions. Often the mind sets its "invisible hands" to work as reliable instruments of social control and development, hands whose work is manifest in the apparently lawful regularities of economic and political systems. The workings of the administrative mind thus calls forth human interaction, but interaction that is largely anonymous and strictly strategic, blind to problems beyond immediate interests. The mechanisms of market economy and pluralist polity, to the extent that they actually operate, are of course not self-regulating; they in principle presuppose, but do not fulfill, the promise of order and progress.[40] Actually, the mechanisms are always subsumed within the framework of the larger administrative apparatus. With a proliferation of complex environmental (and other) problems generated both by these mechanisms and by the rest of the administrative apparatus, the administrative mind falls back upon reductive forms of analysis, but remains unable to perform the measurements and calculations needed to comprehend the problems.

Thinking in Another Direction

In conceptions of an alternative pattern of development, environmental management came to be viewed as potentially a characteristic of the whole, rather than a function of a part controlling the whole. Yet thinking in this other direction was itself—given its holistic focus—so sweepingly comprehensive that it seemed to deny itself any place to begin. Conceptually, the approach seemed capable of recommending only a total transformation—a change requiring a scope and magnitude of power that not only would be fantastic, but that would also violate principles of decentralization and participation that were generally seen as necessary features of an alternative path.[41]

In practice, however, an environmentalist focus on particular problems did emerge. In part, this focus tacitly acknowledged the rationale of administrative compartmentalization: that a problematic complex must, whether or not it constituted a "crisis," somehow be reduced to a set of simpler problems, each of which can become an object of separate attention. At the same time, however, the particular way in which the alternative orientation is decomposed into specific problems shows that how one cuts into a problematic complex is decisive for problem definition.

What is distinctive about an environmentalist orientation is that no problem is assumed, in analysis or design, to be entirely discrete; on the contrary, it is a guiding presupposition that efforts to solve a particular problem will affect efforts to solve other problems. Hence problem-solving designs are elaborated with, as it were, an open boundary; attention is permitted and encouraged to remain devoted to a broader context. From this perspective, the definition of one problem partly defines others; there is, indeed, mutual overlapping. Accordingly, administration must, in technique, process, and structure, match the complexity of these interrelated problems.[42] Although it is clear that thought and practice must somehow be bounded, this approach to problem definition and administration nonetheless attempts to test and stretch these limits through deliberate contextual reorientation—and through designs informed by this effort.[43]

This distinctive approach to context fosters what is in effect a redefinition of conventionally defined environmental problems. The problem of waste disposal, for example, becomes redefined as a problem of waste reduction and recycling. The problem of controlling pesticide pollution is redefined as a problem of developing agricultural patterns that require less pesticide input while, at the same time, utilizing organic nutrients that otherwise end up as waste. Health care expands its focus from cure to prevention, seeking to reduce pollution both in the workplace and beyond while trying, moreover, to encourage healthful dietary patterns—which, in turn, are congruent with the agricultural patterns being developed. Air-pollution control devices on vehicles are seen (at most) as part of the solution to a problem that also requires vehicle redesign to reduce fuel consumption, perhaps the use of different fuels, and even a reform of the entire transportation network—guided by a reconsideration of settlement patterns and work schedules. The problem of meeting increasing energy demand is redefined so that increases are no longer taken as given: the problem becomes one primarily of meeting energy needs through significantly greater reliance upon conservation and efficiency, an effort that complements and reinforces efforts regarding waste, pollution, health, and so on.

What is generally common to environmental problems, as redefined, is that they and their proposed solutions are found by thinking in "another" direction. Such redefinition, indeed, appears risky; for although the new approaches may be insightful, even elegant, they also dispense with guarantees implied by the vision of order and progress, guarantees that depend upon the administrative mind as the coherent locus of comprehension and control. The problem-solving designs—the technical forms—here presuppose an emergent redesign and transformation of the administrative apparatus, anticipating a decentralization and diffusion of responsibility. Although the principle of design for the administrative form thus abandons the "illusion of final authority,"[44] this does not mean that no elements of centralization remain. The point, rather, is that this orientation proceeds by throwing dramatically into question the conventional reflex of relying upon some central, superior authority as the sole agency and ultimate guarantor of direction and coordination. In sum, the guiding outlook is that a new balance needs to be struck between centralization and decentralization, generally favoring the latter. Intrinsic to the problem of defining environmental problems, then, is a challenge of organizational design unsettling to the prevailing form of the administrative sphere. But who is to define and undertake this tremendous task of redesign? Merely to pose the question is to suggest an answer, at least in the negative: no *one*.

Beyond the Administrative Mind?

Thinking in a different direction is the goal of various techniques that have been developed to enhance creative problem-solving capacity in administrative organizations. Here the primary focus is upon ways of thinking that will generate new perspectives and insights: that will identify a dominant concept, reverse the terms of a relationship, review a question in relation to an ambiguous image or statement, imagine a different context.[45] Yet the efforts of creative problem solving have also been extended beyond these various techniques of shifting focus in a thought process. Attention has also been given to processes of interaction, especially in the dynamics of small groups, but also with regard to overcoming the modes of "selective perception"[46] typically generated by differentiation among administrative units. Here organizational designs have been developed to draw differing units and perspectives into closer communication with one another in order to keep organizations attuned to the dynamics and complexities of external contingencies. For planning procedures, indeed, there are designs for encouraging argument and explicitly challenging conventional assumptions.[47] Such innovations—while typically contained within a rather conventional orientation—signal less reliance upon the style of thinking associated with the image of a unified and controlling administrative mind. Indeed, the reliance upon a greater diversity of perspectives points beyond thinking as the analytic activity of an independent mind (cogitation) and draws attention to communication among persons (a form of interaction).[48]

Discursive Openings: An Ambivalent Potential

In the administrative techniques and processes employed in environmental management, we witness some movement from cogitation to interaction—from a monological, self-enclosed process to one that is more open, dialogical. Environmental management here involves discursive openings in such forms as participatory planning, regulatory negotiation, environmental mediation, and public inquiry.[49] These discursive openings are oriented to principles that implicitly challenge the administrative mind and thus are at least suggestive of different administrative forms. However, these innovations do not arise in a vacuum, and within their historical and political contexts, their potential is ambivalent.

Discursive openings point beyond the administrative mind as the organizing principle for environmental management. The prospect is one of moving from a cloistered mode of problem solving to an institutionalization of discourse that would encourage an interplay of differences in defining and resolving problems. Diverging from a rationalistic preoccupation with cogitation in problem solving, such an institutionalization of discourse would foster communicative contexts characterized by a qualitatively freer creation and more equal exchange of ideas than is typical of the administrative sphere. Communication would not be so organized as to absorb differences and block critical insights.

Discursive openings anticipate an institutional form that, with a distinctly more open, decentralized, and participatory orientation, would be conducive to ideas and innovations focused on an alternative pattern of development: an administrative sphere, that is, open to the influence of active, critical public spheres. Yet as narrow spaces in a generally closed world, discursive openings are precarious, always under the threat of being squeezed shut. What weighs against this prospect of closure is the clear message of environmental concern, voiced both by people facing particular threats and by a more or less cohesive network of organizations sharing a broader focus. The administrative apparatus encounters pressure to accommodate these interests, to eliminate their potential for obstruction, to smooth over differences. While often troublesome to the administrative mind, discursive openings thus also provide a convenient resource to promote the incorporation of divergent interests into a more stable consensus. Indeed, administrative units responsible for handling environmental problems find environmentalist pressures useful at various junctures in the policy process, so long as these pressures can be contained within acceptable bounds. Accordingly, support for the institutionalization of discursive innovations—and hence, for a more open process—can come from within the administrative apparatus itself.

This very scope for the expression of environmental concern carries a risk: if institutionalization promotes incorporation, a divergent message can be more or less subtly screened, softened, rendered compatible with the perspective of the administrative mind—or safely ignored. This occurs in an especially subtle manner when the troubling message is translated into a technocratic idiom that deferentially approaches the administrative mind and implicitly presupposes its rationality. Still, those able simultaneously to master and see through the technocratic idiom can make it perform their own tricks, with wit and irony exposing this administrative ritual while propounding a dramatically innovative perspective designed to stretch the administrative mind.[50]

Between Administrative and Public Spheres: Space for Redefining Problems

The administrative sphere offers little space for open discussion, for questioning (much less changing) problem definition. Under the sway of prevailing priorities—and with these being reinforced through the image of the administrative mind—there is little internal impetus to think in a different direction, to break free of clichéd patterns of thought. Contained and organized under this frame of mind, the interactive elements of the administrative sphere are typically reduced to modes of interchange that are variously directive and strategic, depersonalized, even anonymous. Substantial pressure for open discussion does not typically come from within the administrative sphere, but from its periphery or from outside it—from the critical public spheres of civil society, particularly the green public sphere.

The discourse of critical public spheres signals a notable shift from the situation at mid-century when it was possible to portray a cohesive administrative sphere, operating smoothly on the basis of a broad consensus, restricting partisanship to "mutual adjustment," and servicing a quiescent mass society.[51] Subsequent social changes involved the emergence of active publics increasingly capable of monitoring, criticizing, and influencing the operations of the administrative sphere. Demands for openness and participation constitute efforts to overcome a mobilization of bias by pressing peripheral priorities onto and into the administrative sphere—in effect, changing its priorities and creating greater potential for problem redefinition. The administrative sphere, of course, responds by variously repelling, accommodating, and containing these pressures—typically, that is, by changing its mind as little as possible. Discursive openings often emerge from the ambivalent pressures of this context, at a point of division and intersection between administration and society: at the boundary, so to speak, of the administrative and public spheres.[52] At this boundary, pressures for discursive openings signal an attempt at gaining access to perceived key centers of decision making. This effort reflects a realization that it would not be adequate to focus effort only on established legislative bodies or on influencing public opinion.

In terms of organizational design, the creation of discursive bodies connected to the administrative sphere would tend to match internal and external complexity. To the extent that these bodies were not integrated within the flow of administrative decision making, however, their tendency would be only to complicate things, proving variously annoying or irrelevant to administration. Integration within the flow of decision making could, of course, mean absorption—a reduction of the potential complexity.[53] Yet an integration that retained difference would enhance internal complexity in response to the complexity of environmental (and other) problems arising in a wider context. Administrative capacity to redefine problems would be increased through thought and interaction that challenged the hold of prevailing concepts.[54] The capacity to redefine problems, moreover, would amount to a shift in priorities—hence a decisive change in administrative outlook and practice, together with a move toward realigning the apparatus. Problem definition would step beyond the limits of the administrative mind. To cast the main problem in redefining environmental problems simply as one of organizational design would, of course, obscure the political character of the problem. Indeed, the prevailing shape of social power tends to inhibit recognition of this political character as well as to block substantial changes in prevailing priorities.

The Context of Power

An uncritical fixation on misleading notions is itself part of the power alignment of a policy process that systematically renders certain priorities central and others marginal, thereby fostering a particular mode of problem recognition: a "mobilization of bias" that, as part of its operation, tends to deflect attention from itself. This bias is not simply a particular point of view, in other words, but a way of seeing things that is mobilized organizationally to discourage the serious consideration of alternatives. Of the individual, group, and class interests that vie for a hearing in the policy process, those that receive most favored treatment are those that are at once most crucial to the stability of advanced industrial development and most capable of persistently organized expression in an idiom consistent with prevailing presuppositions.[55] These are predominantly interests of institutions in the administrative sphere that possess both the significant incentives and the resources required for advancing their cause effectively. With information a key resource in advancing particular interests, those central to the process have reasons to gain and control information, withholding or releasing it—as it suits their purpose—both from one another and from those on the margins of the process. The effect, as one participant-observer has termed it, is an "*unconscious* conspiracy" to maintain a closed policy process.[56] Broadly based interests, such as those of environmental concern, possess less clearly a potential for effective organization. They have fewer available resources and often speak a language at odds with the main idiom. Simply to squeeze in, to gain entry and a measure of legitimacy, they often find it necessary to reformulate, even censor, their message to accord with the established bias.[57]

Discursive openings could affect developments in different ways—principally, by acting either to absorb pressures within conventionally accepted boundaries or to magnify and expand those pressures. The potential to oppose and expand the administrative apparatus from within is always accompanied by another possibility, that the opposing perspective will be reduced and contained within the apparatus. Discursive openings, nonetheless, constitute an intrusion into the domain of the administrative mind. Increasing the salience of non-programmed features of administrative organizations, these designs loosen the grip of ritual and routine. This is not to predict a particular outcome, but to indicate that what happens becomes less predictable because the control of the prevailing regime becomes less secure. In other words, these innovations involve an accommodation of divergent interests that necessarily carries uncertain prospects for all parties. Plurality tends to displace unity with the unpredictable, unbounded, and inherently fragile character of human action.[58] In the ensuing conflict and coalescence of perspectives, there is an enhanced potential for problems to be redefined beyond conventional bounds.

Discursive openings, however narrow, come in response to actual or anticipated pressures—that is to say, within a context of power—and thus exhibit their ambivalent potential for the administrative sphere. It is thus misleading to think only in terms of *inherent* potential. As responses to pressures from a larger context, such openings are points of intersection between the administrative sphere and the society at large; and as part of this relationship, such openings influence, and remain subject to, a pattern of influences that is susceptible to at least some change. The potential of discursive openings can be assessed only as part of the potential for broader changes to emerge—i.e., only as affecting and being affected by developments in the overall alignment of social power. Even if the context of power is unpromising in light of prevailing priorities, an institutionalization of discursive openings carries a potential that should not be ignored.

Conventional practices have so denigrated discourse that any institutionalization of discursive space—even if part of a cynical effort to manipulate and co-opt oppositional energies—remains notable historically as a venture promoting an institutional capacity at odds with the prevailing framework of the administrative mind. The historical significance of such a venture would certainly be enhanced if it were accompanied and reinforced by emerging changes in the priorities of the administrative sphere. However, an institutionalization of discursive openings would remain significant as a groundwork from which historical possibilities of change might emerge in the future, even if their immediate effect was to reinforce established power and thus inhibit such change.[59]

The administrative sphere typically seeks to promote discursive openings on its own terms, and this establishes a tendency for the simple absorption of pressure, for co-option. However, this obvious tendency can alert those groups and individuals articulating environmental concern to the prospect of co-option in particular cases. Indeed, the record of discursive openings indicates that this prospect can be assessed with regard to procedural issues that often become matters of dispute: concrete issues involving such questions as access to information, the availability of financial aid, timing, the form and sequence of presentations, and the relationship of the process to policy formulation and implementation.[60] Yet the specific issues all revolve about a common point.

Unlike more strictly analytic techniques, discursive openings are *obviously* not neutral elements of an objectively given system. Hence their legitimacy—and even their capacity to absorb and control pressures—is predicated upon an appeal to norms of fairness and openness in communication. Consequently, discursive openings are directly exposed to the potential for critique in terms of these norms.[61] Such critique can inform decisions by potential participants in specific cases about whether to press for a particular discursive forum, to call for procedural change, to withdraw involvement, to stage an alternative discourse, or to make some dramatic protest. In any event, the administrative capacity to absorb pressures through discursive openings is limited; for an achieved consensus can dissolve if the process is perceived to violate significantly the norms of fair and open communication.[62]

The potential for co-option provides a rationale for a general environmentalist suspicion of discursive openings and for doubts—possibly to the point of outright resistance—concerning how they might be formalized and institutionalized. Yet such concern about co-option becomes pressing primarily from a specific vantage point: one that seeks the organization, coordination, and direction of a comprehensive social movement—i.e., implicitly from the viewpoint of an administrative mind that wants secure control over the course of developments, that seeks strategic and tactical unity. Indeed, the potential for co-option might ironically increase to the extent that such unity is achieved; for a singular thrust runs counter to a less manageable diversity. Actually, the sources of environmentalist pressure are not generally cohesive; they are multifarious, cohering at some times but fragmenting at others. This diversity restricts administrative capacity to promote consensus through discursive openings, especially when the procedures proposed are sharply at variance with normative expectations of fair and open communication. Hence protest and refusal by some to participate in a forum could tend to strengthen the position of participants seeking greater openness through procedural changes. The outcome, in any case, is likely to be what no one alone plans.

NOTES

1 See Nancy Fraser, "Rethinking the Public Sphere: A Contribution to the Critique of Actually Existing Democracy," in Craig Calhoun, ed., *Habermas and the Public Sphere* (Cambridge, MA: MIT Press, 1992); Michael Warner, *Publics and Counterpublics* (New York: Zone Books, 2002); Douglas Torgerson, *The Promise of Green Politics: Environmentalism and the Public Sphere* (Durham, NC: Duke University Press, 1999) and "Farewell to the Green Movement: Political Action and the Green Public Sphere," *Environmental Politics* 9.4(2000): 1–19. The literature on public spheres derives from Habermas. It is important to note that, in this usage, a public sphere is a conceived primarily in contradistinction to the state (or what is often termed the "public sector").

2 Gianfranco Poggi, *The Development of the Modern State* (Stanford, CA: Stanford University Press, 1978), p. 142. In attempting to discern broad patterns of development, Poggi tends to disregard national and regional variations. Yet a focus that disregards certain differences does not necessarily deny their potential importance for other relevant inquiries. What I examine here is a general intellectual and institutional background against which such differences might stand out.

3 Chester I. Barnard, *The Functions of the Executive*, 30th anniversary ed. (Cambridge, MA: Harvard University Press, 1968 [1938]), p. 284. For a survey of management theory, see Daniel A. Wren, *The Evolution of Management Thought*, 2nd ed. (New York: John Wiley and Sons, 1979). For a more critical view, see Reinhard Bendix, *Work and Authority in Industry: Ideologies of Management in the Course of Industrialization* (New York: Harper and Row, 1963), esp. pp. 58ff. Images of the administrative mind emerge in a number of variations. For the first attempt to formulate a comprehensive administrative theory, see Henri Fayol, *General and Industrial Management* (London: Pitman Publishing, 1967 [1916]), pp. 24–26 and ch. 5 generally. In regard to medieval theology, see Walter Ullmann, *Medieval Political Thought* (Harmondsworth: Penguin Books, 1975), ch. 4; Ian G. Barbour, *Issues in Science and Religion* (New York: Harper and Row, 1971), pp. 16–23. Descartes was, of course, a key figure in the transition to the early modern period. See *Discourse on Method* (1637) in *The Philosophical Works of Descartes*, 2 vols. (Cambridge: Cambridge University Press, 1975), vol. 1, p. 119, for the famous promise of mastery over nature; pp. 87–88 for suggestions regarding the advantages of a single master. For a relevant discussion of Hobbes, see Douglas Torgerson, "Obsolescent Leviathan: Problems of Order in Administrative Thought," in this volume. Max Weber's account of the rationalization and bureaucratization of the modern world recalls the past while anticipating the future. See Max Weber, *Economy and Society*, 2 vols. (Berkeley: University of California Press, 1978), vol. 1, pp. 217-226; vol. 2, pp. 956–1005, pp. 1381–1469, esp. p. 1402: "An inanimate machine is mind objectified.... Objectified intelligence is also that animated machine, the bureaucratic organization...."

At the top of the mechanized hierarchy, though, one encounters "[t]he 'directing mind,' the 'moving spirit'" which is different from the "mentality of the official" (p. 1403). Weber's ideal-type of bureaucracy thus differs from technocratic administration guided by a systems approach (see n. 4 below). *Cf.* Henry Jacoby, *The Bureaucratization of the World* (Berkeley: University of California Press, 1976), pp. 152ff. Also note the focus on "the mind" in the development of managerial ideologies, esp. the New Thought Movement. See Bendix, *Work and Authority in Industry*, pp. 259ff., 275, 292, 311; also pp. 278, 283, 286, 294, 296, 298ff., 302, 305. With the movement from Weberian bureaucracy to technocracy, the directing mind itself tends to become viewed after the image of the mechanism it directs. The organization first becomes an engineering problem: "The engineer's mind is that of industrialism in its streamlined form." Max Horkheimer, *Eclipse of Reason* (New York: Seabury Press, 1974 [1947]), p. 151. The next step is envisioned in the following: "With recent developments in our understanding of heuristic processes and their simulation by digital computers, the way is open to deal scientifically with ill-structured problems—to make the computer coextensive with the human mind." Herbert A. Simon and Allen Newell, "Heuristic Problem-solving: The Next Advance in Operations Research" (1957), in Herbert A. Simon, *Models of Bounded Rationality*, 2 vols. (Cambridge, MA: The MIT Press, 1983), vol. 1, p. 388. *Cf.* Herbert A. Simon, *The New Science of Management Decision*, rev. ed. (Englewood Cliffs, NJ: Prentice-Hall, rev. ed., 1977).

4 The more traditional "decisionistic" model is distinguished from the increasingly salient "technocratic" model in Jürgen Habermas, "The Scientization of Politics and Public Opinion," in his *Toward a Rational Society* (Boston: Beacon Press, 1971), pp. 63ff. Within this technocratic frame one observes the transition from an earlier focus by technical experts (in scientific management) on achieving efficiency through standardized procedures to a reliance on a more sophisticated systems orientation (in management science). See C. West Churchman, *The Systems Approach*, rev. ed. (New York: Dell Publishing, 1979), chs. 2–3. For an important effort to refine the concept of technocracy, see Wolf V. Heydebrand, "Technocratic Corporatism," in Richard H. Hall and Robert E. Quinn, eds., *Organizational Theory and Public Policy* (Beverly Hills, CA: Sage Publications, 1983). *Cf.* Laurence H. Tribe, "Policy Science: Analysis or Ideology?," *Philosophy and Public Affairs* 2 (1972): 66–110.

5 See William Leiss, *The Domination of Nature* (Boston: Beacon Press, 1974), ch. 2 and pp. 74-76. Faust is of course a key figure in this regard. See also Edward Chase Kirkland, *Dream and Thought in the Business Community, 1860–1900* (Chicago: Quadrangle Books, 1964), pp. 9ff., on an intertwining of spiritualism, myth, religion, and science; and H.V. Nelles, *The Politics of Development: Forests, Mines and Hydro-Electric Power in Ontario, 1849-1941* (Toronto: Macmillan of Canada, 1975), ch. 6, "Hydro as Myth." The phrase "order and progress" was the motto adopted by the early positivist Auguste Comte. See Raymond Aron, *Main Currents of Sociological Thought*, vol. 1 (Garden City, NY: Anchor Books, 1968), ch. 2, "Auguste Comte." On the self-contradiction of the positivist notion of historical progress, see Jürgen Habermas, *Knowledge and Human Interests* (Boston: Beacon Press, 1971), pp. 71ff. *Cf.*, generally, Max Horkheimer and Theodor W. Adorno, *Dialectic of Enlightenment* (New York: Seabury Press, 1972 [1944]).

6 Dwight Waldo, *The Administrative State* (New York: The Ronald Press, 1948).

7 See Poggi, *The Development of the Modern State*.

8 Poggi, *The Development of the Modern State*, chs. 2–4.

9 See Karl Polanyi, *The Great Transformation: The Political and Economic Origins of our Time* (Boston: Beacon Press, 1957), chs. 5–6. Adam Smith was, of course, a key Enlightenment influence in this regard. See Peter Gay, *The Enlightenment: An Interpretation*, vol. 2 (New York: Alfred A. Knopf, 1969); A.L. McFie, *The Individual in Society: Papers on Adam Smith* (London: George Allen and Unwin, 1967), esp. pp. 69, 109ff., 117.

10 Polanyi, *The Great Transformation*, pp. 71–75.

11   Polanyi, *The Great Transformation*, p. 140.
12   Polanyi, *The Great Transformation*, chs. 16 (on land and labor) and 17 (on money).
13   See Poggi, *The Development of the Modern State*, ch. 6. *Cf.* Gerhard Lehmbruch, "Liberal Corporatism and Party Government," in Philippe C. Schmitter and Gerhard Lembruch, eds., *Trends Toward Corporatist Intermediation* (Beverly Hills, CA: Sage Publications, 1979), esp. pp. 148, 154. I am suggesting that the administrative state should be viewed in this manner because doing so draws attention to relationships that one might neglect by taking the conventional boundary between public and private as an ontological given. I do not deny that the conventional boundary remains an important consideration in analyzing concrete relationships; nor would I rule out in principle other conceptualizations that might reveal further neglected relationships. The problem of conceptualizing the state may, indeed, be viewed as involving the same problem, writ large, as that of defining an organizational boundary. See, e.g., Raymond E. Miles *et al.*, "Organization-Environment: Concepts and Issues," *Industrial Relations* 13.3(1974): 244–64; the controversial conception of customers as part of a business organization, seen as a "cooperative system," in Chester I. Barnard, "Concepts of Organization," in his *Organization and Management* (Cambridge, MA: Harvard University Press, 1948); and the proposal for a "figure-ground reversal" in Eric Trist, "A Concept of Organizational Ecology," *Australian Journal of Management* 2.2(1977): 161–75. The identity, hence boundary, of the state—the realm of the "political" as distinct from the "economic"—emerged as a significant issue in the exchange between Miliband and Poulantzas. See esp. Ernesto Laclau, "The Specificity of the Political: The Poulantzas-Miliband Debate," *Economy and Society* 4(1975): 100–01; Nicos Poulantzas, "The Capitalist State: A Reply to Miliband and Laclau," *New Left Review* 95(1976): 81–82.
14   In addition to Weber, see Samuel Haber, *Efficiency and Uplift: Scientific Management in the Progressive Era, 1890–1920* (Chicago: University of Chicago Press, 1964); Samuel P. Hays, *Conservation and the Gospel of Efficiency: The Progressive Conservation Movement, 1890–1920* (New York: Antheneum, 1969); Robert B. Reich, *The Next American Frontier* (Harmondsworth: Penguin Books, 1984), part 2, "The Era of Management, 1920–1970"; John Kenneth Galbraith, *The New Industrial State*, rev. ed. (New York: Mentor Books, 1972); Arthur S. Miller, "Legal Foundations of the Corporate State," and Daniel R. Fusfeld, "The Rise of the Corporate State in America," in Warren J. Samuels, ed., *The Economy as a System of Power*, 2 vols. (New Brunswick, NJ: Transaction Books, 1979), vol. 1.
15   Poggi, *The Development of the Modern State*, pp. 68–85, 104, 112, 124–25.
16   See Jürgen Habermas, *The Structural Transformation of the Public Sphere: An Inquiry into a Category of Bourgeois Society* (Cambridge, MA: MIT Press, 1989 [1962]) and the references cited in n. 1 (above).
17   Georges Lefebvre, "Enlightened Despotism," in Heinz Lubasz, ed., *The Development of the Modern State* (New York: Macmillan, 1964), p. 52.
18   On Bentham in this connection, see Elie Halévy, *The Growth of Philosophic Radicalism* (Boston: Beacon Press, 1955), p. 375. This study of utilitarianism as a form of rationalism is useful in portraying a texture of intellectual relationships stretching back to Hobbes. *Cf.* C.B. Macpherson, *The Life and Times of Liberal Democracy* (Oxford: Oxford University Press, 1977).
19   *Cf.* Harold D. Lasswell, *Propaganda Technique in World War I* (Cambridge, MA: MIT Press, 1971 [1927]), an early attempt to examine propaganda as "a concession to the rationality of the modern world," p. 221.
20   See, generally, John Forester, ed., *Critical Theory and Public Life* (Cambridge, MA: MIT Press, 1985).
21   See Torgerson, *The Promise of Green Politics*, ch. 4.
22   *Cf.* Peter Berger, *The Sacred Canopy: Elements of a Sociological Theory of Religion* (Garden City, NY: Anchor Books, 1969).

23 *Cf.* Herbert A. Simon, "The Changing Theory and Changing Practice of Public
    Administration," in Ithiel de Sola Pool, ed., *Contemporary Political Science* (New
    York: McGraw-Hill, 1967), p. 99; Robert K. Merton, "Bureaucratic Structure and
    Personality," in his *Social Theory and Social Structure*, rev. ed. (New York: The Free
    Press, 1957).
24 See Donald A. Schon, *Displacement of Concepts* (London: Tavistock Publications,
    1963). Also see Ian I. Mitroff, "Systemic Problem-Solving," in Morgan W. McCall, Jr.,
    and Michael M. Lombardo, eds., *Leadership* (Durham, NC: Duke University Press,
    1978); Edward de Bono, *Lateral Thinking: A Textbook of Creativity* (Harmondsworth:
    Penguin Books, 1971); Rollo May, *The Courage to Create* (New York: Bantam Books,
    1976), esp. ch. 5; James G. March, "The Technology of Foolishness," in James G. March
    and Johan P. Olsen, *Ambiguity and Choice in Organizations* (Bergen, Norway: Univer-
    sitetsforlaget, 1976); Jeffrey Pressman and Aaron Wildavsky, *Implementation*, 3rd ed.
    (Berkeley: University of California Press, 1984); David Dery, *Problem Definition in Pol-
    icy Analysis* (Lawrence: University Press of Kansas, 1984).
25 Much work along these lines is conceived in explicitly dialectical terms, influenced in
    particular by C. West Churchman, *The Design of Inquiring Systems: Basic Concepts of
    Systems and Organizations* (New York: Basic Books, 1971). *Cf.* Ian I. Mitroff and Louis
    R. Pondy, "On the Organization of Inquiry: A Comparison of Some Radically Different
    Approaches to Policy Analysis," *Public Administration Review* 43.5(1974): 471–79. See
    also n. 47 below. Aspects of this orientation were anticipated in the early work of Mary
    Parker Follett—e.g., "Constructive Conflict" (1925) in *Dynamic Administration: The
    Collected Papers of Mary Parker Follett*, 2nd ed. (New York: Hippocrene Books, 1977),
    which manifests a dialectical play of concepts. There has also been a complementary
    move to invoke a multiplicity of metaphors for understanding organizations and diagnos-
    ing their problems. See, e.g., Gareth Morgan, *Images of Organization* (Beverly Hills,
    CA: Sage Publications, 1986).
26 See Douglas Torgerson, "Contextual Orientation in Policy Analysis: The Contribution of
    Harold D. Lasswell," *Policy Sciences* 18(1985): 241–61. For Lasswell, all actors are
    guided by an image of "self-in-context" that is either implicit or explicit and that con-
    tains a temporal dimension through a construct of development, an understanding of the
    past and an anticipation of the future. The image of self-in-context may be oriented by a
    developmental construct that is taken for granted or may be informed by multiple con-
    structs that vary greatly in their plausibility and desirability. The likelihood of a future
    prospect may be affected by its formulation in explicit terms since such a formulation
    provides a focus of attention for action.
27 For further characterization of the dispute, see Gideon Rosenbluth, "Economists and the
    Growth Controversy," *Canadian Public Policy* 11.2(1976): 225–39. Of course, this con-
    troversy had a precursor during the early development of economics as certain doubts
    were raised about progress. Here the miserable conditions of early capitalist industrial-
    ization were viewed against the dismal idea of a natural law in which famine would
    continually return as food production failed to keep ahead of population growth. Yet this
    was not to deny progress altogether, for hunger was a "divine sanction": "Malthus ...
    had his own version of the gospel of progress.... Without the stimulus and pressure of
    surplus numbers of people, progress might end and technology stagnate." Donald
    Worster, *Nature's Economy: The Roots of Ecology* (Garden City, NY: Anchor Books,
    1979), p. 151. What this suggests is that the vision of progress was not always a happy
    one; certainly this was the case even with Bentham, the apostle of happiness as "utility."
    The early dispute divided pessimistic and optimistic doctrines of progress; progress
    itself was not questioned. See Halévy, *Growth of Philosophic Radicalism*, pp. 268–76;
    cf. pp. 492–93.
28 See, e.g., Barry Commoner, *The Closing Circle: Man, Nature, and Technology* (New
    York: Alfred A. Knopf, 1971).

29 See Donella H. Meadows *et al.*, *The Limits to Growth* (New York: Universe Books, 1972); also see H.S.D. Cole *et al.*, *Thinking About the Future: A Critique of the "Limits to Growth"* (London: Chatto and Windus Ltd. for the University of Sussex Press, 1973).

30 The formal matrix structure is one device that has been adopted by administrative organizations to balance competing demands from a complex environment. This device violates the principle of unity of command and often elicits resistance; nonetheless, explicit commitment to this traditional principle often coexists with tacit adaptations in the informal structure. See Stanley M. Davis, "Two Models of Organization: Unity of Command versus Balance of Power," *Sloan Management Review* 16(1974): 29–40; P.G. Herbst, *Alternatives to Hierarchies* (Leiden: Martinus Nijhoff, 1976), ch. 3; Jeffrey Pfeffer, *Power in Organizations* (Boston: Pitman Publishing, 1981), pp. 356–63.

31 See Geoffrey Wandesforde-Smith, "The Bureaucratic Response to Environmental Politics," in Albert E. Dutton and Daniel H. Henning, eds., *Environmental Policy* (New York: Praeger Publishers, 1973). *Cf.* Lynton K. Caldwell, *Man and His Environment: Policy and Administration* (New York: Harper and Row, 1975). Some central environmental agency was often to perform a coordinating role, but this task was made difficult by a marginal position in the administrative apparatus and a restricted definition of what constituted "environmental" problems. See, e.g., O.P. Dwivedi, "The Canadian Government Response to Environmental Concern," in O.P. Dwivedi, ed., *Protecting the Environment* (Vancouver: Copp Clark Publishing, 1974), esp. p. 176; Michael J. Whittington, "Environmental Policy," in G. Bruce Doern and V. Seymour Wilson, eds., *Issues in Canadian Public Policy* (Toronto: Macmillan of Canada, 1974), esp. p. 208.

32 Galbraith, *The New Industrial State*, p. 37. *Cf.* Thomas B. Nolan, "The Inexhaustible Resource of Technology," in Henry Jarrett, ed., *Perspectives on Conservation* (Baltimore: The Johns Hopkins Press for Resources for the Future Inc., 1961), esp. p. 66.

33 *Cf.* David Ehrenfeld, *The Arrogance of Humanism* (New York: Oxford University Press, 1978).

34 *Cf.* Theodore Roslak, *Where the Wasteland Ends: Politics and Transcendence in Postindustrial Society* (Garden City, NY: Anchor Books, 1973).

35 For an overview, see Douglas Torgerson, "Environmentalism," in Shepard Krech III, John McNeill, and Carolyn Merchant, eds., *Encyclopedia of World Environmental History*, vol. I (New York: Routledge, 2003), pp. 121–28. Key contributions include Murray Bookchin, "Ecology and Revolutionary Thought" (1965) and "Toward a Liberatory Technology" (1965) in his *Post-Scarcity Anarchism* (San Francisco: Ramparts Press, 1971); E.F. Schumacher, *Small Is Beautiful: A Study of Economics as if People Mattered* (London: Abacus, 1974); David Dickson, *Alternative Technology and the Politics of Technical Change* (Glasgow: Fontana, 1974); Victor Ferkiss, *The Future of Technological Civilization* (New York: George Braziller, 1974); Herman E. Daly, ed., *Toward a Steady State Economy* (San Francisco: W.H. Freeman, 1973); Amory B. Lovins, *Soft Energy Paths* (Cambridge, MA: Ballinger Publishing, 1977). *Cf.* Douglas Torgerson, "Rethinking Politics for a Green Economy: A Political Approach to Radical Reform," *Social Policy and Administration* 36:5(2001): 472–89.

36 See the discussion of "problem displacement" in John S. Dryzek, *Rational Ecology: Environment and Political Economy* (London: Basil Blackwell, 1987), pp. 16ff.

37 See Douglas Torgerson, *Industrialization and Assessment: Social Impact Assessment as a Social Phenomenon* (Toronto: York University, 1980).

38 See n. 31 above.

39 See, e.g., William Ophuls, "Leviathan or Oblivion?," in Daly, ed., *Toward a Steady-State Economy*; William Ophuls, *Ecology and the Politics of Scarcity* (San Francisco: W.H. Freeman, 1977). The idea of an "environmental dictator" was discussed in some environmental groups in the 1970s.

40 See John S. Dryzek, "Complexity and Rationality in Public Life," *Political Studies* 35(1987): 432f. Also see Dryzek, *Rational Ecology*, chs. 7, 9.

41 This tension is evident in Ophuls. *Cf.* Charles Taylor, "The Politics of the Steady State," in Abraham Rotstein, ed., *Beyond Industrial Growth* (Toronto: University of Toronto Press, 1976).

42 See Dryzek, *Rational Ecology*, chs. 3–5; "Complexity and Rationality," pp. 424–42. Also see C.A. Hooker and R. Van Hulst, "The Meaning of Environmental Problems for Public Political Institutions," in William Leiss, ed., *Ecology versus Politics in Canada* (Toronto: University of Toronto Press, 1979); Gareth Morgan, "Cybernetics and Organization Theory: Epistemology or Technique?" *Human Relations* 35.7(1982): 521–38.

43 See Eric Trist, "A Concept of Organizational Ecology," in contrast with Simon's focus on "bounded rationality"—e.g., Herbert A. Simon, *Administrative Behavior: A Study of Decision-Making Processes in Administrative Organization*, 3rd ed. (New York: The Free Press, 1976), esp. pp. xxix-xxx, 82; Herbert A. Simon, "The Theory of Problem-Solving" (1972) in his *Models of Discovery* (Dordrecht, Holland: D. Reidel Publishing, 1977).

44 Mary Parker Follett, "The Illusion of Final Authority" (1926) in *Dynamic Administration*.

45 See n. 24 above.

46 *Cf.* Herbert A. Simon and DeWitt C. Dearborne, "Selective Perception," in Simon, *Administrative Behavior*.

47 See, e.g., Richard O. Mason and Ian I. Mitroff, *Challenging Strategic Planning Assumptions* (New York: John Wiley and Sons, 1981); Ian I. Mitroff and Richard O. Mason, *Creating a Dialectical Social Science* (Dordrecht, Holland: D. Reidel Publishing, 1981); Pfeffer, *Power in Organizations*, ch. 9.

48 The contrast between "interaction" and "cogitation" is made in Aaron Wildavsky, *Speaking Truth to Power: The Art and Craft of Policy Analysis* (Boston: Little, Brown, and Company, 1979). For a critique that discriminates between qualitatively different forms of interaction, see John Forester, "The Policy Analysis-Critical Theory Affair: Wildavsky and Habermas as Bedfellows?," in Forester, ed., *Critical Theory and Public Life*, esp. pp. 266ff.

49 Discursive openings would be central to what I have called a "third face" of policy analysis. See Douglas Torgerson, "Between Knowledge and Politics: Three Faces of Policy Analysis," *Policy Sciences* 19(1986): 33–59. Of a large literature, also see John S. Dryzek, "Discursive Designs: Critical Theory and Political Institutions," *American Journal of Political Science* 31(1987): 656–79; Graham Smith, *Deliberative Democracy and the Environment* (London: Routledge, 2003), ch. 4.

50 See, e.g., Amory B. Lovins, "Cost-Risk-Benefit Assessments in Energy Policy," *George Washington Law Review* 45(1977): 911–43. See also Douglas Torgerson, "Environmental Politics and Policy Professionalism: Agenda-Setting, Problem-Definition, and Epistemology," in this volume.

51 See, e.g., Charles E. Lindblom, *The Intelligence of Democracy: Decision Making through Mutual Adjustment* (New York: The Free Press, 1965). The fundamentally settled world presupposed and reflected in that book stands in contrast to the world "headed for catastrophe" invoked in the opening of Charles E. Lindblom, *Politics and Markets* (New York: Basic Books, 1977), p. 3. His examination of "politico-economic mechanisms" is thus explicitly aimed at finding means of averting an environmental catastrophe. For a further development along these lines, see Dryzek, *Rational Ecology*.

52 The discussion here of the administrative sphere and the public sphere is partly influenced by the treatment of "lifeworld" and "system" in Habermas. See, for a concise discussion, Stephen K. White, *The Recent Work of Jürgen Habermas* (Cambridge: Cambridge University Press, 1988), ch. 5; for a brief, pertinent critique, see pp. 140ff. My view is that elements of the lifeworld "penetrate" the system more fundamentally than Habermas allows—hence the term administrative "sphere" in this article. Moreover, Habermas locates the "administrative system," as he calls it, too readily in the state.

See Jürgen Habermas, *The Theory of Communicative Action*, 2 vols. (Boston: Beacon Press, 1984, 1988), esp. vol. 2, pp. 311, 343f. *Cf.* Torgerson, "Between Knowledge and Politics," p. 51.

53 See Robert H. Socolow, "Failures of Discourse: Obstacles to the Integration of Environmental Values into Natural Resource Policy," in Laurence H. Tribe *et al.*, eds., *When Values Conflict: Essays on Environmental Analysis, Discourse, and Decision* (Cambridge, MA: Ballinger Publishing, 1976); Dryzek, "Complexity and Rationality," p. 433.

54 See Wildavsky, *Speaking Truth to Power*.

55 See Claus Offe, "Political Authority and Class Structures: An Analysis of Late Capitalist Societies," *International Journal of Sociology* 2.1(1972): 73–108; Habermas, *Legitimation Crisis*, pp. 59–68, 136–38. See also Robert R. Alford, "Paradigms of Relations Between State and Society," in Leon N. Lindberg *et al.*, eds., *Stress and Contradiction in Modern Capitalism: Public Policy and the Theory of the State* (Lexington, MA: Lexington Books, 1975). The phrase "mobilization of bias" was presented in E.E. Schattschneider, *The Semisovereign People* (Hinsdale, IL: The Dryden Press, 1975 [1960]) and developed in Peter Bachrach and Morton S. Baratz, *Power and Poverty* (New York: Oxford University Press, 1970), pp. 8, 43, 58. For a discussion of environmental policy framed by the concept of "mobilization of bias," see T.F. Schrecker, *Political Economy of Environmental Hazards* (Ottawa: Law Reform Commission of Canada, 1984). The bias renders some issues "manifest," others "latent," to follow a point developed in William Leiss, "The Political Aspects of Environmental Issues," in Leiss, ed., *Ecology versus Politics in Canada*, pp. 261ff.

56 Douglas Hartle, *The Expenditure Budget Process in the Government of Canada* (Toronto: Canadian Tax Foundation, 1978), p. 122 (original emphasis).

57 See Socolow, "Failures of Discourse," pp. 4–5, 20–22.

58 *Cf.* Hannah Arendt, *The Human Condition* (Chicago: University of Chicago Press, 1958).

59 See John S. Dryzek *et al.*, *Green States and Social Movements: Environmental Politics in the United States, United Kingdom, Germany and Norway* (Oxford: Oxford University Press, 2003) and my review, *International History Review* 26:4 (2004): 924–26.

60 See Torgerson, "Between Knowledge and Politics," pp. 46ff.

61 *Cf.* Ray Kemp, "Planning, Public Hearings, and the Politics of Discourse" in Forester, ed., *Critical Theory and Public Life*.

62 On some problems of consensus formation and maintenance, see Lehmbruch, "Liberal Corporatism," pp. 153–54, 170–72, 180–81.

PART III

The Politics of
Environmental Administration

Environmental administration exists not in the calm, ordered world of the management textbook, but in a world of rough edges. Here environmental problems are defined at the intersection of diverse interests, of forces rife with complexity and variation. This world resists smooth conceptualization and ready comprehension, however much we orient ourselves through inquiry and practice. No general theory or set of specific cases provides an exhaustive and reliable map. Along the corridors of public administration, officials work amid a tangled web of legality, typically forced to respond to well-funded private initiatives while constrained, among other things, by the fingers which hold the public purse-strings. The difficulty is exacerbated because environmental problems often elude the available tools of analysis and management. Turning to concrete issues in the politics of environmental administration, the chapters in Part III focus on matters such as complexity, power, knowledge, class, professionalism, depoliticization, participation, deliberation, and globalization. The chapters employ case material from Europe and Australia as well as the United States and Canada in the context of a range of specific environmental problems. Any effort to revise the agenda of inquiry and practice must keep in view the complexities, dilemmas, and uncertainties of world where politics and administration meet.

8

Class, Place, and Citizenship: The Changing Dynamics of Environmental Protection

Ted Schrecker

Environmental Policy: The Great Retreat

In the early 1990s, environmental protection seemed well established as a political concern. In 1989, *Time* magazine had departed from its usual focus on individual newsmakers by featuring endangered Earth as the Planet of the Year (how many competitors were there?).[1] In Canada, a Conservative environment minister had given a speech in which he described pollution as "the most serious white-collar crime in Canada."[2] The minister's views may not have been shared by his Cabinet colleagues (or even his constituents, since he lost his seat in the next election), but they were at least expressible within the political mainstream. In the United States, the Reagan-era attack on social regulation had coexisted with an expansion of federal criminal enforcement of environmental statutes.[3] In the international arena, the report of the World Commission on Environment and Development (the Brundtland commission)[4] had drawn attention to the interconnectedness of environmental protection and economic activity, calling for a far-reaching transition to sustainable development in which the basic needs of the world's poor would be given priority and the industrialized world would assume special obligations.

The relevance of environmental concerns for political discourse and public administration has changed—and, on the whole, declined dramatically—in the intervening years. Most Canadian governments have systematically retreated from the challenges of environmental protection and sustainable development. In 1990, the Conservative government of Brian Mulroney unveiled a multi-year, multi-departmental Green Plan that was described by two academic observers as "commit[ting] substantial new funds to environmental programs, but [doing] remarkably little to directly clean up or protect the environment."[5] Such measures are perhaps best explained in terms of the amenability of environmental issues to symbolic government responses that may or may not have clearly measurable effects. Shortly after the 1993 election, the Plan was cancelled by the newly elected Liberals with more than 70 per cent of its overall $3-billion budget unspent.[6] For the remainder of the decade, the Liberals were preoccupied with deficit reduction through program spending cuts, including substantial reductions to the budget of Environment Canada, and, in keeping with the ascendant logic of economic integration, the promotion of exports almost at any cost.[7] Especially after the nearly disastrous Quebec referendum of 1995, environmental policy at the national level was also characterized by "the incremental devolution of responsibility over environmental policy to the provinces," creating additional opportunities for subordinating environmental priorities to the interests of regionally important industries.[8] Resistance to using the crucial levers of tax policy to support environmental objectives, even on minor and long-standing issues like the fact that employer-provided public-transit passes are a taxable benefit while employer-provided parking is not,[9] has been a constant.

New federal initiatives, rather like the Green Plan, have reflected a conception of environmental policy in which government functions primarily as an information provider. For example, a national inventory of point-source industrial emissions of a specified list of pollutants (the National Pollutant Release Inventory) is now compiled annually under the authority of the *Canadian Environmental Protection Act.* [10] In 1995, legislative amendments established the office of the Commissioner for the Environment and Sustainable Development within the Office of the Auditor-General, and required that federal departments prepare sustainable-development strategies on a three-year cycle.[11] The latter are of limited practical significance because they cannot normally embody new budgetary or legislative commitments. The Commissioner's office, however, has produced strong criticism of federal government performance—including the retreat from federal jurisdiction—in such areas as protecting water quality in the Great Lakes Basin[12] and managing toxic substances.[13] As the Commissioner's office pointed out in 2001, these two areas of performance are in fact closely related: "Over 23,000 chemicals are currently used in Canada. Of these, 245 are included on the 1999 National Pollutant Release Inventory, and 58 of those are released directly into the waters of Quebec and Ontario. The presence of most of these pollutants is not monitored by Environment Canada in any of the Great Lakes or the St. Lawrence River."[14] Federal environmental policy makers' use of scientific evidence remained idiosyncratic, and apparently subordinated to calculations of political advantage and the economic policy considerations described in the next section of the chapter.[15]

At the provincial level, perhaps the clearest policy shifts occurred in Ontario and British Columbia. Mike Harris's Ontario Conservatives came to power in 1995 on a "Common Sense Revolution" platform consisting of personal and corporate income-tax cuts—the former being more salient in terms of electoral appeal—and reductions in the role and responsibilities of government. Many ministries suffered substantial budget cuts, but Environment was among the worst hit, suffering a reduction of 39 per cent in its operating budget, with corresponding reductions in staff, and 95 per cent in its capital budget between 1994/95 and 2000/01.[16] The rollback of environmental protections involved far more than (de)regulating emission sources and scaling back enforcement activity, which has led to predictable increases in violations.[17] It included major reductions in the scope of environmental impact assessment requirements and a variety of policy measures that had the effect of encouraging automobile use and creating incentives for suburban sprawl.[18] Many environmentally important areas of responsibility, such as capital expenditure on water and sewage treatment plants and operating support for public transportation, were devolved to municipalities. The effect, if not the intent, was a fiscal squeeze for municipalities that created strong incentives to expand local tax bases through development-friendly policies, without any corresponding incentive to consider environmental impacts. In a few cases, such as intensive farming operations, new legislation actively discouraged municipalities from considering those impacts.[19]

British Columbia has a long-standing history of conflicts between conservationists and the resource industries that dominate the economy of the province outside the lower mainland.[20] In 2001, the pro-business Liberals of Gordon Campbell decisively defeated a New Democratic government that had already been accused by environmental organizations of a substantial retreat from the environmental policies adopted during its previous mandate.[21] In its first year, the new government enacted cuts to the budgets of environmental ministries comparable in size to those enacted in Ontario, and announced the weakening of standards and of opportunities for public scrutiny of environmental decision making.[22] Between 2002 and 2004, the Liberals substantially reduced environmental and resource management requirements for the forest industry,[23] which continues to be under severe strain as a consequence of unilateral US tariffs on softwood lumber as well as a long history of over-harvesting.[24]

How can we account for these trends? In what follows, I first explore recent changes in the economic context for environmental policy. I then argue that grudging acquiescence to the new realities of globalization cannot explain the retreat from environmental protection. Rather, it is best understood as part of a much larger and internally coherent discursive shift toward privatization, which must in turn be connected with the changing and polarizing class structure of North American society. This analysis suggests that political support for environmental protection of most kinds will probably continue to decline.

THE ECONOMIC CONTEXT

Governments in all market economies rely heavily on private investment to sustain the economic activity that provides income, employment, and tax revenues.

The effect on the range of policy choices that are considered feasible is summarized by Charles Lindblom's statement that "even the unspoken possibility of adversity for business operates as an all-pervasive constraint on governmental authority."[25] Transnational economic integration ("globalization") has drastically enhanced the leverage of investors with respect to national and subnational policy, by placing jurisdictions around the world into increasingly intense competition not only for product markets, but also for capital investment.[26] A simple but dramatic illustration of the extent of such integration is provided by a study published in 1993 in which two consulting firms were asked to select the world's ten most promising regions for investment in a new, "greenfield" manufacturing facility based on "overall cost competitiveness ... because, as global competition continues to increase, this is the single most important yardstick for the strategic viability of a region."[27] Perhaps as a result of the Thatcher government's relentless efforts to make Britain more business-friendly,[28] the north of England scored highest in each firm's ranking, as did a few other European regions, but 11 out of 20 candidates (with some overlap between the lists) were low-wage regions in China, Latin America, south Asia, and South Africa. Only one North American location, North Carolina, was featured on either list.[29] A decade later, an article in *The Economist* succinctly described contemporary manufacturing in terms of "global supply-chains connecting cheap workers on one side of the world with rich consumers on the other."[30]

For purposes of Canadian public policy, economic integration is first of all a continental phenomenon. The economic logic of restructuring the Canadian economy—or perhaps more accurately, Canada's various regional economies—on a north–south axis was already strong. Continental integration was entrenched and accelerated by the Canada–US Free Trade Agreement (FTA) and the subsequent North American Free Trade Agreement (NAFTA). The effects of continental integration are perhaps most readily observed in Ontario, with an economy heavily reliant on an automotive industry characterized by complex cross-border networks of supplier relationships. Ontario now sends exports equivalent to 32 per cent of the provincial GDP to just four Great Lakes states: Michigan, New York, Ohio, and Illinois.[31] Sustaining this performance requires that Ontario compete not only with those jurisdictions but also with Mexico and the sunbelt states of the US southeast as a location for new investment. This point was driven home in January 2003, when Daimler-Chrysler Corporation was reported to be negotiating for government assistance worth more than $300 million as the price of locating a new assembly plant in Ontario rather than in Mexico or the United States.[32] As an indication of the possible environmental implications, a researcher with Michigan's Center for Automotive Research has been quoted as saying that environmental laws rank first on the list of factors automakers consider in choosing a site for a new plant.[33] If this is true, the effect will be to seriously inhibit policy initiatives perceived by the industry to impose substantial costs relative to those associated with environmental regulation in competing jurisdictions.

Canada's reliance on export-oriented resource industries, a legacy of its historical role as a supplier of resources to a succession of imperial powers, presents distinctive problems for environmental policy. Resource industries such as mining, forest products, and agriculture are the primary source of economic activity in much of Canada outside the Quebec–Windsor corridor, and they account for a substantial proportion of Canada's exports: "Natural resources, including agricultural products, make up 79 percent of Atlantic Canada's merchandise exports, 80 percent of Alberta's, 74 percent of Saskatchewan's, and 77 percent of B.C.'s,"[34] and the one-industry town dependent on a resource industry remains a fundamental feature of the Canadian social and political landscape. As an indication of the increasing vulnerability of resource industries to global competition, Noranda, Inc., announced in January 2003 that it would close a Quebec plant that reclaims magnesium from asbestos tailings just two years after it opened, because of unexpectedly strong competition from Chinese magnesium exports.[35] Globalization, then, intensifies existing pressures to maintain the profitability of resource industries. Few governments will embark on policies that would have the effect of shutting down a town or substantially reducing the throughput of an industry, even when that is a prerequisite for managing the resource on a sustainable basis.[36] The history of (mis)management of the North Atlantic cod fishery demonstrates that it is politically preferable to continue exploitation until "a moratorium [is] decided on by the fish,"[37] or whatever other resource is at issue. Neither corporate managers nor the large-scale institutional investors that dominate contemporary equity markets[38] are likely to have allegiances to any specific regional economy or ecosystem. From their perspective, as from that of any rational investor considering opportunities for portfolio diversification, liquidating the resource and moving on is often the optimal strategy.

The dismantling of environmental protections that began shortly after George W. Bush assumed the presidency in 2001[39] may have significant implications for Canadian environmental policy if, as seems likely, deregulation in the United States achieves the intended result of lowering the cost of doing business or extracting resources. In 2002, a number of firms in the oil and gas industry argued that Canadian ratification of the Kyoto protocol on climate change would mean a shift in new oil and gas investment to the United States, which had repudiated the protocol.[40] This was not a unified stance on the part of the industry; however, it probably contributed to the federal position that "no region or jurisdiction of the country should be asked to bear an unreasonable burden in the realization of our climate change goals,"[41] whatever that means. The cases of the automotive and oil and gas industries indicate that the "discipline of the market" will be applied to environmental regulation, as to various other determinants of investment such as labour costs, with increasing frequency and effectiveness as continental economic integration proceeds.[42] As another illustration, in 1994 an Ontario Ministry of the Environment official explained the province's choice of permissible effluent levels for the chemical industry by saying, "We could say zero discharge but they would all close their plants and move to Mexico."[43]

The reference to Mexico suggests how the asymmetry of the economic relationship among Canada, the United States, and Mexico has been "constitutionalized" by trade agreements[44] because of the extremely high costs that Canada would face in the event of noncompliance or withdrawal. An especially disturbing aspect of NAFTA is the mechanism for resolving disputes between foreign investors and national governments contained in NAFTA's Chapter 11. This mechanism allows foreign (but not domestic) investors to seek compensation before dispute-resolution tribunals, which are closed to the public, for losses associated with a broad (and so far indeterminate) range of government policies that reduce profitability or eliminate business opportunities.[45] This having been said, it is difficult to reliably assess the impact of either economic integration as a whole or specific trade-agreement provisions like Chapter 11 on regulatory outcomes. The bargaining in question normally takes place well out of the public eye. Environmental requirements, which in any event tend to be discretionary and elastic in the Canadian context, are unlikely to function as clearly identifiable deal-breakers, since they are just one cost among many to be considered in making investment decisions. Efforts to assess the impact of trade agreements on environmental policy with reference only to overt government-industry conflicts or to cases that actually proceed to one or another stage of the dispute-settlement process[46] miss this crucial point, and for this reason are of limited relevance to the comprehensive assessment of public policy. In addition, the threat to disinvest, locate new investment elsewhere or take action under Chapter 11 need not be explicit to be effective. It can, and often does, operate instead by way of the mechanism of anticipated reaction.[47]

PRIVATIZATION AND PUBLIC GOODS

Although economic integration creates important constraints on Canadian environmental policy, those constraints do not adequately explain current trends. Far from reluctantly rolling back environmental protections, various Canadian governments have actively embraced an internally consistent reorientation of public policy of which the retreat from environmental protection and sustainability is just one small part. Former prime minister Brian Mulroney confirmed in 2001 that the two continental trade agreements were part of a connected set of policies that also included "the GST [Goods and Services Tax], deregulation, privatization, and a concerted effort to reduce deficits, inflation and interest rates."[48] Post-1995, the federal Liberals continued the Mulroney government's commitment to market-oriented social policy[49] by cutting billions of dollars in transfers to the provinces for health and education and implementing reductions in unemployment insurance eligibility and benefits that generated a $40-billion surplus of revenues over expenditures by the end of 2001/2002.[50] One of the first actions of the Harris government in Ontario was to cut provincial income support rates by 21 per cent and to institute work requirements without any consideration of the potential impact on children and families.[51] Meanwhile, personal income-tax

cuts whose primary beneficiaries were the richest Ontarians cost the public treasury a cumulative $47.6 billion in foregone revenue between 1995 and 2003,
according to the Canadian Centre for Policy Alternatives.[52] In British Columbia,
the Campbell government announced comparable income-tax cuts and welfare
eligibility changes immediately after assuming office.[53]

Legal scholars Brenda Cossman and Judy Fudge, although they do not specifically address environmental issues, describe the conceptual connection among
these various policies in terms of privatization. In this context, the concept must
be understood to include not only the selling-off of government assets like
Crown corporations, but also "a new division of responsibility among the state,
the family and the market for individual and social welfare."[54] This new division
of responsibility proceeds by way of "a range of related strategies that aim to
institutionalize a shift in power relations. These strategies typically invoke a
number of normative claims about the appropriate role of government in the lives
of its citizens,"[55] the most fundamental of which is "the primacy of the market
as the 'natural' and privileged sphere for the delivery of goods and services."[56]
Key among these strategies are reprivatization, "the processes whereby once
public goods and services are being reconstituted as private"; commodification,
in which "once public goods and services are being reconstituted as market
goods and services"; and individualization, in which "a broad range of social
issues," such as health and (un)employment, "is being reconstituted, both with
respect to causes and solutions, in highly individualized terms.... Social and
structural analyses are displaced in favour of individual solutions to individual
problems valorizing individual choice and markets."[57]

In economic theory, the term "public good" has a specific meaning: a "good"
(which can include a service or amenity) that is non-rivalrous (one person's use
does not impair or limit another's) and non-excludable (no one can feasibly be
excluded from its use). The services provided by traffic lights and lighthouses are
standard textbook examples. Since no one could charge individual users for the
services of a traffic light or a lighthouse, relying on markets would mean such
services were drastically undersupplied. On a national scale, defence is the
example most often cited of a pure public good. Historically, environmental
activists have often sought, and argued for, the provision of environmental quality or environmental protection as a public good. Many ecosystem services, such
as the sequestration of atmospheric carbon by forests, can only be provided as
public goods. However, many other environmental benefits *need not* be provided
as public goods. They are best characterized as impure or ambiguous public
goods, which can be supplied by way of various combinations of public provision and private purchase: "Whether—and to what extent—a good is public or
private is often not a given but a matter of policy choice."[58]

Philosopher Nancy Holmstrom therefore reproduces a common error by identifying environmental quality as a public good with respect to which "economics
makes little difference. If the air is polluted, the rich can try to keep moving to
where it is clean, or get the best gas masks, but these are obviously very poor

second bests."[59] Gas masks aside, the rich routinely purchase environmental quality by way of choices about such matters as where they live and how they travel—choices that do, of course, exclude others without the price of admission. Thus, "amenity-driven growth" was part of the vision of the future articulated in a proposal for a protected wildland corridor from Yellowstone to the Yukon (Y2Y): "Substantial financial success in the late 1980s and early 1990s, the boom in the stock market and the rise of current communications technologies have freed people from the monetary and physical constraints experienced by earlier generations, leaving them free to seek the 'mountain amenities' of a healthy environment and easy access to recreation, spectacular scenery and wildlife."[60]

Some kinds and levels of environmental damage are especially difficult to escape. These include air pollution in greater Los Angeles in the 1960s and in many megacities in developing countries today; the effects of ozone depletion; and the genuinely global dispersion of some organic chemical pollutants such as DDT. More recently, attention has been directed to the "endocrine disruption" effects of such chemicals, which have been observed in wildlife; effects on human health are largely unknown, but the possibilities are disturbing.[61] However, these exceptions simply underscore the pervasiveness of the rule, not only in the industrialized world but elsewhere. Especially in the global frame of reference, far more common is exposure to environmental hazards that are quite unequivocally related to poverty.[62]

Amenity-driven growth represents the private purchase of environmental quality, rather than its provision as a public good, just as the gated communities and privately guarded urban enclaves[63] that are becoming a familiar feature of North American metropolitan life represent the private purchase of security against crime. This comparison serves to clarify Kaul's point about the significance of policy choices. Crime protection can instead be provided as a public good, by way of social policies and institutions and policies that avoid the destruction of social cohesion and the creation of "socially toxic environments."[64] However, it seems clear that politically decisive pluralities in North America generally do not favor this option. As the environmental justice movement in the United States has been very effective in pointing out, recently with considerable support from academic health researchers, exposure to many kinds of environmental hazards is concentrated among those people who have fewest economic options.[65] Because studies often fail to take into account multiple exposures to environmental hazards and the cumulative effects of these exposures and stressors unrelated to "environment" as conventionally defined, they almost certainly underestimate the importance of class differences in exposure to destructive social or contextual influences on health.[66] Recent research on housing quality and health underscores this point.[67] The relations between environmental (in)justice and the logic of privatization emerged with special clarity from a 1997 review of research on the siting of polluting industrial facilities in poor and minority US neighborhoods. The authors commented that "if research revealed that current disparities in the siting burdens borne by the poor and minorities resulted from market forces," in other words if communities with the poorest environmental quality end up inhabited mainly by those who cannot afford to move away, "many would argue that government interference in the market would be inefficient or otherwise inappropriate."[68] Holmstrom's limited attention to this point makes the gas-mask trope pernicious rather than merely trivial.

Place, Class, and Environment

Place, then, must play an important role in contemporary analyses of the dynamics of environmental policy and the possibilities for change. In the global frame of reference, the editor of *New Perspectives Quarterly* wrote a decade ago that "Already people merely surviving in places like Bangladesh and across vast stretches of Africa are superfluous from the standpoint of the market. By and large, we don't need what they have; they can't buy what we sell."[69] Manuel Castells is perhaps best known for his descriptions of the largely intangible web of electronic linkages that connect elements of the global economy, and to some extent even define that economy as a "network society."[70] At the same time, Castells is acutely aware of the importance of place and of how power and powerlessness within the global economy manifest themselves on a variety of smaller scales: "Inside each country, the networking architecture reproduces itself into regional and local centres, so that the whole system becomes interconnected at the global level." In the process, geographical districts whose residents are not part of the "process that connects advanced services, producer centres, and markets in a global network" run the risk of becoming "irrelevant or even dysfunctional: for example, Mexico City's *colonias populares* (originally squatter settlements) that account for about two thirds of the megapolitan population, without playing any distinctive role in the functioning of Mexico City as an international business centre."[71]

Irrelevance or dysfunctionality within the global economy is a characteristic not only of districts, but also of the people who inhabit them. Thus, in any number of US cities, the decline and "flexibilization" of manufacturing employment as a result of the interaction of trade liberalization and technological change has left much of the working class unemployed or else reliant on low-wage, insecure jobs as security guards, temporary agency employees, or greeters at Wal-Mart.[72] The proliferation of affluent suburbs and downtown business enclaves and entertainment destinations, coexisting with the stereotypical blighted or abandoned neighborhoods of the "inner city"[73] where the destruction of thousands of units of once-viable housing is viewed as representing a precondition for "renewal,"[74] is just the most clearly visible manifestation of a statistical pattern of increasing spatial segregation along economic lines.[75] According to the logic of privatization, such patterns are simply a consequence of "empowering families to vote with their feet"—and, of course, their wallets—when choosing where to live.[76] (The implications of this logic for environmental justice have already been noted.) Similar patterns of spatial segregation, in particular the concentration of poverty, are beginning to emerge in Canadian metropolitan centers.[77] Although so far the statistical patterns are not as dramatic, we are becoming familiar with the ways in which class separation can be enforced by physical barriers: gated communities, underground shopping concourses with private security guards,[78] and the exclusionary effects of the unavailability of public transportation.[79]

Place and space thus give material form to class inequalities. They are the medium through which environmental amenities are enjoyed and environmental hazards experienced, and they instantiate the contours of power and powerlessness within the global economy. Two scholars who have conducted extensive ethnographic research on the relations among health, race, and place in New York City describe those contours in the following terms:

> No longer are civilizations acting independently. In the modern world, the garbage disposal decisions of one group can radically alter the health of another group, particularly if their community becomes the dumping ground. These decisions, we would posit, are a fundamentally spatial rather than racial process, in which goods are concentrated at the sites that are powerful and wastes are discarded at sites that are weak.
>
> Such efforts to concentrate goods and discard wastes may be thought of as a process of "stripping and dumping," which has transformed the world from one in which many independent communities were each able to create health, into a world dominated by an intercommunity battle for the fundamental goods that make health possible.[80]

Consider, in the Canadian context, how the head of the advertising agency that ran the Ontario Conservatives' 1995 election campaign described a key element of its appeal:

> [T]he suburbanite became much more the mean kind of person, you know, like "look, I'm in the car for an hour and a half, two hours a day, I pay high taxes, I live a stressful life, I want what gets done to benefit me and my family." That kind of attitude. So some of the traditional value systems of universality and "let's take care of the poor first" seemed to move down the hierarchy of priorities, and that group wanted to seize control of their own lives, that was their objective. So issues like tax relief became big. They really weren't the issues of urban Canadians but of suburban Canadians.[81]

If this quotation captures a widespread and deeply rooted political dynamic, and I am convinced that it does, then it goes a long way toward explaining why governments that have most enthusiastically embraced privatization (as the term is used here) have, with the exception of the BC Liberals, each received substantial pluralities of the popular vote in at least two successive elections.[82] At the time of writing, the BC Liberals are in their first term but won almost three out of every five votes cast in 2001. In October 2003, the Ontario Liberals—a party with little in common apart from the name with their BC counterparts—decisively defeated the incumbent Conservatives, winning 46 per cent of the popular vote and 72 of the 103 seats in the provincial legislature. However, because environmental issues were almost invisible during the campaign and because the Conservatives held on to more than 34 per cent of the popular vote, the results do not necessarily indicate a substantial shift in voter orientations on environmental matters. In the US, with two years of the Bush agenda in full view, the Republicans recaptured both houses of Congress in the 2002 mid-term elections.

Explanations of these outcomes that invoke "corporate influence" on the political agenda and the policy process are tenuous, at best. More plausible is the hypothesis that rational (if not necessarily accurate) calculation leads a politically decisive plurality of households to conclude that, on balance, they have more to gain than to lose from the privatization agenda's combination of tax cuts, selective service reductions and regulatory rollbacks. Thus, households with sufficient purchasing power, whether derived from property rights or from their function in the global economy, may be willing to pay a great deal to improve the quality of their own environments or to reduce their exposure to environmental hazards. They will buy bottled water and buy houses and vacation properties in areas well removed from pollutant sources, where environmental quality is capitalized in property values. At the same time, they may resist policies that would socialize the costs of attaining similar goals for a broader segment of the population: the pattern of behavior and political allegiances former US labor secretary Robert Reich has described as "the secession of the successful."[83] Such households may be militant in support of local policy initiatives that protect their own local amenities, yet equally militant in opposition to environmental control measures that might have an adverse impact on their investments—including, for instance, retirement accounts and pension assets held in defined contribution plans by high-income professionals like university professors.

In a somewhat more complicated example that is distinctively important because of how it identifies the relevant cleavages, consider the demonstrably destructive consequences of auto-centered urban development (urban sprawl) in terms of health problems and social exclusion.[84] Consumers in industrialized Europe pay more than twice as much for gasoline as North Americans, with the difference accounted for mostly by differences in taxation.[85] Although a variety of planning tools could be used to reduce or reverse sprawl,[86] by far the simplest approach would involve a gradual but predictable increase in nationally levied gasoline taxes toward European levels. Long before Canadian gasoline taxes (US $0.20/litre in January 2003) approached German levels of US $0.86/litre,[87] the increase would almost certainly generate more substantial and broadly shared environmental benefits than any number of crackdowns on "corporate polluters," in addition to providing a substantial new stream of government revenue. However, suburban municipalities in Canada are in general growing much faster than central cities.[88] Canada has at least 50 per cent more two-vehicle households than no-vehicle households, and more than three out of five households in the top fifth of the income distribution operate at least two vehicles.[89] Furthermore, rapid suburban expansion means that the economic future both of land speculators and of a vocal and politically influential segment of households is inextricably linked with suburban property values and the long-term viability of a low-density, auto-intensive pattern of settlement that is quite literally cast in concrete.[90] Under such circumstances, it is hard to see how the requisite political support for such tax increases could be mobilized, even if their regressive incidence and adverse effects on regional economic competitiveness could be minimized.[91]

CONCLUSION:
FROM CITIZEN ENGAGEMENT TO CONSUMER CHOICE

The preceding discussion presumes that environmental policy preferences and convictions respond primarily to the state of one's own environment. This presumption is an uneasy fit with many people's observed conviction—backed up, in some cases, by cheques written to organizations like the Sierra Legal Defence Fund and the David Suzuki Foundation—that rainforests in British Columbia and the Amazon, or endangered fauna like the golden lion-headed tamarin, should be protected. Such convictions are strongly held even though the people who hold them may never visit either the Amazon or the BC rainforests and will never see a tamarin except in zoos. Neither do the convictions depend on such economic considerations as the possibility that endangered fauna "could be the prime attraction in a future ecotourism industry."[92] Similarly, it is implausible to attribute public concern about the impacts of global climate change on the industrialized world primarily to self-interest.

These phenomena underscore the importance of a point made by Mark Sagoff in a trilogy of articles published in 1981 and 1982: environmental policy must recognize and respect a fundamental distinction between what we want as individual consumers and the kind of society or community we want as citizens.[93] He used the illustration of a class of students presented with a real life proposal to develop a ski resort in a wilderness area (Sequoia National Park). By their own account, the students would probably never visit the wilderness area and were enthusiastic about the recreational opportunities offered by the ski resort. Nevertheless, asked whether the development proposal should proceed, the students' response "was unanimous, visceral and grim. All of the students believed that the Disney plan was loathsome and despicable; that the Forest Service had violated a public trust by approving it; and that the values for which we stand as a nation compel us to preserve the little wilderness we have for its own sake and as an historical heritage...."[94] Sagoff insisted[95] that the distinction between consumers and citizens entails accepting the limits to markets: "The question is whether we should base environmental policy, at least in part, on ideals that people hold and are willing to defend rather than solely on the preferences that they reveal in markets."[96]

Substantial numbers of people appear to believe that environmental policy should be based on such "ideals." The question is whether, and why, they can be expected to provide an adequate political support base and to be willing at least to accept the redistributive consequences. The recent political record is far from encouraging. Elected governments committed to the primacy of markets have remade the North American social policy landscape over the past two decades. Even though she is not writing primarily about the North American context, Zsuzsa Ferge has succinctly described the self-reinforcing dynamic that characterizes the interaction of globalization and domestic retreat from social provision: "With increased income and wealth, the winners are able to spend much more on services of which they are the exclusive users. The former common institutions are destroyed. Of necessity what remains at the service of the losers becomes impoverished and of low quality."[97] As with Reich's discussion of "secession," the critical point here is that globalization's most corrosive consequences for social provision are the result of its effects on *domestic* class structure and political allegiances.

A parallel remaking of the environmental policy landscape (in both literal and figurative senses) is already under way. Place and space not only mediate biophysical exposures, but also provide powerful defining images of inclusion and exclusion. Acknowledging environmental obligations outside one's own locality as meaningful requires at least some sense of a common future: the phrase that provided the title of the Brundtland report. It also requires the existence of a minimally effective mechanism for sharing those obligations. As the rich and the rest of us grow farther apart, statistically and spatially, the idea of a common future strains credulity. And as highly mobile possessors of "human capital" and financial assets are increasingly able to deal with political choices that adversely affect their interests by moving themselves or their assets to jurisdictions that offer higher returns or lower taxes,[98] the effectiveness and legitimacy of political institutions themselves may be undermined. Environmental policy will then increasingly be seen as just another questionable and troublesome governmental intervention in the economy. In the absence of a large-scale environmental disaster with clearly demonstrable health impacts that are largely independent of class, the logic of privatization will dictate that environmental quality is neither regarded as an entitlement or right nor treated as a public good. Rather, it will be regarded as a matter of consumer choice, a good access to which—like foreign vacations or cable television—properly depends on willingness and ability to pay.

NOTES

1 "Planet of the Year: What on Earth Are We Doing?" *Time* 2 Jan. 1989: 18–65.
2 T. McMillan, speech to graduates of Atlantic Police Academy, Charlottetown, Prince Edward Island, October 1986, as cited in "From the horse's mouth," *Alternatives: Perspectives on Society, Technology and Environment* 14.2(May/June 1987): 59.
3 R. McMurry and S. Ramsey, "Environmental Crime: The Use of Criminal Sanctions in Enforcing Environmental Laws," *Loyola of Los Angeles Law Review* 19(1986): 1136–44;

J. Abramson, "Government Cracks Down on Environmental Crimes," *Wall Street Journal* 16 Feb. 1989: B1, B7.

4 World Commission on Environment and Development [the Brundtland Commission], *Our Common Future* (New York: Oxford University Press, 1987).

5 G. Hoberg and K. Harrison, "It's Not Easy Being Green: The Politics of Canada's Green Plan," *Canadian Public Policy* 20(1994): 134.

6 L. Stefanick and K. Wells, "Staying the Course or Saving Face? Federal Environmental Policy Post-Rio," in L. Pal, ed., *Balancing Act: The Post-Deficit Mandate, How Ottawa Spends, 1998–99* (Toronto: Oxford University Press, 1998), p. 251.

7 C.T. Sjolander, "International Trade as Foreign Policy: 'Anything for a Buck,'" in G. Swimmer, ed., *Seeing Red: How Ottawa Spends, 1997–98* (Ottawa: School of Public Administration, Carleton University, 1997), pp. 111–34.

8 Stefanick and Wells, "Staying the Course or Saving Face," p. 254.

9 J. Lorinc, "Seeking Cures for Sick Transit: Nationwide Malady: Cities Call for Sustainable Funding from Ottawa," *National Post*, 15 June 2002.

10 Documentation produced under this legislative mandate is available at <http://www.ec.gc.ca/pdb/npri/npri_home_e.cfm>.

11 L. Juillet and G. Toner, "From Great Leaps to Baby Steps: Environment and Sustainable Development Policy Under the Liberals," in Swimmer, ed., *Seeing Red*, pp. 192-93.

12 *2001 Report of the Commissioner of the Environment and Sustainable Development to the House of Commons* (Ottawa: Office of the Auditor General of Canada, 2001), Chapter 1, §3: "Water." The Commissioner's annual reports are available at <http://www.oag-bvg.ca/domino/oag-bvg.nsf/html/environment.html>.

13 2002 Report of the Commissioner of the Environment and Sustainable Development to the House of Commons (Ottawa: Office of the Auditor General of Canada, 2002), Chapter 1: "Toxic Substances Revisited."

14 *2001 Report of the Commissioner*, ¶ 3.4.16 (see generally § 3.4).

15 T. Schrecker, "Using Science in Environmental Policy: Can Canada Do Better?," in E. Parson, ed., *Governing the Environment: Persistent Challenges, Uncertain Innovations* (Toronto: University of Toronto Press, 2001), pp. 31–72.

16 K. Clark and J. Yacoumidis, *Ontario's Environment and the Common Sense Revolution: A Fifth Year Report* (Toronto: Canadian Institute for Environmental Law and Policy, 2000), pp. 13–14; <http://www.cielap.org/csr5.pdf>.

17 E. MacDonald and J. Roberts, *Cracking Down on Polluters: A Report on Violations of Ontario's Air and Water Pollution Laws* (Toronto: Sierra Legal Defence Fund, March 2004) <http://www.sierralegal.org/reports/cracking_down.pdf>.

18 These measures are described in detail in M. Winfield and G. Jenish, *Ontario's Environment and the Common Sense Revolution: A Four Year Report* (Toronto: Canadian Institute for Environmental Law and Policy, 1999).

19 Clark and Yacoumidis, *Fifth Year Report*, pp. 8, 11. In response to public concern following farming-related contamination of ground water in the town of Walkerton, the Ontario government enacted the *Nutrient Management Act* in 2002. Regulations under the *Act* governing effluents from livestock operations came into force in September 2003 but apply only to large operations (approximately 300 head of cattle or equivalent) and will apply only to new or expanding operations until July 2005; see Canadian Environmental Law Association, "Nutrient Management FAQ," <http://62.44.8.131/faq/cltn_detail.shtml?x=1499>. It therefore remains to be seen whether this initiative constitutes more than a symbolic response.

20 T.A. Hutton, *Visions of a "Post-Staples" Economy: Structural Change and Adjustment Issues in British Columbia,* Paper PI#3 (Vancouver: Centre for Human Settlements, School of Community and Regional Planning, University of British Columbia, January 1994).

21 Sierra Legal Defence Fund, Greenpeace Canada, Sierra Club of British Columbia and BC Endangered Species Coalition, *Betraying Our Trust: A Citizen's Update on Environ-*

mental Rollbacks in British Columbia, 1996–98 (Vancouver: Sierra Legal Defence Fund, 1998); <http://www.sierralegal.org/reports/betray.pdf>.

22 West Coast Environmental Law Association, *The B.C. Government: A One Year Environmental Review* (Vancouver: WCELA, July 2002); <http://www.wcel.org/wcelpub/2002/oneyearreview_final.pdf>.

23 D. Page and A. O'Carroll, *Who's Minding Our Forests? Deregulation of the Forest Industry in British Columbia* (Vancouver: Sierra Legal Defence Fund, May 2002); <http://www.sierralegal.org/reports/Whos_minding_our_forests.pdf>; West Coast Environmental Law Association, *Timber Rules: Forest Regulations Lower Standards, Tie Government Hands and Reduce Accountability*, Deregulation Backgrounder (Vancouver: WCELA, April 2004); <http://www.wcel.org/wcelpub/2004/14098.pdf>.

24 P. Marchak, S. Aycock, and D. Herbert, *Falldown: Forest Policy in British Columbia* (Vancouver: David Suzuki Foundation, 1999), pp. 13–80. For an earlier discussion of the potential impact of plantation forestry in warmer climates on the BC industry, see P. Marchak, *Logging the Globe* (Montreal: McGill-Queen's University Press, 1995).

25 C. Lindblom, *Politics and Markets* (New York: Basic Books. 1977), p. 178; see generally pp. 170–221.

26 Among the best introductions to this topic are R. Boyer and D. Drache, eds., *States Against Markets: The Limits of Globalization* (London: Routledge, 1996); D. Held *et al.*, *Global Transformation: Politics, Economics and Culture* (Stanford, CA: Stanford University Press, 1999); P. Marchak, *The Integrated Circus: The New Right and the Restructuring of Global Markets* (Montreal: McGill-Queen's University Press, 1991); and World Bank, *World Development Report 1995: Workers in an Integrating World* (New York: Oxford University Press, 1995).

27 "Regional Competitiveness: The World's Best Regions," *WorldLink,* November/ December 1993, p. 32.

28 R.W. Stevenson, "Smitten by Britain, Business Rushes In," *New York Times* 15 Oct. 1995: F1, F10.

29 "Regional Competitiveness," pp. 32–34.

30 "A moving story," *The Economist* 7–13 Dec. 2002: 65–66.

31 Calculated from Ontario Exports Inc., *Ontario-Michigan State Trade Factsheet*, July 2001; <http://www.ontario-canada.com/export>.

32 G. Keenan and R. Mackie, "Mexico an option for Daimler plant," *The Globe and Mail* 31 Jan. 2003: B1.

33 Sean McAlinden, as quoted by G. Keenan, "Knowledge-based initiatives seen as auto industry's future," *The Globe and Mail* 23 May 2002: B4.

34 Naomi Klein, "The Real APEC Scandal," *Saturday Night* Feb. 1999: 48.

35 P. Kennedy, "Noranda to mothball Quebec magnesium plant," *The Globe and Mail* 29 Jan. 2003: B1. This example is especially telling and ironic since the plant was built to reclaim magnesium from tailings deposited over decades by asbestos mines in Thetford Mines and Asbestos. The plant was welcomed as a source of employment to replace some of the thousands of jobs once provided by the mines, which are almost completely inactive. Asbestos markets have disappeared as the material's hazards became too widespread to ignore.

36 As would be the case, for instance, with respect to British Columbia's naturally generated forests. See Marchak *et al.*, *Falldown*, pp. 155–70.

37 In the words of a fishery executive quoted by S. Feschuk, "Only One Big Processor Ready for Cod Clobbering," *The Globe and Mail* 3 July 1992.

38 On this point see M. Useem, *Investor Capitalism: How Money Managers are Changing the Face of Corporate America* (New York: Basic Books, 1996).

39 R. Perks, W. Warren, G. Wetstone *et al.*, *Rewriting the Rules: The Bush Administration's Assault on the Environment* (Washington, DC: Natural Resources Defense Council, April 2002); <http://www.nrdc.org/legislation/rollbacks/rollbacks.pdf>.

40 B. Jang, "Imperial Oil executives mince no words on Kyoto or anything else," *The Globe and Mail* 13 March 2002: B9; G. Pitts, "EnCana likely to shift investment if Canada ratifies Kyoto: CEO," *The Globe and Mail* 20 Nov. 2002: B3.

41 *Achieving Our Commitments Together: Climate Change Plan for Canada* (Ottawa: Government of Canada, November 2002), p. 9; <http://www.climatechange.gc.ca/plan_for_canada/plan/pdf/full_version.pdf>.

42 Thus, in 2001, Ontario legalized the 60-hour workweek in the interests of providing employers with greater flexibility in scheduling to meet the demands of "just-in-time" production, without incurring the cost of hiring additional workers.

43 Quoted in D. Westell, "New Rules to Cut Toxic Wastes 47%," *The Globe and Mail* 14 Sept. 1994.

44 L. Panitch, "Globalisation and the State," in Ralph Miliband and Leo Panitch, eds., *Between Globalism and Nationalism: Socialist Register 1994* (London: Merlin Press, 1994), p. 74; *cf.* S. Clarkson, *Canada's Secret Constitution: NAFTA, WTO and the End of Sovereignty?* (Ottawa: Canadian Centre for Policy Alternatives, October 2002); <http://www.policyalternatives.ca>.

45 For an introduction to the application of Chapter 11, see H. Mann, *Private Rights, Public Problems: A Guide to NAFTA's Controversial Chapter on Investor Rights* (Winnipeg: International Institute for Sustainable Development/World Wildlife Fund, 2001).

46 Such as J. Kirton, "Canada-U.S. Trade and the Environment: Regimes, Regulatory Refugees, Races, Restraints and Results," presented at the conference on Rethinking the Line: The Canada–U.S. Border, 23–25 Oct. 2000 (Toronto: Centre for International Studies, University of Toronto, 2000); <http://www.library.utoronto.ca/envireform/pdf/Kirton/Vancouver.pdf>.

47 On the "law of anticipated reaction," see C. Friedrich, *Constitutional Government and Democracy*, rev. ed. (Boston: Ginn, 1946), pp. 589–91. For a description of how the structure of property rights in a market economy gives the owners of capital "the power to define reality" through their investment decisions, see C. Offe, "Some Contradictions of the Modern Welfare State," in *Contradictions of the Welfare State* (Cambridge, MA: MIT Press, 1984), p. 151.

48 B. Mulroney, "What's in Free Trade for Canada?" *The Globe and Mail* 17 April 2001. Because the GST is rebated on exports, it enhances the competitiveness of manufactured exports relative to the situation under the tax it replaced, which applied to all manufactured products regardless of destination, while shifting production costs to domestic consumers. Like most consumption taxes, its incidence is almost certainly regressive.

49 M.G. Cohen, "From the Welfare State to Vampire Capitalism," in P.M. Evans and G.R. Wekerle, *Women and the Canadian Welfare State* (Toronto: University of Toronto Press, 1997), pp. 28–67.

50 M.J. Prince, "From Health and Welfare to Stealth and Farewell: Federal Social Policy, 1980-2000," in L. Pal, ed., *How Ottawa Spends, 1999-2000—Shape Shifting: Canadian Governance Toward the 21st Century* (Toronto: Oxford University Press, 2000), pp. 151–96.

51 I. Morrison, "Ontario Works: A Preliminary Assessment," *Journal of Law and Social Policy* 13(1998): 1–46. "Ontario Works" is the rather Orwellian name given by the Conservatives to Ontario's income supports for its most vulnerable (non-disabled) citizens.

52 H. Mackenzie, *The Money is There: Pre-budget Fiscal Update*, Ontario Alternative Budget Technical Paper no. 6 (Ottawa: Canadian Centre for Policy Alternatives, June 2002), Table 1; <http://www.policyalternatives.ca>.

53 A. Long and M. Goldberg, *Falling Further Behind: A Comparison of Living Costs and Employment and Assistance Rates in British Columbia* (Vancouver: Social Planning and Research Council of British Columbia, December 2002); <http://www.sparc.bc.ca/research/falling_further_behind.pdf>; K. Lunman, "New B.C.

Premier Slashes Income Taxes for all Residents in First Day on the Job," *The Globe and Mail* 7 June 2001.

54 J. Fudge and B. Cossman, "Introduction: Privatization, Law, and the Challenge to Feminism," in B. Cossman and J. Fudge, eds., *Privatization, Law, and the Challenge to Feminism* (Toronto: University of Toronto Press, 2002), p. 18.

55 Fudge and Cossman, "Introduction," p. 20.

56 Fudge and Cossman, "Introduction," p. 19.

57 Fudge and Cossman, "Introduction," pp. 20–22. Another important discussion of this theme is provided by G. Procacci, "Poor Citizens: Social Citizenship versus Individualization of Welfare," in C. Crouch, K. Eder, and D. Tambini, *Citizenship, Markets and the State* (Oxford: Oxford University Press, 2001), pp. 49–68.

58 I. Kaul, "Public Goods: Taking the Concept to the 21st Century," paper prepared for the "Auditing Public Domains" project, Robarts Centre for Canadian Studies, York University (Toronto: York University, 2001), p. 6; <http://www.robarts.yorku.ca/pdf/apd_kaulfin.pdf>.

59 N. Holmstrom, "Rationality, Solidarity, and Public Goods," in A. Anton, M. Fisk and N. Holmstrom, eds., *Not for Sale: In Defense of Public Goods* (Boulder, CO: Westview, 2000), p. 69.

60 R. Rasker and B. Alexander, *The New Challenge: People, Commerce and the Environment in the Yellowstone to Yukon Region* (Bozeman, MT: The Wilderness Society, 1997), p. 1; see also J. Davis, A. Nelson, and K. Dueker, "The New 'Burbs: The Exurbs and Their Implications for Planning Policy," *Journal of the American Planning Association* 60.1(Winter 1994): 45–59.

61 T. Colborn, D. Dumanoski, and J.P. Myers, *Our Stolen Future: Are We Threatening Our Fertility, Intelligence, and Survival?* (New York: Dutton, 1996); T.M. Crisp *et al.*, "Environmental Endocrine Disruption: An Effects Assessment and Analysis," *Environmental Health Perspectives* 106(Supplement 1, 1998): 11–56; D.L. Davis *et al.*, "Rethinking Breast Cancer Risk and the Environment: The Case for the Precautionary Principle," *Environmental Health Perspectives* 106(Sept. 1998): 523–29; E. Knobil *et al.*, *Hormonally Active Agents in the Environment*, Report of the Committee on Hormonally Active Agents in the Environment, [U.S.] National Research Council (Washington, DC: National Academy Press, 1999); G. Solomon and T. Schettler, "Environment and health 6: Endocrine disruption and potential human health implications," *Canadian Medical Association Journal* 163(2000): 1471–76.

62 See, generally, World Resources Institute, United Nations Environment Programme, United Nations Development Programme and World Bank, *World Resources 1998-99: Environmental Change and Human Health* (New York: Oxford University Press).

63 E. Blakely and M. Snyder, *Fortress America: Gated Communities in the United States* (Washington, DC: Brookings Institution Press, 1997).

64 J. Garbarino, "Growing Up in a Socially Toxic Environment: Life for Children and Families in the 1990s," in G. Melton, ed., *The Individual, the Family, and the Social Good, Nebraska Symposium on Motivation* 42 (Lincoln: University of Nebraska Press, 1995), pp. 1–20.

65 For a selection of the recent literature, see G.W. Evans and L. Kantrowitz, "Socioeconomic Status and Health: The Potential Role of Environmental Risk Exposure," *Annual Review of Public Health* 23(2002): 303–31; D. Faber and E.J. Krieg, "Unequal Exposure to Ecological Hazards: Environmental Injustices in the Commonwealth of Massachusetts," *Environmental Health Perspectives*, 110(Supplement 2, 2002): 277–88; S. Foster, "Justice from the Ground Up: Distributive Inequities, Grassroots Resistance, and the Transformative Politics of the Environmental Justice Movement," *California Law Review* 86(1998): 775–841; C. Lee, "Environmental Justice: Building a Unified Vision of Health and the Environment," *Environmental Health Perspectives* 110(Supplement 2, 2002): 141–44; R. Morello-Frosch *et al.*, "Environmental Justice and Regional Inequality in California: Implications for Future Research," *Environmental Health Perspectives*

110(Supplement 2, 2002): 149–54; L. Pulido, S. Sidawi, and R. Vos, "An Archaeology of Environmental Racism in Los Angeles," *Urban Geography* 17(1996): 419–39.

66   Evans and Kantrowitz, "Socioeconomic Status and Health."

67   S.A. Bashir, "Home Is Where the Harm is: Inadequate Housing as a Public Health Crisis," *American Journal of Public Health* 92(2002): 733–38; J.R. Dunn, "Housing and Inequalities in Health: A Study of Socioeconomic Dimensions of Housing and Self Reported Health from a Survey of Vancouver Residents," *Journal of Epidemiology and Community Health* 56(2002): 671–81; L. Freeman, "America's Affordable Housing Crisis: A Contract Unfulfilled," *American Journal of Public Health* 92(2002): 709–12; J. Krieger and D. Higgins, "Housing and Health: Time Again for Public Health Action," *American Journal of Public Health* 92(2002): 758–68.

68   V. Been and F. Gupta, "Coming to the Nuisance or Going to the Barrios? A Longitudinal Analysis of Environmental Justice Claims," *Ecology Law Quarterly* 24(1997): 7–8.

69   N. Gardels, "The Post-Atlantic Capitalist Order," *New Perspectives Quarterly* 10(Spring 1993): 2-3.

70   M. Castells, *The Rise of the Network Society* (Oxford: Blackwell, 1996).

71   Castells, *The Rise of the Network Society*, pp. 380–81.

72   The literature on this trend is too extensive to be canvassed here; perhaps the best introduction is the book version of a *New York Times* series on *The Downsizing of America* (New York: Times Books, 1996). On the spatial implications of industrial job loss, see J.L. Abu-Lughod, *New York, Chicago, Los Angeles: America's Global Cities* (Minneapolis: University of Minnesota Press, 1999); J. Kodras, "The Changing Map of American Poverty in an Era of Economic Restructuring and Political Realignment," *Economic Geography* 73(1997): 67–93; B Warf and R. Erickson, eds., *Globalization and the U.S. City System* [special issue], *Urban Geography* 17.1(1996); D. Wilson, ed., *Globalization and the Changing U.S. City*, Annals of the American Academy of Political and Social Science 551(May 1997). Unfortunately, Canadian research on this topic lags far behind.

73   In addition to the references cited in the preceding note, the best starting points for exploring the growing interdisciplinary literature on metropolitan areas as sites for the interaction of class, place, and inclusion/exclusion in the global economy are M. Polèse and R. Stren, eds., *The Social Sustainability of Cities* (Toronto: University of Toronto Press, 2000), and E.W. Soja, *Postmetropolis: Critical Studies of Cities and Regions* (Oxford: Blackwell, 2000).

74   F.X. Clines, "Philadelphia's Mayor Seeks to Expand City's Revival," *The New York Times* 30 April 2001; T. Rozhon, "Baltimore Stalks Enemy: Old Row Houses," *The New York Times* 13 June 1999.

75   D. Massey, "The Age of Extremes: Concentrated Affluence and Poverty in the Twenty-First Century," *Demography* 33(1996): 395–412.

76   P. Dimond, "Empowering Families to Vote With their Feet," in Bruce Katz, ed., *Reflections on Regionalism* (Washington, DC: Brookings Institution Press, 2000), pp. 249–71.

77   R. Dowling, "Neotraditionalism in the Suburban Landscape: Cultural Geographies of Exclusion in Vancouver, Canada," *Urban Geography* 19(1998): 105–22; M. Hatfield, *Concentrations of Poverty and Distressed Neighbourhoods in Canada*, Working Paper W-97-1E (Ottawa: Applied Research Branch, Human Resources Development Canada, 1997); S. MacDonnell, A. Jackson, F. Ratanshi, S. Schetagne, and P. Smith, *A Decade of Decline: Poverty and Income Inequality in the City of Toronto in the 1990s* (Toronto: United Way of Greater Toronto and Canadian Council on Social Development, 2001); <http://www.uwgt.org/who_we_help/Decade_in_Decline/pdfs/Decade_of_Decline_Final_Report.pdf >; J. Stackhouse, "The New Suburbia," *The Globe and Mail* 8 Oct. 2000: A11, A14–A15.

78   T. Boddy, "Underground and Overhead: Building the Analogous City," in M. Sorkin, ed.,

Variations on a Theme Park: The New American City and the End of Public Space (New York: Hill and Wang, 1992), pp. 123–53.

79 The marginal nature of the constituency for public transportation became clear in at least one Canadian city in 2001, when a lengthy transit strike in Vancouver showed that people who relied on transit were simply too young, old, poor, or disabled to matter much in political terms: see R. Matas, "Strike Not Affecting Most Vancouverites, Poll Finds," *The Globe and Mail* 30 July 2001. On the more dramatic problems that are routine in the US context see e.g. J. Kurth, "Bus System Gaps Punish Workers, Poor," *Detroit News and Free Press* 4 May 2003; E. Mann, "'A Race Struggle, a Class Struggle, a Women's Struggle All at Once': Organizing on the Buses of L.A," in Leo Panitch and Colin Leys, eds., *Working Classes, Global Realities: Socialist Register 2001* (London: Merlin Press, 2001), pp. 59–74; D. Terry, "For Poor of Los Angeles, an Added Burden: The Transit Strike," *New York Times* 13 Oct. 2000.

80 R. Fullilove and M.T. Fullilove, "Place Matters," in R. Hofrichter, ed., *Reclaiming the Environmental Debate: The Politics of Health in a Toxic Culture* (Cambridge, MA: MIT Press, 2000), p. 89.

81 Quoted by S. Dale, *Lost in the Suburbs: A Political Travelogue* (Toronto: Stoddart, 1999), p. 108.

82 This is true not only of the Mulroney and Harris Conservatives and the Chrétien Liberals, but also of Ralph Klein's Conservatives in Alberta.

83 R. Reich, "Secession of the Successful," *New York Times Magazine* 20 Jan. 1991.

84 On health effects see, e.g., M.S. Friedman *et al.*, "Impact of Changes in Transportation and Commuting Behaviors During the 1996 Summer Olympic Games in Atlanta on Air Quality and Childhood Asthma," *JAMA* 285(2001): 897–905; H. Frumkin, "Urban Sprawl and Public Health," *Public Health Reports* 117(2002): 201–17; C.A. Pope III *et al.*, "Lung Cancer, Cardiopulmonary Mortality, and Long-term Exposure to Fine Particulate Air Pollution," *JAMA* 287(2002): 1132–41. On social exclusion see, e.g., R.D. Bullard, G.S. Johnson, A.O. Torres *et al.*, *Sprawl Atlanta: Social Equity Dimensions of Uneven Growth and Development* (Atlanta: Environmental Justice Resource Center, Clark Atlanta University, 1999), and especially P. Dreier, J. Mollenkopf, and T. Swanstrom, *Place Matters: Metropolitics for The Twenty-first Century* (Lawrence: University Press of Kansas, 2001).

85 International Energy Agency, *End-User Petroleum Product Prices and Average Crude Oil Import Costs*, January 2003 (Paris: IEA, Feb. 2003).

86 P. Newman, J. Kenworthy, and P. Vintila, "Can We Overcome Automobile Dependence? Physical Planning in an Age of Urban Cynicism," *Cities* 12(1995): 53-65.

87 International Energy Agency, *End-User Petroleum Product Prices,* Jan. 2003.

88 Statistics Canada, *A Profile of the Canadian Population: Where We Live*, Catalogue no. 96F0030XIE010012001 (Ottawa: Statistics Canada, 2002).

89 Statistics Canada, *Spending Patterns in Canada, 2000*, Catalogue no. 62-202-XIE (Ottawa: Statistics Canada, 2002). Greater precision is not possible without expensive custom tabulations because Statistics Canada reports figures for owned and leased vehicles separately, not indicating the degree of overlap—i.e., it reports the number of households that own two or more vehicles, but does not indicate the number of households that own one vehicle but also lease one.

90 For an earlier exploration of this point with specific reference to a mid-sized Canadian city, see T. Schrecker, "Of Cars, Sustainability and Human Rights: A Canadian Case Study," *CNS: Capitalism Nature Socialism* 7.4(Dec. 1996): 79–97.

91 Addressing the regressive incidence of predictable increases in fuel prices would not be hard to do. For example, a substantial portion of the revenue from gasoline-tax increases could be dedicated to a flat, refundable income-tax credit for every adult tax filer. Avoiding negative effects on the transportation lifelines of continentally integrated industries would be more difficult, but not impossible. One option would be to exempt diesel fuel,

used by most long-distance truckers, from tax increases. Alternatively, a "smart card" system could record the fuel taxes paid in Canada by cross-border truckers; partial fuel tax rebates would automatically be deposited in their, or their employers', bank accounts as the cards were read each time the driver and truck left the country.

92 World Bank, *World Development Report 2003: Sustainable Development in a Dynamic World* (New York: Oxford University Press, 2003), p. 164.

93 M. Sagoff, "Economic Theory and Environmental Law," *Michigan Law Review* 79(1981): 1393–1419; "At the Shrine of Our Lady of Fatima or Why Political Questions are Not All Economic," *Arizona Law Review* 23(1981): 1283–98; "We Have Met the Enemy and He is Us or Conflict and Contradiction in Environmental Law," *Environmental Law* 12(1982): 283–315.

94 Sagoff, "We Have Met the Enemy," p. 284.

95 And has continued to insist—most recently, in "Environmental Economics and the Conflation of Value and Benefit," *Enivronmental Science and Technology* 34(2000): 1426-32.

96 Sagoff, "Economic Theory and Environmental Law," p. 1401 (n37).

97 Z. Ferge, "What are the State Functions Neoliberalism Wants to Eliminate?," in Anton, Fisk, and Holmstrom, eds., *Not for Sale*, p. 200. For similarly thoughtful analyses, see Z. Bauman, *Postmodern Ethics* (Oxford: Blackwell, 1993), pp. 223–50, and M. Bienefeld, "Development Theory: A New Hegemonic Ideology?," in A. Bakan and E. Macdonald, eds., *Critical Political Studies: Debates and Dialogues from the Left* (Montreal: McGill-Queen's University Press, 2002), pp. 209–12.

98 R. Avi-Yonah, "Globalization, Tax Competition, and the Fiscal Crisis of the Welfare State, " *Harvard Law Review* 113(2000): 1573–1676; Bienefeld, "Development Theory."

9

We Just Don't Know: Lessons about Complexity and Uncertainty in Canadian Environmental Politics

Robert B. Gibson

Uncertainty is inconvenient in an administrative state. For administrative purposes the world should be divisible into tidy categories, and what goes on in those categories should be understood by appropriate experts. Or, at the least, it should be open to competent inquiry leading to adequate understanding. Some complexities might be involved and sophisticated methodologies might be required for inquiry and analysis. But, in the end, the world should permit the appropriate experts, armed with the suitable methodologies, to define the problems correctly, to identify the appropriate response options, and to reach the rational conclusions.

Perhaps no informed person today believes the world is actually like this. We have learned that life is messy, intricate, chaotic, and surprising. The past thirty years or so have brought so many failed predictions from credentialed experts, so many hollow assurances from responsible authorities, and so many unanticipated perils, persistent confusions, and grotesque errors that we no longer assume everything is administratively manageable. We expect the experts to disagree. We know that the categories of administrative order are often themselves barriers to comprehension. We presume that decision making is more political than technical, that secrecy is suspect, that forthright public engagement is desirable. It is true that important aspects of the old administrative ways remain, even prevail. Narrow mandates, specious quantification, and impossible standards of proof continue to characterize a good deal of administrative practice. But all this now happens in the face of profound public cynicism about the actual and potential competence of administrative bodies.

Some of this cynicism has arisen because vested corporate interests and associated ideologues have cultivated public doubts about the motives and commitment of government officials. However, cynicism about administrative competence has a more fundamental and legitimate base: growing understanding that the world is complex and uncertain to an extent far beyond all hopes of administrative capability. Nowhere has this understanding been more effectively fostered than in conflicts over environmental concerns. Just about any set of case examples could be chosen to illustrate the problems involved. For the purposes of this exercise, however, four of the most significant environmental controversies of the last three decades in Canada should suffice; the conclusions are applicable in many settings.

LEAD

In Toronto, in 1965, five children living near a secondary lead smelter were treated for lead poisoning.[1] At the time, the assumed danger level for blood lead was 80–100 micrograms per deciliter (g/dL) and only those with blood lead at those levels or higher got much attention. By the early 1970s, 40 g/dL was the accepted threshold. A decade later it was down to 25 g/dL,[2] and there was evidence of biochemical changes affecting child development at 10 to 12 g/dL.[3] The World Health Organization's most recent pronouncement on the matter is a 1996 document, which reports a range of effects, some associated with blood–lead levels in the 5–10μg/dL range, and notes that epidemiological studies have been unable to identify a threshold below which there would be no negative effects on neurological development in children.[4]

Lead, clearly, is a contaminant about which our reasons for concern have grown with advances in our understanding of its effects. As such it is representative of many other contaminants, alone and in combination. Official reaction to evidence of lead poisoning is similarly representative. Throughout the 1960s and 1970s, and even later, authorities were quick with public reassurances of safety, except in the few cases where the then-accepted threshold was crossed. And they were no less quick with reassurances about their commitment to address any serious pollution problems. Both proved dramatically unreliable in the case of the Toronto lead smelters, as they have since in many other instances. The lead smelters case is particularly significant because it began early in the period of recent environmental concern, and because, at least in Toronto, it attracted a great deal of media attention. It was therefore a formative influence on many people's understanding of uncertainties about both health effects and the reliability of government authorities as defenders of the public interest.

While the poisonous potential of lead in large doses was well known in Roman times, the effects of low-level chronic exposures have been more of a mystery. Health damages from heavy occupational exposures—anemia, nervous-system disturbances, and brain damage—have been long recognized, as has the special vulnerability of children. For instance, Britain banned the employment of children under fifteen in lead-using industries a hundred years ago.[5] A persistent difficulty, and a key issue in the Toronto lead smelters case, has been determining what level of exposure and absorption might be safe, especially for children. The chief dangers for children are the subtle effects of lead on brain and nervous-system development—effects that can result in eventual learning difficulties, hearing acuity reduction, attention deficits, behavioral problems, retardation of growth, and slowing of response times. Such effects are clearly important and worrisome but also difficult to distinguish from the influence of multitudes of factors other than lead.

In the Toronto lead smelters case, and in lead regulation generally, there were additional complications. Lead exposure was from multiple sources. Even in the lead smelter neighborhoods during the period of greatest exposure to lead dust and contaminated soils, the accused companies could point to other possible pathways of exposure and poisoning: lead in water pipes; lead in old, peeling house paint; atmospheric lead from vehicles burning leaded gasoline. Moreover, the availability of detailed information did not necessarily resolve things. In a celebrated US debate concerning the attribution of health effects to lead from the combustion of leaded gasoline, well-credentialed scientific and statistical experts from government agencies and affected industries reached directly opposing conclusions from analyses of the very same large database.[6]

These difficulties of cause-effect attribution played an important role in the Toronto lead smelters case. Provincial authorities were hesitant to act forcefully, in part because the law required proof of harm. In October 1973, after tests found three residents of the neighborhood around the Canada Metals plant had dangerously high concentrations of lead in their blood, the provincial environment ministry was finally moved to issue a stop order. But within three days the company, with support from industry experts, had persuaded an Ontario Supreme Court judge to overturn the order on the grounds that no immediate danger had been proven. Critics of the ministry's efforts to defend its order noted that it had failed to make use of easily available evidence and did not call its own experts to counter those of the company.[7] But given the standard of proof required, it is not clear that this evidence and expertise would have prevailed.

The limits of available evidence on lead effects and on exposure attribution were only part of the story behind the government's reluctance to force prompt cleanup of the smelters. While the province's environmental authorities were officially responsible for environmental protection, they were not empowered or inclined by circumstances to act in an adversarial mode against polluters. Environment ministry officials negotiated pollution controls in private with industry representatives, and the latter typically had the advantage of better information, especially about technical options. Members of the concerned public were excluded from these discussions. They were also denied access to information collected by their own government and relevant to their own health, and frequently were treated as perilously irrational and emotional. In one instance, a decade into the public controversies surrounding the Toronto lead smelters, an environment ministry official told the Toronto Board of Health that he had new evidence of emissions problems at one of the smelters but hadn't informed the neighborhood residents because he didn't want to alarm them.[8]

Very slowly, while scientific research gradually lowered the threshold level for lead poisoning, corrective action was taken in the smelter neighborhoods. After thirty years the most heavily contaminated soil had been removed, site dust control had been improved, stack emissions abated, or facilities moved. But the much delayed achievements came only through extraordinary effort by the local residents and with support—media coverage and help from municipal health authorities, environmental law activists, and university researchers—that was not then and is not now often available to beleaguered citizens.[9]

In the course of these frustrations and successes, the Toronto lead smelters case demonstrated a set of important lessons about uncertainty. Chief among these lessons, repeated and reinforced in many other essentially similar environmental controversies over the same period, were these three:

• *Environmental health cause-effect relations can be exceedingly difficult, if not impossible, to prove.* This is the case even when the questions involve a single contaminant acting on a reasonably well-defined population of receptors (e.g., children in specific neighborhoods). Years of research effort and shelves of carefully designed studies may still leave uncertainties about the threshold exposure and ingestion levels beyond which health damage may occur. Indeed, it is not safe to assume there is such a threshold. Because of the multiplicity of sources, it is difficult to link particular sources to particular exposures. And because of the multiplicity of influences on health, it is difficult to link particular exposures to particular health effects.

This discovery raised doubts about the foundations of the legal and regulatory regime for control of contaminants and protection of health. The prevailing regime assumes provability—it assumes that the existence and sources of adverse effects can be established with scientific certainty, at least in cases where these adverse effects are serious enough to merit corrective action. The lead case shows this to be an invalid and dangerous assumption.

• *Additional research on ill-understood contaminant effects can reveal that problems are more serious than initially assumed.* In the lead case, more research with better methodologies and more sensitive tools gradually uncovered a larger set of attributable damages, which occurred at much lower levels of contaminant loading. This has been a common experience with environmental contaminants (radon, asbestos, PCBs, persistent toxic pesticides such as dieldrin and mirex, etc.). Indeed, lead proved to be a less extreme case than many others, perhaps because we had already had millennia of experience with it and its effects. Most of the contaminants that have come to dominate recent public and scientific concern are synthetic chemicals for which humans and ecologies have had little biological preparation.

Here, the lesson from the lead case and other similar experiences has been that what we do not know is great and can certainly hurt us.

• *Expertise is uncertain and assurances are not to be trusted.* The lead case was just one of many experiences, in a host of fields extending well beyond environmental health matters, that undermined public trust in the public authorities over the past four decades. But it was particularly important because it showed that the underlying problems were not merely political (e.g., undue coziness between regulators and regulatees), but also systemic (rooted in the unavoidable complexity and uncertainty of environmental effects). On the surface, the lead case showed that official and expert assurances could be dangerously unreliable. On a deeper level it revealed that any such assurances *had* to be unreliable—there was not and could not be a firm base for confidence. Decisions to act or to hesitate could not be made solely on information and expertise. Priorities, interests, and choices were necessarily involved. Open involvement of those affected by such decisions was therefore needed, not just because the officials might be untrustworthy or inexpert, but also and more fundamentally because in uncertainty there is choice and the choosers should include those who will have to live with the results.

Budworm

Throughout the mid-1970s, much of eastern Canada was embroiled in lively debates over the acceptability of spraying chemical pesticides to control the spruce budworm. The center of controversy was New Brunswick, a province that was heavily dependent on the forest industry and that had already been spraying against the budworm for a couple of decades. But the budworm battles extended also to Newfoundland, to parts of Quebec and Ontario, and to Nova Scotia, especially Cape Breton, where the Swedish owners of the economically crucial Port Hawkesbury pulp mill were demanding a (government-funded) spray program that would douse most of the island.

Spruce budworm is an indigenous resident of the spruce/fir forests of eastern North America. Historically it emerged in outbreaks recurring cyclically every 30–60 years.[10] During these outbreaks large numbers of budworm would feed on mature trees for four to eight years; then the populations would collapse to levels that could be controlled by insectivorous bird predation until new spruce/fir growth reached sufficient maturity and density to support a new outbreak.[11] Hoping to protect harvestable mature trees and perhaps even break the cycle of destruction, New Brunswick began an insecticide spray campaign. In the first year, 1952, 80,000 hectares were sprayed and an estimated 95 per cent of the budworms were killed.[12] The initial assumption was that the spraying would be needed only for a few years, after which the budworm populations would collapse following the historical cycle.[13] But by maintaining foliage and protecting harvestable trees, the spraying also maintained budworm food supplies, permitting a permanent outbreak.[14] And so both spraying and budworm infestation became continuing phenomena, essentially symbiotic.

By 1976, the budworm outbreak covered over half the province: 3.9 million hectares—almost the entire vulnerable forest of New Brunswick—were identified as "requiring protection."[15] As the area of infestation and spray expanded, so did the public controversy. Not surprisingly, the bulk of public and media attention was focused on the human health and ecological effects of the spray chemicals.[16] For the first decade and a half, New Brunswick used DDT against the budworm. In 1968, six years after the revelations about DDT in Rachel Carson's *Silent Spring,* the province switched to organophosphate insecticides, chiefly fenitrothion. The organophosphates were much less persistent than DDT, but they too had negative effects on non-target species,[17] including birds that would otherwise have been budworm predators. Moreover, a variety of human health threats were associated with, or attributed to, the spray chemicals, including the emulsifiers used in the aerial applications. As in the lead case, the health-effects data were limited and open to debate. The several complexities included the usual problems: ill-understood sicknesses, multiple possible causes and contributing factors, and competing interests involved in interpreting the results.

In the budworm controversies, the uncertainties regarding health effects were accompanied by a set of equally perplexing difficulties concerning forest dynamics and management options. While these received much less public attention than the health-related issues, they were no less important as sources of lessons about complexity, uncertainty, and their political implications.

For forest management, the key issues centered on the inconvenience of nature and the apparent absence of a management option that would establish a forest that fitted with industrial and economic expectations. The industrial and economic demand was for a constant and predictable flow of sawlogs and pulp fiber to the mills. A forest with young and mature trees in nicely balanced age classes would have served nicely. Unfortunately, this was not the natural reality of the spruce/fir forest. The actual forest was of trees mostly the same age, the product of a dynamic cycle of budworm-driven collapse and regeneration.[18] For the New Brunswick forest industry, and for provincial forestry officials, the apparent challenge was to break this cycle and the evident solution was to knock out the budworm, or at least reduce its consumption of fir and spruce to commercially insignificant levels.

By the mid 1970s it was quite clear that the problem was not going to be resolved through an ever-expanding aerial insecticide bombardment. The spraying was protecting trees but supporting a permanent infestation. There were always budworm survivors and plenty of moths from the forests upwind from the province to reinvigorate local populations where the spraying was especially effective. The costs of spraying were becoming unmanageable as the areas to be covered expanded and as insecticide prices and application costs rose with the price of oil.[19] The non-target effects and risks to human health threats were straining public tolerance. Moreover, industry too was facing undesirable side effects. There were fewer sawlogs because the quarter-century of spraying had protected dense stands of small trees at the expense of the larger trees that sawmills needed. And forest-regeneration costs were rising because the permanent infestation conditions, combined with changes in harvesting practices, damaged seedlings that would have provided natural regeneration.[20]

Some traditional foresters and spray opponents advocated gradual management efforts to establish and maintain more species-diverse and mixed-age forests.[21] These would, they hoped, be less vulnerable to budworm outbreaks. But there was little ground for confidence that this ideal but unnatural-for-the-area forest would be safe from serious budworm damage or that it could be achieved without harvest and employment cuts in the forest industry.[22]

Finally, at the end of the 1970s, the New Brunswick forestry interests decided, effectively, to respect the complexity of the case and adopt a different approach to forest management. Instead of focusing on the simple target of expanding timber supply and the simple strategy of attacking the budworm threat to supply, the province initiated a shift to "integrated adaptive management"—recognizing the forest as a dynamic system beyond confident predictability.[23] Management efforts would be assisted by sophisticated modeling and forecasting and attempts at long-term planning, but errors would be expected; monitoring and adjustment would be continuous. Moreover, the concept saw that forest management had to serve multiple objectives and that public choices, not just expert knowledge, were involved.

Implementation of this approach has proven difficult.[24] Gordon Baskerville, who played a central role in the shift to adaptive management, has reported particular problems in changing the basic rules of official behavior and in defining multiple goals that are both biologically possible and socially acceptable.[25] Concerning the former, Baskerville observed, "Bureaucracies have great difficulty with adaptive management, for it requires admitting, 'I don't know; I must learn,' and this results in removing the standard reference point in a bureaucracy."[26] Concerning the latter, he said, "The problem is one of establishing public expectations that are consistent with public willingness to allow/permit/enforce long-term efforts to make management work in the forest."[27] Both problems center on the need for individual and institutional learning about complex systems and associated uncertainties, and for acceptance of a world without simple solutions and predictive confidence.

Appreciation of complex system realities has been the particular contribution of the New Brunswick budworm case to the set of lessons about uncertainty. Like the lead controversies, the budworm battles involved concerns that could not be resolved simply through the application of more science. The many confident assurances of managerial success were also firmly contradicted by evident failure. But the budworm case added some new lessons too:

• *Practical problems emerge in socio-biophysical systems that are both complex and dynamic.* The failure of the spraying program—its inability to beat back the budworm infestation, and its increasing costs as the infestation spread and side effects emerged—demonstrated that the complexity and minimal predictability of forest dynamics had to be recognized and respected. In New Brunswick the budworm are a normal component of a larger system of collapse and renewal. For industries wanting a steady flow of pulpwood and sawlogs, it would be more convenient if the natural forest had tidy age distribution and if perturbations such as insect infestations could be eliminated through deft chemical intervention. But that was not and is not the reality of the actual forest in New Brunswick, or of biophysical systems generally.

The New Brunswick case has been influential in the understanding of complex systems. On the basis of this case and studies of similar systems in a host of other places, C.S. Holling has presented the key common finding as a general rule:

> The very success in managing a target variable for sustained production of food or fiber apparently leads inevitably to an ultimate pathology of less resilient and more vulnerable ecosystems, more rigid and unresponsive management agencies, and more dependent societies. This seems to define the conditions for gridlock and irretrievable resource collapse.[28]

Holling suggests that while we can and should work to enhance our understanding of biophysical and socio-economic/political systems, their future states will always remain beyond confident prediction. In such circumstances, tentative, reversible, and modest interventions, implemented with careful monitoring and adjustment, are likely to be most suitable.[29]

• *The realities of complex and dynamic systems will frustrate interventions that presume simple cause-effect relations.* New Brunswick's eventual conclusion was not so much that the budworm had to be approached differently as that forest management had to be reformed. This too offered an important lesson. Because of the broader systemic complexities involved, the problem focus had to be expanded to encompass the key systemic elements. Here, as in many other instances,[30] potential resolution depended on escaping from the initial managerial box.

• *Inevitably, this recognition of a broader range of considerations also entails involvement of a larger set of interests, more evident trade-offs, and less chance that the relevant experts could provide correct answers.* While expertise remained important, it was mostly useful for revealing constraints and helping to identify potentially viable options. Deciding what to do—how to respect the dynamic complexity of the ecological system and how to sort through the relative merits of competing management options with uncertain implications—was not a matter for mere expertise. It was a matter of public choice and applied ethics.

ACID RAIN

By the 1980s, the scale of environmental concerns had grown. Canadians still confronted a plethora of local and regional environmental concerns, most of them within the potentially effective jurisdiction of municipal or provincial authorities or particular national agencies. But bigger problems were winning more attention. These included worries about damage to the stratospheric ozone layer, about the possible carcinogenic and teratogenic effects of some widely used synthetic chemicals and process by-products, about global losses of species diversity, and about climate destabilization due to increasing atmospheric concentrations of carbon dioxide and other greenhouse gases. Here the problem and the necessary responses were—and remain—international. This larger scale brought a consequential amplification of the usual challenges of delineating effects, identifying sources, attributing responsibility, understanding relevant system components, and predicting their behavior if adjusted. It also added a layer or more of complexity and uncertainty concerning strategies for mobilizing appropriate responses.

Continental and global environmental concerns had been recognized and addressed before. The pioneering movement against atmospheric nuclear testing in the 1950s, for example, had demonstrated the ability of an activist public to push a modicum of reason on the world of geopolitics. But in the early 1980s, the peculiar complexities of international environmental problems and responses were still not deeply appreciated. For Canadians, the most telling lessons were to be learned from experience with acidic deposition, known more familiarly though less accurately as acid rain.[31]

Precipitation is normally a little acidic. But when the usual atmospheric chemistry is complemented by compounds such as sulfur dioxide and nitrogen oxides from industrial facilities and other anthropogenic sources, the acidity of rain and snow can increase significantly. The consequent ecological effects, especially on poorly buffered aquatic systems and vulnerable forests, can be dramatic. Local effects of sulfurous emissions were recognized in antiquity and had long been evident in places such as Sudbury, Ontario, where decades of smelter discharges had created a landscape famously selected for training Moon-bound astronauts. Response to these local problems included construction of very tall stacks for release and assumed dispersal of the pollutants of concern. By the late 1960s, however, scientists were reporting evidence of acidification far from local sources.

The Scandinavians were the first to push for international action on the long-range transport of acidifying emissions. In the 1950s and 1960s they had identified acidification damage, due in part to pollutants discharged by their more heavily industrialized European neighbors.[32] Sweden's concerns about acid rain were a prime motive for their decision to host the first UN conference on the environment in 1972.[33] The countries most responsible for acidifying emissions, the United Kingdom in particular, spent the next decade and a half arguing that greater scientific certainty was needed to justify commitments to a substantial abatement effort.[34]

In the late 1960s Canadian scientists, too, had documented lake acidification due to atmospheric deposition. In 1972, University of Toronto biologists Richard Beamish and Harold Harvey published detailed and dramatic evidence of acidification in the La Cloche mountain lakes of Killarney Park, 80 kilometers west of Sudbury.[35] In 1977, the pH of snowfall near Dorset, just outside Algonquin Park, was measured at 2.97, the acidity of vinegar.[36] But Ontario, a major source as well as victim of these acidifying emissions, was not quick to respond. By the 1980s, there was easily enough research evidence to show that acid rain had caused widespread environmental damage, particularly to aquatic ecosystems, and that it threatened to cause much more.[37] A Canadian Parliamentary committee recognized in 1981 that acid rain was a disaster in the making and that to forestall it, immediate and decisive actions were needed.[38] Deciding just what to do was more difficult.

Much of the problem was with complexities and uncertainties familiar at least since the experience with lead. Governments must induce or force those responsible for individual sources of polluting emissions to carry out costly abatement programs. In each case, government officials must decide not only whether to compel abatement, but also how much, by whom, how quickly, and despite what costs. Emitters would—and did—insist that abatement requirements are not justified unless there is proof beyond a reasonable doubt, not just that significant damages are occurring, but that the measurable environmental benefits of individual proposed abatement requirements will be greater than the costs of abatement. The position taken by Dr. Stuart Warner of Inco Ltd. in a 1979 statement to an Ontario Parliamentary committee was typical: "The scientific community is gearing up to acquire the necessary understanding of acidic precipitation. We believe it would be inadvisable to make important, regulatory decisions before this information is available. Doing so could result in a net loss to Ontario."[39]

Such information was not and could never be available. The basic chemical and ecological and human health factors, processes, and interrelationships influencing acid-rain effects were and are far too numerous, subtle, intricate, and difficult to distinguish one from another. By the mid 1980s, after a decade or more of substantial research effort in affected jurisdictions, there was relatively reliable information about only a few of the larger-scale damages that acid rain had caused or exacerbated. There was no adequate basis for describing with precision and confidence the nature, extent, and timing of future damages given various emission scenarios or the likely gains from various kinds and intensities of abatement effort.[40] By 1998, Canadian authorities felt able to make an important gross calculation—the "critical load" sulfur levels for various ecoregions in southeastern Canada—but they judged the nitrogen cycle too complex even for such broad calculations.[41] A 2001 US review of advances in understanding acid rain concluded that while major gaps in understanding still remained, the new evidence had generally uncovered "greater environmental impact than previously projected."[42]

As with lead, more research led to more worries, while full understanding of processes, damages, costs, and options for corrective action remained far out of reach. In the lead case, however, the polluters and their victims were neighbors under the jurisdiction of a single provincial authority. The uncertainties and trade-offs could be addressed internally. With acid rain, international action was evidently needed, including action by jurisdictions that were responsible for significant emission sources but were not themselves particularly vulnerable to the effects.[43]

In Europe, the Scandinavian countries were most vulnerable to acid-rain damage, and the main emission sources were in the United Kingdom and other heavily industrialized parts of northern Europe. In North America the main sources were in the US Midwest and Ontario, while the most vulnerable forests and lakes were in Ontario, Quebec, the Maritime provinces, and the US northeast. Ontario was in an almost unique position as both villain and victim.

Even for a predictably ambivalent actor, Ontario was slow to move on the abatement of acidifying emissions. In the case of the Inco Ltd. smelter in Sudbury, the continent's largest and most infamous source of sulfur dioxide emissions, government officials retreated several times from the demanding requirements of a 1970 Minister's order requiring reduction of sulfur dioxide emissions to 750 tons per day.[44] Representatives of the provincial Ministry of the Environment appearing before a legislative committee examining Inco abatement options in 1979 argued that they could not, on the basis of existing information, justify compelling the company to reduce its emissions below the then-current rate of 3,600 tons per day. They also stated that because of the importance of pollutants from sources outside the province it was not clear that further abatement at Inco Sudbury would reduce acid-rain damages in Ontario.[45] Eventually, media attention and expressed public concerns in the province intensified the political attractiveness of abatement requirements to the point where action was unavoidable. In 1985 the old target was reinstated, with 1995 set as the compliance deadline.[46]

There are several explanations for the slowness of Ontario's abatement response. These involve usual problems with the legal expectations for proof of damage and established cause-effect relations, the established regulatory preference for cooperative relations with regulatees, and the disinclination to take stern action against corporate powers, especially if they are important employers or are otherwise economically and politically powerful. In the case of acid rain, it was also clear that the environmental benefits would be less immediate and perceptible than the costs of abatement and that the beneficiaries would be more dispersed and less well connected politically than the recipients of abatement orders. But no less important were considerations beyond Ontario.

Acid-rain decision making in Ontario was confounded by the fact that a significant portion of domestic acid loadings originated in the US Midwest. Ontario government officials in the 1970s and early 1980s concluded that stringent abatement requirements in the province would be unfair to Ontario polluters, who would be subject to requirements not imposed elsewhere. They also concluded that, given the significance of foreign emission sources upwind from Ontario, unilateral measures would not ensure a substantial reduction of acid-rain damages in the province.[47]

A key question, then, was how best to promote concerted international action. If acid-rain damage could be prevented effectively only through joint Canada-US abatement initiatives, Ontario had to consider whether exemplary abatement action would assist in negotiations with the Americans, or merely put the province at an economic disadvantage. Here too there were many added complications. The relevant negotiations were not just a matter between Ontario and the US Midwest states. Several northeastern American states and Canadian provinces downwind from Ontario were involved as acid-rain victims. Both the Canadian and US federal governments had roles to play as mediators between domestic emitters and receivers and as negotiators between nations. Industrial and environmentalist lobbies weighed in. The North American negotiations were paralleled and influenced by similar deliberations in Europe, and the immediate acid-rain considerations were surrounded by a wide range of other associated issues, interests, ideological predilections, and possible trade-offs. Thus the acid-rain case raised an additional whole category of uncertainties—the strategic uncertainties surrounding interjurisdictional political pressures, motives, and influence. This proved to be a field of complex system behavior presenting predictive challenges equal to any in the biophysical realm.

Throughout the 1980s, acid-rain discord was a major irritant in Canada–US relations.[48] For reasons of ideology and raw interest politics, the Reagan administration was willing only to support research, which it then manipulated.[49] The Canadian government continued to raise the issue, complementing legal and political pressure from acid-damaged states in the US northeast and lobbying by US environmentalists. An unprecedented grouping of Canadian environmental organizations structured themselves as the Canadian Coalition on Acid Rain and set up an office in Washington as the first ever Canadian body formally registered as a lobby group in the US.[50] Gradually, increasing numbers of legislators were persuaded that acid rain was a problem, and eventually some openings appeared as the Reagan era ended, but it took a full decade. Finally, in 1990, the US Congress passed a set of amendments to the US *Clean Air Act* that set targets for substantial sulfur dioxide cuts and established an ambitious emissions-trading scheme to facilitate implementation. This was followed in 1991 by a Canada–US Air Quality Agreement.[51] It is conceivable, perhaps even likely, that some other set of political strategies would have worked more quickly. Even in retrospect, however, there is no way of knowing. The complexities involved are simply too great.

The much-belated US and Canadian actions required major reductions in sulfur dioxide emissions. Canada had decided in 1985 to cut eastern Canadian emissions to 30 per cent below 1980 levels and achieved 54 per cent reduction by

1997. The US 1990 *Clean Air Act* target—a 40 per cent cut from 1980 levels by 2010—seems likely to be reached.[52] In both countries, industrial opponents of acid-rain action had claimed that such requirements would be economically ruinous. Governments were quick to agree, at least initially. This was in part because they failed to examine the companies' claims or the available abatement options very closely. But even careful study was no sure route to confidence about technological possibilities and associated costs.

In part because of the successful use of a market-based approach to emission regulation, implementation of the US requirements proved to be surprisingly inexpensive. Moreover, a 1998 US report to Congress concluded that quantifiable benefits in the areas of human health and visibility alone might well be greater than the costs of compliance.[53] The Canadian story is similar. In 1979, Inco Ltd. had claimed that significant abatement would cost "billions of dollars" and had warned darkly of job losses.[54] By 2001, the company, still in good health, had cut emissions to about a fifth of the 1979 levels and was accepting a provincial order to chop out another 34 per cent.[55] No one foresaw that in 1979.

The acid-rain problem has not been solved. Recent reviews suggest that substantial further emission reductions are still needed in both Canada and the US. A 2001 US study concluded that electric utility emissions would need to be cut another 80 per cent beyond the 1990 US requirements to permit significant ecological recoveries.[56] Public and media attention has long since drifted to other areas of concern. But one of these is smog, a similarly regional problem that is attributable largely to long-distance transport of pollutants including sulfur and nitrogen oxides.

In a 1981 assessment of the complexity of acid-rain politics in the United States, B.A. Ackerman and W.T. Hassler observed that the environmental movement coincided with "the decline of an older dream—the image of an independent and expert administration creatively regulating a complex social problem in the public interest."[57] That dream, like so many others in environmental administration, evaporated in conflicts among experts and between completing interests over how to interpret incomplete information and what to do in the face of uncertainties about ecological and human health effects, contributions from multiple sources, and potential abatement options and their costs. The case of acid rain did not introduce these problems, but it underlined the possible extent and depth of the relevant uncertainties. And it did so with a phenomenon that in its international character, its delayed effects, and multiple other complexities, represented the new wave of subtle, insidious, and global threats. More important, the acid rain case confirmed the role of political choice. In the international acid rain conflicts, the key uncertainties were about what political strategies would be most effective, and the key lessons were about the importance of political arrangements.

• *In environmental controversies, especially where international factors are at work, the most vexing uncertainties may be about suitable political strategies. At* the beginning of the North American debate on what to do about acid rain, many participants may have seen it as a contest over the scientific, technological, and economic facts. By the end, the story was essentially and transparently political. Facts, or at least interpretations of the available evidence, were involved, certainly. But what happened was determined by the nature of the authoritative political institutions, by the ideologies of the politically powerful, and by the distribution of political power.

GENETICALLY MODIFIED ORGANISMS

Today, the most serious Canadian environmental issues typically involve the full set of complexities and uncertainties that characterized the lead, budworm, and acid rain cases, further enriched by matters of scale and ethics. All the big concerns are characterized by toxicological and/or ecological difficulties, intricate interdependencies among social and biophysical systems, and unavoidable roles for moral and political choice. Most now are also shared with the rest of the world. The toughest challenges (e.g., preservation of ocean fish stocks and stabilization of global atmospheric chemistry) are wholly global in character and consequence and substantially global in necessary response. Many other big issues are largely within domestic competence (e.g., management of hazardous wastes and protection of old-growth forests) but evidently require global-scale scientific, economic, and political effort to spur action.[58] In virtually all cases, questions about justice have become as important as questions about truth.

While no one issue can adequately represent all the challenges in this diverse congregation of Canadian and global environmental issues, how to regulate genetic engineering research and applications is a good contender. Biotechnology, especially the use of recombinant DNA techniques to modify an organism's genetic code, serves many different scientific, commercial, and military objectives. Among the major areas of established and potential activity are

- genetic engineering of humans to eliminate fatal or debilitating genetically transferred illnesses, to avoid other undesirable characteristics or conditions, or to enhance desired qualities;
- genetic engineering of other animals for improved quantity or quality of current food products (e.g., more meat and milk), for novel products (e.g., recombinant proteins) or materials (e.g., more or thicker wool), for xenotransplantation purposes (especially replacement organs for humans), or for other human health gains (e.g., production of pharmaceuticals in eggs, or alteration of pets to reduce allergens, or modification of insects such as mosquitoes to limit disease vectors or reduce crop damage);[59]
- genetic engineering of food plants for greater productivity or product quality, including through greater pest resistance and hardiness;[60]
- genetic engineering of microbes in liquids, soils, animals or the atmosphere for industrial, ecological, and military purposes (e.g., bacteria to concentrate

minerals, detoxify hazardous wastes or improve farm-animal productivity; and viruses to kill forest or agricultural pests, to serve as military weapons or for defense research).[61]

Each of these current and potential applications has stirred some measure of controversy. While not all have been initiated or proposed in Canada, this country is likely to be affected, positively and negatively, by the intended and unanticipated effects of applications elsewhere. Proper consideration of concerns raised by genetic engineering therefore involves attention to the full package as well as the individual applications, and to the nature of and prospects for response options around the world. For our immediate purposes here, however, it may be sufficient to look at just one illustrative part of the larger story: Canadian deliberations on the regulation of food biotechnology—transgenic crops and genetically modified food products.

Recombinant DNA technologies were first developed in the early 1970s and food-crop applications date back at least to the mid 1980s when work began on genetic modification of crops for resistance to particular herbicides.[62] While there were controversies from the outset and serious Canadian debates on the associated policy issues in the 1980s,[63] the main regulatory responses did not emerge until the 1990s. Both the controversies and the regulatory deliberations continue today, with no appreciable abatement of enthusiasm on the part of biotechnology advocates or diminution of worries on the part of the technology's detractors.

The Canadian federal government's initial interest was largely promotional. The National Biotechnology Strategy, announced in 1983, focused on boosting the Canadian biotechnology industry's economic prospects. Regulatory controls were left to a variety of existing agencies and tools provided in legislation predating the science of genetic modification. This approach was maintained a decade later when Canada introduced a more formal regulatory framework for biotechnology that specified responsibilities for nine federal departments.[64] In the news release accompanying announcement of the new framework, the tension between promotion and regulation remained evident. The release concluded that the new framework would "enable the biotechnology industry to maximize opportunities while minimizing concerns about human health and safety and the environment."[65]

Subsequent years brought little evidence of diminishing concerns, in Canada or elsewhere.[66] Government and industry claims about safety were undermined by the evident unreliability of earlier reassurances on other topics. Moreover, biotechnology initiatives were poised to become more ambitious and more worrisome. While the first generation of genetically modified food crops had involved transfer of individual genes and a focus on a few selected traits (e.g., insect resistance or reduced herbicide vulnerability), the industry was moving towards more complex multiple-gene transfers.[67] Facing growing public concern about an increasingly significant part of the economy, the Canadian government moved in early in the present decade to initiate major reviews of the regulatory approach to food biotechnology.

After years of biotechnology promotion, the federal government had no hope of carrying out a publicly credible review itself. It turned instead to other bodies, especially a multi-stakeholder Canadian Biotechnology Advisory Committee (CBAC) representing a wide range of biotechnology interests, including some critical and independent voices, and an Expert Panel on the Future of Food Biotechnology appointed by the Royal Society of Canada at the request of the federal ministers with major food biotechnology responsibilities.[68] Referring regulatory issues to such bodies was in itself no innovation; governments had often appointed more or less independent bodies to provide advice on matters of environmental dispute. Back in 1974 in the lead case, for example, the province of Ontario had established a special task force of three eminent scholars to examine the human health effects of lead exposure.[69] In the food biotechnology case, however, the independent review bodies have been distinguished by their broader scope and explicit attention to matters of uncertainty and ethics.

The deliberations on food biotechnology regulation have also been unusual as anticipatory exercises. Critics have expressed concern that the recent moves towards effective regulation in this area come more than a decade after the federal government began enthusiastic promotion of biotechnology. But unlike the more typical lead, budworm, and acid rain cases, where regulatory action and process reform came after serious problems had been forced into the light, genetic engineering applications have been examined as *potential* problems, prior to any evident disasters. Biotechnology has won attention not because of its effects but because of its risks.

Advocates of ambitious genetic engineering research and applications argue that the technology will bring important environmental as well as economic benefits. These include the promise of more food from less land, greater nutritional value, engineered suitability for marginal or degraded soils and difficult climates, and reduced needs for chemical pesticides, nutritional supplements, antibiotics, and other medicines. Some biotechnology supporters claim that engineered food crops and animals offer the only viable path to agricultural sustainability.[70] Such claims have been consistently challenged and countered by critics pointing to the technology's potential negative effects.

Food biotechnology risks have been variously described and categorized. The Royal Society's Expert Panel used three categories: the potential risks to the health of human beings, animals, and the natural environment; to social, political and economic relationships, and values; to fundamental philosophical, religious or "metaphysical" values held by different individuals and groups.[71] The list of anticipated or possible human, animal, and environmental health risks is long and diverse. Significant items include

- the introduction of novel or increased concentrations of toxicants and allergenic proteins in foods for human consumption;[72]

- the loss of food-source diversity due to concentration of global food production on a small number of highly engineered seeds and animals, with associated losses of other food and non-food genetic resources and compromises of potential sustainability;[73]
- deleterious secondary effects on animals that are modified to increase production of commercial products such as growth hormones;[74]
- the possibility that animals engineered for disease resistance will become reservoirs (carriers) of diseases to which humans are vulnerable;[75]
- the likely disruption of highly complex and ill-understood microbial communities on which "higher" life forms depend;[76]
- prospects for released transgenic plants becoming "superweeds" directly or though natural hybridization with indigenous plants;[77]
- damages from targeted pest insects that develop greater resistance to insecticides genetically introduced and incorporated into transgenic crops;[78] and
- the danger of fish hybridization and other ecological disruptions from transgenic fish that escape from aquaculture enclosures.[79]

Social, political, and economic issues center on concerns about the potential for inequitable distribution of the benefits, risks and other costs, and possible compromises of democratic choice opportunities for individuals and communities. It is widely expected that expanded reliance on biotechnology in agriculture will be accompanied by increasingly globalized food systems and increasingly concentrated multinational corporate control over the seed industry. This has stirred fears that small farmers and poor nations will face greater challenges, including reduced food self-sufficiency.[80] Other concerns in this category include damages to organic farming due to contamination of organic farming products through transgenic plant transfers, and due to enhanced resistance of insects to *Bacillus thuringienses*, the key non-chemical insecticide used in organic farming;[81] inadequate attention to the most desirable applications from a sustainability perspective (e.g., detoxification of hazardous wastes) because most innovation in the field is driven by corporate commercial objectives rather than commitment to the long-term public interest; basic conflicts of interest within government agencies playing the dual roles of regulators and promoters;[82] and denial of public choice due to refusals to label genetically modified foods.

Deep ethical concerns (philosophical, religious, or metaphysical) have also been raised in debates about food biotechnology. These include discomfort with what biotechnology does to the conception or boundaries of what is "natural," opposition to further commodification of animals, offences against religious or moral convictions, and perceptions that the interventions involved in genetic engineering go too far, in the sense that they introduce fundamental uncertainties with possibly enormous but unpredictable consequences.[83]

All these concerns involve uncertainties. In some cases, the key uncertainties are about the likelihood or potential severity of feared adverse effects. In others the main issues are whether the anticipated benefits will provide adequate compensation for the new costs and risks, especially for those most vulnerable to the negative side of biotechnology effects. There are also questions about whether regulatory intervention is the most appropriate response. While advocates and critics of biotechnology may claim to be confident about the significance or triviality of the risks involved, the independent and multi-stakeholder review bodies, which have the best claims to general credibility, have clearly recognized that the essential questions are about uncertainties and therefore choices.

The important choices include those to be made among the various available approaches to risk. The Royal Society Expert Panel, in particular, noted important differences among the available risk assessment options. Evaluations that simply trade off risks/costs against anticipated benefits, for example, are likely to be less conservative than approaches that judge some categories of risks, or risks over certain thresholds, to be unacceptable.[84] Similarly, comparative evaluations of individual transgenic and conventionally bred crops permit less ambitious responses than comparisons of alternative agricultural systems (e.g., industrial agriculture versus more sustainable low-input agriculture).[85]

Throughout its report, the Expert Panel stressed that the identification of potential risks is not purely a question of science:

> It is now generally recognized in the scholarly literature on the nature of risk analysis that many aspects of the task of assessing the magnitude of technological risks and managing them within the limits of safety involve judgments and decisions that are not themselves strictly scientific. They involve value judgments related to such issues as the appropriate way to handle uncertainties in scientific data and results, assignment of the burden of proof among stakeholders in risk issues, standards of proof, definition of the scope of the risk issue (e.g. should human error be considered part of the risk of the technology?), and, of course, the central issue ... of what levels of risk should be considered "acceptable."[86]

In face of the uncertain risks, the Expert Panel recommended adoption of a precautionary approach favoring avoidance of risks to human and environmental well-being, especially where the damages may be significant and irreversible, even where the evidence is indicative rather than fully persuasive.[87] It recognized, however, that there are competing possible approaches to precaution and that choices are involved in this as well.

Perhaps most significantly, both the Expert Panel and Canadian Biotechnology Advisory Committee reviews recognize that ethical issues are important factors to be addressed in biotechnology decision making. This is not an aberrant position on their parts. Ethical considerations have played a significant role not only in public debates on biotechnology but also in governmental deliberations. Canadian federal agencies and advisory bodies have assembled a sizable collection of detailed studies of ethical issues raised by biotechnology, and while the federal government is still wrestling with how best to respond to the social, political, and deep moral concerns listed above, it has clearly accepted that these are legitimate components of public policy deliberations on biotechnology.[88]

Thus on several grounds Canadian food biotechnology deliberations have brought us, or at least they represent, another step forward in the understanding of uncertainties. Three major lessons are evident—all of them about choices:

• *While great emphasis is placed on scientific knowledge, essentially all key issues involve choice; they require political and ethical decisions.* In biotechnology, with its evident disruptions of what is "natural," the role of moral choice may be easier to see. But recognizing it in this case encourages a more general awareness of the necessary link between uncertainty and choice.

• *A key set of choices centers on whether and how to adopt a precautionary approach in the face of uncertainty.* This too has been widely accepted in the public policy discussions on food biotechnology. While the meaning and implications of the precautionary principle are debated, the concept has been established in the language and agenda of regulation. Perhaps unwillingly and certainly despite their prevailing promotional inclinations, Canadian federal authorities have helped ensure rigorous consideration of the meaning of, and need for, a precautionary approach to biotechnology regulation.[89]

• *A precautionary approach to profound uncertainties may entail consideration of comprehensive, systemic alternatives as well as specific restrictions and adjustments.* In the food biotechnology case, the policy discussion has recognized broad choices—not just among particular options for approval or rejection, but also between different systems of agriculture. Much of the public debate has been framed as a choice between confidence in economic and scientific capabilities and a precautionary favoring of less invasive and ambitious approaches to nature and well-being. While such fundamentally contrasting options were presented in some earlier cases (for example, in the budworm debates when spray opponents proposed alternative approaches to forest management), the biotechnology debates have been remarkable for the extent of attention given to basic systemic choices, globally as well as nationally.

These observations are about the public policy debates on food biotechnology. The regulatory response so far has not met the standards of understanding and precaution set in the public debates or the independent reviews. The government continues to be a biotechnology booster. Recent public consultation documents have avoided attention to potential negative effects and have depicted public concerns about risks as the product of insufficient understanding.[90] The Expert Panel report criticized the existing regulatory and decision process for genetically modified food products for relying on ad hoc regulatory requirements, being overly focused on individual food constituents rather than whole foods, being inadequately clear about evaluative criteria, lacking independent peer review and public transparency, being open to inappropriate uses of standard risk assessment approaches, and tending to misuse the concept of "substantial equivalence" to permit approaches based on optimistic assumptions.[91] The Expert Panel also pointed to the weak base of ecological baseline information and independent research on biotechnology issues, due in part to the increasing commercialization of university-based scientific research on biotechnology.[92] Similarly, though less comprehensively, CBAC recommended greater transparency and public involvement, called for assessments that withstand the scrutiny of independent experts, and advocated precautionary actions, long-term monitoring, broader and more rigorous field-trial assessments, as well as attention to distributional effects and respect for traditional knowledge, religious beliefs, and other social and ethical issues.[93]

How much influence the recent reviews and public debates will have on regulatory practice remains to be seen. While the government's response to the Expert Panel's report and recommendations included some important commitments,[94] further discussions and implementation steps remain ahead. The test of progress in appreciation of uncertainty, however, does not rest wholly on immediate government response. It is significant enough that the public deliberations and the independent reviews have set a more advanced agenda.

CONCLUSIONS FROM THE FOUR CASES

The lead, budworm, acid rain, and biotechnology cases were both influential in their times and merely representative of a host of other environmental controversies. The four were chosen for discussion here in part because they reveal a range of uncertainty issues and span the past three decades in a way that permits consideration of how the understanding of uncertainties has evolved. But they are not atypical cases. Essentially the same findings would have emerged if, for example, mercury, forest fire, cod, and climate change had been chosen instead. Through the four cases and many similar experiences, large and small, understanding of uncertainty in Canadian environmental politics has expanded and deepened. While relevant adjustments to administrative practice have come more slowly, the results have certainly changed the context for environmental politics in this country, probably irreversibly.

The basic lessons have been about complexity, systemic interrelations, and choice. In all four cases, concerns about human health and ecological effects could not be resolved through science and other applied expertise alone. The key problems were not typified by simple cause-effect relations amenable to proofs beyond a reasonable doubt. In the lead case, sophisticated research eventually revealed the naiveté and arrogance of initial assurances of safety, showing that a suspected but difficult-to-prove problem was much more harmful than had been claimed. The budworm case presented a further stark lesson about how ecological systems (and our own interrelationships with them) are intricate and dynamic in non-linear ways, how this tends to frustrate simple, heavy-handed interventions, and how it might be easier to adjust our approaches to management to nature than to adjust nature to our managerial preferences. In the acid-rain battles, uncertainties in the science of biophysical effects were clearly intertwined with uncertainties of political strategy. On a matter of international significance, dramatic ecological effects and a range of other damages to health and property, difficulties of effect prediction, attribution, and evaluation were visibly treated as mere pawns in debates evidently rooted in conflicting political ideologies and interests. Finally in the food biotechnology deliberations, there are signs that the cumulative lessons from earlier experience have combined with instinctive concerns about a technology of unprecedented intrusion. Unlike the earlier controversies about appropriate reactions to existing problems, we now have, with biotechnology, anticipatory attention to possible effects that cannot possibly be predicted, or ruled out, with much confidence. The result has been a focus on precaution, complemented by at least the beginnings of awareness that the key choices involved may not be about particular applications and restrictions but about broad systemic alternatives—agriculture systems that are essentially global and manipulative, or ones characterized by diversity and adaptive capacity, or other broad approaches combining these two or otherwise designed to serve valued ends. Accordingly in the food biotechnology case, we are seeing explicit attention not just to the role of political choice but also to the foundations of such choice: that is, ethics.

Of course, the dynamic complexity of biophysical and social systems, the limitations of actual and possible knowledge, and the roles of political power and moral choice have been present throughout. What has changed, what continues to grow and deepen, is our awareness of these factors. This is to be celebrated. Nevertheless, the gains should not be overrated, since the challenges to be faced are also growing and deepening. The difficulties surrounding decisions about genetic engineering are clearly more daunting than those raised in the lead-poisoning era. And this is just an indication of the larger problem. The pace and scale of biospheric changes due to human activities are increasing, with consequent implications including greater complexity and uncertainty.[95]

For the administrative state none of this is good news. Simple solutions, expert authority, stable rules, specific mandates, and confidence in the basic path of progress are all undermined. A reality of dynamic, systemic complexity demands integrated, flexible, and adaptive response. Pervasive uncertainty demands open and deliberative decision making. Unavoidable choice demands explicit critical attention to the distribution of power and advantage, and to the fundamental values involved. At the same time, it is clear that more or less authoritative and administrative organizations are here to stay. They are necessary in any conceivably viable future. Certainly reliance on custom, market exchange and conscious moral decision—the other main options—will not be sufficient. The question, then, is how the necessary accommodations will be made.

NOTES

1 C.C. Lax, "The Toronto Lead-Smelter Controversy," in William Leiss, ed., *Ecology versus Politics in Canada* (Toronto: University of Toronto Press, 1979), p. 58.

2 Barbara Wallace and Kathy Cooper, *The Citizen's Guide to Lead: Uncovering a Hidden Health Hazard* (Toronto: NC Press, 1986), pp. 5–11.

3 Joel Schwartz *et al., Costs and Benefits of Reducing Lead in Gasoline: Final Regulatory Impact Analysis* (Washington, DC: US EPA Office of Policy Analysis, Feb. 1985).

4 World Health Organization, *Guidelines for Drinking Water Quality*, 2nd ed., vol. 2, *Health Criteria and other Supporting Information* (Geneva: WHO, 1996), pp. 254–75; see also Ontario Ministry of the Environment and Energy, *Scientific Criteria Document for Multimedia Environmental Standards Development—Lead* (Toronto, MOEE, 1994).

5 Ross Howard, *Poisons in Public: Case Studies of Environmental Pollution in Canada* (Toronto: Lorimer, 1980), p. 98.

6 The conflict is described in Beth Savan, "Sleazy Science," *Alternatives* 13.2(April 1986): 13–15.

7 Howard, *Poisons in Public*, pp. 104-105; C.C. Lax, "The Toronto Lead-Smelter Controversy," pp. 62–64.

8 Russel Boyd to the Toronto Board of Health, April 1979, reported in Howard, *Poisons in Public*, p.123.

9 Howard, *Poisons in Public*, pp. 96–130; C.C. Lax, "The Toronto Lead -Smelter Controversy," pp. 58–63.

10 Gordon Baskerville, "The Forestry Problem: Adaptive Lurches of Renewal," in Lance H. Gunderson, C.S. Holling, and Stephen S. Light, eds., *Barriers and Bridges to the Renewal of Ecosystems and Institutions* (New York: Columbia University Press, 1995), p. 46.

11 C.S. Holling and Lance H. Gunderson, "Resilience and Adaptive Cycles," in Lance H. Gunderson and C.S. Holling, eds., *Panarchy: Understanding Transformations in Human and Natural Systems* (Washington, DC: Island, 2002), p. 30.

12 Elizabeth May, *Budworm Battles: The Fight to Stop the Aerial Insecticide Spraying of the Forests of Eastern Canada* (Halifax: Four East Publications, 1982), p. 74.

13 Baskerville, "The Forestry Problem," p. 51.

14 Baskerville, "The Forestry Problem," p. 52.

15 Baskerville, "The Forestry Problem," p. 69.

16 See, for example, May, *Budworm Battles*; Howard, *Poisons in Public*, pp. 43–70.

17 Baskerville, "The Forestry Problem," p. 55.

18 Baskerville, "The Forestry Problem," esp. pp. 60–67.

19 Baskerville, "The Forestry Problem," pp. 57–58.

20 Baskerville, "The Forestry Problem," pp. 62–63.

21 See, for example, May, *Budworm Battle*, p. 48.

22 There was already evidence of overcapacity in the New Brunswick forest industry, especially due to the impending shortage of spruce sawlogs. Baskerville, "The Forestry Problem," p. 80, reports, "Forecasts indicated the forest could continuously support about 80% of installed capacity."

23 Baskerville, "The Forestry Problem," pp. 78–85.

24 Baskerville, "The Forestry Problem," pp. 85–87.

25 "Establishing a real intersection of what is biologically possible with what is socially acceptable in terms of goals remains a major problem." Baskerville, "The Forestry Problem," p. 87.

26 Baskerville, "The Forestry Problem," p. 88.

27 Baskerville, "The Forestry Problem," p. 89.

28 C.S. Holling, "What Barriers? What Bridges?," in Gunderson *et al.*, eds., *Barriers and Bridges*, p. 8.

29 Holling, "What Barriers?," p. 8; Holling and Gunderson, "Resilience and Adaptive Cycles," p. 30.

30 Major examples of environmental problem solving requiring broader definition of initial concerns have included shifts from garbage-dump replacement to waste management, and from electricity generation to energy demand-and-supply management.

31 "Acid rain" is the popular shorthand for wet and dry deposition of acids or acidifying compounds originating from anthropogenic emissions. Sulfur and nitrogen oxide emissions are the chief contributors, but many pollutants and pathways are involved.

32 Ross Howard and Michael Perley, *Acid Rain: The North American Forecast* (Toronto: Anansi, 1980), pp. 124–25.

33 John McCormick, *Acid Earth: The Global Threat of Acid Pollution* (London: Earthscan, 1985), p. 70.

34 McCormick, *Acid Earth,* pp. 86–100.

35 R.J. Beamish and H.H. Harvey, "Acidification of the La Cloche Mountain Lakes, Ontario, and Resulting Fish Mortalities," *Journal of the Fisheries Research Board of Canada* 29(1972): 1131–43.

36 Howard and Perley, *Acid Rain,* p. 29.

37 For the North American evidence see, e.g., United States-Canada Memorandum of Intent on Transboundary Air Pollution, *Interim Report* (Feb. 1981), report of Work Group 1, Impact Assessment; for the European evidence see, e.g., L.N. Overrein *et al., Acid Precipitation: Effects on Forest and Fish,* final report of the SNSF project 1972–1980 (Oslo, Dec. 1980).

38 See Canada, House of Commons Sub-Committee on Acid Rain, *Still Waters: The Chilling Reality of Acid Rain* (Ottawa: 1981).

39 Dr. Warner's statement is quoted in Ontario Legislature Standing Committee on Resources Development, *Final Report on Acidic Precipitation, Abatement of Emissions from the International Nickel Company Operations at Sudbury, Pollution Control in the Pulp and Paper Industry, and Pollution Abatement at the Reed Paper Mill in Dryden* (Toronto, Oct. 1979), p. 25. See also Walter Curlook (president and chief executive officer, Inco Metals Company), "Remarks at the Ontario Ministry of the Environmental Public Meeting to Discuss Proposed Control Order" (Sudbury, 4 June 1980).

A similar statement was made four years later in the UK by Lord Marshall, the head of Britain's electric power utility: "Since electricity is essential for everyone, this [costly requirements to cut emissions from thermal electric generating plants] will effectively lower everyone's standard of living and it would be tragic to do this without understanding exactly what we are accomplishing." Qtd. in McCormick, *Acid Earth,* p. 90.

40 A survey of the complexities was provided by, e.g., D. Drablos and A. Tollan, eds., *Ecological Impact of Acid Precipitation,* proceedings of an international conference, Sandefjord, Norway, 11–14 March 1980 (Oslo, Oct. 1980). A more narrowly focused examination of these problems with reference to one category of emissions sources is provided in Brian E. Felske and Associates Ltd., *Sulphur Dioxide Regulation and the Canadian Nonferrous Metals Industry* (Ottawa: Economic Council of Canada Technical Report No. 3, 1981), esp. chs. 2, 9.

41 Canada, *Supporting Document for the Canada-Wide Acid Rain Strategy for Post-2000* (Halifax: Federal/Provincial/Territorial Ministers of Energy and Environment, 19 Oct. 1998), p. 8.

42 Charles T. Driscoll, G.B. Lawrence, A.J. Bulger, T.J. Butler, C.S. Cronan, C. Eagar, K.F. Lambert, G.E. Likens, J.L. Stocklard, and K.C. Weathers, *Acid Rain Revisited: Advances in Scientific Understanding since the Passage of the 1970 and 1990 Clean Air Act Amendments* (Hanover, NH: Hubbard Brook Research Foundation/Science Links, 2001), p. 11.

43 By the 1980s there was research certainty on the long-distance transport of acidifying pollutants. Abnormally acidic precipitation had been identified thousands of kilometers from contributory sulfur and nitrogen oxide emission sources. The many major and countless minor sources were located in and subject to a variety of jurisdictions and

some of the most serious deposition effects were in areas distant from the emission sources. Consequently, abatement efforts in jurisdictions with major emission sources might have limited domestic benefit while environmental protection efforts in areas vulnerable to acid rain damages might be ineffective in the absence of concerted action in upwind source areas. On the long-range transport of these pollutants see, e.g., Organization for Economic Cooperation and Development, *The OECD Programme on Long Range Transport of Air Pollutants: Measurements and Findings* (Paris, 1977), and United States-Canada Memorandum of Intent on Transboundary Air Pollution, *Interim Report* (Feb. 1981), Report of Work Group 2, Atmospheric Modelling. On variable vulnerabilities and the need for concerted action see, e.g., Sub-Committee on Acid Rain, *Still Waters,* esp. pp. 14–16.

44 The 1970 order was issued in response to the local effects of sulfur dioxide emissions. More distant acid-rain effects were not then considered.

45 See Felske, *Sulphur Dioxide Regulation,* pp. 159–65; Ontario Standing Committee on Resources Development, *Final Report on Acidic Precipitation,* pp. 37–39, 50; and Howard and Perley, *Acid Rain,* pp. 133–46.

46 Ontario was no less hesitant to insist on maximum feasible abatement of emissions from other major sources, including Ontario Hydro's coal-fired generating plants. See Howard and Perley, *Acid Rain,* pp. 129–33; Sub-Committee on Acid Rain, *Final Report on Acidic Precipitation,* p. 40.

47 See Andrew R. Thompson, *Environmental Regulation in Canada* (Vancouver: Westwater Research Centre, 1981), esp. pp. 33–41; and Howard and Perley, *Acid Rain,* pp. 153-60.

48 McCormick, *Acid Earth,* pp. 148–51.

49 David W. Schindler, "A View of NAPAP from North of the Border," *Ecological Applications* 2.2(1992): 124–30.

50 The archives of the Canadian Coalition on Acid Rain are now housed in the University of Waterloo library. See <http://www.lib.uwaterloo.ca/discipline/SpecColl/acid/index.html>.

51 Canada, *Supporting Document,* p. 2.

52 Canada, *Supporting Document,* pp. 2-3.

53 United States National Science and Technology Council Committee on Environment and Natural Resources, *National Acid Precipitation Assessment Program Biennial Report to Congress: An Integrated Assessment* (Silver Spring, MD: NAPAP, May 1998), executive summary; <http://www.nnic.noaa.gov/CENR/NAPAP/NAPAP_96.htm>.

54 Howard and Perley, *Acid Rain,* pp. 122, 138.

55 See Inco Limited, News Release, "Inco Proposes CDN\$100 Million Investment for a 34 Percent SO2 Reduction in Sudbury," 7 Sept. 2001. <http://www.inco.com/mediacentre/news/default.asp?posting_id=612>. Ontario Ministry of the Environment, News Release, "Sulphur Dioxide Emission Reductions: INCO and Falconbridge ordered to reduce total emissions and ground level concentrations," 6 Sept. 2001; <http://www.ene.gov.on.ca:80/envision/news/090701mb.htm>.

56 Driscoll *et al.*, *Acid Rain Revisited,* p. 21.

57 B.A. Ackermann and W.T. Hassler, *Clean Coal/Dirty Air* (New Haven, CT: Yale University Press, 1981), p. 1.

58 Even on concerns such as urban sprawl and water quality where little explicit international effort has been apparent, global-scale learning has played an important role.

59 Royal Society of Canada Expert Panel on the Future of Food Biotechnology, Conrad Brunk and Brian Ellis, co-chairs, *Elements of Precaution: Recommendations for the Regulation of Food Biotechnology in Canada,* prepared at the request of Health Canada, Canadian Food Inspection Agency and Environment Canada (Ottawa: Royal Society of Canada, 2001) <http://www.rsc.ca/english/index.html>, pp. 24–29; Canadian Biotechnology Advisory Committee, *Improving the Regulation of Genetically Modified Foods and other Novel Foods in Canada: report to the Government of Canada Biotechnology Ministerial Coordinating Committee* (Ottawa: CBAC, Aug. 2002); <http://www.cbac-

cccb.ca/documents/en/cbac.report.pdf>, annex 3; United States National Resource Council, Board on Agricultural and Natural Resources, Board on Life Sciences, *Animal Biotechnology: Science Based Concerns* (Washington, DC: National Academies Press, 2002), especially ch. 1 and 5 (pre-publication version: <http://books.nap.edu/books/0309084393/html/index.html>).

60   RSC Expert Panel, *Elements of Precaution,* pp. 20–21, 24ff.; CBAC, *Improving the Regulation,* annex 3.

61   RSC Expert Panel, *Elements of Precaution,* pp. 23–24; CBAC, *Improving the Regulation,* annex 3; Eileen Choffnes, "Bioweapons: New Labs, More Terror?," *Bulletin of the Atomic Scientists* 58.5(Sept./Oct. 2002), pp. 28–32.

62   Roger Wrubel, "The Promise and Problems of Herbicide-resistant Crops," *Technology Review* (May/June 1994), pp. 57–61.

63   The Medical Research Council of Canada had issued safety guidelines for laboratory experiments involving genetic engineering in 1977, but broader deliberations came later. One early document was the Science Council of Canada's 1980 report, J. Miller *et al.*, *Biotechnology in Canada: Promises and Concerns.* The Science Council followed this in 1984 with a report looking particularly at genetic modification of food crop seeds: T.F. Funk, *Examination of Policy Issues Related to the Adoption of Biotechnology Research by the Canadian Seed Industry* (Ottawa: Science Council of Canada, 1984).

64   The new strategy was approved in principle in early 1993 (see Government of Canada, "Federal Government Agrees on New Regulatory Framework for Biotechnology," News Release, 11 Jan. 1993, plus "Backgrounder: A Federal Regulatory Framework for Biotechnology") and formally announced in 1998 (see Government of Canada, "Federal Government releases new Biotechnology Strategy," News Release, 6 Aug. 1998). See also RSC Expert Panel, *Elements of Precaution*, ch. 2.

65   Government of Canada, "Federal Government Agrees on New Regulatory Framework."

66   Care, experience, and regulation have reduced some concerns about laboratory and controlled environment work with genetically modified organisms, such as recombinant microbes in the fermentation industry. Concerns about open environment releases, potential human health effects, and broad ecological and socio-economic implications have generally expanded. See RSC Expert Panel, *Elements of Precaution,* p. 34.

67   RSC Expert Panel, *Elements of Precaution,* pp. 14, 20–22.

68   The members of these two bodies are listed in their respective reports. See CBAC, *Improving the Regulation*, p. iv; and RSC Expert Panel, *Elements of Precaution,* opening page. CBAC, established in 1999, replaced an earlier federal advisory committee that included only executives of biotechnology companies and university researchers in the field.

69   The Committee members were H. Rocke Robertson, former principal of McGill University; Donald Chant, the University of Toronto zoologist who founded Pollution Probe; and Frank DeMarco, dean of engineering at the University of Windsor. See Lax, "The Toronto Lead-Smelter Controversy," pp. 65–69, 71.

70   Howard A. Schneiderman and Will D. Carpenter, "Planetary Patriotism: Sustainable Agriculture for the Future," *Environmental Science and Technology* 24.4(April 1990), pp. 466–73.

71   RSC Expert Panel, *Elements of Precaution*, p. 3. The Expert Panel respected its mandate to focus on "human, animal and environmental health" concerns, but recognized that "they are only a small part of the debate. There are also the other categories of important questions having to do with the economic costs and benefits of agricultural biotechnology, the social impacts on societies at different stages of technological and social development, environmental and social ethics, as well as deeply held philosophical and religious convictions about human interventions in nature" (p. 4). A similarly broad range of issues was recognized by the Canadian Biotechnology Advisory Committee, *Improving the Regulation*, pp. 43–47.

72 RSC Expert Panel, *Elements of Precaution*, pp. 44–74, 82-84.
73 RSC Expert Panel, *Elements of Precaution*, pp. 94–95; 129–31.
74 RSC Expert Panel, *Elements of Precaution*, pp. 87ff., found such effects on "morphol-ogy, respiratory capacity and locomotion" are the rule in the case of fish. The most reported concerns have surrounded use of engineered bovine somatotropin (rBST) in dairy cattle to enhance milk production. See, for example, Tony Hiss, "How Now, Drugged Cow?," *Harper's Magazine* 289 (Oct. 1994), pp. 80–90. Also RSC Expert Panel, *Elements of Precaution*, pp. 100–101.
75 RSC Expert Panel, *Elements of Precaution*, pp. 93–95.
76 RSC Expert Panel, *Elements of Precaution*, pp. 107–15.
77 RSC Expert Panel, *Elements of Precaution*, pp. 121–32. In the prairie provinces, canola cultivars engineered for resistance to various herbicides have individually and as hybrids already become a significant weed problem (RSC Expert Panel, *Elements of Precaution*, p. 122).
78 RSC Expert Panel, *Elements of Precaution*, pp. 139-41.
79 RSC Expert Panel, *Elements of Precaution*, pp. 150-70.
80 RSC Expert Panel, *Elements of Precaution*, p. 5.
81 RSC Expert Panel, *Elements of Precaution*, pp. 127, 139.
82 Michael McDonald, *Biotechnology, Ethics and Government: A Synthesis*, prepared for the Canadian Biotechnology Advisory Committee, Project Steering Committee on Incor-porating Social and Ethical Considerations into Biotechnology (Oct. 2000) <http://www.cbac-cccb.ca/english/ethical/sections.aro?exp=Research>, p. 2.
83 Ethical concerns raised in papers prepared for the federal government in the late 1990s are surveyed in McDonald, *Biotechnology, Ethics and Government*; see also RSC Expert Panel, *Elements of Precaution*, pp. 6–7, 93.
84 RSC Expert Panel, *Elements of Precaution*, p. 5.
85 RSC Expert Panel, *Elements of Precaution*, p. 29.
86 RSC Expert Panel, *Elements of Precaution*, p. 8.
87 RSC Expert Panel, *Elements of Precaution*, pp. 194–207.
88 This is not peculiar to Canada. In a discussion of "fourth-hurdle" public policy concerns about proposed products (in addition to safety, quality, and efficacy), McDonald (*Biotechnology, Ethics and Government*, p. 19) notes that distribution, equity, and com-munity interest considerations are receiving increased attention, including incorporation in Norwegian biotechnology legislation.
89 See, especially, Canada, *A Canadian Perspective on the Precautionary Approach/Princi-ple: Discussion Document* (Ottawa, Sept. 2001); and a response: Stuart Lee and Kather-ine Barrett, "Comments on *A Canadian Perspective on the Precautionary Approach/ Principle: Discussion Document*" (Science and Environmental Health Network, 28 March 2002); <http://www.sehn.org/canpre.html>.
90 See Susan Sherwin, *Towards an Adequate Ethical Framework for Setting Biotechnology Policy*, prepared for the Canadian Biotechnology Advisory Committee, Stewardship Standing Committee (Ottawa: CBAC, Jan. 2001), pp. 4–5, 14 <http://www.cbac-cccb.ca/english/ethical/sections.aro?exp=Research>.
91 RSC Expert Panel, *Elements of Precaution*, pp. 36–38, 47–48, 165, 177–91, 211–18.
92 RSC Expert Panel, *Elements of Precaution*, pp. 190, 215–17.
93 CBAC, *Improving the Regulation*, pp. 14–48.
94 Canada, "Action Plan of the Government of Canada in response to the Royal Society of Canada Expert Panel Report, *Elements of Precaution: Recommendations for the Regula-tion of Food Biotechnology in Canada*," 23 Nov. 2001.
95 Gilberto C. Gallopín, Silvio Funtowicz, Martin O'Connor, and Jerry Ravetz, "Science for the Twenty-First Century: From Social Contract to the Scientific Core," *International Journal of Social Science* 168(2001): 219–29.

10

Environmental Politics and Policy Professionalism: Agenda Setting, Problem Definition, and Epistemology

Douglas Torgerson

Environmentalism has emerged as a dissident social movement, throwing into question comfortable assumptions about progress that have sustained the pattern of development characteristic of the advanced industrial order. Through the combination of its reformist as well as radical tendencies, environmental politics has made a mark on the contemporary political landscape, affecting not only the terms of public discourse, but also key features of the policy process. In a pattern that may hold for other social movements as well, environmentalism has worked an influence on the world of policy professionalism, shaping the focus of attention in three related, though distinguishable, ways: through *agenda setting*, *problem definition*, and *epistemology*.[1] The setting of the policy agenda is a question of which matters, out of many possibilities, become focal issues and which matters are instead screened out. Defining a policy problem has to do with the particular way in which attention is focused, that is, with the perspective that frames a problem and thus sets the range of solutions that can be imagined or legitimately entertained. Epistemology, finally, concerns what is to be deemed relevant and warranted knowledge in the policy process, a consideration that in turn influences both agenda setting and problem definition. In this chapter, we will examine the advent of environmentalism in terms of this tripartite scheme, focusing particular attention on the emergence of the issue of toxic waste.

Despite its prevailing image as a technocratic enterprise, policy professionalism has long harbored internal differences of method and commitment, and these have become increasingly visible against the backdrop of dissident social movements.[2] Inclined in favor of affiliation with established order, policy professionalism might appear irrevocably at odds with any dissident orientation. Indeed, the background to the advent of policy professionalism is clearly marked by a wish to prevent the fearful consequences of disruptive social tensions. Nonetheless, professional policy theory and practice now contain significant anti-technocratic and anti-scientistic tendencies that are congruent with the goal of expanding participation in policy deliberations while promoting democratic political and social life.[3]

In terms of agenda setting, the environmental movement brought to attention general concerns, specific issues, and particular elements of evidence typically ignored or neglected by the industrialism characteristic of policy professionalism and conventional perspectives generally. Environmentalism also introduced distinctive ways of framing and defining policy problems, amounting to what might be termed environmentalist problem *re*definition. Finally, the environmental movement has provoked epistemological controversy to challenge prevailing conventions and suggest new, or at least revised, standards as to what can legitimately count as relevant evidence and knowledge in the policy process.

POLICY PROFESSIONALISM
AND ENVIRONMENTALIST DISSENT

A festive, unruly atmosphere characterized the first Earth Day in 1970, as environmentalism made a dramatic entry into the political spotlight of advanced industrial society.[4] The event evoked fears of ecological catastrophe but also brought hopeful visions of nature and humanity in harmony. Convinced that the direction of advanced industrial society was significantly flawed, environmentalists debated the options of radical action or reform but generally shared a concern that their efforts could fall prey to co-optation by the prevailing institutions of government and industry. Indeed, many sharply oppositional features of environmentalism were smoothed over as the 1970s advanced.

Government confidently portrayed new rules and agencies as the solution to the environmental crisis, industry vigorously defended itself against disturbing demands, and the domain of environmental professionalism grew significantly. The core of this institutional response to environmentalism, as Samuel Hays has emphasized, was a call to reason: contentious environmental politics, supposedly a source of irrationality and policy stalemate, should give way to "centralized direction by technical experts"[5] who would provide "the central language of public discourse over environmental policy."[6]

Voices of a dissident environmentalism were constrained by a language of policy professionalism. As a leading primer in the field declares, policy analysis provides "a discipline for working within a political and economic system, not for changing it."[7] Policy professionalism is mainly concerned with making "minor adjustments in existing mechanisms."[8] This narrow focus is useful, it has been claimed, because "expertise and decision-making technologies" have become necessary for a "technical process of government" ruling out public participation: "It is clearly a job for experts and for all the sophisticated information handling and management techniques that can be brought to bear on it."[9] In his critique of the disciplinary foundations of policy professionalism, Laurence Tribe emphasized its attachment to an "objectivist ideal" and its reliance upon an "antiseptic terminology" tending to reinforce an image of neutrality and to anesthetize moral feeling: "To facilitate detached thought and impersonal deliberation, what more plausible path could there be than to employ a bloodless idiom, one as drained as possible of all emotion?"[10] In the professional focus, then, there is a foreshortening of perspective, in which moral, political, and historical contexts are thrown out of proportion. Professional policy discourse provides an adjunct to established order, facing its problems and speaking its language.

The professional orientation tends to constrain those elements of environmentalism that would draw attention to new problems and would speak a new language. The professional world of environmental policy nonetheless expanded and became institutionalized in a manner that reflected as well as resisted the influence of environmentalist dissent. Dissident environmentalism has not simply been constrained by policy professionalism, that is, but has worked its own influence on the world of the policy professional. This influence is most obvious in that environmentalist concern has been firmly institutionalized on the agenda of public policy deliberations. Once the environment made it onto the agenda of policy processes in advanced industrial society, environmentalist challenges were in the offing as well at the levels of problem definition and epistemology.

AGENDA SETTING:
ENVIRONMENT BECOMES AN ISSUE

Although the administrative state has consistently adopted policies to advance the cause of industrialization, relatively little attention was given to the environmental consequences of these policies until the emerging environmental movement made it into the public spotlight in the late 1960s. Earth Day, as inaugurated in 1970, marked a culmination of extraordinary environmentalist agitation and legislative response that saw unlikely public figures suddenly seem eager to support the environmentalist cause, though not always for long.[11] The environment had made it high onto the public policy agenda in dramatic fashion, but the question remained as to how long this prominence would last.[12]

From an environmentalist perspective, the environment constituted an enormous blind spot for industrialization. Placing the environment securely on the policy agenda meant somehow institutionalizing a focus on the environment. Changes in the state administrative apparatus helped to serve this purpose by placing the "environmental" symbol prominently in the titles and mandates of agencies that were either entirely new or created by a realignment of previously existing administrative units. Another chief means to the end of keeping a focus on the environment was environmental impact assessment, a visible influence of environmentalism on procedures in public policy.

Although environmental impact assessment—and related innovations such as technology assessment and social impact assessment—have often been appropriately criticized for a propensity to become little more than technocratic rituals, these practices are not always easily contained. They bring attention in a routine way to matters that before would have remained invisible, and this altered focus of attention has the potential to influence the flow of policy considerations while promoting entry to the process of interests and perspectives that would previously have been excluded.[13] Environmental impact assessment has thus been described as a "worm in the brain," as possessing the "subversive" potential[14] of "making bureaucracies think."[15]

Once the environment becomes an issue, there remains the question of what particular problems are to be addressed. How is *environment* to be understood? By the time of the first Earth Day, concern was primarily focused on air- and water-pollution issues. The following decades, however, were to witness a burgeoning of the range of environmental issues, many related to new industrial processes and consumer products emerging in the postwar era.[16] Early environmentalist moves, both in terms of popular agitation and public policy, remained marked by an industrialist tendency toward linear thinking and narrowly conceived solutions. Attention was focused on the "end of the pipe," on installing filters on existing equipment or finding ways of diluting pollution. Little focus yet was directed to the redesign of techniques and activities in light of wider patterns and cycles of eco-systemic relationships. Greater attention turned in this direction as new environmental issues began to crowd onto the policy agenda.

Of the new issues, one of the most striking was that of toxic wastes. This largely remained a non-issue throughout the early rise of the environmental movement and the institutionalization of an environmental focus in public policy: "Early air-and water-pollution laws were debated and enacted without awareness or consideration of what to do with the waste materials once we stopped dumping them in the air and water."[17] Nonetheless, hardly more than a decade after the first Earth Day, Al Gore could call the toxic waste problem "the centerpiece of the environmental movement."[18] During the 1970s, a number of environmentally concerned legislators in the United States were effective in passing pieces of legislation relevant to toxic waste management.[19] However, there was little public attention to the issue and little administrative inclination toward effective enforcement. In a 1980 speech recalling the early days of the Environmental Protection Agency (EPA), a senior official gave this portrayal:

Few seemed to care, within or outside of EPA. That included the major public interest groups or the environmental community which were still apparently intoxicated by the bold regulatory moves in air and water pollution which engaged the passions and interests of the leaders of the new Agency.

That was the way it was ... not many people gave a damn about waste, hazardous or otherwise.[20]

The disposal of toxic wastes did not become a major concern until after 1978 when, especially with the citizen activism and publicity surrounding the case of Love Canal, past practices of toxic waste storage and disposal were drawn sharply into question. The toxic waste problem entered dramatically onto the public agenda, as a grassroots anti-toxics movement emerged and public officials began to respond.[21] There remained a question, however, of how the toxic waste problem was to be defined.

PROBLEM DEFINITION:
THE CASE OF TOXIC WASTES

Environmentalism contains a propensity not only to recognize, but also to define problems in ways that depart from prevailing tendencies in policy professionalism. Environmentalist problem definition—or, more to the point, redefinition—proceeds from a focus on complexity, particularly on the interdependent and cyclical features of natural systems. Similarly, such problem redefinition is often characterized (in a manner similar to creative problem solving) by the reversal of a key relationship in the formulation of the problem. Prominent examples of such reversal in environmentalist problem redefinition are to be found in Rachel Carson and Amory Lovins, both of whom advocated changes in policy orientation. For pest control, Carson counseled reliance upon the complexity of biological systems rather than upon a reduction of complexity with poison chemicals.[22] In crafting his idea of a "soft path," Lovins redefined the energy problem as one that called chiefly for enhancing efficiency rather than increasing supply.[23]

Environmentalist problem definition can further be illustrated concretely by examining the case of toxic wastes. Focusing attention on toxic wastes itself constituted a significant reframing of environmental problems. Yet, even as toxic wastes emerged prominently on the policy agenda, the characteristic policy response amounted largely to an extension of past practice. The problem, that is, remained defined primarily in terms of disposal. The environmentalist response reversed a key relationship by asking first not where and how to dispose of wastes, but how to reduce them to a minimum at source and then how to reuse and recycle them.

There was, of course, good reason to promote better disposal. The past had seen some extraordinary mismanagement in the disposal of toxic wastes: "corporate managers, in companies large and small, strong and weak, ... chose to abandon wastes all over the countryside. When they have been apprehended, their defense has been that, however bad their practices were, they were established and standard at that time."[24] Of course, not only were corporations involved here; so too were government officials, who were inclined to see toxic wastes "as an insignificant after-effect of industrial production." Before Love Canal, governmental attention to toxic wastes was a matter of "random competence and interest": "Officials working on the problem of toxic wastes struggled unnoticed and often alone."[25] The upshot was a *de facto* public policy allowing industry to avoid the costs of careful disposal.[26]

As toxic wastes came onto the public policy agenda, it became apparent that past disposal practices had generated a massive problem, a lapse in administrative control that ran against common expectations of how the industrial world was supposed to develop. Re-establishing a smooth pattern of industrial development meant a massive, expensive project of finding and cleaning up past mistakes[27] while making sure that future disposal practices would be methodically planned and controlled. How the future was to differ from the past was, nonetheless, basically simple: disposal would now receive much more careful attention and would be addressed with more effective techniques.

With this form of problem definition, a major difficulty emerged to confront policy professionals, who typically encounter great resistance when attempting to site improved hazardous waste treatment and disposal facilities. The situation has spawned a vast policy literature on the NIMBY (not-in-my-backyard) Syndrome and related administrative frustrations: "From a managerial perspective, ... protestors are simply incapable of appreciating the information they are being given.... The typical remedy ... is the injection of greater expertise into the policy process...."[28] Resistance to siting proposals is typically portrayed as a threat both to sound governance and to environmental quality. Those who resist facility siting are pictured as emotional, self-interested minorities imposing their will on the majority. Toxic wastes are an inevitable by-product of industrial society, an unavoidable price all must pay for its benefits. The question is how to build new, technically sophisticated treatment and disposal facilities as expeditiously as possible.

Opposition to the siting of new facilities can, however, lay claim to its own rationality. Since the past record of toxic waste management shows a glaring ineffectiveness, residents can offer significant reasons why they should doubt the competence and commitment of those who propose a disposal site in their area. The difficulty is exacerbated by the fact that professionals can no longer simply rely upon unchallengeable claims that they know best, for they have no monopoly on the relevant knowledge. The members of effectively organized and sophisticated environmental groups now have the capacity to uncover errors and weaknesses in site plans. Indeed, they "have frequently shown that the industry has simply not done its technical homework."[29] Moreover, environmentalists can readily point to a preoccupation with disposal as evidence of a conventional blind spot symptomatic of the perspective which, guiding the path of industrialization to date, helped to turn toxic waste into a major problem in the first place.

By taking the generation and disposal of wastes for granted, the industrialist perspective ignores the potential that environmentalists claim for reduction, reuse, and recycling. In opposing particular siting decisions, both environmental activists and local residents can thus appeal to the rationality of a more coherently designed system of industrial processes and products in which toxic materials would not typically end up as wastes creating significant disposal problems. The guiding idea would be "to integrate the waste fully into the web of industrial relationships."[30] Designing and implementing such a system becomes, from this viewpoint, the real problem—while preoccupation with disposal is seen as an extension of past errors and a convenient way to ignore the real problem.

An environmentalist redefinition of the toxic waste problem is supported by an historical focus on how toxic wastes were created and neglected as industry advanced. While administrative organizations, both public and private, proceeded under the banner of reason and progress, the full nature and consequences of their activities obviously escaped attention and control. How might the problem of toxic wastes—and its attendant dangers and costs—have been avoided in the first place? Asking this question not only renders dubious the past rationality of the administrative organizations that have presided over the process of industrialization, but also suggests a problem orientation for the future: how to reform the industrial system so as to dispose safely of toxic wastes while also minimizing the generation of such wastes. In advancing this orientation, environmentalism questions the conventional fixation on disposal and redefines the toxic waste problem particularly in terms of reduction. Redefining the problem in this way follows the general environmentalist focus on interdependencies—a focus that brings activities and relationships to attention in terms of cyclical and eco-systemic patterns.[31]

The environmentalist definition of the toxic waste problem was long neglected by the professional approach.[32] In order to focus fully on the problem in environmentalist terms, indeed, professionalism would have to escape an orientation rooted deeply in the institutions of advanced industrial society. A partial impetus in this direction has, nonetheless, been supplied by comprehensive systems concepts of environmental management that have been advanced in recent decades. Another impetus for movement in this direction has been citizen resistance to toxic waste management proposals. In this regard, the supposed emotionalism of the NIMBY Syndrome may provide an opportunity for a more "rational" response to the toxic waste problem than professionalism could achieve if left to its own devices.[33]

Environmentalism does not deny that safe disposal is an immediate concern, given the past accumulation of wastes and a mode of economic activity that routinely adds to it. The question is how necessary attention to disposal can be combined with significant attention to—even an emphasis on—reduction. The conventional outlook typically ignores the fact that any program for the disposal of toxic wastes is unavoidably related to the future generation of such wastes. How such a program is designed is liable to either discourage or encourage the generation of wastes. Implicit in past practice was a policy of setting the costs, to be borne by the generator for toxic waste disposal, at virtually nil. The environmentalist redefinition of the problem seeks to avoid this. A focus on reduction rather than disposal in problem definition promotes a planning orientation that would see significant costs of toxic wastes borne by producers in order to promote a decisive break with past practices.[34]

EPISTEMOLOGY: THE CHALLENGE TO SCIENTISM

Groups at the grassroots level, expanding into a coherent anti-toxics movement in the wake of Love Canal, have been able to point out clear evidence of public and private mismanagement of toxic wastes. It is obvious that no one was really in control or knew what was happening: "government knew very little about the magnitude of the hazardous waste problem as it embarked upon regulating it."[35] At the same time, these groups have widely protested dangers arising from exposure to toxic concentrations in the environment. Here, however, the grounds for protest have not been so clear-cut. Indeed, the dangers claimed by these groups have not generally been supported by scientific research based upon established presuppositions.[36]

One possible response to the situation would be for anti-toxic groups to fold their tents, admit they have been wrong or alarmist, just as many policy professionals might like to think. Another response would be to exalt the role of common sense and community-based experience, to hold that these—not scientifically grounded expertise—possess the "definitive wisdom."[37] In examining this situation, Sylvia Tesh has drawn the conclusion not that environmental concerns have here failed the test of science, or that direct experiential knowledge can lay claim to the final word. Instead, she re-examines science from an environmentalist perspective, arguing that common-sense understandings of the world permeate scientific practice.[38] Here environmentalism reinforces the insight that notions of legitimate knowledge emerge from a social context, that modern science specifically is a social construction in which both questions and answers are influenced by implicit assumptions.[39]

Tesh maintains that, in assessing environmentalist concerns, epidemiology has been marked by assumptions of a "pre-environmentalist" cultural context conducive to industrial development: "In standard epidemiological practice the questions one asks, the studies one designs, the rules of evidence one obeys, and the interpretation one gives to results all start from the pre-environmentalist premise that the ambient environment is healthful and the scientist's task is to look for evidence to the contrary."[40] This pre-environmentalist premise itself, however, is not a scientific finding, but a matter of common sense—precisely the type of common sense that has supported the advance of industrialization. Environmentalism challenges this common sense with a perspective that could provide a different orientation for epidemiological practice—a viewpoint presupposing that the environment has indeed already been polluted, thereby shifting the burden of proof: "A new, environmentalist epidemiology might ... choose another tack entirely. Instead of presuming that nature is clean and looking for evidence to the contrary, as the null hypothesis requires, investigators might start from the assumption that nature is *polluted* and look for evidence to the contrary.

Such a tack would shift the burden of proof from those who would clean up the environment to those who would endanger it."[41]

The reversal Tesh proposes as the basis of an environmentalist epidemiology can be construed as a matter of problem definition since it constitutes a reframing and redefinition of the research problem. However, problem definition here clearly involves epistemological questions related to scientific practice. As Tesh poses the issue, the practical difference between employing pre-environmentalist and environmentalist assumptions is one of shifting "the burden of proof." A further issue that arises here is how to decide where the burden of proof should be placed. Tesh's position is that environmentalist assumptions are better suited to a science that seeks the prevention of disease.[42] What her argument reveals, in any case, is that the choice of assumptions is not one for which scientific expertise possesses any ultimate authority; non-experts thus have a legitimate say in the choice. The epistemological orientation of policy professionalism thus confronts a challenge from within, from considerations arising from its own presuppositions. As the epistemic authority of scientism is thrown into doubt, any coherent policy professionalism must reconsider how policy questions can legitimately be posed and addressed. As we shall see in the next section, this opens the door to a dissident professionalism and its concern with the communicative context of policy deliberations.

Tesh's examination of a particular toxic waste issue offers an illustration of how change at the level of problem definition can anticipate such an epistemological challenge: attention is focused on the broader social and cultural contexts that enter into the construction of scientific practices, together with their application to policy problems. In both agenda setting and problem definition, environmentalism challenges conventional ideas and attitudes that have supported the advance of industrialization. Yet change at these levels can, in principle, be incorporated within technocratically oriented policy professionalism. Once environment has been placed on the agenda, it can be addressed with conventional techniques—even though the scope of concerns thus raised tends to make the limitations of such techniques rather obvious. Similarly, once problems have been redefined to take into account broader cycles of activities and relationships, planning and management can settle into conventional routines—even though the process of problem redefinition may have seen a disruption of those routines and may suggest advantages in altering them. At the level of epistemology, however, the scientistic foundation of technocratic notions is itself challenged in a way that throws into question the premises of industrialization.

The effective management of toxic wastes, we have seen, came as an afterthought to the industrial world and the administrative state. What became strikingly obvious was how little was known about the problem during, to use Tesh's term, a "pre-environmentalist" period: how little attention had been devoted to the generation and handling of toxic waste not only by private corporations, but also by agencies directly charged with public obligations. Why was the toxic waste problem so strikingly neglected? An answer to this question must go beyond references to the capitalist drive for profitability or government incompetence and connivance. An answer requires attention to pre-environmentalist assumptions about what makes knowledge legitimate and relevant in a policy context.

Policy professionalism takes its cue from scientism—the positivist celebration of science as the only source of genuine knowledge—and regards scientifically grounded expertise as both the basis of its authority and the means of effective governance in the technologically complex society that scientific achievements make possible. Challenges to scientism often begin with the pointed observation that *faith* in science is not itself a form of scientific knowledge.[43] Indeed, this faith has been secured within a modern cultural context that has granted the scientific enterprise an authority and prestige that it could not claim for itself without violating its own epistemological premises. Within the context of a progressively rationalized culture, the emergence of industrialization was supported by the conviction that modern science and technology offered the means for humanity to dominate nature, to achieve mastery—as Max Weber put it—of "all things by calculation."[44] As rationalized techniques and processes of administration promoted this mastery through an ensemble of state agencies and private corporations, a "commonplace" conviction emerged to inspire confidence in the capacity of modern society and technology to confront successfully whatever challenges the future might bring: i.e., "a high measure of certainty that problems have solutions before there is knowledge of how they are to be solved."[45]

Although this industrialist conviction has been reinforced by impressive technological achievements, these have typically depended upon a focus attending to a strictly delimited set of variables. Success has thus come from systematic inattention to the complexities and ambiguities of a broader context. The administrative organizations of advanced industrial society, moreover, have exhibited a "bounded rationality" secure in the belief that the world is "mostly empty"—that contextual interdependencies and uncertainties are largely irrelevant to administrative decisions.[46] Problems can thus be rationally isolated, addressed, and solved through highly selective attention by administrative organizations, aided by scientific experts. This presupposition, necessary if scientism is to be creditable in the context of policy problems, has early roots in the emergence of the modern age, as nature and administration came to be understood in terms of the central metaphor of mechanism: "The rationalization of administration and of the natural order was occurring simultaneously. Rational management in the social and economic spheres helps to explain the appeal of mechanism as a rational order created by a powerful sovereign deity. As Descartes wrote ... in 1630, 'God sets up mathematical laws in nature as the king sets up laws in his kingdom.'"[47] Environmentalism, by directing attention to neglected contexts, poses a challenge to a long cultural tradition underpinning the project of industrialization. From an environmentalist perspective, technological development based upon narrowly focused analysis exhibits an enormous blind spot of industrialism: technology worked to the extent that one could ignore its side-effects, but environmentalism announced a crisis—one perhaps threatening the very survival of humanity—that consisted precisely in an accumulation and interaction of previously neglected side-effects.

This environmentalist perspective was reinforced not only by public perceptions of environmental deterioration, but also by developments within scientific discourse—particularly ecology and systems theory—that focused attention upon complex interdependencies and made it increasingly difficult to restrict analytic attention within narrow boundaries. The simplifying assumptions and reductive moves of technocratically oriented policy professionalism become less convincing once the vagaries of an uncertain context become obvious. When administration is made to think outside its conventional boxes, the fragility of its bounded rationality is exposed: administrative organizations are faced with a "gross increase in ... *relevant uncertainty.*"[48] Moreover, as mechanistic metaphors become insufficient guides to a complex terrain, attention turns to the possibility of designing "holistic" institutions in which inner and outer complexity would adequately match one another.[49]

Ecology was one of the sources in the twentieth century inspiring a holistic approach to nature that recalled an earlier organicism. With the rise of the mechanistic world order, organicism was sharply attenuated, compromised, nearly eclipsed: the universe came to be seen in terms of discrete elements that could be clearly known, assembled and disassembled, with particular things treated as separate from everything else. Under the influence of a holistic orientation, environmentalism tends to challenge the mechanistic outlook: "Ecology necessarily must consider the complexities and the totality. It cannot isolate the parts into simplified systems...." It focuses attention instead on "cyclical processes" and "the interconnectedness of all things."[50]

Environmentalism, although significantly influenced by the modern natural sciences and informed by systems-theoretic concepts, also questions the whole mode of objectification characteristic of modern epistemology. Although ecology often exhibits features typical of modern scientific disciplines, the scope and nature of its concerns also often rule out convincing causal explanations, thereby frustrating the quest for predictability and control. Ecology, indeed, does not simply remain the name for a scientific discipline, but is conceived as a path to ecological consciousness—a sensitivity attuned to natural interdependencies, informed by a reconceptualization of the human/nature relationship, and guided by attitudes and values that prize the natural world for its own sake.[51] Ecological consciousness is thus subversive of both the subject-object dualism of modern epistemology and the value-neutral, reductionist scientism dependent on it. The new way of looking at things lends credence to local and traditional knowledge, to new metaphors of the biosphere (e.g., the "Gaia hypothesis"), and to esthetic and moral judgments.[52]

Ecological consciousness is clearly at odds with a technocratically oriented policy professionalism. Yet the epistemological influence of environmentalism on policy professionalism is unlikely to be particularly visible in terms of promoting some sudden conversion to ecological consciousness that would dramatically alter the character of deliberations in established policy arenas. Such influence has greater likelihood of being exerted in more subtle ways. One such way—as we have seen in the toxic waste case—is through modes of problem definition that, although they pose no direct threat in principle to prevailing analytic practices, promote a focus of inquiry in which the epistemological sufficiency of these practices is thrown into question. Another way is through critique of the supposed rationality of policy professionalism. The notion of rationality prevalent in professional circles has indeed been squarely contested—portrayed as overly narrow and simplistic—by dissident figures championing a broader conception. Environmentalism offers an important dimension to such critique.

Evidence of environmental damage often tends to undermine the exuberant confidence that has inspired the advent of the industrial order. Lapses in control—as in the case of toxic wastes—signal that the rationality of this order is not necessarily to be taken for granted. Indeed, this rationality can be challenged in the name of an "ecological rationality" necessary for any viable society. What is at stake here is the "life-support value of ecosystems": "The preservation of the life-support systems on which human beings depend is a precondition to the continued existence of society itself and its institutional forms...."[53] Ecological rationality can be understood in terms of "an order of relationships among living systems and their environments"[54] within which any human society must somehow fit. A society becomes "ecologically irrational" when it fails to fit, when its forms of epistemic authority and institutional practice threaten the eco-systemic relations on which it relies.[55]

The quest for ecological rationality is not altogether new, but informs past efforts at resource management that, dating to incipient stages of industrialization, became especially prominent during the Progressive era in the United States as early conservation policies were inspired by a "gospel of efficiency."[56] These efforts, however, typically remained guided by pre-environmentalist presuppositions; in particular, they lacked much appreciation of the enormous natural and social complexities that the rise of industrialism tended to override and obscure: there was little humility in the face of uncertainty and ignorance.

Even as environmentalism came to be celebrated with the first Earth Day in 1970, the quest for ecological rationality was at times supported by an epistemic confidence lending credence to the notion that environmental problems could be solved through reliance on the very forms of thinking and institutional design that had supported the rise of industrialization. Various authoritarian and technocratic modes of governance were advanced as necessary solutions to an escalating environmental crisis in which human beings were rapidly destroying their niche in the biosphere. Quite early on, however, William Leiss was able to formulate the conundrum of any such neo-Hobbesian proposal: "a concern with ecology necessarily becomes part of a *social* movement" which, if it faces up to the environmental destruction wrought by established power, cannot avoid "challenging the authoritarian decision-making powers vested in corporate and governmental institutions."[57]

Ecological rationality cannot have recourse to the reductive moves and simplifying assumptions that allowed scientism to gain its epistemic authority in the course of industrialization. It is at this point that the most telling level of epistemic challenge emerges: experience with environmental problems throws into question the assumption that scientific procedures can supply the knowledge necessary to handle such problems. The concept of "trans-scientific" issues, for example, draws attention to questions of key policy relevance that can be framed in conventional scientific terms but are entirely impractical to answer through scientific procedures.[58] The overall problem, as Robert Gibson argues, is one not only of uncertainty, but of enormous *ignorance* as well: it is not a matter of "gaps" in knowledge, but of a "general darkness with scattered pinpoints of light." What Gibson, in effect, suggests is that ecological rationality is inseparable from "an attitude of environmental humility": an orientation guarding against problems that arise when humans fail "to respect the complexity and vulnerability of the environment, and to appreciate the limits of human knowledge and understanding."[59] He argues against the common notion that we are "near the point at which properly supervised and directed scientists and administrators, assisted by specialized experts, could identify the right responses to most policy problems." These beliefs are exposed as "dangerous fictions" when one considers "evidence of environmental abuse" from "toxic releases" and in similarly complex issues such as "acid rain," "the greenhouse effect," and "holes in the ozone layer."[60]

Since the challenge to scientism is cast in terms of socially constructed institutional practices, the challenge does not remain narrowly epistemological but emerges as also being societal and institutional. The problem of "respecting ignorance and uncertainty,"[61] as Gibson puts it, indicates that "the self-confidence of large-scale industrial societies is unfounded" and suggests a "distant and difficult goal of establishing societies that respect the boundaries imposed by human ignorance."[62] For the moment, however, efforts to promote institutional designs consistent with environmental humility must confront the difficulties posed by established policy processes. Here key tasks involve enhancing "the transparency of decision making," exposing "the breadth of expertise and understanding used," promoting "an institutionalization of openness to scrutiny," and incorporating diverse "critical perspectives."[63] With particular reference to the toxic waste issue, Bruce Williams and Albert Matheny have similarly advocated establishing the conditions for a "policy dialogue," emphasizing that such a dialogue requires "strong citizens" able to exercise a "right-to-know" in gaining access to information previously shielded from public view. In the context of such a dialogue, they maintain, serious attention can shift from the mere disposal of toxic wastes to ways of reducing them at source.[64] Pursued with such a societal and institutional focus, the epistemological challenge to scientism raises the possibility of a reorientation within policy professionalism, of practices that—

while concerned with immediate issues of reform—are also attuned to a larger agenda animated by a spirit of dissent.

POLICY DISCOURSE
AND DISSIDENT PROFESSIONALISM

Policy professionalism has at times faced the problem of counter-expertise: experts siding with the voices of dissent, aligning themselves with social movements opposed to established social and political order. The resulting politics of expertise, however, carries with it an implicit questioning of the role of expertise itself, drawing attention to issues in which non-expert, as well as expert, opinion is clearly relevant.[65] The response among some policy professionals has been to introduce innovations that clearly depart from scientistic and technocratic presuppositions, such that a significant current of opinion has emerged to promote approaches to policy discourse that are emphatically anti-scientistic and anti-technocratic. This current of opinion, clearly influenced by social movements such as environmentalism, constitutes a voice of dissent within policy professionalism.[66]

Dissident professionalism reinforces challenges to prevailing forms of agenda setting, problem definition and epistemology. A key question that arises in connection with these challenges is how to create an appropriate forum for policy discourse in which both non-expert and expert opinion are relevant. Tesh, for example, focuses on the burden of proof as a key concept for promoting an environmentalist epidemiology relevant to concerns posed by the anti-toxics movement. Her deployment of this concept links the framework of science with that of jurisprudence and suggests the possibility of a variation on the model of a "science court," one not restricted to experts judging clearly factual questions, but involving citizens as well as experts in deliberating upon a range of issues that cannot be neatly demarcated in advance by a fixed epistemological position.[67] Just as important as expert opinions, in such a context, are those opinions that draw attention to expert bias.

The problem of expert bias, when recognized and taken seriously within policy professionalism, throws the edifice of scientism into question. In this regard, Giandomenico Majone has recommended a "generalized jurisprudence."[68] Focusing particularly on the assessment of technological development, Majone has maintained that open criticism and public debate are necessary to counteract a central bias of experts: "Technical experts are naturally biased in the assessment of proposals and are more likely to be sceptical of any evidence of possible adverse effects than someone less committed to that particular project. The initial assumption is that the innovation will achieve what the innovator claims for it and that it will have no negative consequences that could reduce the attractiveness of its practical implementation." Majone's conclusion is that "technological expertise cannot be relied upon to discover the characteristic risks and social implications of new technologies."[69] Indeed, in the case of energy policy, especially as involving nuclear power, Amory Lovins similarly maintains that "too much expertise tends to obscure rather than illuminate the basic questions at issue."[70]

Such observations can be applied more broadly to the prevailing pattern of development in advanced industrial society. As we have seen, environmental impact assessment was advanced—along with technology assessment and social impact assessment—as a way of coming to grips with neglected difficulties in this pattern of development, or at least as a kind of "worm in the brain" unsettling to the normal boundaries of administrative rationality. Nonetheless, expert bias often appears here both as an unquestioning attitude toward the prevailing pattern and as a tendency to constrain inquiry according to scientistic notions. Thomas Berger, who headed one of the most significant exercises in impact assessment, drew attention to such expert bias as obscuring "the nature of human affairs"[71] and pointed inquiry in a different direction:

> If you are going to assess impact properly, you have to weigh a whole series of matters, some tangible, some intangible. But in the end, no matter how many experts there may be, no matter how many pages of computer print-outs may have been assembled, there is the ineluctable necessity of bringing human judgement to bear on the main issues. Indeed, when the main issue cuts across a range of questions, spanning the physical and social sciences, the only way to come to grips with it and to resolve it is by the exercise of human judgement.[72]

The inquiry Berger headed was significant not so much for the exercise of judgment by an individual, however, as for the process of inquiry itself, which brought citizens and experts together in a forum that tended to equalize their standing.[73]

In such a context, the focus of attention breaks decisively with the framework of a technocratically oriented policy professionalism: "The supreme analytic achievement," as Majone puts it, "is no longer the computation of optimal strategies, but the design of procedural rules and social mechanisms for the assessment of incomplete and often contradictory evidence."[74] With this proposal we encounter, within policy professionalism, an epistemological shift from scientism to "discursive design," as Dryzek has suggested.[75] Similarly, according to Fischer, the shift involves decreased faith in the epistemic authority of technocratic experts together with an enhanced context of policy and public discourse that encourages the development by citizens of "participatory expertise."[76] Such a communicative shift, or "argumentative turn," has especially been advanced within the policy literature through the advent of a dissident policy professionalism that decidedly departs from positivism by posing a challenge to conventional epistemology and commitment.[77]

Dissident policy professionalism constitutes a tendency that both reflects the influence of dissident social movements such as environmentalism and renders policy professionalism more receptive to that influence. By itself, of course, this tendency has but an ambivalent potential in terms of challenges to established power relations. [78] Directly contesting the identity and purpose of policy professionalism, nonetheless, the dissident current constructs policy inquiry not as a fixed instrumentality, but as a site of contention. Historically, indeed, policy discourse has not emerged with a fixed identity insulated from context, but has always been a site of contention where different interests and perspectives are brought to bear.[79] Although scientism did seek to fix the identity of policy professionalism as a technocratic instrument based on an authoritative epistemology, the dissident voice disrupts that identity by promoting participatory expertise and designs for open discourse tending to anticipate a more vigorously democratic public life.

NOTES

1 For relevant discussions in the policy literature, see the following: Robert W. Cobb and Charles D. Elder, "The Politics of Agenda Building: An Alternative Perspective for Modern Democratic Theory," *Journal of Politics* 33(1971): 892–915; David Dery, *Problem Definition in Policy Analysis* (Lawrence: University Press of Kansas, 1985); John W. Kingdon, *Agendas, Alternatives, and Public Policies* (Boston: Little, Brown, 1994); David A. Rochefort and Roger W. Cobb, "Problem Definition: An Emerging Perspective," in David A. Rochefort and Roger W. Cobb, eds., *The Politics of Problem Definition: Shaping the Policy Agenda* (Lawrence: University Press of Kansas), pp. 1–31; Mary Hawkesworth, "Epistemology and Policy Analysis," in William N. Dunn and Rita M. Kelly, eds., *Advances in Policy Studies since 1950* (New Brunswick, NJ: Transaction Publishers 1995), pp. 295–329. Environmentalism draws attention to the category of nature in a way that advances a critique of industrialism. See Douglas Torgerson, *The Promise of Green Politics: Environmentalism and the Public Sphere* (Durham, NC: Duke University Press, 1999). Feminism draws attention to the category of gender in a way that advances a critique of patriarchy. From feminist contributions to the policy literature, this critique can be seen to involve agenda setting, problem definition, and epistemology: e.g., Mary Hawkesworth, "Policy Studies Within a Feminist Frame, *Policy Sciences* 27(1994): 97–118; Martha A. Ackelsberg, "Feminist Analyses of Public Policy," *Comparative Politics* 24(1992): 477–93; Diane Gibson and Judith Allen, "Parasitism and Phallocentrism in Social Provisions for the Aged," *Policy Sciences* 26(1993): 79–98; Stephanie S. Rixecker, "Expanding the Discursive Context of Policy Design: A Matter of Feminist Standpoint Epistemology," *Policy Sciences* 27(1994): 119–42.

2 For a relevant treatment of policy professionalism, see Donald A. Schön, *The Reflective Practitioner: How Professionals Think in Action* (New York: Basic Books, 1983), esp. pp. 338–54. Cf. John L. Foster, "Professional Models for Policy Analysis," *Administration and Society* 12(1981): 379–97. Also see the early and influential characterization of the policy field as a technocratic venture by Laurence H. Tribe, "Policy Science: Analysis or Ideology?," *Philosophy and Public Affairs* 2(1972): 66–110.

3 See Douglas Torgerson, "Democracy through Policy Discourse," in Maarten A. Hajer and Hendrik Wagenaar, eds., *Deliberative Policy Analysis: Understanding Governance in the Network Society* (Cambridge: Cambridge University Press, 2003), pp. 113–38. Also see Douglas Torgerson, "Policy Analysis and Public Life: The Restoration of *Phronesis*?," in James Farr, John S. Dryzek, and Stephen T. Leonard, eds., *Political Science in History: Research Programs and Political Traditions* (Cambridge: Cambridge University Press, 1995), pp. 225–52; John S. Dryzek and Douglas Torgerson, "Democracy and the Policy Sciences," *Policy Sciences* 26(1993): 127–37.

4   See Douglas Torgerson, "Environmentalism," in Shepard Krech III, John McNeill, and Carolyn Merchant, eds., *Encyclopedia of World Environmental History*, vol. 1 (New York: Routledge, 2003), pp. 121–28.

5   Samuel P. Hays, *Beauty, Health and Permanence: Environmental Politics in the United States, 1955–1985* (Cambridge: Cambridge University Press, 1989), p. 394.

6   Hays, *Beauty, Health and Permanence*, p. 412.

7   Edith Stokey and Richard Zeckhauser, *A Primer for Policy Analysis* (New York: W.W. Norton, 1978), p. 4.

8   David Easton, *The Political System: An Inquiry into the State of Political Science*, 2nd ed. (New York: Alfred A. Knopf, 1971), p. 81.

9   Emmanuel G. Mesthene, *Technological Change: Its Impact on Man and Society* (New York: Mentor, 1970), pp. 79–80.

10 Tribe, "Policy Science," pp. 97–98.

11 See Torgerson, "Environmentalism."

12 For an early statement on the fortunes of environmentalism, see Anthony Downs, "Up and Down with Ecology—The 'Issue Attention Cycle,'" *The Public Interest* 28(1972): 38–50.

13 See, e.g., Laurence H. Tribe, "Technology Assessment and the Fourth Discontinuity: The Limits of Instrumental Rationality," *Southern California Law Review* 46(1972–73): 617–60; Douglas Torgerson, *Industrialization and Assessment: Social Impact Assessment as a Social Phenomenon* (Toronto: York University, 1980), ch. 7.

14 Robert V. Bartlett, "Ecological Reason in Administration: Environmental Impact Assessment and Administrative Theory," in Robert Paehlke and Douglas Torgerson, eds., *Managing Leviathan: Environmental Politics and the Administrative State* (Peterborough, ON: Broadview Press, 1990), p. 82.

15 Serge Taylor, *Making Bureaucracies Think: The Environmental Impact Statement Strategy of Administrative Reform* (Stanford, CA: Stanford University Press, 1984).

16 See Barry Commoner, *The Closing Circle* (New York: Alfred A. Knopf, 1971).

17 Samuel S. Epstein, Lester O. Brown, and Carl Pope, *Hazardous Waste in America* (San Francisco: Sierra Club Books, 1982), p. 37. Toxic wastes, strictly speaking, are only the most dramatic form of hazardous wastes. However, the distinction is not pertinent to the purposes of this essay.

18 Albert Gore, Jr., "Foreword" to Samuel S. Epstein, Lester O. Brown, and Carol Pope, *Hazardous Waste in America* (San Francisco: Sierra Club Books, 1982), p. x.

19 See Bruce A. Williams and Albert R. Matheny, *Democracy, Dialogue, and Environmental Disputes: The Contested Languages of Social Regulation* (New Haven, CT: Yale University Press, 1995), Part II, "Hazardous Waste Policy: Regulatory Failure and Grass Roots Response," esp. pp. 98ff.

20 Thomas F. Williams, deputy director, EPA Office of Public Awareness, quoted in Williams and Matheny, *Democracy, Dialogue, and Environmental Disputes*, p. 98, from Mary Worobec, "An Analysis of the Resource Conservation and Recovery Act," *Environment Reporter* 22 Aug. 1980, p. 634. Also see Richard Ripley, "Toxic Substances, Hazardous Wastes, and Public Policy: Problems in Implementation," in James P. Lester and Ann O'M. Bowman, eds., *The Politics of Hazardous Waste Management* (Durham, NC: Duke University Press, 1983), pp. 24–42.

21 Williams and Matheny, *Democracy, Dialogue and Environmental Disputes*, ch. 7, provide a particularly useful discussion of the rise of the anti-toxics movement. On Love Canal, see Adeline Gordon Levine, *Love Canal: Science, Politics, and People* (Lexington, MA: Lexington Books, 1982).

22 Rachel Carson, *Silent Spring* (Boston: Houghton Mifflin, 1994).

23 Amory Lovins, *Soft Energy Paths: Toward a Durable Peace* (Cambridge, MA: Ballinger Publishing, 1977).

24 Epstein, Brown, and Pope, *Hazardous Waste in America*, p. 357.

25 Epstein, Brown, and Pope, *Hazardous Waste in America*, p. 181.
26 See T.F. Schrecker, *Political Economy of Environmental Hazards* (Ottawa: Law Reform Commission of Canada, 1988).
27 On the misadventures of Superfund in the United States, see Williams and Matheny, *Democracy, Dialogue and Environmental Disputes*, pp. 101ff.; also see Robert Paehlke and Douglas Torgerson, "Toxic Waste and the Administrative State: NIMBY Syndrome or Participatory Management?," in Robert Paehlke and Douglas Torgerson, eds., *Managing Leviathan: Environmental Politics and the Administrative State* (Peterborough, ON: Broadview Press, 1990), pp. 259–81; Steven Cohen and Marc Tipermas, "Superfund: Preimplementation Planning and Bureaucratic Politics," in Lester and Bowman, eds., *The Politics of Hazardous Waste Management*, pp. 43–59.
28 Williams and Matheny, *Democracy, Dialogue and Environmental Disputes*, p. 167; also see Barry Rabe, *Beyond Nimby: Hazardous Waste Siting in Canada and the United States* (Washington, DC: Brookings Institution, 1994).
29 Joe Castrilli, "Hazardous Wastes Law in Canada and Ontario," *Alternatives: Perspectives on Society and Environment* 10.2/3(1982): 55. Also see Paehlke and Torgerson, "Toxic Waste and the Administrative State."
30 Robert A. Frosch, "Industrial Ecology: A Philosophical Introduction," *Proceedings of the National Academy of Sciences U.S.A.* 89(1992): 800.
31 See John S. Dryzek, *Rational Ecology: Environment and Political Economy* (London: Basil Blackwell, 1987), ch. 3.
32 See Robert Paehlke and Douglas Torgerson, "Toxic Waste as Public Business," *Canadian Public Administration* 35(1992): 339–62; Rabe, *Beyond Nimby*.
33 See Paehlke and Torgerson, "Toxic Waste and the Administrative State"; Williams and Matheny, *Democracy, Dialogue and Environmental Disputes*, chs. 7–8; Andrew Szaz, *Ecopopulism: Toxic Waste and the Movement for Environmental Justice* (Minneapolis: University of Minnesota Press, 1994).
34 For a discussion of some complexities that arise in this connection, see Paehlke and Torgerson, "Toxic Waste as Public Business."
35 Williams and Matheny, *Democracy, Dialogue and Environmental Disputes*, p. 96.
36 Sylvia N. Tesh, "Environmentalism, Pre-environmentalism and Public Policy," *Policy Sciences* 26(1993): 2–7.
37 Sylvia N. Tesh and Bruce A. Williams, "Identity Politics, Disinterested Politics, and Environmental Justice," *Polity* 28(1996): 297.
38 Tesh, "Environmentalism," pp. 8–13.
39 Tesh and Williams, "Identity Politics," pp. 299ff.
40 Tesh, "Environmentalism," p. 9.
41 Tesh, "Environmentalism," pp. 13–14 (original emphasis).
42 Tesh, "Environmentalism," p. 14.
43 See, e.g., Jürgen Habermas, *Knowledge and Human Interests*, Jeremy Shapiro, trans. (Boston: Beacon Press, 1971), esp. pp. 4, 67.
44 Max Weber, "Science as a Vocation," in H.H. Gerth and C. Wright Mills, eds. and trans., *From Max Weber: Essays in Sociology* (New York: Oxford University Press), p. 139. Also see William Leiss, *The Domination of Nature* (Boston: Beacon Press, 1974); Carolyn Merchant, *The Death of Nature: Women, Ecology and the Scientific Revolution* (New York: Harper and Row, 1983).
45 John Kenneth Galbraith, *The New Industrial State*, 2nd rev. ed. (New York: Mentor Books, 1972), p. 37.
46 However much "bounded rationality" may be ascribed to intrinsic limitations of human individuals and collectivities, it is characteristically accentuated in administrative organizations, where Simon first identified it. See Herbert A. Simon, *Administrative Behavior: A Study of Decision-Making in Administrative Organization*, 3rd ed. (New York: The Free Press, 1976), esp. pp. xxix–xxx; cf. John S. Dryzek, "Complexity and Rationality in

Public Life," *Political Studies* 35(1987): 424–42. Lasswell's stress on contextual orientation may be regarded as an effort to press against such boundaries; see Douglas Torgerson, "Contextual Orientation in Policy Analysis: The Contribution of Harold D. Lasswell," *Policy Sciences* 18(1985): 241–61.

47 Merchant, *Death of Nature*, p. 205, quoting a letter from Descartes to Mersenne of 15 April 1630.

48 F.E. Emery and Eric Trist, "The Causal Texture of Organizational Environments" (1965), in F.E. Emery, ed., *Systems Thinking*, rev. ed., vol. 1 (Harmondsworth: Penguin Books, 1981), p. 254 (original emphasis); also see Eric Trist, "A Concept of Organizational Ecology," *Australian Journal of Management* 2(1977): 161–75.

49 C.A. Hooker and R. van Hulst, "The Meaning of Environmental Problems for Public Political Institutions," in William Leiss, ed., *Ecology versus Politics in Canada* (Toronto: University of Toronto Press, 1979), pp. 131–34. Cf. Frosch, "Industrial Ecology."

50 Merchant, *Death of Nature*, p. 293; cf. chs. 4, 8, 9, 10. Yet, there is an important distinction between ecology as a scientific discipline and the influence that certain ideas drawn from ecology have had in a broader cultural context. Commoner, e.g, in *The Closing Circle*, pp. 29–42, popularized four now famous "laws of ecology"; he called them "informal," and no one would seriously regard them as "scientific laws." As a scientific discipline, ecology is heterogeneous and not necessarily governed by great unifying ideas. The practices of scientific ecology appear to be substantially influenced by particular political and institutional contexts. See Stephen Bocking, *Ecologists and Environmental Politics: A History of Contemporary Ecology* (New Haven, CT: Yale University Press, 1997), esp. ch. 8.

51 Donald Worster, *Nature's Economy: The Roots of Ecology* (Garden City, NY: Anchor Press, 1979) portrays the tension between scientistic tendencies in ecology and the rise of ecological consciousness. On the latter, see esp. John Rodman, "Four Forms of Ecological Consciousness Reconsidered," in Donald Scherer and Thomas Attig, eds., *Ethics and the Environment*, (Englewood Cliffs, NJ: Prentice-Hall, 1983), pp. 82–92.

52 See, e.g., Milton M.R. Freeman, "The Nature and Utility of Traditional Ecological Knowledge," in Chad Gaffield and Pam Gaffield, eds., *Consuming Canada: Readings in Environmental History* (Toronto: Copp Clark, 1995), pp. 39–46; John Visvader, "Gaia and the Myths of Harmony: An Exploration of Ethical and Practical Implications," in Stephen H. Schneider and Penelope J. Boston, eds., *Scientists on Gaia* (Cambridge, MA: The M.I.T. Press, 1993), pp. 33–37; Rodman, "Four Forms of Ecological Consciousness Reconsidered."

53 John S. Dryzek, "Ecological Rationality," *International Journal of Environmental Studies* 21(1983): 5, 8; also see Dryzek, *Rational Ecology*, chs. 3–5.

54 Robert V. Bartlett, "Ecological Rationality: Reason and Environmental Policy," *Environmental Ethics* 8(1986): 229.

55 Dryzek, *Rational Ecology*, p. 245.

56 See Merchant, *Death of Nature*, ch. 10; Samuel P. Hays, *Conservation and the Gospel of Efficiency: The Progressive Conservation Movement, 1890–1920* (New York: Antheneum, 1975).

57 Leiss, *The Domination of Nature*, p. 22.

58 For the formulation of this concept, see Alvin M. Weinberg, "Science and Trans-Science," *Minerva* 10(1972): 209–22. For some striking applications involving a critique of technocratic policy professionalism, see Lovins, "Cost-Risk-Benefit Assessments in Energy Policy," *George Washington Law Review* 45(1977): 911–43, esp. pp. 920ff.

59 Robert B. Gibson, "Respecting Ignorance and Uncertainty," in Erik Lykke, ed., *Achieving Environmental Goals: The Concept and Practice of Environmental Performance Review* (London: Belhaven Press, 1992), pp. 158, 173.

60 Robert B. Gibson, "Out of Control and Beyond Understanding: Acid Rain as a Political Dilemma," in Robert Paehlke and Douglas Torgerson, eds., *Managing Leviathan: Envi-*

ronmental Politics and the Administrative State (Peterborough, ON: Broadview Press, 1990), p. 243.

61 Gibson, "Respecting Ignorance and Uncertainty."

62 Gibson, "Out of Control and Beyond Understanding," p. 253.

63 Gibson, "Respecting Ignorance and Uncertainty," p. 167

64 Williams and Matheny, *Democracy, Dialogue and Environmental Disputes*, pp. 177 ff., 193, 196, 200–03.

65 See Schön, *The Reflective Practitioner*, pp. 338–54; Frank Fischer, *Technocracy and the Politics of Expertise* (Newbury Park, CA: Sage Publications, 1990). Also see Aat Peterse, "The Mobilization of Counter-Expertise: Using Fischer's Model of Policy Inquiry," *Policy Sciences* 28(1995): 369–73.

66 See Torgerson, "Democracy through Policy Discourse."

67 One possibility is a variation on the "science court" that is deliberately designed to avoid constraints on participation suggested by conventional legal practice. See Frank Fischer, "Citizen Participation and the Democratization of Policy Expertise: From Political Theory to Practical Cases," *Policy Sciences* 26(1993): 165–87.

68 Giandomenico Majone, "Technology Assessment and Policy Analysis," *Policy Sciences* 8(1977): 174.

69 Giandomenico Majone, *Evidence, Argument and Persuasion in the Policy Process* (New Haven, CT: Yale University Press, 1989), pp. 5–6.

70 Amory B. Lovins and John H. Price, *Non-Nuclear Futures: The Case for an Ethical Energy Strategy* (Cambridge, MA: Ballinger Publishing, 1975), p. xix.

71 Thomas Berger, *Northern Frontier, Northern Homeland: The Report of the Mackenzie Valley Pipeline Inquiry*, 2 vols. (Ottawa: Supply and Services Canada, 1977), vol. 1, p. 161.

72 Berger, *Northern Frontier, Northern Homeland*, vol. 2, p. 229.

73 See D.J. Gamble, "The Berger Inquiry: An Impact Assessment Process," *Science* 199(1979): 946-52.

74 Majone, "Technology Assessment and Policy Analysis," p. 174.

75 See John S. Dryzek, "Policy Analysis and Planning: From Science to Argument," in Frank Fischer and John Forester, eds., *The Argumentative Turn in Policy Analysis and Planning* (Durham, NC: Duke University Press, 1993), pp. 213–32. Also see John S. Dryzek, "Discursive Designs: Critical Theory and Political Institutions," *American Journal of Political Science* 31(1987): 656–79.

76 See Frank Fischer, *Technocracy and the Politics of Expertise*, and "Participatory Expertise: Toward the Democratization of Policy Science," in William N. Dunn and Rita M. Kelly, eds., *Advances in Policy Studies since 1950* (New Brunswick, NJ: Transaction Publishers, 1992), pp. 351–76.

77 See Frank Fischer and John Forester, eds., *The Argumentative Turn in Policy Analysis and Planning*; Hajer and Wagenaar, eds., *Deliberative Policy Analysis*.

78 See Torgerson, "Democracy through Policy Discourse."

79 See Douglas Torgerson, "Policy Analysis and Public Life," and "Power and Insight in Policy Discourse: Postpositivism and Problem Definition," in Michael Howlett, and David Laycock, eds., *Policy Studies in Canada: The State of the Art*, Laurent Dobuzinskis (Toronto: University of Toronto Press, 1996), pp. 266–98.

11

Depoliticizing Environmental Politics: Sustainable Development in Norway

Ingerid S. Straume

Environmental politics in Norway has undergone several significant discursive shifts over the past decades.[1] The field of environmentalism has expanded to include more participants and a wider range of issues while, at the same time, the definition of central problems has been the subject of much dispute and negotiation. Environmentalism itself has been transformed from being a special interest of the few—a feature of group membership—to becoming a naturalized, uncontested aspect of organized social life. Nowadays, actors from all spheres of society are involved in some kind of environmentalist agenda. In turn, the environmentalist agenda has become a mediating field containing very different strategic interests, and more social conflicts have been assimilated into environmental discourse. In recent years, the developments in Norwegian environmental politics have become too complex to be reduced to one story. Nonetheless, certain ideological patterns stand out as historically significant. This chapter will focus on one such pattern, namely the systematic tendency to conceptualize societal, structural issues as matters concerning the individual as a private person. A process of "structural individualization"[2] is at work in Norwegian environmental discourse, and the consequence is a depoliticization of environmental politics.

My critique of structural individualization is based on the premise that environmental problems should be understood first and foremost as problems of society, of a certain organization of human cohabitation, namely industrialized society. In earlier times, during the more politicized period of the 1970s and early 1980s, this was a virtually self-evident premise of environmentalist debate. In contrast, in Norwegian policy today, researchers' reports and government strategies tend to downplay the structural side of environmental problems. Furthermore, to the extent that environmental problems *are* regarded as structural problems today, the tendency is to pose *the individual as responsible* for the system. The individual is seen as having created the system by her choices—in elections as well as in daily practices—as upholding it, and eventually as being the agent responsible for altering the system. The Norwegian Ministry of the Environment made the focus on the individual explicit in its recommendations for a National Strategy for Sustainable Development:

> Although in earlier times the industry was held responsible for environmental problems, we now see that the individuals' consumer lifestyle will be a new challenge for the near future. This will have consequences for the shaping of future policy and strategic measures.[3]

What kind of "new challenge" might the Ministry of the Environment be referring to? Leaving issues of substance aside, I think this redefinition of the individual/society nexus has deep political implications—the bottom line being the power balance between authorities and their subjects. With structural individualization, the burden of the problems is being discursively relocated from industry as the site of production to the individual as site of consumption.[4]

In this chapter, I will examine the depoliticization of environmental politics in Norway by giving particular attention to the turn from traditional environmental protection toward sustainable development in the country. I will especially highlight the individualizing tendency in policy documents and local community projects that led to the first National Action Plan for *Agenda 21*, launched in the fall of 2003. What should concern us about the individualization of environmental politics is that the shift of attention from the level of structures to the private sphere of the individual—as the roots of environmental problems come to be seen as located in people's minds and hearts—makes it increasingly difficult to practice politics. As we shall see, democracy is undermined, weakened by a discrediting of the *demos*.

AGENDA 21 IN NORWAY: ENVIRONMENTAL POLITICS AND SUSTAINABLE DEVELOPMENT

Norway is often thought of as an "environmentalist" nation.[5] The country is blessed with spectacular scenery and is rich in natural resources, especially fish, lumber, and oil. Of course, Norway is often associated with "sustainable development" because one of its prime ministers, Gro Harlem Brundtland, headed the United Nations commission that helped to make the term a household word. Within the country, indeed, the notion of sustainable development was well received in official circles. There is a high degree of incorporation of the environmental movement within the state, especially in the Ministry of the Environment, and throughout the years Norwegian politicians have frequently proclaimed that Norway should take a leading role in environmental matters. Whenever environmental and development issues are concerned in international fora, Norway does tend to speak loudly, pushing for international commitments and agreements.[6]

At home, however, the situation is rather different. Norway has in fact often been slow to implement national environmental objectives, particularly in the realm of sustainable development. The country has been found "markedly deficient" here, "clearly off the pace" when compared with other nations in the OECD: all in all, Norway lacks governing mechanisms for sustainable development.[7] Norway's advances in matters of sustainable development seem to be mostly at the level of *technology development* and *rhetoric*, and as Morten Nordskag comments in a thorough evaluative study, "the gap between normative political commitment and the realisation of change is disturbingly large."[8]

It would be unwise to treat lightly the discrepancy between action and words in Norwegian environmental policy. On the surface, the deficit may seem merely to indicate delay, weakness or incompetence, shortcomings that could be remedied technically by increasing effort and doing more of the same. This would make for a rather benign diagnosis, namely that of a state that really wishes to do more. I would suggest, however, that the deficiency is better viewed as a functionally significant, if not intentional, *act*: one that serves the very real purpose of exercising control and preserving the status quo. There are three aspects to this point. First, when the authorities declare bold "visions" and "goals" that are unrealistically high, they are in effect outbidding potential critics. Second, with the same maneuver, the need to show any substantial results is postponed to a distant future. With the spotlight on individual matters, finally, individuals—not the established social structure—can be held responsible if, and when, results fail to materialize. The overall effect is that social and political processes become obscured in a way that makes it difficult to criticize conventional policy measures.

Norway's approach to *Agenda 21*—the international implementation plan for sustainable development adopted at the Rio Earth Summit in 1992—can serve as a case in point.[9] The country's role in the *Agenda 21* process has been characterized as being "constructive" yet primarily "geared towards international adaptation and national advantage, not national change for sustainable development."[10] Here the main focus will be on how the Norwegian approach to *Agenda 21* illustrates, and contributes to, the depoliticization of environmental politics. We shall be looking at three central policy documents: the Ministry of the Environment's *recommendations* for a strategy for sustainable development,[11] the national *strategy* for sustainable development,[12] and the national *action plan* for sustainable development.[13]

The depoliticization of environmental politics is, of course, not something unique to Norway: the tendency is already part of *Agenda 21* itself as an international agreement. The announced goals of *Agenda 21* are all good and worthy, and any suggestion of conflicting interests is conspicuous by its absence. As sociologist Stephen Yearley has pointed out, the objective of sustainable development is so obviously good and rational that it seems nobody could reasonably disagree with its desirability: "[S]ustainable development colonizes environmental policy by offering an objective from which one apparently could not wish to diverge."[14] The Brundtland Commission's goal—a form of development that "seeks to meet the needs and aspirations of the present without compromising the ability to meet those of the future"[15]—has something unquestionable about it. With a basic agreement on goals taken for granted, however, little or no room is left for political debate. According to Yearley, the virtual impossibility of dissent promotes the assumption that political discussions about the aims of societal development are superfluous. Thus the authorities may concern themselves simply with means.

The depoliticizing tendencies of *Agenda 21* became pronounced in Norway as the country started the implementation of a "Local Agenda 21"[16] in the middle of the 1990s. Norway's approach to *Agenda 21* has been significantly influenced by these lines from the international agreement:

> Each local authority should enter into a dialogue with its citizens, local organizations and private enterprises and adopt "a local Agenda 21." Through consultation and consensus building, local authorities would learn from citizens and from local, civic, community, business and industrial organizations and acquire the information needed for formulating the best strategies. The process of consultation would increase household awareness of sustainable development issues.[17]

"Local Agenda 21" advocates communicative strategies to implement *Agenda 21*, starting with the level of local authorities (municipalities). The Norwegian Local Agenda 21 (LA21) was conceived as basically an apolitical project, dominated by the terms implementation, information, consensus-building, management by objectives, strategy, and so on. A central question for the authorities in charge has been how to mobilize the population, especially households, in a "common effort." The main strategies are partnerships and consultation. In the international agreement, as seen from the above quotation, a Local Agenda is envisioned as a two-way learning process: Authorities would learn and acquire information, while households would reach increased awareness. This increased awareness would arise *through the activity of the consultation process itself*—not *via* information from the authorities. When it came to working out strategies for implementation in Norway, however, this changed.

Dialogue may be given some lip service in the opening lines of policy documents, but actual practice can be better seen by looking at a case. In particular, we may look at the pilot project Sustainable Local Communities, which was linked to Norway's LA21. The official aim of this three-year project was to gather knowledge about what sustainable production and consumption might imply at the level of local municipalities. A global perspective on the local handling of resources should provide indications of both impediments to, and practical opportunities for, the advancement of sustainable production and consumption. Central to the project was "broad local participation," involving different interest groups and civilian participants, as well as dialogue between local and central authorities.[18] Sociologist Anne Bregnballe followed the pilot project from beginning to end (1996–1999), focusing on one sub-project in one particular city. [19] Although leaders of the project and national assessments have called this project a success, Bregnballe reports that the citizen participants deemed it a failure. When talking to Bregnballe, the citizens voiced an interest in community matters, in political creativity, and in the global aspects of sustainable development. The project leaders believed, however, that such matters were not fit to be raised with the citizens. They assumed that the citizens were not really interested in the central aims of the project. In the view of the authorities, citizens needed to be encouraged, mobilized, and—above all—supplied with information. A potential dialogue thus became one-way "communication." Although the citizens had expected to participate in common activities involving both private and community life, they were instead constituted as the receiving end of information from leaders and experts. The substance of the information involved relatively traditional, isolated actions that could be performed at home, by the households. The citizen's own opinions were, according to Bregnballe, *not* welcomed at *any* stage of the process. Their views of the matters had no official outlet because no arena for public activity was established. This lack of communication and the narrow views of authorities largely reduced this pilot project in sustainable development to the delivery of information about waste management and environmental purchasing.

Most of the citizens left the project rather quickly, much to the disappointment of the project leadership. However, this event did not lead the authorities to reexamine their assumptions or the design of the project. On the contrary, the preconceptions guiding the project were strengthened. From the perspective of the authorities, it turned out that the public was indeed difficult to mobilize in a common effort for sustainable development.[20] Bregnballe's findings match the conclusions of researchers who conducted an official evaluation of the project as a whole: "We are left with a strong impression that the current focus within [Norwegian] environmental policy is on the role of the individual to influence the composition of the consumption."[21] These researchers concluded, moreover, that local authorities identified a major part of the problem they faced with the public to reside at the level of *attitudes*.[22]

It is clear that, in failing to initiate a proper public dialogue, the relevant authorities did not seriously take up *Agenda 21*'s idea of promoting cooperation among civil, state, and commercial agents. With the premise that everybody wants a sustainable development—at least when they have been sufficiently enlightened and informed—the central question became simply one of *how to mobilize* the population. As the call for dialogue had now been reduced from political to instrumental terms, the preferred approach became delivery of information.

Local Agenda 21:
Public Dialogue without Politics

A major part of the resources spent on Norway's LA21 have indeed been for information, in the form of written material, meetings, workshops, round-table conferences, and the like.[23] Very often, as in Project Sustainable Local Communities, the information given to the public has been about consumption and waste management. Bregnballe's study showed that what the project leaders substituted for dialogue did not create enthusiasm among the public. Because the authorities construed the participants as essentially atomistic agents within the private sphere, the participants were afforded no communal fora in which to develop and voice their own viewpoints. Efforts to promote public participation were geared at mobilizing people as *consumers*, not as *citizens*. The appeal to the individual in the role of consumer is also evident in the National Strategy and National Action Plan for Sustainable Development: whenever the public is mentioned in these documents, it is portrayed merely as a collection of consumers in need of information.[24] There is a current, general trend of authorities to appeal to the public in a way that reduces sustainable development to a private matter for individuals and households. Furthermore, there is an accompanying tendency to downplay political dialogue, which becomes clear in the following recommendation from the Ministry of the Environment:

> We recommend that the strategic work puts emphasis on describing the current situation, trends and challenges, and *thereafter* aims for a broadly based process of consultation in order to identify long-term, common goals and possible challenges. We find it essential that the concerned ministries make a combined effort to develop new solutions in order to *ensure the necessary anchoring and ownership* to the measures.[25]

By defining the situation first and *thereafter* asking for involvement, however, authorities could at best make only a half-hearted invitation for citizens to participate. The main purpose of this "broadly based" consultation process is to produce a sense of "ownership" among the public. In other words, the point is to *fabricate legitimacy* for policy measures that have been determined in advance, without public involvement. Such an approach to participation was also advanced in Norway by the environmental policy research group ProSus.[26] In their guidelines for implementing LA21 in Norway from 1999, ProSus researchers state that "[w]ithout a broad-based process of participation to generate support for change, we do not think it will be possible to reach the goal of a sustainable development."[27] However, LA21 should not be "dialogue-for-the-sake-of-dialogue."[28] The dialogue should be a means to achieve sustainable development and should be limited to that. To this end, ProSus advocated the coupling of dialogue with the technique of management by objectives.[29] Public participation and involvement was conceived in instrumental terms, as a means to facilitate implementation. It is true that, as the building of public consensus becomes a matter of management, an instrumentalist conception of citizenship might aid in producing the legitimacy of a sense of ownership, but it will not promote an active citizenry. Lack of public enthusiasm is perhaps not the worst possible outcome, however, from the viewpoint of authorities. At least a lot of complexity and potentially unruly activity is ruled out.

As shown in Bregnballe's study and as indicated in other reports,[30] public participation in *Agenda 21*-processes typically does not live up to expectations of democratic citizenship. The absence of citizen involvement is more often than not interpreted in official circles as signifying low interest in political matters and a lack of community orientation. However, as Bregnballe's studies also indicate, these interpretations are more the prejudices and self-fulfilling prophecies of authorities and experts than anything essential to the public. Explanations have often been sought in clichés about the *demos*, clichés that rely on the presupposition that the individual necessarily accords with the self-centered, possessive image of economic doctrine. The Ministry of the Environment claims that, in present-day society, "Self-interest, like e.g. health and personal well-being, is becoming more important as motive force for action and political standpoint than the concern for society as a whole."[31] The Ministry therefore recommends that information campaigns about health, well-being, and the like should be the method of communication with the population in matters of sustainable development.[32] Conspicuous by its absence is any effort to engage the public in a way that would activate concerns about common interests or elicit political debate and action.

Over the years, the ProSus research group has made several assessments of Norwegian national policy relating to *Agenda 21*. After monitoring the implementation of Local Agenda 21 for many years, ProSus researchers reached this conclusion: "Experience from both rural and urban municipalities points at the participatory aspect of LA21 as being *particularly difficult to handle*."[33] On this basis, the researchers suggest that authorities *reduce* their ambitions for participation, thereby reducing the "democratic aspect" of LA21, in order to better "cope with the challenges" it presents.[34] LA21 continues to be framed in terms of management by objectives, but this time however, participation is no longer seen as instrumental to success—by, for example, creating "ownership"—but as a potential *hindrance*.[35] However, it is hardly surprising that people are reluctant to contribute their viewpoints to "cooperation" or "dialogue" so long as their viewpoints are inspected, sorted, and possibly replaced by more proper ones. Also, the interpretation of ProSus and the authorities misses a key democratic point. The lack of popular enthusiasm for LA21 processes is not lack of political interest, but the opposite: people want real dialogue and an influence in things that matter.

The depoliticization of environmental politics evident in the Norwegian experience with sustainable development projects should also be linked to the dominant discursive framework at the time *Agenda 21* was received in Norway. This was the discourse of ecological modernization,[36] a key aspect of which is the so-called win-win principle. What is good for the environment, this principle holds, is usually good for business (as in the efficient use of energy and other resources). When sustainable development was introduced as a new policy concept in Norway, it was largely promoted as a *win-win ecomodernist reform*, thus ruling out radical possibilities and intensifying the depoliticizing tendencies already present in the Brundtland Report and *Agenda 21*.[37]

Environmental policy documents became a lot less depressing in the 1990s than they had been before, because it was no longer considered necessary to make sacrifices in terms of comfort, profit, or standard of living. With win-win ecomodernization, the possibility of a fundamental incompatibility between different interest spheres in society disappeared from discourse. The weak organizational division between interest spheres in Norway fits hand-in-glove with the win-win aspect of ecomodernization. Business, public administration, and civil society were all perceived as supporting the same thing: sustainable development. The interests of normally conflicting social spheres not only became compatible, but also came to be perceived as in essence the *same*. Rational principles of production—producing more with less—were then discursively located at the center of solutions for all kinds of environmental problems. It accordingly became easier for commercial actors and state authorities to legitimize the pursuit of economic goals. The framework of win-win environmentalism thus contributes to the depoliticization of environmental politics by deflecting attention from issues whose discussion might challenge the economic foundation of a society dependent on resource extraction and high-consumption lifestyles in the context of advanced capitalism.

STRATEGY WITHOUT PRIORITIES: DEPOLITICIZING ENVIRONMENTAL POLITICS

The depoliticization of environmental politics in Norway has become especially pronounced in recent years with trends in official documents and the belated creation of a National Action Plan for *Agenda 21*. To depoliticize something so clearly political, however, is sure to generate problems. Conflicts may be covered over, but paradoxes remain, as we shall see—particularly as both the individual and democracy itself get the blame for environmental problems.

The first Norwegian action plan for Sustainable Development—a "National Agenda 21"—was completed in the fall of 2003, eleven years after Rio. This followed the launch by the Royal Ministry of Foreign Affairs of the long-awaited first Norwegian National Strategy for Sustainable Development[38] in August 2002, a few weeks before it was to be presented at the World Summit for Sustainable Development in Johannesburg. The Strategy has been the subject of much critique from the environmental movement, and it is debatable whether this document should be called a strategy at all, as it contains very little in terms of specific goals and means of reaching them (proposals, proposed effects of strategic measures, etc.).[39]

The Strategy was not formed in accord with the recommendations of Rio in that there was a very limited process of involvement, cooperation, and mutual learning.[40] The explicit main objective of the Strategy is to ensure economic and social welfare "within a sound environmental framework."[41] However, structures are not up for discussion and possible restructuring. At *no point* in the Strategy is there any suggestion of possible conflicts between environmental goals and economic or social welfare. The key to consolidating environmental and economic goals is the principle of "ecoefficiency"—"producing more from less."[42] Adopting with the other Nordic countries the goal of a transition to sustainable development by 2020,[43] the Norwegian strategy seeks to do away with potential conflict through a perpetual win-win situation: "the Nordic countries *will complete the transition* to sustainable development in which economic growth *has been decoupled* from increasing pressure on the environment and increasing resource consumption."[44] The desired decoupling of economic growth from resource depletion *will be achieved*, it is further stated, as the Nordic countries "seek to promote the demand for cleaner products and remove barriers to trade for environmentally friendly and resource-efficient technologies. They will also seek to play a leading role in research in this field."[45] No doubt, there are environmental gains in replacing existing products and processes with more ecoefficient ones. To a certain extent this approach might meet its expectations—but the blind spots and risks are large. Most important, simply assuming a win-win situation risks downplaying serious problems. Potential conflicts are, for example, downplayed by the Strategy in the following proposals:

- Ensure economic growth in one of the richest countries in the world[46]—and at the same time eradicate extreme poverty and hunger.[47]

- Reduce climate emissions[48]—while increasing the production (extraction) of oil and natural gas[49]—and manage the petroleum resources for the maximum economic benefit.[50]

- Muster public participation and collective efforts—without promoting the political role of the citizen. There is *no mention* of the "citizen" in the strategy, even in sections where the issues are democratic procedures and public participation. Instead, there is much reference to the "consumer."

The Strategy endorses many goals without examining possible contradictions among them. The problem is not so much the content of the various proposals and the frequent use of economic justifications for protection of the environment, but the failure to establish explicit priorities. The lack of critical analysis obscures potential conflicts and allows a harmonious picture in a manner that reinforces the legitimacy of the status quo.

An environmental policy strategy may be formulated in a way that enables the government to uphold legitimacy while, at the same time, promoting the institutions and practices that produce environmental problems. This possibility is especially enhanced if the causes of the problems, and the responsibility for creating solutions, are discursively located as *external* to official institutions. Such an impression will manage to uphold legitimacy, exempt the authorities from criticism, and fend off political demands for the restructuring of central institutions. The Strategy is crafted in a way that creates precisely this impression.

If business as usual is maintained in the economic management of the nation *and* the desired environmental results fail to appear, then some discursive move is needed to save the authorities from embarrassment and a consequent loss of communicative power. Problems must be discursively located outside the authorities' sphere of responsibility *and* outside the market. How is this to be done? By blaming "the individual."

CONSUMPTION AND LIFESTYLE: PROBLEMS OF "MARKET SOCIETY"

In the Norwegian mass media over the past decade or so, the focus on environmental problems has been in terms of individuals' consumption and lifestyle. Journalists and commentators frequently identify "market society" and "consumer culture" as *main causes* of environmental problems. The tendency to advance the same diagnosis in official policy documents becomes especially evident in efforts to guide public dialogue. Yet this type of problem formulation is bound to present a paradox to national policy makers. As authorities are forced to address "market society" and "consumer culture" as *unwanted* phenomena, the conceptual basis of the policy orientation promoting the nation's economy tends to be undermined. With a national economy heavily dependent on the circulation and transportation of goods—and, in the case of Norway, on extraction of fossil fuels—how can the authorities fight market society and consumerism? Doing so would mean a rejection of official goals and practices and a phasing out of structural dependencies. Promoting the continued extraction of fossil fuels in the face of the climate crisis does, indeed, require much rhetorical hocus-pocus.

Environmental policy programs in Norway have recently turned toward matters of identity, culture, and health. These are all matters that concern the individual and that belong to the private sphere. Health, the most recent matter to be emphasized,[51] is spoken of as a matter of individual self-interest. As shown earlier, the Ministry of the Environment even makes this aspect of health its central interest as a way of promoting "political" mobilization. This turn in environmental policy helps to shift attention away from the complex, interdependent relationships that constitute the environment, toward the well-being of individualized human beings. At the same time, the focus on the individual means that, in the view of the Ministry, members of the public will understand themselves and be aroused and mobilized only in terms of private self-interests—not on behalf of the community, as citizens concerned for the future, or as people who care enough about nature and society to act.

Of the two major problems identified in the Norwegian discourse, it is striking how most attention goes to "consumer culture" and significantly less to "market society." Indeed, consumer culture tends to be criticized not in terms of a collective culture but as a problem that can be reduced to—and blamed on—selfish, narrow-minded individuals.[52] Such an over-emphasis on individuals to the neglect of societal structures is, as we shall shortly see, connected to an attack on democracy. What is overlooked and undermined is the chance for the creation of a democratic society that would involve the activity of political citizens, working for the common good and critically examining social structures on a continuing basis.[53]

The leading idea of *Agenda 21*—the integration of environmental and developmental concerns—did in fact suggest the importance of a structure. With sustainable development on the agenda, systemic structures are addressed in a much more radical way than when environmental problems are regarded in isolation. Since 1997, the principle of sustainable development was supposed to be an underlying principle for *all* Norwegian national policy programs,[54] and this principle indicates a need for a shift in organization and ideology toward a systemic perspective. As long as environmental problems were regarded in isolation, they could be addressed one by one, without attention to systemic structural changes. Sustainable development, however, requires a deeper, more thorough investigation into the workings of economic structures, decision processes, international relations—in short, a total systemic debate concerning laws, norms, and institutions.

How is it that individuals come to be seen as responsible for structural matters? In the Norwegian case, the problem cannot entirely be laid at the doorstep of officials. There is a reductionist tendency to blame the individual within environmental ideology itself, and official discourse has readily incorporated and adapted thought fragments from this tendency. Norwegian environmental authorities are known to have close personal, financial, and organizational ties with the environmental movement's voluntary organizations as well as with research institutes and centers.[55] During the 1990s, many Norwegian non-governmental organizations have become increasingly dependent on financial support from the state.[56] At the same time, the Ministry of the Environment has been able to enhance the legitimacy of official policy by drawing upon convenient themes of depoliticization and individual responsibility within environmentalism itself. [57]

To illustrate the point, we can look the ideology of a grassroots movement—The Future in Our Hands—which gathered much support in Norway in the 1970s and has been influential ever since. This movement is strongly critical of the workings of the world economy for fostering an unfair distribution of global resources. Yet, according to the movement's founder Erik Dammann, the central thought of the movement was the following assumption: "[I]f enough [individuals] demonstrated their will to change by getting off the merry-go-round of consumption, politicians would be forced to alter their strategy from [economic] growth to global solidarity and environmental responsibility."[58] Although structural change was the objective, individual change in lifestyle was the means. The original intention was political—but the consequences were quite the opposite. Now, in critical retrospect, Dammann calls himself naive for not taking into account "structural force" (*systemtvang*), particularly in the form of macroeconomic institutions. Expecting global structural changes to arise more or less directly from the actions of individuals was just expecting too much. Unfortunately, Norwegian officials have long warmly embraced this image of the individual's importance. As already suggested, this image serves very well to veil the workings of power structures and managerial techniques.[59] In this way of thinking, individuals are responsible for environmental problems, and they will be blamed further if the problems are not solved.

Herein we find the basis for an attack on democracy. Over the past three or four decades a recurring claim, especially by political scientists, has been that the environmental crisis is too serious a matter to be left to democratic procedures such as voting. Some have claimed that there is not enough time to wait for the public to reach the right decisions. Some have pointed out that the parliamentary system itself is too restraining or complicated—based on compromises between interest groups, and some simply have no confidence in the judgment of the public. One proponent of the rather widespread latter view is the Norwegian political scientist T.C. Wyller. Gravely concerned about the environmental future of the earth, Wyller claims that "the democratic system has itself added fuel to the fire. Economy and lifestyle decide, and the system elements of democracy influence."[60] According to Wyller, the democratic system is desirable only if citizens' attitudes are changed: "Democracy is an excellent system, provided that people use it right.... There is nothing the matter with the majority principle, only with the majority."[61] Even though the main source of the problem, in Wyller's view, lies with the economy, he still blames democracy. This position is based on a mechanistic conception of "democracy" in which democratic procedures are regarded as the "channel" for expressing the subjective states of citizens. A basic assumption here is that *present society is a fully instituted democracy*. From this assumption, he infers that the democratic subjects have, more or less purposefully, created *this* specific society and its environmental problems. The easy conclusion, then, is that democratic subjects either are not interested enough, or at present are incapable of, fostering an environmentally responsible better society and therefore require the rational guidance of officials. However, if the premise that democracy is sufficiently instituted in today's society turns out to be false, the rest of Wyller's argument becomes dubious. It may be that more, not less, influence by the people is needed. To imagine this possibility means to depart from the conventional focus that blames structural problems on individuals and seeks solutions in the mobilization of individuals primarily through private motives. We are then looking at a strengthening of the *demos* that would reverse the depoliticization of environmental politics.

A DISEMPOWERED DEMOS?

Even though officials find it convenient to blame the individual-as-consumer for environmental problems, the role of the consumer is vital to the larger system, as becomes obvious at moments of crisis. In the chaotic times following September 11, 2001, the mayor of New York and the US President desperately encouraged people to buy goods and spend money. Ironically, they turned private consumption into a public duty with the message: "Be a good citizen: Shop!"—"Want to do something for your country? Shop!" Campaigns against selfish consumerism may be significant in belittling the potential for a critical and active *demos*, but consumer culture is in fact a necessary part of the prevailing economic structure. Consumerism is regularly reinforced by the prevailing structure, aided by the active intervention of officials when consumer demand falters.

When, as in the case of Norway, the individual and private areas of social life become the focus of administrative attention, democracy is undermined. A central democratic principle is reversed as public policy is directed at altering the thoughts, values, and preferences of the *demos*. For democratic public policy should be informed by an active *demos*—not by a *demos* under the direction of officials. In such a context of official direction, the *political as such* slips out of sight. The power practices at work are repressive, but not overtly so; precisely because they are not openly authoritarian, these repressive practices are able to reinforce their own strength by cultivating the passivity of political subjects and veiling the potential of political action.

Western society is supposedly democratic, and its citizens have supposedly chosen democratically to create precisely the society they have: market society. Accordingly, the private, isolated individual—stripped of citizen-capacity and political community—is not only made responsible for all the wrongs of the system, but is also blamed for not changing it. For administrative officials, research and strategic measures focusing on people's *attitudes* constitute ways to distribute guilt, exercise control, avoid blame, and preserve the status quo. The power of this system is enhanced through discursive and managerial techniques that disempower political subjects. The result for the *demos* is guilt and loss of creative power.

Official admonitions of the need for individuals to change have an aura of common sense because they fit with much that is taken for granted in a consumer-oriented society. Environmental problems are portrayed as unwanted offspring of this society, which threaten its promise of a good society. At the same time, however, these very problems serve to justify central institutions of the society. The continuous generation of environmental problems helps to legitimize administrative paternalism, while keeping the public passive with guilt. What remains obscured is the possibility that solving environmental problems would require a structural change that would replace the production of consumers by the development of active citizens. To fully entertain this possibility would mean violating what is nearly a tabooed insight in official environmental discourse: that it is not the individual, but society as a collectively organized structure, that produces environmental problems. By blaming the individual, the self-representation of the society is protected so that the prevailing social order can be preserved. The source of environmental problems is thus located outside the society proper in the wayward, anti-social tendencies of individuals. For the prevailing social structure, however, intense private demands from the consumer are—far from being anti-social—in fact necessary to ensure stable order and functioning. The individual consumer is thus in a bind as consumption is both promoted and blamed. The depoliticization of environmental politics helps to maintain this bind by blocking the way out.

NOTES

1 My deep thanks to Doug Torgerson for his insightful assistance in matters of language, phrasing, and clarification.

2 The term individualization has been used with very different meanings. Here it signifies a concept much like that of Ulrich Beck in *Risk Society* (London: Sage, 1992): Individualization is a sociological process whereby the individual is freed from traditional and collective settings and left to his or her own resources, made responsible for managing all aspects of his or her life.

3 The Norwegian Ministry of the Environment, National Strategy for Sustainable Development *(Nasjonal strategi for bærekraftig utvikling*, Oslo, 2001), paragraph 1.3 (author's translation).

4 In reality there has, of course, been little structural change in the turnover of goods. The major difference from the 1970s industrial production is that the pollution is less visible at the site of the factory, but reveals its face at a much later stage, as "junk," wrapping, etc., after having entered people's homes.

5 Together with Sweden, Germany, the Netherlands, and Japan, Norway has been named as one of a very few "clean, green countries" (John S. Dryzek, *The Politics of the Earth* [Oxford: Oxford University Press, 1997], p. 137).

6 Especially in the fields of developmental aid, climate protection, and biodiversity, Norwegian representatives have made a considerable effort to put into place and strengthen international regimes (William Lafferty and Morten Nordskag, "Concluding Perspectives on Governing for Sustainable Development in Norway," in W.M. Lafferty, M. Nordskag, and H.A. Aakre, eds., *Realizing Rio in Norway. Evaluative Studies of Sustainable Development*, [Oslo: ProSus, 2002], p. 180).

7 Lafferty and Nordskag, "Concluding Perspectives," pp. 179–80.

8 Morten Nordskag, "Improving Decision-Making for Sustainable Development? The Role of Science and Information," in Lafferty *et al.*, eds., *Realizing Rio in Norway*, p. 103.

9 *Agenda 21: Action Plan for the 21st Century* is a recommended program for international cooperation for a sustainable development, which was produced at the United Nations Conference on Environment and Development in Rio de Janeiro in 1992. This conference was, in turn, a follow-up to the Brundtland Report (World Commission on Environment and Development, *Our Common Future* [Oxford: Oxford University Press, 1987]). Some 177 nations signed the *Agenda 21*, agreeing to work for a global shift in the years to come. The nations' follow-up to the Rio accords is constantly being monitored and evaluated—recently at the World Summit for Sustainable Development in Johannesburg in August 2002.

10 Lafferty and Nordskag, "Concluding Perspectives," p. 173.

11 The Norwegian Ministry of the Environment, *Nasjonal strategi for bærekraftig utvikling* (Oslo, 2001).

12 The Royal Norwegian Ministry of Foreign Affairs, *National Strategy for Sustainable Development* (Oslo, 2002).

13 The Norwegian Ministry of Finance, *Nasjonal handlingsplan for bærekraftig utvikling* (Oslo, 2003).

14 Stephen Yearley, *Sociology, Environmentalism, Globalization* (London: Sage, 1996), p. 133.

15 World Commission on Environment and Development, *Our Common Future*, pp. 1–13, §49.

16 The term "Local Agenda 21" signifies Chapter 28 in *Agenda 21*. The chapter is only three pages out of about 700, yet it has by far received the most attention in the Norwegian reception of the *Agenda 21*.

17 United Nations, *Agenda 21, The United Nations Programme of Action from Rio* (Geneva: United Nations 1993), ch. 28.3.

18 Statens Forurensningstilsyn (Norwegian Pollution Control Authority), *Bærekraftige lokalsamfunn. Prosjektplan* (Oslo: Statens Forurensningstilsyn, 1996), p. 6.

19 Anne Bregnballe, *Når opplysning blir hindring. Legfolk og fagfolk i dialog om utviklings-og miljøpolitikk.* Doctoral thesis, Department of Political Science, University of Oslo, July 2004.

20 Bregnballe, *Når opplysning blir hindring*, p. 229.

21 C. Aall, W. M. Lafferty, T. Bjørnæs, *Kartlegging av hindringer i prosjekt Bærekraftige lokalsamfunn* (Oslo: Norwegian Pollution Control Authority, Report 99:01, 1999), p.27. The researchers continue: "The challenge, consequently, lies in *extending* the perspective to include structural conditions and recognise the necessity of reducing the level of consumption in some areas."

22 Aall *et al.*, *Kartlegging*, p. 25.

23 The quantity of press coverage, workshops, conferences, and especially information material has been an important success criterion for LA21 in Norway. Even in local projects where environmental problems like fossil fuel emissions and garbage production have *increased*, Local Agenda 21 has still been regarded as a success due to the application of these criteria (H.J. Müller, "Miljøbyen—allmenningens komedie?," in Ann Nielsen, ed., *Miljøsosiologi* [Oslo: Pax Forlag, 1997]).

24 Cf. Norwegian Ministry of Finance, *Nasjonal handlingsplan*, paragraph 1.6.4.

25 Norwegian Ministry of the Environment, *Nasjonal strategi for bærekraftig utvikling*, section 2, "Political Challenges" (author's translation, emphasis added).

26 ProSus—Program for Research and Documentation for a Sustainable Society—is an officially funded, strategic research program with the mandate to monitor and stimulate the Norwegian follow-up to the Brundtland Commission's recommendations. The research group produces both evaluative assessments and recommendations for Norway's implementation of *Agenda 21*. In 1998, ProSus was appointed by the Ministry of the Environment to work out guidelines for implementation of Local Agenda 21 in Norway, presented in the report by T. Bjørnæs and W.M. Lafferty, *Innføring av lokal Agenda 21 i Norge* (Oslo: ProSus, 1999).

27 Bjørnæs and Lafferty, *Innføring av lokal Agenda 21*, p. 14 (author's translation).

28 W.M Lafferty, C. Aall and Ø. Seippel, *Fra miljøvern til bærekraftig utvikling i norske kommuner—Overgang fra MIK til Lokal Agenda 21*, Rapport nr. 2/98 (Oslo: ProSus, 1998), p. 16.

29 Lafferty *et al.*, *Fra miljøvern til bærekraftig utvikling*, p. 121.

30 Cf. T. Bjørnæs and I.T. Norland, "Local Agenda 21: Pursuing Sustainable Development at the Local Level," in Lafferty *et al.*, eds., *Realizing Rio in Norway*.

31 Norwegian Ministry of the Environment, *Nasjonal strategi for bærekraftig utvikling*, paragraph 1.2 (author's translation).

32 Norwegian Ministry of the Environment, *Nasjonal strategi for bærekraftig utvikling*, paragraph 2.

33 Bjørnæs and Norland, "Local Agenda 21," p. 58 (emphasis added).

34 Bjørnæs and Norland, "Local Agenda 21," p. 58.

35 In the here much quoted volume *Realizing Rio*, different researchers at ProSus take a serious look at the Norwegian Government's governing practices in matters of sustainable development, ten years after Rio. In sum, the researchers express disappointment. It would of course be relevant to ask whether ProSus's own recommendations have in some way contributed to the poor results—as their guidelines have been central to Norwegian authorities' implementation of *Agenda 21*—but that is not an issue in the assessment.

36 See, e.g., Maarten Hajer, *The Politics of Environmental Discourse* (Oxford: Oxford University Press, 1995), and John S. Dryzek, *The Politics of the Earth* (Oxford: Oxford University Press, 1997). Over the past decade, there have been debates about the ideological contents of ecological modernization, especially along the lines of strong versus weak versions (Dryzek, following Peter Christoff) or reflexive versus non-reflexive ecomodernization (Hajer). I shall not engage in these discussions but merely comment on principles that are common and necessary for both the weak and the strong type, but not sufficient for strong/reflexive ecomodernization.

37 A crucial distinction between ecomodernization and sustainable development is that the latter has a strong focus on global and temporal social equity. The Norwegian policy documents that introduced sustainable development as a policy principle initially failed to encompass this "developmental" dimension, and focused on environmental issues only, most importantly in The Norwegian Ministry of the Environment, *White paper 58 (1996–97), Miljøvernpolitikk for en bærekraftig utvikling. Dugnad for framtida* (Oslo, 1997).

38 Royal Norwegian Ministry of Foreign Affairs, *National Strategy for Sustainable Development*.

39 *Cf.* ProSus, *Skisse til Nasjonal Agenda 21: Kommentarer og anbefalinger fra Program for forskning og utredning for et bærekraftig samfunn*, Arbeidsnotat (*Working Paper*) 1/2003, (Oslo: ProSus, 2003).

40 Eivind Hovden and Solveig Torjussen, "Environmental Policy Integration in Norway," in Lafferty *et al.*, eds., *Realizing Rio in Norway*, p. 36.

41 Royal Norwegian Ministry of Foreign Affairs: *National Strategy for Sustainable Development*, p. 40.

42 Royal Norwegian Ministry of Foreign Affairs: *National Strategy for Sustainable Development*, p. 36.

43 *New Bearings for the Nordic Countries* (Nordic Council of Ministers, 2001).

44 Royal Norwegian Ministry of Foreign Affairs: *National Strategy for Sustainable Development*, p. 36 (emphasis added).

45 Royal Norwegian Ministry of Foreign Affairs: *National Strategy for Sustainable Development*, p. 36.

46 Royal Norwegian Ministry of Foreign Affairs: *National Strategy for Sustainable Development*, pp. 8, 39.

47 The Strategy commits to the Millennium Development Goals (United Nations, 2000), and highlights goal no. 1, where a subtarget is to "halve the proportion of people whose income is less than one dollar per day by 2015" (Royal Norwegian Ministry of Foreign Affairs: *National Strategy for Sustainable Development*, p. 8).

48 Royal Norwegian Ministry of Foreign Affairs: *National Strategy for Sustainable Development*, pp. 22–23, 37, 39.

49 Royal Norwegian Ministry of Foreign Affairs: *National Strategy for Sustainable Development*, pp. 24, 39. The Strategy elaborates on how to manage the revenues of the petroleum industry, the Government Petroleum fund. It enters a discussion on levels of public spending, interest rates, budget balance and future pension expenditure. Not once does the Strategy discuss *whether* the oil should be extracted and sold—only how to manage the revenues.

50 Royal Norwegian Ministry of Foreign Affairs: *National Strategy for Sustainable Development*, pp. 25, 40. ProSus researchers Lafferty and Nordskag comment that the gap between rhetoric and performance is "at its strongest and most consequential" in the area of energy consumption and fossil fuels emissions. Here, Norway is "seriously at odds" with virtually *all* the standards applied in the research (Lafferty and Nordskag, "Concluding Perspectives," p. 180). As they also point out, this is *the* area where Norway bears a special responsibility toward the rest of the world, and to future generations, due to the nation's wealth (which stems from its abundant natural energy resources, its technical and knowledge resources, and—on the negative side—its high energy consumption per capita).

51 *Cf.* a recently instigated research program in the the Norwegian Research Council called "Environment and Health."

52 More subtle, but no less discrediting to the *demos*, are well-meaning attempts to understand the consumer on her own premises: "consumerism" as "identity construction."

53 For a thorough argument in favor of politicization of environmental issues, see Douglas Torgerson, *The Promise of Green Politics: Environmentalism and the Public Sphere* (Durham, NC: Duke University Press, 1999). See also the works of Cornelius Castoriadis for a more general discussion of political creativity and radical democracy.

54 The Norwegian Government's White Paper 58 (1996–97), *Miljøvernpolitikk for en bærekraftig utvikling* (Oslo: The Ministry of the Environment, 1997).

55 See, e.g., John Dryzek *et al.*, *Green States and Social Movements* (Oxford: Oxford University Press, 2003).

56 Dryzek *et al.*, *Green States and Social Movements*. See also K. Strømsnes and P. Selle, eds., *Miljøvernpolitikk og Miljøvernorganisering mot år 2000* (Oslo: Aschehoug, 1996).

57 The thought that environmental problems are caused by "wrong attitudes" has a long and honourable history in Norwegian environmentalism—from its cultural and ideological roots in pietism, via deep ecology to the Norwegian adaptation of ecological modernization. The central idea is that actions "spring" from a set of beliefs and values, seated in the individual's consciousness. It follows from this idea that, in order to change behavior and actions, the values must be altered first. Thus, the nodal point for societal change remains the individual and his or her system of beliefs and values.

58 E. Dammann, "Et helhetssyn på alternativbevegelsenes utfordringer foran tusenårsskiftet," in K. Strømsnes and P. Selle, eds., *Miljøvernpolitikk og Miljøvernorganisering mot år 2000* (Oslo: Aschehoug, 1996), p. 115.

59 *Cf.* Michel Foucault's concept of *"gouvernmentalité"* as developed in his "Governmentality," in G. Burchell, C. Gordon, and P. Miller, eds., *The Foucault Effect* (London: Harvester Wheatsheaf, 1991).

60 T.C. Wyller: *Demokratiet og miljøkrisen* (Oslo, Universitetsforlaget 1999), p.39 (author's translation).

61 Wyller: *Demokratiet og miljøkrisen*, p. 76 (author's translation).

12

Democratic Deliberation and Environmental Policy: Opportunities and Barriers in Britain[1]

Graham Smith

Deliberative democracy has emerged as one of the most serious and influential theoretical challenges to conventional liberal democracy. Although vigorous debate continues about the precise meaning of deliberative democracy, its main institutional principle is clear: greater participation by citizens in debates about public problems increases the democratic legitimacy of decision-making processes. The institutionalization of inclusive and unconstrained democratic dialogue among free and equal citizens is widely viewed as the most defensible method of achieving legitimacy in collective decision making and in sustaining forms of political authority.[2] The growing interest in deliberative democracy from within green political theory adds a further rationale: environmental policy developed through democratic deliberation is not only more legitimate in a normative sense but also is likely to be more effective in an instrumental sense; that is, it is more likely to result in environmentally sustainable policy. But, if deliberative democracy has so much to offer, why has it not been fully institutionalized?

After briefly considering the significance of deliberative democracy in green political theory, this chapter examines in detail the limited extent to which democratic deliberation has been institutionalized within the environmental policy process in Britain. Although the focus is on one country, the overall pattern of institutionalization is likely to be similar in other liberal democratic polities despite differences in detail. What we find in the current British situation is the emergence of notable opportunities for democratic deliberation on environmental policy, but also significant barriers. These barriers mean that, despite much in the way of hope and rhetoric, the full institutionalization of democratic deliberation in environmental policy is far from an immediate prospect. However, reflecting on the failures as well as the successes helps to clarify what this institutionalization might mean in practice and indicates the challenges that should be expected in attempting to enhance deliberation within the environmental policy-making process.

DELIBERATIVE DEMOCRACY AND GREEN POLITICAL THEORY

Theories of deliberative democracy are having a quite profound effect on green political thought. A roll call of contemporary green political theorists would highlight a significant level of commitment to the deliberative ideal and a widespread belief that the institutionalization of democratic deliberation would lead to policy making that is both more legitimate and more environmentally sustainable.[3] With regard to the latter, deliberative institutions are perceived to have an epistemological advantage over other approaches to social choice because of their ability to respond to the complexity, uncertainty, and problems of collective action associated with many contemporary environmental problems.[4] Inclusive and unconstrained democratic dialogue increases the capacity of a political system to lessen the problem of bounded rationality: "the fact that our imaginations and calculating abilities are limited and fallible."[5] More ecologically rational policy decisions are likely to emerge by drawing on the knowledge, experience, and capabilities of differently situated actors.

Democratic deliberation improves information flows by actively engaging numerous voices, including those individuals and groups with direct experience of the effects of environmental change. Too often decision makers are far removed from the impact of their decisions: the experience, knowledge, and perspectives of those whose practices are more attuned to the changes in local ecosystems are not articulated in the policy process. Deliberative institutions promise an ingenious mechanism through which the application of scientific and technological knowledge and expertise might be democratically regulated—an institutional setting within which the divisions between "expert" and "lay" knowledge can be challenged and reformulated.[6] Similarly, deliberative arrangements are more likely to overcome coordination and collective action problems that lie at the heart of many environmental problems: evidence suggests that a period of dialogue prior to decision making reduces the likelihood of free-riding in the provision of public goods.[7]

This epistemological defense of deliberative democracy is often presented alongside an ethical argument about the types of preferences that prosper under deliberative conditions. It is argued that democratic deliberation provides motivation and encouragement to articulate preferences and justifications that are "public-spirited" in nature. David Miller, for example, stresses the "moralizing effect of public discussion": deliberation will tend to eliminate irrational preferences based on false empirical beliefs, morally repugnant preferences that no one is willing to advance in the public arena, and narrowly self-regarding preferences.[8] For greens, the moralizing effect of deliberation offers the opportunity to emphasize the public-good character of many environmental problems and to expose and challenge the narrowly self-interested grounds of many environmentally degrading and unsustainable practices, together with the powerful interests that promote such practices. It offers a context in which preferences and values are not treated as incorrigible, but as an object of reflection, challenge, and possible reformulation.

Robert Goodin has argued that deliberative institutions offer the most likely mechanism through which people can be induced to internalize nature's interests. Greens (who have already incorporated nature's interests) will have a voice to challenge environmentally insensitive decisions and offer alternative proposals. Further, the public-spirited character of deliberation means that there is also likely to be "anticipatory internalization" of green ethical arguments by participants: "discursive democracy ... creates a situation in which interests other than your own are called to mind."[9]

Goodin's argument relates directly to a further attraction of deliberative democratic theory: its association with a strong conception of citizenship. Greens have seen much promise in the more active deliberative conception of citizenship for the development of an ecological ethos and the practice of ecological stewardship.[10] It is not simply participation *per se* that is important to an expression of such democratic citizenship, but rather a particular form of civic engagement that encourages the public articulation, defense, and revision of judgments. Democratic deliberation offers conditions under which citizens will encounter and reflect upon ecological knowledge and values and will be more likely to internalize these in their judgments and practices. As Robyn Eckersley argues, "Public spirited deliberation is the process by which we learn of our dependence on others (and the environment) and the process by which we learn to recognize and respect differently situated others (including non-human others and future generations)."[11]

The institutionalization of democratic deliberation promises much: the articulation of, and reflection on, environmental values and knowledge in the policy process; more legitimate and environmentally sensitive policy outcomes; and a more environmentally aware citizenry. This is certainly an enticing theoretical idea of how political engagement should progress. However it appears a long way removed from the actual nature of the policy process in contemporary liberal democratic states. The rest of this chapter will focus on the extent to which democratic deliberation has been institutionalized within the environmental policy process in Britain, paying particular attention to the institutional barriers that thwart institutionalization.

FRAGMENTATION AND DIFFERENTIATION: THE BRITISH POLICY PROCESS

In the study of political systems there is a common and unfortunate tendency to treat "the state" as a single, unitary actor and a belief that the analysis of the policy process will yield an identifiable center of power. Although the traditional model of political accountability—based on the sovereignty of Parliament—remains an important mode of justification within British politics, the actual reality of decision making is far more complex.

The complexity of the policy-making process is perhaps best captured in the governance and policy network literature, where it is recognized that a wide range of groups and organizations are involved in the political decision-making process, not only officials from different levels of government, but also government agencies, privatized utilities, private companies, voluntary organizations, community groups, and so on.[12] The contemporary political system is best characterized as differentiated, disaggregated, and fragmented. Different parts of government focus on different policy issues and have different interests. In their classic study of the British political system, *Governing Under Pressure*, Jeremy Richardson and Grant Jordan attempt to characterize such differentiation:

> Policy making in most Western democracies has ... become compartmentalized. The policy-making map is in reality a series of vertical compartments or segments—each segment inhabited by a different set of organized groups and generally impenetrable by "unrecognized groups" or by the general public.[13]

The most obvious manifestation of differentiation is the number of government departments dealing with different policy issues, for example, the economy, industry, agriculture, health, education, environment, and so on. But even within these departments, policy making is further differentiated into specialist policy arenas (sometimes referred to as "policy subsystems"), typically involving close relationships between government officials and pressure groups. The environment ministry, for example, is home to a number of policy arenas such as pollution control and wildlife conservation, each attracting the attention of different pressure groups. Policy arenas are always home to policy networks that can take the form of a highly exclusive "policy community" involving only a small number of actors able to frustrate major changes, or an "issue network" in which there is more competition of ideas and a wider range of interests involved in debates.[14] As David Marsh and Rod Rhodes argue,

> Government is fragmented, and in many cases, individual departments and a powerful interest have developed a *common* interest and policy, and the network fosters the mutual interests of its members against outsiders. The pattern of policy making is essentially elitist.... There is clear structural inequality in the access of interests to, and their influence over, government policy making.[15]

The strongest policy communities are typically those dominated by either producer or economic interests (for example, agriculture) or by professionals (for example, health). Where no other group has access, such communities have rightly been termed policy monopolies.[16] Environmentalists have frequently found themselves in opposition to some of the most widely recognized and powerful policy monopolies that developed in the second half of the twentieth century. Two of the best documented were the near-exclusive relations between officials from the Ministry of Agriculture, Fisheries and Food (MAFF) and representatives of the National Farmers' Union (NFU) and between officials of the Department of Transport and the British Road Federation.[17] Where such exclusive policy communities exist, they are able to exercise a high degree of power, containing and constraining the policy agenda and policy outcomes.

The governance literature highlights the extent to which policy networks are autonomous and self-governing. This is not to suggest that the "core executive"—the group of actors and institutions at the heart of central government—does not attempt to coordinate and steer the whole range of government business.[18] However, the extent to which the core executive is actually able to coordinate policy making is a matter of contention. There is an ongoing debate as to whether we are witnessing the "hollowing out of the state": changes in the structure and practice of government, including, for example, the privatization of services, the introduction of new public management techniques, and the loss of functions to European Union institutions, have increased the degree of fragmentation and created new difficulties in steering the policy-making process.[19] However, against this background, the core executive has found new ways to increase its capacity to coordinate and steer.[20] For example, the Blair Labour government introduced cross-cutting units such as the Social Exclusion Unit and Performance and Innovation Unit into the Cabinet Office in an attempt to coordinate the government's response to policy issues that cross departmental and policy arena boundaries.

Even with such developments within the core executive, much day-to-day policy making remains the province of policy networks. When the core executive attempts to coordinate activity across policy issues it often finds itself in conflict with departments that have historically developed their own patterns of work, relationships with other actors, and specific ways of framing policy problems.[21] Departments and policy networks are typically resistant to change and attempts at coordination. Summarizing the results of a series of empirical studies of policy networks in Britain, Marsh and Rhodes ominously note that they "are conspicuously silent on the accountability of networks. They describe a system of private government subject only to the most tenuous forms of accountability."[22] As Gerry Stoker argues, "There is a divorce between the complex reality of decision-making associated with governance and the normative codes used to explain and justify government."[23]

DEALING WITH THE ENVIRONMENT IN A DIFFERENTIATED POLITY

Given the differentiated nature of the policy process, what are the implications for environmental policy? Although since 1994 British governments have published sustainable development strategies that explicitly aim to integrate environmental considerations across all areas of policy,[24] it is fair to say that the environment tends to remain compartmentalized, just like most other policy issues: there is a particular department that has functional responsibility for environmental issues. In some ways this is desirable: better there be a part of government that has a direct interest in environmental issues, an institutional arena for developing environmental policy even when the issue-attention cycle focuses elsewhere. However, this apparent advantage can at the same time be a drawback. There is an assumption that environmental problems can be dealt with discretely, divorced from the concerns of other departments, be they fiscal, agriculture, health, or transport policy.

Such compartmentalization is endemic and exemplifies the "limits of the administrative mind."[25] The prevailing political and administrative arrangements shape the way in which governments define and respond to environmental problems. Individual environmental problems are typically defined in isolation rather than being seen as deeply interconnected with other policy issues. Rather than recognizing that environmental problems may constitute a challenge to contemporary development patterns, it is simply assumed that environmental problems can be effectively managed by a functionally differentiated administration.

The ability of existing policy networks (in particular tight policy communities) to frame policy issues and shape the choice of policy instruments means that environmental interests—whether from within the environment ministry or environmental pressure groups—have little meaningful opportunity to influence many policy arenas that directly affect the environment. For much of the second half of the twentieth century, the policy communities surrounding, for example, fiscal, agriculture, and transport policy, were relatively impenetrable to environmental interests. Their impact on the environment was generally ignored. For example, the House of Lords Select Committee on Sustainable Development, established in March 1994, called the Treasury to account for its apparent lack of interest in sustainable development. This, it seems, was "the first occasion on which the Treasury had sent a team to defend its contribution to environmental protection before a parliamentary committee."[26] Even though the government had recently launched its sustainability strategy in response to the 1992 Rio Earth Summit, the Treasury's attitude showed that action on developing new fiscal policies to protect the environment had been negligible. The Treasury took the view that such policy should be developed by the environment ministry. Solutions to complex environmental problems require more creative, imaginative, and coordinated responses than the current functional differentiation of the state appears able or willing to promote.

Administrative reforms since the early 1990s have provided the opportunity for environmental interests to have an impact on previously exclusive policy communities, but these reforms also highlight the extent to which the government has found it difficult to deal with environmental issues. On assuming power in 1997, the Labour government amalgamated the Department of the Environment into a "super-ministry," the Department of Environment, Transport, and the Regions (DETR). This re-organization was applauded by environmentalists on the grounds that one department would now be responsible for environment, transport, land-use planning, and local and regional government.[27] The potential for integration and dialogue across policy issues had increased. Although this potential represented both the growing influence of environmental interests inside and outside government and the end of the policy monopoly around road-building policy, the new department lasted less than four years. It was seen as simply too large to effectively manage the different and varying demands placed upon it.

A perception that the 1997 re-organization was actually driven by political expediency rather than environmental commitments was reinforced when the government responded to the foot-and-mouth policy disaster that began in 2000 by merging environment with agriculture. After the 2001 general election, the Department of Environment, Food, and Rural Affairs (DEFRA) was established. The significance of this restructuring is difficult to judge. On the one hand, it can be seen as a recognition that a sustainable agricultural policy is needed, one in which environmental concerns are as important as producer interests. The long-established agricultural policy monopoly has been broken up. On the other hand, there is some disquiet amongst environmentalists. The creation of DEFRA is perceived as a knee-jerk reaction to the agricultural crisis. In the long term, the re-organization may well damage environmental governance: the DETR was a prestige ministry that offered meaningful opportunities to integrate environmental concerns into transport, regional and local government, and land-use planning policy.[28] The environment as a policy issue seems to be passed around the administrative apparatus like a hot potato. Will environment be moved again when the issue-attention cycle moves on and the environmental impact of another area of policy is recognized?

Successive administrations have at some level attempted to overcome the differentiated and fragmented nature of their response to environmental issues. In the early 1990s the Conservative administration established the Cabinet Committee on the Environment and the Cabinet Sub-Committee of Green Ministers.[29] These committees are an explicit attempt to steer environmental governance from within the core executive, drawing in ministers from across government in an attempt to coordinate activity across disparate departments. The Cabinet Committee, made up of senior ministers from different departments, is chaired by the Deputy Prime Minister and reports directly to the Prime Minister. However it is difficult to judge the effectiveness of the committee because its activities are shrouded in secrecy: agendas are not published, meetings are held in private, and little information about outcomes is made public. In a recent parliamentary report, the Cabinet Committee was heavily criticized for its lack of transparency and for "not driving the Government's pursuit of sustainable development nor acting in a positive way to unearth and deal with related policy conflicts."[30]

Each department is required to appoint a Green Minister who then becomes a member of the Cabinet Sub-Committee of Green Ministers. Green Ministers have the responsibility of promoting sustainable development across government and specifically within their own departments through the use of environmental appraisals and other instruments. The activities of the Green Ministers have also been subject to criticism. The suspicion that the Sub-Committee's standing and impact under the Conservatives was highly limited was confirmed when it was revealed that the ministers had met only seven times in the five years from 1992 to 1996.[31] Under the Labour administration more administrative support has been provided. However, there is still little evidence of any meaningful impact on the practice of individual departments and policy arenas. For example, one of the objectives of the Green Ministers is to promote the use of environmental appraisals in their own departments: by early 2001, only 55 appraisals had taken place across government, 45 of which had been within the environment ministry.[32] In principle a network of ministers championing environmental concerns in each department is highly desirable, but in reality the ministers are relatively junior and environmental considerations are secondary to their primary departmental responsibilities. Disparate departmental interests continue to trump any cross-departmental commitment to sustainable development.

A further institutional reform was the establishment of the Sustainable Development Unit (SDU) within the DETR in 1997, with the explicit aim of spreading good practice across all government departments. However, unlike other specialist units such as the Social Exclusion Unit, the SDU was never placed in the core executive. Rather the sustainable development policy network found itself relatively marginalized and caught up in the reorganizations of the environment ministry.

This characterization of policy making and administrative restructuring presents a picture much removed from the ideal deliberative process outlined at the beginning of this chapter. The deliberative ideal points towards a policy process that is open to all affected interests and that proceeds through reasoned democratic dialogue. In contrast, the current policy process is highly differentiated and fragmented into policy arenas, with structural inequalities in access and influence. Where attempts have been made to coordinate environmental governance they have lacked sustained political leadership and impact, failing to effectively challenge established interests and policy networks. However, despite these inhospitable tendencies, successive governments have made limited attempts to embed forms of democratic deliberation in environmental decision making, particularly by consciously structuring spaces that draw in a more diverse range of actors to deliberate about environmental policy. Reflecting on these developments may help us to be clearer about the institutional barriers that weigh against increasing the deliberative capacity of the environmental policy process in Britain and other liberal democracies. Three developments in deliberation will be investigated: reforms within Parliament, institutional mechanisms to engage environmental pressure groups, and experiments in broader public participation.

Deliberative developments within Parliament

On taking office in 1997, the Labour government fulfilled a long-standing promise by establishing the Environmental Audit Committee (EAC) in the House of Commons. The EAC has a cross-party membership of 15 backbench Members of Parliament and has a scrutiny function: reviewing and assessing the contribution of the government and its various departments and agencies to environmental protection and sustainable development. To fulfill this function the EAC takes evidence from ministers and officials, but also from outside experts and interested parties.

The EAC has provided a highly visible and consistent location for debate and deliberation on environmental policy. In a relatively short time the EAC has become highly adept at examining major government policies and scrutinizing their contribution to sustainable development.[33] However, it concedes that it has not managed to effectively audit the government against the government's own targets—first, because the government has provided few targets, and second, because the EAC lacks the resources to fulfill all its objectives. Just as the work of the Public Accounts Select Committee (arguably the most powerful parliamentary scrutiny committee) is supported by the National Audit Office, the EAC argues that it needs an equivalent independent environmental audit facility in order to bridge the audit gap.[34]

The EAC offers an interesting site for democratic deliberation. The cross-party membership provides the opportunity for scrutiny, drawing on diverse perspectives on the environment. It is one of the few ongoing fora where ministers and officials are required to provide evidence in public. It also allows interested parties to offer evidence on the issues the EAC is scrutinizing. Typically the EAC requests submissions from major pressure groups and experts, but the wider public can also provide evidence for consideration. However, the deliberative capacity of the EAC is limited. Even when witnesses are called to give evidence in person, they find themselves being cross-examined; unlike the members of the committee, they are not allowed to engage in deliberation proper. That said, the transparency of the EAC's proceedings certainly adds a deliberative element to the environmental policy-making process, even if it is a relatively peripheral scrutiny function.

Engaging environmental organizations

Since 1994, the British government has developed formal mechanisms to engage environmental pressure groups in deliberations about sustainable development. One of the problems facing such groups in wishing to influence government policy is the sheer number of policy arenas and networks that have an impact on the environment. Environmental pressure groups have had much success developing effective relations with government officials within policy arenas in the environment ministry and certain specialist policy networks in other departments. However, the fragmentation and differentiation of policy making and the hostility toward environmental interests in many policy communities make it difficult to effectively engage across all relevant issues. Groups such as Friends of the Earth and Greenpeace have been forced to adopt a "twin-track" strategy—using their influence where they have access to policy networks and engaging in direct action in other areas. For example, Greenpeace's famous direct action against the deep-sea disposal of the Brent Spar was partially the consequence of the lack of access to the tight policy monopoly between officials from the Department for Trade and Industry and oil companies. Given that Greenpeace felt that it was excluded from the decision-making process on the disposal of oil platforms, the organization briefly occupied the Brent Spar in an attempt to generate public interest in the issue. The stunt successfully galvanized public action, particularly in Germany, and Greenpeace was able to reverse the decision.[35] Again the highly public direct actions against the planting of genetically modified organisms that have been undertaken by a variety of environmental organizations are in part a response to the lack of access to, and influence on, official decision-making processes.

The exclusionary character of many policy networks and direct action responses reinforce a classic pluralist vision of the policy process. Interest groups (including different interests within government itself) are competing to influence the policy-making process, utilizing whatever resources they have at their disposal. This is a long way removed from the deliberative ideal, which envisages affected interests engaging in a dialogue rather than direct competition.

An ambitious attempt to integrate environmental organizations into the policy process in a more formal, deliberative fashion was introduced initially by the Conservative government in 1994. Two new advisory bodies were created: the British Government Panel on Sustainable Development and the United Kingdom Round Table on Sustainable Development. The Panel comprised a group of five prominent and highly experienced individuals, appointed by the Prime Minister, whose role was to provide authoritative and independent advice on strategic issues and priorities for attaining sustainable development. The Panel's yearly reports contain detailed work and submissions in areas where it contends that the government lacks a coordinated approach.

Of more interest from a deliberative perspective, the Round Table embodied a "stakeholder" philosophy and aimed to involve the most significant organizations in the sustainable development debate from across the public, private, and voluntary sectors. Its membership included representatives of central and local government, the business and industrial sector, voluntary groups, and the scientific and academic communities. In order to work efficiently, the Round Table broke up into smaller sub-groups to develop its recommendations, often drawing in expert advisers and other interested parties into deliberations. The stakeholder structure was seen as important in order

to encourage discussion on major issues of sustainable development between people who approach them from different positions and who have different responsibilities. Members will be able to compare notes on what is being done in different sectors, to develop a better understanding of the problems faced by others, and to see how far a common perspective might be developed on various issues.[36]

Achieving broad consensus on contentious issues was seen as the goal of the organization. The Round Table produced a relatively impressive number of reports, some of which attracted short-term media and government attention, although its status within broader policy-making processes remained ambiguous. At times the Round Table was openly critical of government responses to its work.

The publication in 1999 of the Labour government's sustainable development strategy, *A Better Quality of Life*, led to a re-organization of this external machinery, with the two advisory bodies merging into the Sustainable Development Commission (SDC) chaired by the well-known environmentalist Jonathan Porritt. Like the Round Table before it, the SDC draws together representatives from across different sectors in an attempt to generate a common understanding of the demands of sustainable development: "The Commission's main role is to advocate sustainable development across all sectors in the UK, review progress towards it, and build consensus on the actions needed if further progress is to be achieved."[37]

Although it will take time to assess the impact of the SDC, its creation is an extremely interesting development. First, its function is explicitly deliberative—drawing together a range of different interests in the search for common perspectives and consensus on the way forward. Its ethos is far removed from the competitive spirit of interest-group pluralism. Second, the SDC is sponsored by the Cabinet Office and reports to the Prime Minister, the First Minister in Scotland, the First Secretary in Wales, and the First and Deputy First Ministers in Northern Ireland. Whereas the earlier Round Table was viewed as an advisory body for the environment ministry, it is significant that the SDC is sponsored from within the core executive and is thus less likely to be marginalized to the same extent as its predecessor.

Should such a stakeholder arrangement be viewed as an exemplary way to institutionalize democratic deliberation? Certainly a number of deliberative theorists have shown an interest in stakeholder processes such as mediation.[38] The attraction is obvious: organizations that represent a range of different and at times conflicting interests are brought together in a search for common understandings and collective solutions. But there are limits to an arrangement such as the SDC; most notably, it does not directly engage citizens in deliberations. Established environmental pressure groups and other organized interests are members of the SDC and participate in deliberations. But pressure groups are generally not internally democratic: the involvement of members is often limited to simply paying membership fees. Should deliberation be institutionalized not only between elites (in fora such as the SDC), but also between elites and the rank and file members of constituent organizations—even, indeed, among the rank and file of these organizations?[39] The lack of such institutionalized deliberation is not necessarily a problem fatal to democratic concerns. Given the complexity of contemporary societies, citizens do not have the time, desire, or expertise to engage continually in the critical scrutiny of political and scientific authority. The activities of environmental pressure groups are part of the accepted political division of labor. As Mark Warren suggests, "One important function of public pressure groups in a democratic setting is that they constitute a critical and attentive public."[40] But the deliberative potential of this stakeholder arrangement may still pose a problem on at least two grounds.

First, mainstream environmental organizations are not entirely representative of the plethora of environmental perspectives. There are a range of marginalized groups and communities whose environmental values and commitments are not well represented by established environmental pressure groups and whose interests are therefore not articulated in official stakeholder fora.[41] Second, the institutionalization of deliberation across the membership of interest groups may be necessary to avoid a gap between the common understanding generated within elite forums and the opinions of rank-and-file members who are not party to the deliberations. Theories of deliberative democracy assume that dialogue may lead to the transformation of opinions and preferences. But much of the attraction of environmental pressure groups to their supporters is their uncompromising stance on environmental issues. Tensions may well exist between the idea of group representation in stakeholder forums and the requirement within deliberative democracy for representatives to be open to the possibility of transformation.[42] The SDC is a welcome and important development, but it remains an elite forum and should not be viewed as the panacea of deliberative design.

Arguing for public participation

If we take the deliberative ideal seriously, then the establishment of neither the Environmental Audit Committee nor the Sustainable Development Commission achieves the desired levels of inclusiveness. They are clearly a vast improvement on the often highly exclusive policy networks that populate the policy-making landscape and potentially improve the deliberative capacity of the policy process. However, many affected interests remain excluded from deliberations, and there are few opportunities and incentives for citizens to directly engage in the policy process. The two most recent national sustainable development strategies have little or nothing to say about citizen engagement.[43] Discussions of the development of environmental citizenship are limited to promoting environmental education in schools and broader public awareness campaigns. The British government has not paid systematic attention to citizen engagement in the environmental policy processes. This does not mean there has been no interest at all from within government circles: there is growing pressure from a range of different sources to broaden forms of participation and deliberation and to engage citizens in a more constructive political manner. There appears to be a growing recognition that citizens are increasingly alienated from the environmental (and other) decisions made in their name and that their direct involvement in the policy process would increase the legitimacy of political authorities.

At the international level, *Agenda 21*—inaugurated at the Rio Earth Summit in 1992—advocates the principle of democratic renewal, stressing the need for political institutions to expand their capacity to support increased participation: "One of the fundamental prerequisites for the achievement of sustainable development is broad public participation in decision-making."[44] The direct involvement of citizens in decentralized action for sustainable development is promoted as particularly central to the effectiveness of Local Agenda 21.[45]

The deliberations in Rio directly led to the "Convention on access to information, public participation in decision-making and access to justice in environmental matters," otherwise known as the Aarhus Convention, signed by the member states of the regional United Nations Economic Commission for Europe (UNECE) in 1998. The Convention explicitly draws on Principle 10 of the 1992 *Rio Declaration on Environment and Development*, which stresses that transparency, public participation, and access to justice are preconditions for achieving sustainable development. The Convention not only recognizes that "citizens must have access to information, be entitled to participate in decision-making and have access to justice in environmental matters," but also acknowledges that "citizens may need assistance in order to exercise their rights." Enhancing the transparency and accountability of public authorities is seen as fundamental, as is expanding the capacity of institutions to promote participation. In line with the arguments of green deliberative democrats, the Convention argues that environmental benefits will flow from increased participation:

> in the field of the environment, improved access to information and public participation in decision-making enhance the quality and the implementation of decisions, contribute to public awareness of environmental issues, give the public the opportunity to express its concerns and enable public authorities to take due account of such concerns.[46]

The Aarhus Convention came into force in October 2001, and the first meeting of the parties took place in October 2002. It is unclear how much effect the Convention will have in practice, although Kofi Annan, the UN Secretary General, argues that "the Aarhus Convention is the most ambitious venture in environmental democracy undertaken under the auspices of the United Nations. Its adoption was a remarkable step forward in the development of international law."[47]

This international promotion of citizen engagement and deliberation within environmental decision making is mirrored in three official advisory reports in Britain that focus particularly on policy issues involving scientific uncertainty. In its 1998 report, *Setting Environmental Standards*, the Royal Commission on Environmental Pollution argues that traditional forms of consultation, such as opinion polling, do not adequately capture and articulate environmental values. In terms that resonate with the arguments of deliberative theorists, the Royal Commission argues:

Parliaments are able to express public attitudes and values to some extent. Nevertheless, governments should use more direct methods to ensure that people's values, along with lay knowledge and understanding, are articulated and taken into account alongside technical and scientific considerations.... A more rigorous and wide-ranging exploration of people's values requires discussion and debate to allow a range of viewpoints and perspectives to be considered, and individual values developed.[48]

Along similar lines, a report by the influential House of Commons Select Committee on Public Administration makes the specific case for the introduction of more deliberative mechanisms to engage the public in the policy-making process. The report states that, rather than using techniques such as opinion polling that seek only a "snapshot" based on pre-defined questions framed by policy makers, the emphasis should shift to more deliberative procedures: "We believe that deliberative techniques should be routinely employed to explore the views of citizens on appropriate issues of scientific uncertainty."[49]

Finally, a report by the Parliamentary Office of Science and Technology— *Open Channels: Public Dialogue in Science and Technology*—provides an overview of the arguments for increased deliberation and the use of innovative engagement techniques:

Around the world there is widespread and growing interest in engaging the public in more deliberative and inclusive processes linked to policy and decision-making. This is occurring for a number of reasons, but principally in response to a wider social trend away from automatic deference to, and trust in, institutions of authority. Increasingly, public dialogue is being applied in many areas, including science, technology, engineering and medicine; central and local government; health planning and education.[50]

Innovations in public participation

The reports discussed above all explicitly promote the idea of enhancing citizen deliberations within the environmental policy process as well as specifically recommending innovative techniques such as citizens' juries, consensus conferences, and deliberative opinion polls as methods for embedding such deliberations.[51] These particular deliberative techniques share a number of features: a cross-section of the population is brought together for three to four days to discuss an issue of public concern; citizens are exposed to a variety of information and hear a wide range of views from witnesses whom they are able to cross-examine; and the fairness of the proceedings is entrusted to an independent facilitating organization. There are, however, important differences. First, there are variations in the number of citizens who participate. Deliberative opinion polls involve over 200 citizens. In comparison, a citizens' jury or consensus conference will typically involve only between 12 and 25 citizens.[52] Second, to select citizens, deliberative opinion polls and citizens' juries use some form of random sampling procedure. Because of the relatively small size of most citizens' juries, citizens are often selected using stratified random sampling to ensure that different demographic, and at times attitudinal, criteria are fulfilled. The sheer size of a deliberative opinion poll means that stratification is unnecessary. Consensus conferences differ again in that volunteers are recruited through advertisements and make written applications from which the panel is selected on the basis of socio-demographic criteria. Thus the first stage of the procedure is self-selecting. The final important variation concerns the outcomes of the different models. With juries and consensus conferences, citizens come to *collective* decisions after a period of deliberation and provide a series of recommendations as a group. By comparison, at the end of the deliberative opinion poll, the *individual* views of citizens are recorded and collated.

There have been a small number of experiments in Britain using these techniques, although relatively few in the area of environmental policy and with negligible involvement by central government. Much of the support for these mechanisms is drawn from experience in the rest of Europe and the United States. The available evidence indicates that citizens take their role seriously and are willing and able to reflect on different evidence and perspectives. Citizens involved in the juries, conferences, and polls become better informed and many of their preferences and judgments change. There is also some indication that citizens are more civically minded and active well after the process ends. Empirical backing is emerging to support the theoretical claim made for the transformative and educative power of democratic deliberation. Independent facilitators play an important role in ensuring inclusiveness, encouraging an ethos of mutual respect and defending against domination and manipulation by witnesses or participants during deliberations.[53]

Deliberative opinion polls have not been used in Britain in the area of environmental policy. However, they have been run by public utilities in the state of Texas to fulfill a requirement for public participation in resource planning.[54] The results from the first three utility polls offer interesting reading. Participants were presented with four "first choice" options (renewable energy, fossil fuel plants, investment in energy conservation, or buying and transporting energy from outside the service territory), and significant changes in opinion occurred over the period of the deliberations. Before deliberation, renewable energy had been the first choice, but considerable support later shifted to energy conservation. Although there was a dramatic rise in the number of citizens who were willing to pay extra for more investment in renewables, conservation was seen as an even more cost-effective solution and became the first option. Reflecting on the results of the utility polls, James Fishkin argues that they "highlight the fact that on issues where the public has not invested a lot of time and attention, the changes are likely to be large because the public is arriving at a considered judgment where previous responses would have represented only 'top of the head' views or even 'nonattitudes' or nonexistent opinions."[55]

Citizens' juries, which have been run and promoted since the 1970s in both Germany (where they are known as planning cells) and the United States, have been used more recently in Britain. In Germany they have had the most political impact. A range of government bodies and agencies commission planning cells on a number of different policy issues, such as planning, energy, and transport policy, at the same time agreeing to take planning cell recommendations into account in decisions. The original architects of the process, Peter Dienel and Ned Crosby, have both argued that the model is particularly useful in engaging citizens directly in environmental policy making.[56] Two citizens' jury experiments in Britain, one on the creation of wetlands in the Fens and one on waste management in Hertfordshire, produced recommendations that take environmental concerns more seriously than much existing policy and broadly support the view that citizens are willing and able to deliberate about fairly complex and detailed environmental issues.[57]

The interest in consensus conferences derives mainly from experience in Denmark, where the Danish Board of Technology has run them regularly since the 1980s. Consensus conferences are perceived as an effective means of incorporating the perspectives of the lay public within the assessment of new and often controversial scientific and technological developments that raise serious social and ethical concerns. The lay panel's recommendations have no statutory authority, but have sometimes had direct impact on the legislative process in the Danish parliament. For example, the recommendations of the panel on genetic engineering in industry and agriculture led to the exclusion of transgenic animals from the first governmental biotechnology research and development program.[58] Experiments with consensus conferences have also occurred in the Netherlands, New Zealand, Switzerland, and Britain, although without the level of media and public interest or the political impact observed in Denmark. The first United Kingdom National Consensus Conference (UKNCC), hosted by the Science Museum in November 1994, was on plant biotechnology. The conference was meant "to contribute to public debate and policymaking by providing insight into public perception of agricultural and food biotechnology in Britain."[59] Unfortunately, there was a lack of a formal link to any public body or policy-making process, negligible political or public interest, and criticism of the scope of the questions and the choice of witnesses.[60] Even though the report was relatively sympathetic to the biotechnology industry, the lay panel recommendations expressed a number of significant reservations about the way the technology was being developed, concerns that foreshadowed the public backlash against biotechnology a few years later. The second UKNCC, in May 1999, was on radioactive waste management.[61] On this occasion the Environment Minister, Michael Meacher, who was present to receive the citizens' panel report, stated in his response that "there is no question of this report disappearing into oblivion. I think it's going to be listened to extremely carefully.... This is an issue which has bugged this country for decades and I think opening it out, getting citizen involvement, is exactly the right way to try and resolve it."[62] Representatives from government, the nuclear industry, and environmental pressure groups were highly supportive of the process and impressed with the panel's deliberations. For example, even though he did not agree with all the conclusions, Charles Secrett, Executive Director of Friends of the Earth, did praise "the common sense" of the lay panel's analysis and "the process by which they arrived at these recommendations."[63]

Consensus conferences, citizens' juries, and deliberative opinion polls are certainly significant innovations in citizen participation and provide carefully crafted settings within which citizens are able to engage in often controversial policy deliberations. However, the techniques should not necessarily be viewed as a panacea for citizen engagement: concerns can rightly be raised about the manner in which powerful institutions might manipulate these experiments by setting the agenda and selectively responding to recommendations. Organizers and advocates of these deliberative techniques appear well aware of these potential problems and have attempted to respond to these challenges in a number of creative ways. The independence of the facilitating organization is fundamental here, and organizers are often fastidious in their attempt to draw together a range of stakeholders to help select relevant questions and evidence. In the consensus conference model, the panel of citizens is brought together for preparatory weekends during which they have the opportunity to be involved in the selection of expert witnesses and key questions. In the citizens' jury process, citizens are typically given the opportunity to call new witnesses as they deliberate and learn about the issues under consideration. The problem of authorities selectively adopting recommendations is somewhat ameliorated in citizens' juries in Germany and Britain, where a pre-jury contract is usually drawn up between the independent facilitating organization, the commissioning body, and the jurors, requiring the commissioning body either to act on the jury recommendations or to give reasons why it has decided not to act.

There are also justified concerns that only a small number of citizens are involved in the process. There is obviously a balance to be struck between numbers participating and the protection of deliberation: these experiments prioritize the achievement of a structured and protected deliberative space. It is also important that the citizens involved not be perceived as representing the population in the strong sense: no group of citizens can accurately mirror all the standpoints and views present within the wider community, and there is a danger of creating the false expectation that participants will represent the views of citizens who have socio-demographic characteristics similar to their own. The primary task of participating citizens should instead be understood in terms of *deliberation* rather than *representation*. The democratic value of these deliberative techniques rests on drawing a range of citizens together so that they are able to reflect upon a wide variety of experiences and perspectives.[64]

THE BRITISH GM DEBATE

Following public hostility to the introduction of genetically modified (GM) foods and crops in Britain, a government advisory body, the Agriculture and

Environment Biotechnology Commission (AEBC), was influential in persuading the government of the need for a widespread public debate on the future of GM technology. The AEBC's suggestions offer one possibility of how deliberative techniques—in this case consensus conferences—could be blended with broader public deliberations. Explicitly drawing on ideas from the reports by the Royal Commission on Environmental Pollution and the Parliamentary Office of Science and Technology (discussed earlier) and experience in Denmark and the Netherlands, the AEBC argued that any credible public debate needs to be carefully structured and facilitated independently of government.

The AEBC conceived of a number of stages to the core program of the debate: first, creating an independent steering board to run a series of local workshops around the country where citizens frame the issues for deliberation; second, commissioning a short film punctuated by questions arising from the workshops to be used as the basis of a series of debates around the country in local community groups; and third, inviting representatives from these groups to regional and national events to discuss the issues further. A series of focus groups was also envisaged to run alongside this process to analyze changes in opinion as debate progressed.[65] Beyond this core program, the AEBC was also keen to draw these debates together in one or more consensus conferences:

> The consensus conferences would add a further valuable element to the debate. They also unlike focus groups have a public dimension (public audiences and the media are usually invited to the later sessions) which could stimulate wider public discussion. In addition, like the focus groups, they would provide a means of benchmarking the local, regional and national debate and so add to the richness of the analysis of public views and the comparison of public engagement techniques employed in the debate.[66]

Margaret Beckett, the Secretary of State for the Environment, Food, and Rural Affairs, accepted the need for a national GM debate and stated in response to the AEBC recommendations, "The Government wants a genuinely open and balanced discussion on GM. There is clearly a wide range of views on this issue and we want to ensure all voices are heard."[67]

The national debate took place in June 2003 and was complemented by independent scientific and economic reviews of the technology.[68] But how seriously did the government take this innovative public initiative? First, the public debate took place after the scientific and economic reviews were completed. Sir Tom Blundell, Chair of the Royal Commission on Environmental Pollution, voiced a key concern: "It seems impossible that the values articulated in [the public debate] could inform the science review or the … economic study."[69] Second, the funding provided by the government was inadequate because it did not allow the independent steering group to organize all the elements of the proposed dialogue. After originally offering only £250,000, DEFRA doubled the funding. But even this larger amount did not cover the cost of the suggested core program, and the consensus conferences were abandoned as too expensive (the most recent consensus conference in Britain alone cost £100,000). Third, it remains unclear precisely how the debate might actually affect GM policy; indeed, fears were expressed that "the debate is in danger of ending up as a meaningless exercise that could further undermine confidence in GM foods."[70] These aspects of the British GM debate illustrate how the realization of potential opportunities for meaningful and effective citizen engagement is often unfulfilled.

Barriers to Institutionalizing Democratic Deliberation

Although we are witnessing the emergence of nascent deliberative spaces within the British environmental policy process, it is clear that there are a number of barriers to the effective institutionalization of democratic deliberation. There are specific problems about how to actually construct deliberative spaces: who, for example, should be involved, at what point in the policy process, and with how much influence? These are difficult questions, and the examples offered in this chapter—the Environmental Audit Committee, the Sustainable Development Commission, and experiments in citizen engagement—offer interesting and contrasting practical examples of how these questions might be tentatively answered. To a certain extent it is a matter of experimentation. This is a relatively new endeavor: given the complexity of the policy process, different mechanisms will need to be tried and tested.

However, there is a broader problem. To what extent are senior government figures and other powerful interests actually committed to embedding deliberative spaces within the policy process? The three highly favorable national-level reports supporting the institutionalization of citizen engagement are all from advisory and scrutiny bodies outside the core executive—the Royal Commission on Environmental Pollution, the Parliamentary Office of Science and Technology, and the Select Committee on Public Administration. It is fairly easy for powerful interests to ignore such reports. We began, indeed, by characterizing the policy process as one of differentiation and fragmentation, with policy making the preserve of more or less exclusionary policy networks. What incentive do these powerful actors have to open up the policy process if they are concerned where deliberations might lead? Deliberation by its very nature can unsettle existing power relations and open up policy issues to contestation. This is likely to be particularly uncomfortable for the core executive and strong policy communities that wish to control the agenda and direction of policy development. The pressure to open up dialogue usually faces stronger pressure to contain debate. This resistance to increasing deliberation is further engendered amongst those interests hostile to environmental considerations because of the evidence that the outcome of most deliberative processes tends to be more environmentally sensitive than existing policies.[71] Powerful interests have much to lose.

The government remains supportive of increased citizen participation at a rhetorical level. However, when it comes to actual practice there is less enthusiasm. Much of the government's lack of enthusiasm is couched in terms of cost: institutionalizing democratic deliberation is expensive. The government's inadequate funding of the public debate on GM technology mirrors its less than enthusiastic response to the recommendations of the Select Committee on Public Administration discussed earlier: the Cabinet Office at the heart of government simply repeats the line that deliberative techniques are generally too expensive.[72] However, in response the Select Committee has reaffirmed its commitment to deliberative techniques, arguing that the government's attitude "fails to take proper account of the cost—sometimes a very high cost—which can be attached to rushed government decisions based on contested scientific judgments."[73] The widespread negative public reaction to the government's support for GM technology, potentially compounded by its inadequate support for the GM debate, is one such area where the long-term cost of ignoring public concerns and values may be extremely high.[74]

Within green political theory there is some skepticism as to whether the institutionalization and embedding of deliberative spaces within the policy process can take place: deliberative institutions within or involving the state may simply be a contradiction in terms. Theorists such as John Dryzek argue that deliberative institutions are liable to be co-opted and absorbed by the state: extra-constitutional imperatives (such as the protection of capital accumulation) limit the scope for democratic authenticity in the institutions of the state.[75] The analysis offered within this chapter demonstrates a more complex picture. The administrative apparatus of the state is highly differentiated and fragmented. There are certainly powerful interests and policy communities that are hostile to the embedding of democratic deliberation and that will actively resist or attempt to co-opt any emerging deliberative institutions and experiments. However there are also vocal advocates of institutionalizing deliberation and citizen participation who view such experiments as vital to the development of legitimate forms of policy making, particularly around controversial scientific and technological issues. Deliberation has become a site of contestation within the state itself. It remains an open question to what extent a green and authentically democratic state can be conceived as a reasonable prospect. Is it reasonable to envisage the emergence of an activist green state effectively engaging with citizens and the institutions of civil society and protecting deliberative spaces within the policy process?[76] The nascent deliberative designs that have emerged in Britain certainly do not go far in realizing such a goal, but—if we take the goal to be possible—they do at least help in suggesting what it might look like and what the barriers to achieving it are likely to be.

NOTES

1   The author would like to thank Doug Torgerson for his perceptive comments on an earlier version of this chapter.

2 On the nature of deliberative democracy, see contributions in, e.g., Seyla Benhabib, ed., *Democracy and Difference: Contesting the Boundaries of the Political* (Princeton: Princeton University Press, 1996); James F. Bohman and William Rehg, eds., *Deliberative Democracy* (Cambridge, MA: MIT Press, 1997); Jon Elster, ed., *Deliberative Democracy* (Cambridge: Cambridge University Press, 1998); Michael Saward, ed., *Democratic Innovation: Deliberation, Representation and Association* (London: Routledge, 2000); Maurizio Passerin D'Entreves, ed., *Democracy as Public Deliberation: New Perspectives* (Manchester: Manchester University Press, 2002). There are ongoing debates about whether deliberative democracy should be viewed as a complete, self-contained theory (or model) or simply as a desirable ingredient of democracy. See, e.g., Michael Saward, "Less than Meets the Eye: Democratic Legitimacy and Deliberative Theory," in Saward, ed., *Democratic Innovation*; Judith Squires, "Deliberation and Decision-Making: Discontinuity in the Two-Track Model," in D'Entreves, ed., *Democracy as Public Deliberation.*

3 See, e.g., John Barry, *Rethinking Green Politics: Nature, Virtue and Progress* (London: Sage, 1999); John Dryzek, *Deliberative Democracy and Beyond: Liberals, Critics, Contestations* (Oxford: Oxford University Press, 2000); Robyn Eckersley, "Deliberative Democracy, Ecological Representation and Risk: Towards a Democracy of the Affected," in Saward, ed., *Democratic Innovation;* Robert E. Goodin "Enfranchising the Earth and its Alternatives," *Political Studies* 44(1996): 835-49; Tim Hayward, *Political Theory and Ecological Values* (Cambridge: Polity, 1998); Graham Smith, *Deliberative Democracy and the Environment* (London: Routledge, 2003).

4 John S. Dryzek, *Rational Ecology: Environment and Political Economy* (Oxford: Blackwell, 1987).

5 James D. Fearon, "Deliberation as Discussion," in Elster, ed., *Deliberative Democracy*, p. 49. See also Douglas Torgerson, "Limits of the Administrative Mind: The Problem of Defining Environmental Problems," in Robert Paehlke and Douglas Torgerson, eds., *Managing Leviathan: Environmental Politics and the Administrative State* (Peterborough, ON: Broadview Press, 1990).

6 Frank Fischer, *Citizens, Experts, and the Environment: The Politics of Local Knowledge* (Durham, NC: Duke University Press, 2000); David Schlosberg, *Environmental Justice and the New Pluralism* (Oxford: Oxford University Press, 1999); Ulrich Beck, *Risk Society* (London: Sage, 1992).

7 Dryzek, *Rational Ecology*, p. 211. See also Elinor Ostrom, "A Behavioral Approach to the Rational Choice Theory of Collective Action," *American Political Science Review* 92(1998): 1–22.

8 David Miller, "Deliberative Democracy and Social Choice," *Political Studies Special Issue: Prospects for Democracy* 40(1992): 54–67.

9 Goodin, "Enfranchising the Earth and its Alternatives," p. 847.

10 See Barry, *Rethinking Green Politics*; Douglas Torgerson, *The Promise of Green Politics: Environmentalism and the Public Sphere* (Durham, NC: Duke University Press, 1999).

11 Eckersley, "Deliberative Democracy, Ecological Representation and Risk," p. 120. See also Peter Christoff, "Ecological Citizens and Ecologically Guided Democracy," in Brian Doherty and Marius de Geus, eds, *Democracy and Green Political Thought* (London: Routledge, 1996).

12 For a summary of the governance literature, see Gerry Stoker, "Governance as Theory: Five Propositions," *Governance* 155(1998): 17–28; Jon Pierre, ed., *Debating Governance* (Oxford: Oxford University Press, 2000); Rod Rhodes, *Understanding Gover-*

nance: Policy Networks, Governance, Reflexivity and Accountability (Buckingham: Open University Press, 1997).

13 Jeremy Richardson and Grant Jordan, *Governing Under Pressure: The Policy Process in a Post-Parliamentary Democracy* (Oxford: Martin Robertson, 1979), p. 174.

14 David Marsh and Rod Rhodes, *Policy Networks in British Government* (Oxford: Clarenden Press, 1992). Richardson and Jordan introduced the term "policy community" in their earlier work, but the Marsh and Rhodes framework provides a more systematic analytical framework. On its further development see David Marsh, ed., *Comparing Policy Networks* (Buckingham: Open University Press, 1998).

15 Marsh and Rhodes, *Policy Networks in British Government*, p. 264.

16 Frank Baumgartner and Bryan Jones, *Agendas and Instability in American Politics* (Chicago: University of Chicago Press, 1993).

17 Martin Smith, *The Politics of Agricultural Support in Britain* (Aldershot: Dartmouth, 1990); Mick Hamer, *Wheels Within Wheels: A Study of the Road Lobby* (London: Routledge and Kegan Paul, 1987).

18 The term "core executive" covers "the complex web of institutions, networks and practices surrounding the prime minister, cabinet, cabinet committees and their official counterparts, less formalized ministerial 'clubs' or meetings, bilateral negotiations and interdepartmental committees. It also includes coordinating departments, chiefly the Cabinet Office, the Treasury, the Foreign Office, the law officers, and the security and intelligence services." Rod Rhodes, "From Prime Ministerial Power to Core Executive," in Rod Rhodes and Patrick Dunleavy, eds, *Prime Minister, Cabinet and Core Executive* (London: MacMillan, 1995), p. 12.

19 Rhodes, *Understanding Governance.*

20 Ian Holliday, "Is the British State Hollowing Out?," *Political Quarterly* 71(2000): 167–76; Andrew Taylor, "Hollowing Out or Filling In? Taskforces and the Management of Cross-cutting Issues in British Government," *The British Journal of Politics and International Relations* 2(2000): 46–71.

21 Denis Kavanagh and David Richards, "Departmentalism and Joined-Up Government: Back to the Future?," *Parliamentary Affairs* 54(2001): 1–18.

22 Marsh and Rhodes, *Policy Networks in British Government*, p. 265.

23 Stoker, "Governance as Theory," p.19.

24 For a discussion of the content and impact of the Department of Environment's *Sustainable Development: The UK Strategy* (London: HMSO, 1994) and the Department of Environment, Transport, and the Regions' *A Better Quality of Life: A Strategy for Sustainable Development for the United Kingdom* (London, 1999), see James Connelly and Graham Smith, *Politics and the Environment: From Theory to Practice*, 2nd ed. (London: Routledge, 2003), pp. 309–18. The government's 1999 strategy and annual reports can be found at <http://www.sustainable-development.gov.uk>.

25 See Torgerson, "Limits of the Administrative Mind."

26 Environmental Data Services, "Treasury Put to Test over Sustainable Development," *ENDS Report* 242(1995): 29.

27 A number of explanations have been offered as to why this amalgamation of departments took place. The Labour government inherited a road-building policy that was both fiscally draining and environmentally unpopular: it was the transport policy of earlier Conservative administrations that led to an unprecedented wave of anti-road direct action across Britain. See, e.g., Brian Doherty, "Paving the Way: The Rise of Direct Action Against Road-Building and the Changing Character of British Environmentalism,"

Political Studies 47(1999): 95–120. The creation of the super-ministry was also a way of rewarding the Deputy Prime Minister, John Prescott, with a suitably powerful department.

28 For a discussion of these concerns, see House of Commons Environmental Audit Committee, *Department Responsibilities for Sustainable Development* (London: HMSO, 31 Jan. 2002). Environmental Audit Committee reports can be found at <http://www.parliament.uk/parliamentary_committees/environmental_audit_committee.cfm>.

29 The two committees were initially proposed in the 1990 White Paper *This Common Inheritance* (London: DOE, 1990). This was the first white paper on the environment from a government led by Margaret Thatcher after more than a decade in office.

30 Environmental Audit Committee, *The Greening Government Initiative 1999* (HMSO: London, 23 Feb. 1999), paragraph 12.

31 Environmental Data Services, "Green Ministers who Barely Meet," *ENDS Report* 263(1996): 24.

32 Cabinet Sub-Committee of Green Ministers, *Greening Government Third Annual Report* (London: Cabinet Office, 27 Nov. 2001) <http://www.sustainable-development.gov.uk/sdig/reports/index.htm>.

33 The reports of the Environmental Audit Committee can be found at <http://www.parliament.uk/parliamentary_committees/environmental_audit_committee.cfm>.

34 Environmental Audit Committee, *Environmental Audit: The First Parliament* (London: HMSO, 9 Jan. 2001), paragraphs 75–78. See also Andrea Ross, "Greening Government: Tales from the New Sustainability Watchdog," *Journal of Environmental Law* 12.2(2000): 175–96.

35 For a detailed discussion of the Brent Spar incident, see Grant Jordan, *Shell, Greenpeace and the Brent Spar* (Basingstoke: Palgrave, 2001).

36 Department of the Environment, *Sustainable Development: The UK Strategy*, p. 235.

37 <http://www.sd-commission.gov.uk>. Details of the work of the Sustainable Development Commission and previous reports by the Panel and Round Table can be found on the Commission's website.

38 John S. Dryzek, *Discursive Democracy: Politics, Policy, and Political Science* (Cambridge: Cambridge University Press, 1990), pp. 53–58; John Forester, "Envisioning the Politics of Public-Sector Dispute Resolution," *Studies in Law, Politics and Society* 12(1992): 247–86; Smith, *Deliberative Democracy and the Environment*, pp. 81–86.

39 Jane Mansbridge, "A Deliberative Perspective on Neocorporatism," in E.O. Wright , ed., *Associations and Democracy* (London: Verso, 1995).

40 Mark Warren, "Deliberative Democracy and Authority," *American Political Science Review* 90.1(1996): 46–60.

41 See, e.g., Schlosberg, *Environmental Justice and the New Pluralism*; Douglas Amy, *The Politics of Mediation* (New York: Columbia University Press, 1987).

42 Nancy Rosenblum, *Membership and Morals* (Princeton, NJ: Princeton University Press, 1998), pp. 343–46.

43 Department of the Environment, *Sustainable Development*; Department of the Environment, Transport, and the Regions, *A Better Quality of Life*.

44 United Nations Conference on Environment and Development (UNCED), *Agenda 21* (New York: United Nations, 2001), Chapter 23.

45 UNCED, *Agenda 21*, Chapter 28. For more details on *Agenda 21* and Local Agenda 21, see Connelly and Smith, *Politics and the Environment*.

46 The full text of the Aarhus Convention can be found at <http://www.unece.org>.

47 Department of Environment, Food, and Rural Affairs (DEFRA), *Achieving a Better Quality of Life: Review of Progress towards Sustainable Development: Government Annual Report 2001* (London: DEFRA, 2002).

48 Royal Commission on Environment and Pollution, *Setting Environmental Standards* (London: HMSO, 1998), paragraphs 7.17 and 7.23. The Royal Commission on Environmental Pollution is an independent standing body established in 1970 to advise the Queen, the Government, Parliament, and the public on environmental issues. See <http://www.rcep.org.uk>.

49 Select Committee on Public Administration, *Sixth Report on Public Participation: Issues and Innovations* (HMSO: London, 2001), paragraph 53. See <http://www.publications.parliament.uk/pa/cm/cmpubadm.htm>.

50 Parliamentary Office of Science and Technology (POST), *Open Channels: Public Dialogue in Science and Technology* (London: POST, 2001), p.19. See <http://www.parliament.uk/post.htm>.

51 The following analysis draws heavily on Smith, *Deliberative Democracy and the Environment*, pp. 77–102, and "Taking Deliberation Seriously: Green Politics and Institutional Design," *Environmental Politics* 10.3(2001): 72–93.

52 In Germany, a number of juries have been run concurrently or in series. To date, the largest project involved 500 citizens from all over Germany.

53 For evidence of the impact of deliberation on citizens, see references in Graham Smith and Corinne Wales, "The Theory and Practice of Citizens' Juries," *Policy and Politics* 27(1999): 295–308; "Citizens' Juries and Deliberative Democracy," *Political Studies* 48.1(2000): 51–65; Smith, *Deliberative Democracy and the Environment* and "Taking Deliberation Seriously."

54 James S. Fishkin, *The Voice of the People* (New Haven, CT: Yale University Press, 1997), pp. 200–03; Center for Deliberative Polling, *Deliberative Polling Blue Book* (2002), <http://www.la.utexas.edu/research/delpol/bluebook/summary.html>.

55 Fishkin, *Voice of the People*, p. 202.

56 Ned Crosby, "Citizen Juries: One Solution for Difficult Environmental Questions," in Ortwin Renn, Thomas Webler, and Peter Wiedermann, eds, *Fairness and Competence in Citizen Participation* (Dordecht: Kluwer, 1995); Peter Dienel and Ortwin Renn, "Planning Cells: A Gate to 'Fractal' Mediation," in Renn *et al.*, eds., *Fairness and Competence in Citizen Participation*.

57 Jonathan Aldred and Michael Jacobs, *Citizens and Wetlands: Report of the Ely Citizens' Jury* (Lancaster: Centre for the Study of Environmental Change, 1997); Richard Kuper, "Deliberating Waste: The Hertfordshire Citizens' Jury," *Local Environment* 2.2(1997): 139–53. In Britain, the Institute for Public Policy Research (IPPR), the King's Fund Policy Institute, and the Local Government Management Board (LGMB) introduced the idea of citizens' juries by promoting and sponsoring a series of juries in the mid-to late 1990s. These were typically conducted in conjunction with local government or health authorities, two institutions often criticized for failing to engage their local populations. See Anna Coote and Jo Lenaghan, *Citizens' Juries: Theory into Practice* (London: IPPR, 1997); Shirley McIver, *An Evaluation of the King's Fund Citizens' Juries Programme* (Birmingham: Health Services Management Centre, 1997); Declan Hall and John Stewart, *Citizens' Juries in Local Government: Report from the LGMB on pilot projects* (Luton: LGMB, 1997).

58 Lars Klüver, "Consensus conferences at the Danish Board of Technology," in Simon Joss

and John Durant, eds., *Public Participation in Science: The Role of Consensus Conferences in Europe* (London: Science Museum, 1995).

59 Simon Joss and John Durant, "The UK National Consensus Conference on Plant Biotechnology," *Public Understanding of Science* 4(1995): 195–204; UK National Consensus Conference, *Lay Panel Preliminary Report* (London: Science Museum, 1994).

60 Derek Purdue, "Contested Expertise: Plant Biotechnology and Social Movements," *Science as Culture* 5.4(1996): 526–45; POST, *Open Channels: Public Dialogue in Science and Technology*, p. 10.

61 Jane Palmer, ed., *UK National Consensus Conference on Radioactive Waste: Final Report* (Cambridge: UKCEED, 1999). For information on the second UKNCC, see <http://www.ukceed.org>.

62 Palmer, ed., *UK National Consensus Conference on Radioactive Waste*, p. 96.

63 Palmer, ed., *UK National Consensus Conference on Radioactive Waste*, p. 100.

64 Smith and Wales, "Citizens' Juries and Deliberative Democracy," pp. 56–57; Jeffrey Abramson, *We, The Jury* (New York: Basic Books, 1994), p. 11.

65 Agriculture Environment and Biotechnology Commission (AEBC), "A Debate about the Issue of Possible Commercialisation of GM Crops in the UK" (Letter to the Secretary of State for the Environment, Food and Rural Affairs), 26 April 2002, paragraphs 14–32. See <http://www.aebc.gov.uk/aebc/subgroups/public_attitudes_advice.shtml>.

66 AEBC, "A Debate about the Issue of Possible Commercialisation of GM Crops in the UK," paragraph 35.

67 AEBC, "Public Dialogue on GM: UK Government Response to AEBC Advice Submitted in April 2002," 26 July 2002, <http://www.aebc.gov.uk/aebc/subgroups/public_ attitudes_debate_gov_response.shtml>.

68 At the time of writing the results of the debate have not been released. For details on the GM debate, see <http://www.gmpublicdebate.org>.

69 Antony Barnett and Mark Townsend, "Blair Adviser Attacks Labour BM Crops 'Fix,'" *The Observer* 13 April 2003: 8. It also appears that the results from the government's three-year farm-scale trials of GM crops will be delayed and will not be available for discussion during the debate.

70 Mark Townsend and Antony Barnett, "GM Debate Plan is 'On the Brink of Collapse,'" *The Observer* 10 Nov. 2002: 11.

71 Smith, *Deliberative Democracy and the Environment*, pp. 77–102.

72 Cabinet Office, "Government Memorandum In Response To The Public Administration Select Committee's Sixth Report On Public Participation: Issues And Innovations," in Select Committee on Public Administration, *Public Participation: Issues and Innovations: The Government's Response to the Committee's Sixth Report of Session 2000-01* (HMSO: London, 2001), paragraph 17. See <http://www.publications.parliament.uk/pa/cm/cmpubadm.htm>.

73 Select Committee on Public Administration, *Public Participation: Issues and Innovations*, paragraph 8.

74 See, e.g., the two research reports produced by the Economic and Social Research Council: "Global Environmental Change Programme," *The Politics of GM Food: Risk, Science and Public Trust* (Swindon: ESRC, 1999), and *Risky Choices, Soft Disasters: Environmental Decision-Making Under Uncertainty* (Swindon: ESRC, 2000). Both can be accessed at <http://www.gecko.ac.uk>.

75 Dryzek, *Deliberative Democracy and Beyond*; "Discursive Democracy vs. Liberal Constitutionalism," in Saward, ed., *Democratic Innovation*.
76 See, e.g., Barry, *Rethinking Green Politics*; Smith, *Deliberative Democracy and the Environment*.

13

Outside the State:
Australian Green Politics and the
Public Inquiry into Uranium

Timothy Doyle

Gone are the days of progressive green policy making in Australia. After being at the vanguard of environmental policy making during the 1970s, Australian environmentalists are experiencing difficult times at the start of the millennium. The federal government is run by a conservative coalition (comprising the Liberal and National parties) with very strong ties to the corporate sector, most specifically to powerful extractive industries, such as mining and forestry.[1] The state has now largely abandoned a commitment to independent science. Increasingly, Australia is regarded in international circles as an environmental pariah, with its anti-environmentalist stance on climate change at the Kyoto and subsequent The Hague summits most widely known. Whereas once environmentalists sought to influence policy makers, in classical pluralist and neo-corporatist styles, this different context has led environmentalists to construct newer ways of influencing public policy, to develop different paths of playing environmental politics, often bypassing the state as axis point, as convener.

After mapping out recent changes in Australian environmental policy making and describing the current practices of the uranium industry, this chapter will concentrate on one specific case of alternative green politics forged outside the state: the creation of the Public Inquiry into Uranium.[2] This case is viewed in the broader context of similar inquiries and fora both in Australia and elsewhere.

This broader context of policy-relevant inquiries and fora signals some notable experimentation with deliberative processes that poses some challenge to what Deborah Stone has called the "rationality project" of conventional approaches to public policy. There is a move away from the conventional reliance upon analyses by established experts toward forms of deliberation involving citizens. This move also creates an opening to throw into question the market model of society that is largely taken for granted by disciples of the rationality project:

> Society is viewed as a collection of autonomous, rational decision makers who have no community life. Their interactions consist entirely of trading with one another to maximize their individual well being. They each have objectives and preferences, they each compare alternative ways of attaining their objectives, and they each choose the way that yields the most satisfaction. The market model and the rational decision-making model are thus very closely related.[3]

The very process of deliberation by citizens implicitly opposes the premise that "there is no such thing as society" (as Margaret Thatcher once put it). Citizen deliberation is, indeed, based on the premise that it is possible for a democratic citizenry to debate and weigh issues in terms of a meaningful public interest. However, it is common for such deliberative experiments to remain linked to the state in such a way that they are ineffective as citizen fora. The powerful intersection of state and business interests typically screens out or marginalizes divergent perspectives.

The Public Inquiry into Uranium arose to directly counter the dominance of such forces in Australia by encouraging the public expression of marginalized voices, particularly those of environmentalists. Significantly, these voices did not call for alternative green "ways of knowing," but demanded rationality and objective science, including the challenges that can come from ecological analyses. The implicit point here is that the conventionally approved rationality project (as Stone terms it) is itself impossible when the state abandons a commitment to independent science and allows business forces to dominate the policy process. Too often, these forces are interested only in the kind of narrowly focused research and analysis that is needed to maintain and expand their operations. At the same time, whenever inconvenient or troublesome information is encountered, it is typically ignored or suppressed. What is obviously lacking is the kind of comprehensive monitoring of business ventures and their impact that would allow for the meaningful use of ecological science to protect the environment.

Australian environmentalists certainly have not come to endorse the rationality project, but their demands at the Public Inquiry implicitly suggest that the project is clearly incoherent in a context where the policy process is biased in favor of developments promoted by state and business interests. Here any rationality depends on confronting the conventional orientation with divergent perspectives that are interested in a more thorough comprehension and control of what is done to the environment. This does not mean departing from science, but rather promoting scientific activity that is independent enough of dominant forces to seek out troublesome information and to analyze what is being done to the environment, not in fragmented terms, but in a manner that is informed by the "subversive" science of ecology. This kind of independence cannot be gained simply by adhering to the rationality project's call for expert analysis, but depends on the loud and dramatic entry into public debate of environmentally informed voices, uncontrolled by the state and not intimidated by business. The Public Inquiry, as we shall see, was a step in this direction.

AUSTRALIAN ENVIRONMENTALISM AND THE STATE: THREE PHASES

The relationship of Australian environmentalism to the state-centered policy process can be understood in terms of three distinct phases (Table 1):[4] a period of exclusion, a period of inclusion, and a period of circumvention. The initial period includes the first twenty years of the "modern movement," from the 1960s until the mid-1980s. During most of this era, Australia had conservative federal governments, but the period included the important Whitlam Labor government of 1972–75. The first period saw the movement playing outsider politics. Environmental concern was largely based on direct, oppositional dissent to the state's ideology of unrestrained exploitation of the environment. Environmentalists, on the whole, were considered deviant "folk devils," regardless of whether their demands were radical or reform-oriented. Radical environmentalists demanded revolutionary changes, considering the state as incapable of bringing about sufficient social and ecological reforms. These activists concentrated on mass mobilization techniques and strategies. Their actions did not seek a direct effect on the policy process but had indirect significance through an influence on public opinion. More reformist environmentalists, though still very much on the outside, demanded legislative change to enable the state to manage the environment more effectively. Their major strategy was one of lobbying elites. They succeeded to the extent that an unprecedented range of legislation was passed during these early days, particularly in the 1970s. Conflict-oriented public policy models, such as pluralism, fit with the environmentalist initiatives of this outsider politics.

By the mid-1980s the "accord-style" of politics, championed by Labor prime minister Bob Hawke, began to dominate environmental policy making. Sustainable and multiple use began to dictate environmental management in the second period. This ideology was developed predominantly by business interests in a bid to incorporate environmental concern into business-as-usual. Still, this era saw the emergence of many cross-sectoral, round-table fora set up by the state that included some real efforts to provide representative and scientific management of nature and its resources. The second period began after the mid-1980s, and it can be characterized in terms of corporatist models of power. Although the radical wings of the movement continued to play oppositional, outsider politics in this period, many other parts of the movement began to deal more closely with the state at this stage, engaging in an insider politics. Dominant and mainstream

TABLE I   Three Periods of Environmentalism in Australia

Period	Date	Dominant ideology	Models	Strategies
1	1960s to mid-1980s	Unrestrained use	Pluralism /conflict (outsider politics)	Dissent/mass mobilization and lobbying of govt. Responding to govt.
2	mid-1980s to mid 1990s	Sustainable and multiple use	Corporatism (insider politics)	Working with govt. to formulate and implement environmental policy
3	mid-1990s to present	Wise and sequential use	Decentered (bypassing the state)	Working directly with or against business and other sectors

green non-governmental organizations (NGOs) became incorporated into the Labor government's policy-making processes and agendas.

The third and current period, beginning in the mid-1990s, describes the most recent trends during the re-emergence of conservative politics under Prime Minister Howard. In the third period, "wise" and sequential use began to dominate state management initiatives. What this means in practice is that the government continually advocates free-market, radical libertarian solutions to environmental problems, diminishing the role of active public and community sectors in environmental monitoring, regulation, and problem solving. At the same time, the input of large corporate interests into the shaping of government policy is ever increasing. The free-market ideology, already anticipated even by the Labor Party, now takes a far purer form under the Coalition and threatens environment movements directly. The Coalition is advocating US-style resource-management techniques and decision-making styles fashioned and promoted by the "wise use" movement. Under wise use, the days of government-centered, pluralist, and corporatist-style decision making are no more. The roles of labor unions, the public service, and "independent" or "bureaucratic" science have been minimized. The market place was deemed "natural" under sustainable use; now wise use builds on this premise, in effect reversing it to argue that nature itself is a free market.

Environmentalism is again on the outside, but with a difference. Now it is not just a matter of being excluded from a state-based policy process and working to get on the inside. Now there is a move to a more decentered approach in the sense that the state is no longer viewed as the center of the action. The state is, to an extent not seen before, bypassed in favor of working directly with or (perhaps more commonly) against business and other potent social forces.

The Attack Upon the Public Service
and "Independent Science"

With the state retreating from past responsibilities, it is no longer the hub of the action. The case of South Australia—the home, as we shall see, of the Public Inquiry into Uranium—is significant here. The state now presents itself as a corporation. Recently in South Australia, both the Department of Primary Industry (PIRSA) and the Department of Environment, Housing, and Aboriginal Affairs (DEHAA) have undergone a structural transition to a purchaser/provider model, which has been echoed in numerous other bureaucracies under free-market governments elsewhere in Australia and the world.[5] The purchaser/provider model dictates that the purchaser, or client, is no longer the public. Each bureaucratic division's client is now its own departmental director and policy advisers. The director purchases the services from his or her own employees. When these services can be more efficiently and effectively purchased outside of the bureaucracy, the director outsources them. Where once the public would demand that the public service act in its interests, now the bureaucracy must satisfy its own top managers, who, in South Australia, are sometimes political appointees of a party whose interests are often inseparable from those of big business. The bureaucracy must now provide the "correct" information that will lead to profitable outcomes. In effect, business becomes the client and government becomes its service provider.

The attack on traditional public service has also been accompanied by a thorough offensive against independent science. In many ways independent science complements the concept of a separate, permanent state, performing a monitoring and moderating role in the processes of capital production, accumulation, and consumption. Whatever the limitations of bureaucracy and positivist science, both have provided an alternative force to the excesses of capitalism. Just as an autonomous state is often seen as interfering in radical, free-market environmental solutions, "independent" science has also been seen as a barrier to market-based outcomes.

The funding and political support for the Commonwealth Science Industry Research Organization (CSIRO), traditionally the nation's largest state-run science organization, has been dramatically slashed in real terms under Howard's neo-liberal economic regime. Generally, however, the attack on science is more subtle, masked in the changes to the philosophy of government already alluded to in the discussion of the purchaser/provider model of the public service. Fewer permanent scientific officers are being employed, with more and more services being outsourced to industry-friendly consultants.

An exemplary case of this process is found in the South Australian Public Service. Originally, scientific officers were hired by the Native Vegetation Assessment Branch of DEHAA to independently assess applications for native vegetation clearance. Over recent years these permanent employees have been replaced by temporary employees provided by a "temp agency." The permanent employees of the state had infrastructural and institutional support to embark upon research and to make recommendations without fear or favor. It is fairly obvious that the careers of temporary officers are far more susceptible to political manipulation. Of a previous twelve scientific assessment officers in the branch, in 1999 there were only three full-time and one part-time permanent scientific officers left. Another recent trend in the same branch is even more disturbing. The agency has now been restructured as an environmental consultancy. This "consultancy" has performed its own "rapid assessments." For an additional cost, certain companies can have the normal assessment procedures fast-tracked, delivering the proponent, more often than not, market-based (favorable) outcomes. Mildara Blass, an Australian wine-making giant, is one company to have pursued rapid assessment in this way. The boundaries of public service and private consultancy are blurred here, as are those between independent and market-led science/non-science. In this manner, outsourcing becomes insourcing.

Despite official rhetoric, this political situation, coupled with a weak Native Vegetation Act, has led to a dramatic increase in both legal and illegal native vegetation clearance in South Australia. This situation is particularly significant in a state where in some areas as little as two per cent of native vegetation remains. In a news release, the Conservation Council of South Australia, South Australia's peak environmental organization, stated:

> In March, 1495 trees and 19 ha of native vegetation were recommended for clearance approval.... Large applications are currently going through the system, applications for high value vegetation which include old trees, which would take hundreds of years to replace. The Native Vegetation Council [the statutory body which administers the Act] seems powerless to stop this endless stream of destruction.[6]

The broader political context both reflects and defines movement initiatives. It must be said, however, that the majority of movement initiatives have been reactive over all three periods. The movement has rarely dictated terms, though there have been some telling exceptions, as we shall see when we turn to the case of the Public Inquiry into Uranium. Before that, however, we should examine the significant of the uranium industry for environmental politics in Australia.

THE URANIUM INDUSTRY AND ENVIRONMENTAL POLITICS IN AUSTRALIA[7]

The lack of independent science and open decision making created by an overly close relationship between the state and big business has led to Australian citizens being ill-informed and left out of crucial environmental policy decisions. What has happened in the uranium industry over the past decade offers the clearest example of this.

Let us consider an extraordinary document. The Roxby Downs Indenture Ratification Act established an agreement between the South Australia (SA) Government and Western Mining Corporation (WMC)—originally as a joint venture with British Petroleum. Drawn up by the Liberal government in June 1982, the agreement gave Western Mining enormous powers. It underlined the government's obligation to facilitate WMC with access to Great Artesian Basin water free of charge. In the driest state on the driest continent on Earth, the value of this gift from the government to the company is inestimable. Next, the Act overrode a range of pre-existing Aboriginal heritage and environmental legislation. But even more astonishing was the fact that the Act gave WMC and the SA Government the right to withhold all information pertaining to the operation of the mine from the public unless both parties agreed to release it. This created a formal policy, as well as a culture, of secrecy in the uranium industry in Australia that has endured up until the present day. This secrecy ultimately forced the Australian public to create its own inquiry into the operations of the industry in the late 1990s.

Despite the reality of the Roxby Indenture, there have been some attempts by both the state and the mining corporations at least to appear interested in public opinion. In April 1996, this factor, coupled with a bid to open the legislative gates to the nuclear industry, saw the Senate (the federal upper house of parliament) call for an inquiry conducted by a Select Senate Committee into Uranium Mining and Milling (Senate Committee); but even before the inquiry had started, the-then Minister for the Environment, Senator Robert Hill, had stated that the inquiry would be of limited value and would not affect his environmental assessment of new mine applications.[8] According to the Nuclear Issues Coalition, one of the foremost anti-nuclear organizations in Australia, the Senate Inquiry was merely a means of fast-tracking the state/industry objectives, and any promotion of public input was meant as no more than political window-dressing. NIC argued that

- the Senate Inquiry hearings were never publicly advertised;
- some pro-nuclear organizations, which did not make a submission, were invited to present evidence at the hearings, and the evidence presented (e.g., overheads) was not incorporated into the transcripts;
- some anti-nuclear organizations that made submissions and requested a hearing were not even notified about the hearings, let alone invited to present evidence;
- the schedule of hearings in the city of Adelaide was changed at the last moment and environmental organizations were not notified of the changes;
- the Chair of Senate Inquiry, Senator Grant Chapman, criticized the environment movement for "being long on assertion and short on evidence" before they had presented their evidence and then did not stay to question the evidence;
- the SA Government was six months late in making its written submission and gave its verbal evidence to the Senate Inquiry in Canberra, rather than in

Adelaide, two months after the Conservation Council of SA and Friends of the Earth had appeared before the Senate Inquiry in Adelaide;
• and, most important, there was an inadequate amount of independent scientific evidence presented at the Senate Inquiry.

The common means of public participation in decision making during this period are closely controlled by the big companies themselves, rather than provided by the state. Australian uranium companies like WMC have taken a leaf out of the books of US chemical and extractive companies such as Texaco. In the early 1990s Texaco created a series of Citizens' Advisory Panels (CAPs) in a bid to engage the public on tours of the plant sites and to help "create an atmosphere of trust between the community and Texaco." As Texaco "community relations" executive Gary Graham states, "We are aware that the citizens are looking over our shoulders."[9]

Apart from WMC creating similar tours of its rapidly expanding Olympic Dam site at Roxby Downs, it has also adopted the US model of corporate-controlled round-table decision making, which emerged from the wise use movement. The wise use movement has been assiduous in its promotion of round-table, consensus decision making. The round-table idea follows the "win-win" image of an essentially non-conflictual politics. A fine example of avoiding conflict through round tables is afforded by the case of the Quincy Library Group. The town of Quincy, in the Sierra Nevada range in California, formed this group in 1993 ostensibly to resolve resource conflicts between timber and environmental interests, as well as government agencies.[10] Meetings were held in the town library so people would not yell at each other. Wise use and multiple use models are based on the premise that everyone will win in the market, including the environment, if quiet negotiation between conflicting interests and values takes place. The Quincy Library Group has been extremely successful in promoting its wise use round table, resulting in victories for resource extractive industries. It has been hailed as a model of resource decision making right across the US. The federal Quincy Library Group Forest Recovery and Economic Stability Act of 1997 emerged from this process. It orders the US secretary of agriculture to hold a five-year pilot project based on Quincy-style decision making in three national forests in the Sierra.

Although it appears to uphold democracy, the round table is deeply exclusive. All decisions are handed over to "local" people. The definition of local is telling, however, as it includes multinational companies and their management teams (because they are employers in the local community) but excludes representation from national environmental organizations. Consequently, industry is markedly over-represented, creates agendas and bottom lines, sets terms of reference, and receives acclaim for achieving community consensus, with all the legitimizing imprimaturs associated with this process. The notion of "localism," of course, fits in nicely with the discourses relating to "bioregions," "grassroots," and "participative decision-making": concepts widely endorsed by environmentalists.

This further diffuses opposition. Sierra Club chair Michael McCloskey's 1995 memo to the club's board comments on this cleverly contrived exclusionist process:

> Industry thinks its odds are better in these forums.... It has ways to generate pressures on communities where it is strong, which it doesn't have at the national level.... This re-distribution of power is designed to disempower our (national environmental) constituency, which is heavily urban.... Big business has a game-plan of pursuing this approach to get out of the clutches of the tough federal agencies.... A lot of people on the left have been taken in because it is a touchy, feely approach that plays to those with romantic notions about localism and self-control. They forget they're disempowering most of the people who have a stake in the issue.[11]

Consensus is more easily achieved by limiting the domain of stakeholders. These round tables are also formed by business, not the state (although sometimes it is a shared task, with the division between private and public sectors, again, almost imperceptible). The pluralist and even corporatist notions of state-initiated coordination, mediation, and monitoring of such processes are no longer useful in understanding these recent innovations. The state is no longer the axis point in negotiations between conflicting interests.

The example of WMC's Olympic Dam Community Consultative Forum process is straight out of a US wise use manual.[12] Although the odds are stacked even more against environmentalists than in the old government-led round tables of the previous period, some activists argue that if they do not engage the corporation and the state here, then their chances of being involved in any decision-making process are almost non-existent. If they remain outside the process, others, such as the World Wide Fund for Nature, willing to provide the "green stamp" will be summoned. Another option, mass mobilization campaigns, has its own problems when the focus of the campaign—in this case the mine site is in an arid zone—is not seen as esthetically marketable (like the Kakadu uranium mine in Australia's Northern Territory).

In the specific case of the Community Consultative Forum (CCF), "local people" are usually corporate employees in the town. There are no representatives in the Forum from the working population of Roxby Downs (over 1,000 workers) other than managers. Both the Construction Forestry Mining and Energy Union and the Australian Workers Union operate on the site, but neither union nor non-union workers were asked to sit on the Community Consultative Forum. Of significant interest, however, is the virtual exclusion of Aboriginal peoples from the process. Only one indigenous representative was chosen from the community, and this was done without consultation. Responding to a letter from the Conservation Council in February 1998, the Minister for Primary Industries, Natural Resources and Regional Development justified the inclusion of only one Aboriginal member on the CCF as follows:

It was not easy to resolve the matter of an appropriate level of Aboriginal representation on the CCF. I am advised that there are at least seven different Aboriginal organizations with substantial interest in the matters to be discussed by the CCF. I believe it would be impractical to include representatives from all the organizations and choosing only two or three groups could offend those omitted.[13]

The Minister was placed in a very difficult position due to the prior activities of WMC. It appears that WMC has exploited Aboriginal differences by supporting the establishment of small Aboriginal groups that have challenged the rights of the traditional owners: the Kokotha and Arabunna peoples. Regardless of the maneuverings of WMC, in June 1994, 80 elders from various regions of central Australia met at Port Augusta and determined that the Arabunna people were the traditional custodians of the area in question. A committee of spokespeople and elders was nominated and confirmed in association with the South Australian Government. WMC has consulted only perfunctorily with this committee. Having succeeded in confusing traditional ownership issues, WMC used this confusion to justify non-consultation with "local blacks."

Community groups that do attend these "consultation meetings" often defend "poor process" under wise use on the basis that they have been given singular access to important information. This argument does not apply in the case of Roxby. Information provided to the Community Consultative Forum was usually taken from the WMC public relations "show bag," ranging from readily accessible annual reports to documents with colorful covers presenting the results of corporate self-monitoring. This same information proved to be largely the same as the independent "scientific evidence" that had been presented at the Senate Inquiry.

Obviously all community-based groups have to decide whether or not they wish to be involved in governmental and corporate round tables. After some discussion, the Conservation Council of South Australia decided to participate in the Roxby consultations on a temporary basis. The validity of participation was constantly re-evaluated. One of the reasons why conservation stakeholders finally withdrew from the process in the late 1990s, after a year, was that the governmental representatives rarely spoke at the "round tables," leaving this task to corporate public-relations executives. The "last straw" for the two environmental representatives came when they sent a list of written concerns to the "independent chair," Stephen Walsh QC. WMC's public relations officer Richard Yeeles responded to this formal letter on behalf of the chair. From his response, it was clear that the supposedly "independent position" of the Community Consultative Forum was actually the same as the corporate position. This is in keeping with the fact that most "independent" scientific "facts" were generated by the corporation.

Participating in such fora can, nonetheless, have some limited benefit for community groups. Participation provides an opportunity for such groups to make their goals and strategies more explicit and coherent. Also, it gives these groups a better understanding of the public-relations operating techniques of large companies. Finally, it affords them a better understanding and appreciation of the context of power: a bigger political picture is presented to them. Of course, in deciding to participate, it is best that groups also recognize the limited usefulness of doing so and should pursue complementary options to influence policy outcomes.

Many environmentalists who have contributed to state-run inquiries or industry-provided round tables are now looking at new ways of creating avenues of public participation in environmental policy making concerned with the specifics of the rapidly expanding Australian uranium and nuclear industries. One such example was the establishment of a people's inquiry into uranium, an attempt to make the "public inquiry" process *more public.*

THE PUBLIC INQUIRY INTO URANIUM

The Public Inquiry into Uranium was the outcome of a strategy meeting held in mid-1996. At that strategy meeting the Nuclear Issues Coalition (NIC) addressed the problem of how to deal with a new federal government that was pro-nuclear and anti-environment. NIC decided that the forthcoming 1997 SA state elections would be its best chance for alerting the public to the dangers posed by the government-nuclear industry alliance and that a public inquiry before the election would provide information and publicity to help it make an impact at the election. Initially the focus of the Inquiry was WMC's mine at Roxby Downs, which was undergoing a two-stage expansion. It soon became clear, however, that Roxby Downs was by no means the only nuclear threat looming in the near future. As a consequence, NIC widened the terms of reference of the public inquiry to include all aspects of the mining, processing, export, and use of uranium.

The Public Inquiry into Uranium was sponsored by a large array of groups and organizations, including minor political parties, church groups, women's groups, peace groups, and a plethora of environmental interests (see Table 2). South Australia has a long history of involvement in the nuclear industry. It was appropriate, therefore, that it should be the site of the inquiry into all aspects of the nuclear industry. In the case of the public inquiry, environmental organizations, and others drawn from the community sector, set up its own round table. Thus a community alliance chose to mimic the inquiry mechanism of the state in its bid to pursue its own goals. There were also substantial differences between the Senate Committee and the Public Inquiry. The former, as we shall see, had limited itself to a narrowly defined agenda and its membership was exclusive. By concentrating on just procedural issues confined to the actual milling and mining of uranium, the Senate Committee ignored the broader role of WMC and other uranium-mining companies in the nuclear fuel cycle. The Public Inquiry opened this Pandora's box, refusing to isolate mining activities from nuclear weapons, the

TABLE 2   Organizational Sponsors of the Public Inquiry

Australian Conservation Foundation (SA Branch)
Australian Democrats
Australian Greens (SA)
Australian Nursing Federation (SA Branch)
Australian Peace Committee
Australian Women's Party
Conservation Council of SA
Democratic Socialist Party
Economic Reform Australia
Friends of the Earth
Green Party SA
HEMP SA
Uniting Church
Women's International League for Peace and Freedom

treatment and storage of nuclear waste, or the development of alternative energy options.

Submissions to the Public Inquiry into Uranium were called for and the hearings were announced through notices in *The Adelaide Advertiser.* Both written and verbal submissions were also called for by personal written invitation.[14] In the case of WMC, five written invitations were sent out. The Public Inquiry into Uranium received a total of 25 submissions from all states and territories except Queensland. These submissions were from environmental and political organizations as well as from individuals. Verbal presentations made to the Inquiry were followed by questions from the Panel, and the entire proceedings were recorded by audiotape. Transcripts from the recordings were made available to the witnesses for correction. The audience had the opportunity to question the witnesses through Dr. John Coulter, a former federal government senator, and ex-president of the Conservation Council. The report of the Public Inquiry into Uranium is the culmination of the above evidence, including written and verbal submissions, material tabled by witnesses, questions from the audience, and the results of the Panel's research and discussions.

The public inquiry model is similar to various forms of public participation that have emerged in North America, parts of Europe, and Australia in recent years, such as *people's inquiries, citizens' juries* and *citizens' forums.* Hendriks describes the basic characteristics of these more deliberative democratic processes as follows:

While there are some differences between these processes, they seek to bring together a small panel of randomly selected lay citizens together to deliberate on a policy issue. After hearing from and questioning a number of experts such as academics and interest groups, the citizens' panel develops a set of written recommendations. This document then feeds into the policy process either directly (for example, tabled in parliament) or indirectly through wide public dissemination.[15]

Most public inquiries, such as the aforementioned Senate Committee, are constructed by the state. Often these are closely affiliated to the traditions of the law, with quasi-adversarial processes dominating and with expert witnesses called from interests representing the "pro" and "con" positions. Sometimes these inquiries are overseen by one person, almost taking on a judicial role, and sometimes they are run by a panel, such as the case of many senate inquiries.

People's inquiries, such as the Public Inquiry, are different in the sense that there is an attempt to get citizens involved in the policy process at the outset, thus providing for an early deliberative democratic input by laypersons, rather than simply making submissions or otherwise responding to the findings of policy-making elites. In this sense, people's inquiries, juries, and forums are attempts to "get democracy in early."[16] The Public Inquiry was a hybrid mixture of the more "democratically pure" citizens' juries and the more traditional Senate Committee inquiry that had preceded it. Some elements of the Senate Committee inquiry were mimicked, particularly those that reflected the clear political orientation of that committee. Members of the Panel that heard the evidence and oversaw the writing of the final report were hand-selected, not randomly chosen. The five panel members included the present president and two past presidents of the Conservation Council of South Australia, which is that state's peak environmental organization, an umbrella of sixty other green organizations. Of the other two members, one was an Aboriginal activist and past participant in the Sizewell Public Inquiry in the UK, and the other was an editor of the environmental magazine *Chain Reaction*. The Panel, therefore, was dominated by volunteer environmentalists with professional occupations such as academics and scientists.

This hand selection of the panel makes the public inquiry model distinct from the *citizens' jury* model of public participation, which has become popular in recent times. In a study of innovations in public participation and environmental decision making in the Great Lakes region, Konisky and Beierle emphasize the importance of citizens' juries being politically neutral, with the jury pool being randomly selected "to ensure that the sample matches the demographic and/or attitudinal characteristics of the population at large."[17] Similarly, in a study of citizens' juries in the UK and Germany, Milne, like Hendriks, also stresses the importance of a neutral facilitator and writes that jurors are "chosen randomly from the electoral register or selected by age, sex, and class to give a representative cross-section of the local population."[18]

Once panels are chosen, rather than randomly selected, the question presents itself: Who makes this selection? The answer to this question in the context of the Public Inquiry is that the terms of reference for the inquiry and its initial organization were overseen by a non-governmental organization, the Nuclear Issues Coalition (NIC), rather than by the state or a corporation. In this manner, the

Public Inquiry was not politically neutral from its inception. When asked about the political nature of the Public Inquiry selection process, the Convener of NIC, Dennis Matthews, defended this decision on several counts, again comparing the Public Inquiry to the Senate Committee process:

> The Senate Committee was hand-picked by a pro-nuclear industry minister, and stacked with senators, which supported, and have shares in the industry. As a result, the people had no real input into the process, and environmental and independent scientific information was not adequately considered. We are not naïve enough to imagine that any committee, however randomly selected, has no political leanings. This whole "objective balance" idea favors the powerful. We are unashamed environmentalists, and we want the social and environmental implications of the expansion of the nuclear industry to be considered. So we make no apologies for setting our terms of reference, and selecting our expert panel. Besides, our panel members are not paid ... they have no vested financial interests in the outcome. And, anyway, the environmental movement has a tradition of honest, open decision-making. We don't just talk about being *transparent,* we are.[19]

The citizens' jury model and any such attempt at impartiality are based on a misreading of the context of power. There is no democratic level playing field, but an oligarchical structure of state and industry that blocks full consideration of divergent voices. Hence the impartiality is a pretense, and there is no space for a "rational" discussion in which all relevant perspectives are considered. Achieving such a space would be a matter of struggle. Efforts like the Public Inquiry resist the silencing and marginalization of divergent voices. Another point is that "impartial" design could serve to homogenize a divergent perspective. Those who hold the perspective and have developed it need to be able to speak and argue for themselves if the message is to get through: "rationality" depends on this.

Of course, the hand-selected panel members had to be of such standing to meet subsequent approval of a huge variety of interested individuals and other community organizations that contributed to the Inquiry. All "stakeholders" were invited to take part, but on this occasion the agenda and minimal rules for entry had been established by environmentalists and other community activists—not by the state or extractive industries.

It was thus not surprising that the Public Inquiry did not attract any corporate input. Also, only one government agency, the Office of the Supervising Scientist (Environment Australia), made a submission and presented evidence at the hearings. In letters to the Public Inquiry, both corporations and state officials explained their absence by referring to their past contributions to the earlier Senate Committee inquiry. The refusal of corporations and other powerful interest groups to operate outside their own fora and their own terms of reference, however, is a usual occurrence in deliberative, democratic fora, where their control is limited.[20]

The issue of science and the objectivity of "facts" are common to citizens' juries.[21] Hendriks writes, "In interest group dominated processes such as stakeholder roundtables and advisory committees, arguments focus around the establishment of 'hard' scientific truths, resulting in a series of expert and counter-expert claims."[22] One fascinating outcome of people's inquiries is that importance is given to community-generated information, which does not normally comprise hard science. This alternative, non-scientific information did appear at the Public Inquiry and was received with respect. But, interestingly, the importance of science, rather than the valuing of community-generated knowledge, proved paramount. Science was not cast as "expert" knowledge that, serving the interests of the state and big business, was hostile to citizen-based knowledge.[23] The community groups and individuals testifying at the Inquiry instead made constant reference to the need for independent science in the absence of sufficient "objective accounts." In this manner, science was made an ally of the people's inquiry, rather than an enemy. This occurrence can be partly explained by the lack of state-created, objective science about the nuclear industry so that the companies themselves almost totally control "fact production" as well as the monitoring of their operations. During this third period of environmental management in Australia, the state's ability to provide independent science has, as previously noted, been vastly reduced. In the absence of independent science, the Panel of the Public Inquiry, apart from hearing submissions, had to seek out scientific papers in a bid to access some of the limited scientific facts. Particularly in the case of water management, the issue of the lack of "objective science" arose several times during the Public Inquiry.

LACK OF INFORMATION: THE WATER ISSUE AND THE INQUIRY

Mining uranium requires the extraction of water in volumes of almost unimaginable magnitude. In the past, Western Mining Corporation has drawn its water from Borefield A (also referred to as Wellfield A), derived from the antique waters of Australia's Great Artesian Basin. From March 1996 to March 1997, WMC withdrew an average of 14.2 million liters a day (mil l/day) from Borefield A, which is 100 kilometers north of the mine. Only 5 mil l/day were used in the township of Roxby Downs. Already, this draw down has had major effects on certain mound springs. Baker writes,

> The pressure depletion caused by this removal rings the death knell for nearby mound springs. Two mound spring complexes, Gosse and Fred, were severely damaged during the sinking of monitoring bores. Since operations began Beatrice Spring has almost dried up and two others, Venable Spring and ... Pricilla Spring have completely dried up.[24]

The South Australian government submission to the Senate Committee on Uranium Mining and Milling attempted to down-play these decreases in spring flows, but still admitted the demise of several:

in some areas the rate of draw down was greater than expected and approached the limits imposed by the Special Water License. In addition the reduction in flows at some springs (notably Bopeechee) was greater than anticipated. These effects were found to be due in part to geological structures not identified at the time the initial modeling took place.[25]

WMC also admits a reduction in certain springs, but does so in such a way as to justify further withdrawals from other GAB sources. WMC's 1994–1995 Environment Progress Report reads,

Another issue arises because at Olympic Dam we draw water, via an underground pipeline, from the Great Artesian Basin.... We draw up to 15 megaliters a day from Wellfield A which is near a range of naturally occurring mound springs. In recent years we have monitored and published a decline in the flow rate at the nearby Bopeechee Spring System.... This underlines the need to bring the second well field on line as soon as possible.[26]

The profound lack of independent and publicly available scientific data on water management became apparent in the course of the Public Inquiry. The concerns raised by the Australian Conservation Foundation (ACF) in its submission are indicated in the following exchange from the public hearings of the Inquiry:

THE CHAIRMAN: I think there are a number of questions in relation to mound springs and water there. I think you had another question on that Clare.

CLARE HENDERSON: David, I was interested in getting some idea, given these impacts on the mound springs, of what sort of modeling has been undertaken to assess future impacts, and in your view how adequate is that monitoring that has been undertaken?

DAVID NOONAN: Again, the monitoring that has been undertaken has basically been by Western Mining or the companies that it has contracted. It is again a case, I suppose, of their claiming that they are commissioning independent studies. The approvals that were given by Government were based on information that was made public, and this is a very limited subset of the information that was available to Government from the Company. For instance, at the approval of Borefield B, the only information available to the public was a 20 years modeling projection of the impact on the Great Artesian Basin and on the mound springs of the water extraction that Western Mining's uranium mine is dependent on. On that basis, the Government granted a 40-year water license. The South Australian public are committed to provide free fossil water to Western Mining, up to 42 million liters a day each day every day for the next 40 years. However, within Government they had access to modeling papers that analyzed the impacts on the Great

Artesian Basin and the mound springs for a period of 50 years, and that information was withheld from the public. It was also withheld from Parliament, whether deliberately or through circumstance, and that information was not available to members of the South Australian Parliament in late 1996 when they were to address the amendments to the Roxby Indenture Act.

THE CHAIRMAN: Do you have any information for this panel as to what is contained in those secret documents?

DAVID NOONAN: We cannot anticipate the detail of the figures that it may nominate, but the trends are fairly obvious. For instance; back in the early 80s it was predicted, under the modeling at that time, that Borefield A, the first borefield that Western Mining's Roxby Downs was dependent on, would operate for some 20 years, and now we find some 10 years later that Borefield A is at the point of exceeding its legal compliances as to the extent of the draw-down effect that it causes, and you should realize that the new Borefield B that was instigated by the company was not, as the public was told, required for the expansion of the uranium mine but was actually required by the company to maintain the current levels of production at Roxby Downs, because the borefield that they were relying on (Borefield A) was reaching the limit of its legal compliance.

It thus seems that some information about water management of the GAB and the mound springs has not been disclosed to the public in its entirety. The Roxby Action Collective (RAC) and the Friends of the Earth presented a submission to the Public Inquiry that raised similar concerns:

WMC are engaged in an extensive monitoring program of the Mound Springs and the information being gathered is useful in gaining a better understanding of the workings of the springs. However, the monitoring program is questionable when what in fact is being monitored is the demise of the springs brought about by WMC operations. Since WMC began taking water from the springs in 1983 two springs have dried up completely. At Venable Spring, a pump with two solar panels is still not producing flowing water. Other springs in the area, particularly Beatrice and Bopeechee, have drastically reduced flows. In November 1995 WMC began pumping .02 million liters of water a day into the aquifer in the vicinity of Bopeechee Spring. In April 1996 there had been no improvement in flows from the spring. It is not known if the springs are replenished by water flow or by pressure and the experiment at Bopeechee is an attempt to determine this.[27]

This quotation indicates again that much of the monitoring is controlled by the company. Another key issue that the Roxby Action Collective and Friends of the Earth referred to relates to the sometimes undue powers given to WMC under the aforementioned Indenture Act, which promotes secrecy by operating companies and the state government:

> We are concerned with the role of "Project Notices," a provision under Clauses 6 of the Indenture Act, whereby changes in design to those set out in the Environmental Impact Statement and assessments are permitted. The subject of these notices have no provision for independent or public review, therefore the original role of the EIS is negated or compromised. We question the commitment by the operators to the protection and management of the environment if changes can be made in secret.... Project Notices in relation to Borefield A, allowed the construction of three pumps on the edge of Lake Eyre South, the effect of which impacted on the depletion of water from springs in the area.[28]

Accordingly, the RAC/FoE submission called for the advertisement of "project notices" to allow access for interested parties into the decision-making process.

Both ACF and RAC/FoE stressed the inadequacy of existing knowledge and how, due to this inadequacy, ecological modeling and subsequent long-term management is fraught with difficulties. In addition, they reinforced a view advanced time and again throughout the Inquiry: that prior assessment of the nature of the mound springs, the GAB, and the long-term effects on them created though massive water extraction, has been insufficient.

The appeal here, repeatedly made during the Inquiry, was for independent science, rather than non-scientific, community-generated information and other "ways of knowing." The emphasis on the need for independent science came in the absence of state-controlled, bureaucratically manufactured baseline data. The environmental community in Australia argues that ecological solutions crucially depend on the availability of relevant independent knowledge, rather than information collected for business motives.

This problem is well exemplified in the Simpson Desert Regional Reserve Ten Year Review, another attempt at managing the arid lands of South Australia, including mining and pastoral interests. The South Australian Government outsourced, or let go of, the review to a private consultant, Resource Monitoring and Planning Pty Ltd. The consultant requested any "information regarding relevant activities of the numerous stakeholders in the area over the last 10 years, and some basic descriptive background material."[29] In a response to this management/public relations company, Vera Hughes, state coordinator of The Wilderness Society, writes,

> The ecological quality of the Simpson Desert Regional Reserve over the past ten years is impossible to assess given the lack of scientific data currently available. We simply have no credible means of measuring the impact of exploitation. From your letter, it is clear the focus of your concern is on

gathering this data any way you can. Basing studies on data provided by vested interests may be better than nothing. Or, it may not. If the attempt to assess the viability of the regional reserve for conservation is sincere, ongoing scientific data must be gathered and interpreted by independent parties. If this data has not been gathered on an on-going basis, a thorough and rigorous audit of the Reserve is not possible.[30]

In an interesting book dedicated to a discussion of the politics of local knowledge, particularly in the environmental realm, Fischer asks the question: "Do most citizens have the knowledge and the intellectual wherewithal to contribute meaningfully to the complex policy decisions facing an advanced industrial society?"[31] One lesson that forcefully emerged from the Public Inquiry for the community can be expressed in the words of one of its five Panel members: "when the state relinquishes the responsibility of providing or adequately funding the compilation of base-line scientific data upon which to establish a management regime, each stakeholder whistles in the dark."[32]

CONCLUSIONS

The ideology of wise use has pushed the environment movement into confusion. The politics of wise use, in its brutal depiction of nature as marketplace, coupled with the decline of the central resource management role of the state, has driven Australian environmentalists to the edge. Although some of the corporatist strategies of the second period remain, these negotiating round tables are now increasingly defined and dominated by business. Conventional public policy texts are inadequate in their analysis of environmental and resource conflicts under Australian governments. Texts such as Bridgeman and Davis's *Australian Policy Handbook* (1998)[33] still attribute the central role to an independent state, almost ignoring the invasive power of business while providing an ideological framework in which wise-use-style, win-win round tables derive substantial credibility. These rational comprehensive-style texts operate on the widely accepted and unquestioned premise of the rationality project that the appropriate *"model of society* ... is the market."[34]

Unfortunately for the environment movement, the current political context is far worse than the first period, when concern about the environment was being forged into a political force. Now the movement's strategies and tactics are largely a known quantity, and the public relations industry's opposition to green political theory and activism is extremely sophisticated, supported by large amounts of money emanating from the private sector.

This frontal attack on the movement has, however, given its younger and more radical networks new life. This "new life" is currently found in the re-emergence of broad-based community coalitions, as exemplified by the 1997 Public Inquiry into Uranium. These broad coalitions will be a flourishing reality for Australia in future years because many citizens are searching for new ways to contribute to a polity increasingly bereft of environmental leadership or even accessible ways of making environmental voices heard within government.

The Public Inquiry into Uranium proved to be a tremendous educational tool because information about the uranium industry was—and remains—highly inaccessible. Although it concentrated on WMC's operation at Roxby, the Inquiry also adopted a broad focus on gathering evidence on industry operations relating to the full nuclear fuel cycle, to health and safety issues, and to control of information.[35] The Inquiry also fostered solidarity among community groups, something that is important because this is often the only source of power these participants possess. An excellent form of theater, moreover, the Inquiry attracted good media coverage.[36] Along with numerous ethical questions, issues of information and scientific "objectivity" and of the usefulness of deliberative fora re-emerged in the public realm.

Finally, the Public Inquiry encouraged marginalized voices, mostly environmentalists, who stressed, at the same time, alternative forms of knowing, alongside the need for more orthodox, but independent science. This kind of independence cannot be gained simply by adhering to the rationality project's call for expert analysis, but depends on the entry into public debate of informed voices, uncontrolled by the state and not intimidated by business. The Public Inquiry was radical, part of a longer-term environmental struggle. As a model for public education and symbolic politics, it most importantly showed the potential for public deliberation as a form of action confronting the powers that be.

NOTES

1 Australia is a federation of states, each with its own state government.

2 In 1997, at the time of the Public Inquiry into Uranium, the author served as both a Select Panel member, as well as co-chair of the Inquiry. He was primarily responsible for drafting the final report, which was published in November of that year. At the same time he served as president of the Conservation Council of South Australia, which is that state's principal environmental organization.

3 D. Stone, *Policy Paradox: The Art of Political Decision Making* (New York and London: Norton, 1988), p 9.

4 This table and the argument detailing three distinct periods of Australian environmentalism was first presented in T. Doyle, *Green Power: The Environment Movement in Australia* (Sydney: University of New South Wales Press, 2000), esp. part two.

5 A more detailed account of these changes in the operational style of the SA governmental bureaucracy, and their structural impacts on independent science, were first described in Doyle, *Green Power*, chs. 11 and 12.

6 Conservation Council of South Australia, press release, 20 April 1998.

7 A full chronology depicting the activities of the uranium industry in South Australia has been adapted from T. Doyle and D. Matthews, "Playing Green Politics Outside the State: The Public Inquiry into Uranium," presented to the Ecopolitics XI Conference, University of Melbourne, 1998.

8 *The Australian* 19 April 1996.

9 G. Morris, "Texaco," *Chemical Week* 150.23(17 June 1992): 112.

10 Sierra Club, "Local Control a Smokescreen for Logging," *The Planet: The Sierra Club Activist Resource* 1(1997); <www.sierraclub.org/planet/199711/Delbert.html>.

11 P. Mazza, "Cooptation or Constructive Engagement?: Quincy Library Group's Efforts to Bring together Loggers and Environmentalists under Fire," August, 1997, p 3, at <http://www.cascadia@tnews.com>.

12 The author served as one of two "conservation stakeholders" on the Olympic Dam Community Consultative Committee. Full details of this account first appeared in a chapter written by the author: "Roundtable Decision Making in Arid Lands under Conservative Governments: The Emergence of 'Wise Use,'" in K. Walker and K. Crowley, eds., *Environmental Policy Two: Studies in Decline and Devolution* (Sydney: University of New South Wales Press, 1999), ch. 7.

13 R. Kerin, Minister for Primary Industries, South Australia, letter to the Conservation Council of South Australia, 24 April 1998.

14 Evidence presented to the Panel included verbal submissions from The Australian Conservation Foundation (SA Branch), the Conservation Council of SA, the Roxby Action Collective (Victoria), Friends of the Earth, the Spencer Gulf Environmental Alliance, Margaret Dingle, the Women's International League for Peace and Freedom, the Australian Women's Party, Peter Schnelbögl (NSW), and the Office of the Supervising Scientist.

15 C. Hendriks, "Institutions of Deliberative Democratic Processes and Interest Groups: Roles, Tensions and Incentives," *Australian Journal of Public Administration* 61.1(2002): 65.

16 J. Dryzek and D. Torgerson, "Democracy and the Policy Sciences: A Progress Report," editorial, *Policy Sciences* 26(1992): 127–37, p. 128.

17 D. Konisky and T. Beierle, "Innovations in Public Participation and Environmental Decision-Making: Examples from the Great Lakes Region," research note, *Society and Natural Resources* 14(2001): 815–16.

18 K. Milne, "Citizen's Juries are an Attractive, Democratic Idea," *New Statesman* 30 August 2002: 8–9.

19 D. Matthews, Nuclear Issues Coalition Convener, personal interview, 22 May 1997.

20 P. Dienel and O. Renn, "Planning Cells: A Gate to Practical Mediation," in O. Renn, T. Webber, and P. Wiederman, *Fairness and Competence in Citizen Participation* (Boston: Klewer Academic, 1995), pp. 127–28.

21 Hendriks, "Institutions of Deliberative Democratic Processes and Interest Groups," p. 70.

22 Hendriks, "Institutions of Deliberative Democratic Processes and Interest Groups," p. 69.

23 F. Fischer, *Citizens, Experts, and the Environment: The Politics of Local Knowledge* (Durham, NC, and London: Duke University Press, 2000).

24 S. Baker, "An Obituary for Pricilla," *Environment South Australia* 4.1(1995): 22–23.

25 South Australian Government, "Submission to the Senate Inquiry on Uranium Mining and Milling," 1996, p. 9.

26 Western Mining Corporation, "Environment Progress Report" (Melbourne: WMC Limited, 1994–95), p. 14.

27 Roxby Action Collective, quoted in the Select Panel of the Public Inquiry into Uranium, "The Report of the Public Enquiry into Uranium" (Adelaide: CCSA, Nov. 1997), pp. 1–40.

28 Roxby Action Collective, "The Report of the Public Enquiry into Uranium."

29 Resource Monitoring and Planning Pty Ltd, personal communication, 17 Aug. 1998.

30 V. Hughes, The Wilderness Society, letter to R. Playfair, 17 Sept. 1998.

31 Fischer, *Citizens, Experts, and the Environment*, p. ix.

32 Doyle, *Green Power*, ch. 12.

33 P. Bridgeman and G. Davis, *Australian Policy Handbook* (Sydney: Allen and Unwin, 1998).

34 Stone, *Policy Paradox*, p. 9.

35 Select Panel of the Public Inquiry into Uranium, "The Report of the Public Enquiry into Uranium."

36 Although the Inquiry was deliberately positioned before a state election, the participants did not directly seek to influence which elected officials would ultimately gain power. Rather, the media circus and interest surrounding the election was seen as an ideal platform from which the silence cloaking the uranium industry could be challenged.

14

Participation and Agency: Hybrid Identities in the European Quest for Sustainable Development[1]

Andrew Jamison

Technology has become the great vehicle of *reification*—reification in its most mature and effective form. The social position of the individual and his relation to others appear not only to be determined by objective qualities and laws, but these qualities and laws seem to lose their mysterious and uncontrollable character; they appear as calculable manifestations of (scientific) rationality. The world tends to become the stuff of total administration, which absorbs even the administrators.

Herbert Marcuse, *One-Dimensional Man* (1964: 168–69)

INTRODUCTION

In the course of the 1990s, the ideas and practices of environmentalism lost whatever politically mobilizing force they might earlier have had, and largely came to resemble what Herbert Marcuse, in his classic text of the 1960s, termed the stuff of total administration. The redefinition of environmental politics as an ambiguous quest for sustainable development can be seen as a form of reification, bringing environmental politics under the control of the established order and its administrative apparatus and making environmental problems amenable to the instrumental procedures of technological rationality. What had seemed for many of us in the 1970s to be a broad social movement out to save the planet from further environmental destruction and ecological deterioration has given way to a much more amorphous, and socially acceptable, political agenda and range of practical activity. The "environmental movement" has been effectively stripped of its underlying meanings and motivations and largely transformed into institutions and professions. The visionary ideas of political ecology and the utopian practices of appropriate technology have become a fragmented array of institutional, intellectual, and practical activity, what I have termed the making of green knowledge.[2] In this paper I explore some of the cultural dynamics of these transformation processes in terms of the human agency involved in this multifarious shift in political agenda and practical focus. Borrowing a term from postcolonial studies, I will try to identify some of the "hybrid identities" that have emerged in the European quest for sustainable development.

At the level of discourse, the ideas of environmental protection or, as they have come to be redefined in the 1990s, sustainable development, have increasingly taken on an ideological or rhetorical character. In the northern European countries, where the environmental movements of the 1970s were among the most visible and politically significant of any in the world, environmental ideas have become deeply embedded in the language games and discourse coalitions that have been characterized as ecological or reflexive modernization.[3] Within national governments in Germany, Great Britain, the Netherlands, and the Scandinavian countries, as well as at the European Commission, the dominant policy documents have come to be framed within the terminology—and mindset—of business management, and there has developed a repertoire of so-called market-oriented environmental policies that, among other things, attempt to encourage private companies to develop "cleaner technologies," institute environmental management and accounting systems, and devise strategies for "green product" innovations.[4]

When it was first formulated in the 1980s, the doctrine of sustainable development was seen to represent a new approach to environmental politics that was cooperative and constructive, by which environmental concerns were to be integrated into all other areas of social and economic life. As formulated in the so-called Brundtland report, *Our Common Future*,[5] sustainable development was seen to necessitate the combination of environmental protection with economics and management and, as such, the development of methods and techniques for measuring, assessing, and accounting for the environmental and resource implications of production and consumption patterns, communication and transportation infrastructures, educational and welfare programs, and even social and political interaction. Environmental politics, the report contended, needed to embrace and eventually encompass the entire range of social and economic issues, and there was a need for everyone to be involved, to *participate*.

In the course of the 1990s, the meanings of the term—and of the ideas of environmental politics more generally—gradually shifted from the visionary to the mundane, or, as Karl Mannheim once put it, from the utopian to the ideological.[6] Whereas a utopian vision "orients conduct towards elements which the situation, in so far as it is realized at the time, does not contain,"[7] an ideology, at least for Mannheim, is a more closed and exclusive set of ideas. Ideologies serve to systematize and provide a sense of order—imputing an overarching logic to a set of ideas—whereas utopias are inherently something quite different, serving at best to inspire or encourage the imagining of alternative "logics" and possibilities, and at least questioning the dominant and socially accepted logic or forms of rationality.[8] History is full of examples of shifts from utopias to ideologies, from the visionary to the realistic, from the imaginary to the scientific, and it is perhaps helpful to view the discursive journey of environmental politics as yet another closing in of the visionary, and a narrowing of the collective imagination.

That discursive journey can be traced from the visions of the early 1970s—the programmatic report to the UN Conference on the Human Environment in 1972, *Only One Earth*, jointly authored by an economist, Barbara Ward, and a biologist, Rene Dubos; the manifesto-like *Blueprint for Survival* that launched the journal *The Ecologist*; and perhaps especially the widely-read *Limits to Growth*, which brought to the world's attention the startling results of computer-based prognostications of patterns of resource and energy use—to the intergovernmentally negotiated agreements of the 1980s and 1990s: the Kyoto protocol on climate change, and, not least, *Agenda 21*, the document that emerged from the UN Conference on Environment and Development in Brazil in 1992.

In the world of public policy, the open-ended and all-encompassing visionary thought of the 1970s—the "care and maintenance of a small planet," as Ward and Dubos put it in the subtitle of their book—has, in the course of the journey, been broken down into sectorally separated and administratively specific programs and projects—sustainable technology development, ecological agriculture, green product innovation, industrial ecology, sustainable transport, energy efficiency, and so on. In the rarefied world of academic thought, new-fangled "green political theorists" have devoted many a book-length treatment to elucidating the interrelationships between the various components of environmental politics and the standard political grammar of justice, power, and democracy.[9] Indeed, in the course of the 1990s, all the academic disciplines—from history to sociology, from biology to physics—have been encouraged on numerous occasions to consider their "role" in contributing to an understanding of sustainable development and in making their particular science, and sometimes even science in general, more sustainable. Among influential politicians and their expert advisers, sustainable development has come to be embedded in the emerging language of *governance* and *deliberation*, suggesting that what is required if societies are to be sustainable is nothing less than a whole new way of thinking about politics, which can transcend the cleavages of class and nation: a new ideology "beyond left and right."[10]

On a practical level, the various activities that have been associated with, or characterized by, a desire to bring about more sustainable paths to social and economic development have largely left behind the space of civil society, or the wider "public sphere" where social movements are to be found, to enter instead into the rather more circumscribed confines of public administration and corporate management. The poorly funded and loosely organized activities of the 1970s have tended to give way to more formalized and well-subsidized projects, at the same time as those taking part in what might be termed the quest for sustainable development have tended to assume more narrowly defined professional and/or vocational identities. In the 1970s, "participation" in regard to environmental politics was for many people a primarily voluntary activity, a matter of individual commitment and personal engagement, in large measure a means to express one's sense of civic or public concern in relation to one or another environmental problem or environmentally deleterious project. Whether driven by fear and foreboding for the future or by a sense of solidarity with the non-humans with whom we share the planet, the emerging environmental consciousness, as in many if not all social movements, allowed disparate individuals to find common cause in a public space of their own creation.[11]

By the end of the 1990s, that movement space had largely disappeared. There had emerged instead a range of new, more delimited spaces, or arenas in both the public and private spheres—corporate departments of environmental management, administrative offices of sustainable development, entire industrial branches of renewable energy, even green think tanks, such as the Wuppertal Institute in Germany—which fundamentally altered the conditions of participation. Thereby, both the possibilities for directly taking part *in* one or another activity, as well as the opportunities for feeling part *of* environmental politics, became more limited. There was a transition, in other words, from a kind of open-ended process by which environmental politics had formed a social movement's underlying "collective identity" to a more enclosed set of discourses and practices that were organized largely in the form of externally funded projects, which had meaning more or less only for those directly involved in them, or who had a direct interest in them, often of a commercial nature.

In the following, I want to identify some of the main agents, or forms of agency, that have been involved in this process of cultural transformation, as I have come to recognize them in the course of my own recent research in Europe. The agency that seems particularly significant in the making of green knowledge, the cognitive dimension of environmental politics, is what can be characterized as mediation: bringing people together in new networks, creating communicative or deliberative spaces, or transferring ideas and practices from one place to another in activities of interpretation or translation. What is involved at the personal level is often a process of *hybridization*, or hybrid identity formation, which is remarkably similar to previous periods in history when emerging ideas and practices struggled to win acceptance and support. Both the so-called scientific revolution of the seventeenth century and the emergence of socialism in the nineteenth century involved similar processes of hybridization and hybrid identify formation, by which ideas and practices that had developed in social movements were appropriated by the broader culture.[12]

Hybrid identities are much discussed in the literature on post-colonialism, signifying a "third space" of cross-cultural communication and a seedbed of fertile creative invention.[13] In regard to science, technology, and the environment, Bruno Latour has come to define our technoscientific age in terms of the proliferation of hybrid mixtures of the human and the non-human,[14] or what Donna Haraway has intriguingly characterized as "cyborgs."[15] My use of the term in relation to the quest for sustainable development is meant to emphasize the transcending of boundaries—discursive, institutional, and/or practical—that is the main cultural work of many an agent of change. By elucidating some of the cognitive components of these hybrid identities, we might be better able to know how to readjust our educational and research institutions so that they might more effectively, and appropriately, foster the making of green knowledge.

My reflections are based, in large measure, on two projects supported by the European Commission: PESTO, or Public Participation and Environmental Science and Technology Policy Options, which I coordinated from 1996 to 1999; and TEA, or the Transformation of Environmental Activism, coordinated by Christopher Rootes from 1998 to 2001, for which I served as the Swedish partner.[16]

A CULTURAL APPROACH TO PARTICIPATION

In the PESTO project, we made use of an analytical framework by which the relations between various actors and institutions involved in the world of environmental science and technology policy making are conceptualized in terms of ideal-typical categories of "policy cultures" or policy domains.[17] Each culture has its own particular principle, or policy perspective, as well as its own favored approach, or policy style: its particular way of doing things. Each culture also has its own characteristic ethos, or value system, which helps shape the ways that policies and programs are implemented and carried out in practice. The framework has been developed in order to be able to explore dimensions, or aspects, of policy making that are seldom examined explicitly, namely the various "cultural tensions" that come into play, as those who represent or embody the different perspectives and value systems enter into interaction and negotiation with one another. Policy making, according to this approach, is seen to be based on a conflict of interests among different "actors" and their institutions and recognizes the importance of transcending or resolving those conflicts through processes of mediation and negotiation in the making of policy decisions (Table 1).

The PESTO project consisted of three main stages, or work-packages as they are called in the language of the European Union. First, we described the historical development of environmental science and technology policy in our respective countries, with a particular emphasis on the ways in which the general public had been involved, or allowed to participate, in policy-making processes.[18] In our historical accounts, we found interesting differences among our sample of countries: in Sweden and Britain, for example, public participation was much less conspicuous and explicit than it was in Denmark and the Netherlands, both in terms of the "theory" and the "practice," the ways in which it was talked about, and the ways in which it was carried out. The Netherlands and Denmark had produced a number of innovative procedures in the name of public participation in environmental science and technology policy—science shops and state bodies

TABLE I   Cultural Tensions in Policy Making[19]

Policy Culture

	State	Market	Civil society
Principle	social order	economic growth	public accountability
Style	formal	entrepreneurial	personal
Ethos	bureaucratic	commercial	democratic

for technology assessment, for example—while such innovations were absent in Britain and Sweden. Similarly, the academic investigation of participatory approaches to science and technology policy was an area of some significance in Denmark and the Netherlands, while in Britain and Sweden, there had been far fewer studies and far less opportunity for such research to be conducted. In Sweden and Britain, the education of scientists and engineers was relatively free from any social or cultural ingredients, while in Denmark and the Netherlands, engineering students were exposed, as part of their normal educational experience, to courses in science, technology and society, or the history of technology, or environmental studies. There had thus developed, in Denmark and the Netherlands, somewhat more appropriate institutional and intellectual frameworks for making participation happen when the doctrine of sustainable development was articulated in the late 1980s.[20]

Our second work-package was an attempt to explore the relations between public participation and environmental science and technology policy through case studies in the different countries. We wanted to investigate some of the specific forms that participation had taken in somewhat more detail, by focusing on particular themes: the role of non-governmental organizations, local Agenda 21, sustainable transport, the role of entrepreneurship in environmental science and technology policy.[21] The general ambition was to problematize public participation by studying it in different contexts, so that we might be better able to characterize some of the underlying conditions that were at work in the various activities. The transformations within environmental organizations—from the "protest" organizations that had been so active in the movements against nuclear energy in the 1970s to the more complex and variegated division of labor that characterized environmental activism in the 1990s—was especially noticeable. In the TEA project, we discovered that this was a more general process that had characterized environmental activism across Europe and, indeed, in North America as well: a process of institutionalization or normalization.[22]

In the PESTO project, our third work-package focused explicitly on networks of environmental management, both in the private sector and in the academic world, and not least in the emerging space of academic-industrial interaction. By interviewing a wide range of people active in these networks of ecological mod-

TABLE 2   Some Conditions for Participation, according to the PESTO project

- spaces for interaction across societal domains
- processes of communication across "discourses" and disciplines
- enlightened civil servants
- organizational bridge builders
- political support "from above"
- mobilization of traditions "from below"

ernization, or green business, we sought to increase our understanding of the types of brokerage that took place within the networks. What was actually taking place in terms of mediating, facilitating, and interpreting, that is, in terms of human change agency?

This kind of research is somewhat different from the dominant forms of research in the social sciences. I have come to characterize it as "action-oriented" in that it is problem-driven rather than discipline-driven, and focuses on ongoing, dynamic processes. Its findings thus take the form of intersubjective insights rather than objective facts, lessons that can be learned from different examples rather than "iron laws" that have a universal validity. More specifically, what research like PESTO and TEA can help understand are the conditions that make participation possible, the kinds of contingencies and contextual factors that appear to be necessary for participation to have some cultural significance, however small or fleeting that might be (see Table 2).

On the one hand, we discovered the crucial need for new sorts of public spaces or, perhaps better, social interfaces, where interaction could take place across the domains or policy cultures. Such social interfaces as the cross-ministerial Sustainable Technology Program in the Netherlands, the agencies of technology assessment associated with national and regional governments, the local Agenda 21 offices in many municipalities, and, not least, the ad hoc projects and networks that have been created to deal with specific issues—all these provided opportunities for participation. On the other hand, there was a need for communication and cross-fertilization across disciplines and "discourses." The spaces had to be filled with meaning, with projects and interactive workshops and conferences. Lay people and experts, bureaucrats, and businessmen, needed to be brought together into communication and dialogue: the image of the round table and the notion of "stakeholder dialogue" were recurrent aspects of the participatory activities that we studied.[23]

In most of the projects of public participation that we investigated, we also noted the importance of support both from "above" and "below," that is, the importance of top-down initiative meeting bottom-up engagement. The quest for sustainable development, as we came to understand it in action, seems to require the active involvement of some centrally placed public authorities—whom we can think of as enlightened civil servants—as well as a receptive local base of support. People cannot be forced to participate in environmental politics. It seems that, for participation to happen, they need to feel that their participation contributes to, or is connected to, some other political project. The enlightened civil servants are important as promoters of social innovations; they serve to translate a new approach or method or concept into the relevant public (or private) context. In creating the so-called Infralab or Infrastructural laboratory in the Netherlands, for example, where local citizens are brought into the decision-making processes around new transportation projects, it was an official at the Ministry of Transportation who realized that things had to be done differently: a new structure was called for if the concerns of the public were to be taken into account. In the "green guides" program in Denmark, as well as in other projects of urban ecology that the Danish government instituted in the 1990s, civil servants in the Ministry of the Environment were given the task of making participation happen. It was necessary for public officials to break out of their normal routines: to innovate, think differently, and envision new possibilities. Enlightened civil servants, often together with people who work for a non-governmental organization, have served to bring a kind of professionalism, and often crucially valuable official connections, into a wide range of projects.

At the same time, there need to be bridge builders, people who can facilitate interaction and catalyze processes of communication across the various social divisions and boundaries. In the quest for sustainable development, particular combinations of competencies are called for: linking natural science with social science, engineering with empowerment, ethics with economics, and, not least, environmental concern with professional management.

In the contemporary world, this knowledge making is increasingly being taken on by campaigning organizations or ad hoc networks that have been established for particular campaigns or events in order to address particularly pressing global environmental issues. They tend to operate within particular sectors or interest areas. There are climate action networks and climate change panels, renewable energy networks and intergovernmental programs, organic agriculture networks, ecological design networks, as well as environmental justice networks. In many cases, the networks bring together people working in professional organizations and institutions with local activists and personal environmentalists. The difficulty is in sustaining these kinds of networks and temporary activities and keeping them from being taken over by the large, transnational NGOs such as Greenpeace or the World Wildlife Fund or, for that matter, by business firms and their networks, such as the World Business Council for Sustainable Development.

THE FORMING OF HYBRID IDENTITIES

In cognitive terms, what seems to be involved in the quest for sustainable development is the making of new forms of knowledge, what I have come to

TABLE 3   Hybrid Identities in Sustainable Development

Networkers	
• horizontal	e.g., Johan Schot (Greening of Industry)
• vertical	e.g., Jacqueline Cramer
Translators/interpreters	
• transdisciplinary generalists	e.g., Fritiof Capra
• public intellectuals	e.g., Arne Næss
Facilitators	
• consensus-makers	e.g., Lars Klüver (Danish Technology Board)
• social innovators	e.g., Robin Grove-White
Brokers	
• product champions	e.g., Donald Huisingh
• project managers	e.g., Karl-Henrik Robert (Natural Step)

characterize as green knowledge. Like the new mode of knowledge production identified by Michael Gibbons and his collaborators,[24] green knowledge is often carried out in networks rather than traditional scientific disciplines, and it tends to be organized in ad hoc or temporary projects rather than in more traditionally defined research programs or the puzzle-solving paradigms of what Thomas Kuhn so famously termed "normal science."[25] Green knowledge is usually produced in relation to specific contexts of application or action and thus takes its point of departure in problems with which the researcher feels a sense of engagement; it is rarely the disinterested kind of inquiry that Robert Merton once characterized as central to the modern scientific enterprise.[26] Like many other new fields of knowledge production in the contemporary world—genetic engineering, gender studies, nanotechnology, cognitive science, cultural studies—green knowledge also involves the formation of a number of "hybrid identities" or emergent social roles, which bring together types of competence and expertise that have previously been separated from one another. In this sense, environmental politics embodies, or is grounded in, a new kind of synthesizing cognitive praxis that brings together different kinds of insights and expertise, interests and competencies, and methods and experiences into new combinations.

I will now describe some of these hybrid identities by briefly recounting the activities of some of the people I have come across in the course of my recent research. Each story is meant to illustrate one exemplary type of hybrid identity. There are certainly other ways to talk about these matters, but it seems that if we are to grasp the cultural significance of sustainable development, we must at least in part begin to identify what is going on at the personal level (Table 3).

Obviously, the types of identity are not mutually exclusive, but they do require somewhat different kinds of competence and expertise in order to be carried out effectively. They also require a congenial cultural climate for providing opportunities for hybridization and combination.

Johan Schot, trained as a historian of technology at the Erasmus University in Rotterdam, and one of the first people in Europe to work as a consultant in the field of environmental management and cleaner technologies, is a good example of a horizontal networker, that is, a person who works across the policy cultures or domains in his or her networking activity. Throughout his career, Schot has combined his various interests in creating networks and projects that have been influential in the quest for sustainable development. He was one of the co-founders of the Greening of Industry network (GIN), which has organized a series of international conferences and workshops where academics, business people, government officials, and environmental activists could exchange experiences and discuss the various elements of industrial environmental management and sustainable technological development. Schot's hybrid identity includes an organizational competence, as well as particular intellectual components that have been put together into new conceptual and methodological combinations.

Whereas Schot's networking activities—first GIN and more recently the European history of technology network, Tensions of Europe—have tended to be horizontal, in bringing people together from different countries and different professions, vertical networking often involves a different kind of hybrid identity formation. People who work as environmental managers or environmental accountants within particular organizations or companies are good examples of the ways in which an environmental or biological expertise is being combined with a managerial or organizational expertise. Schot's former colleague, Jacqueline Cramer, who has helped the Dutch firms Unilever and Philips establish environmental product policies, has combined her education in ecology and her personal background as an environmental activist with communicative and educational skills in her particular form of "vertical" networking. What is central to the vertical networking identity is the carrying of one or another sort of environmental competence into unfamiliar territory, the bringing inside of knowledge that was previously considered to be outside, even foreign, to the particular organization or company, and then devising ways to institutionalize that green knowledge.

The translators, or interpreters, are more like what Mannheim once termed free-floating intellectuals, in that they are often people who combine ideas from different academic disciplines or fields of knowledge and struggle to retain their independence from formal or established institutions. The physicists-turned-environmentalists Amory Lovins, Fritiof Capra, and Vandana Shiva are good examples of this kind of hybrid identity; they apply their trained competence in generalization and abstraction to the world of environmental politics. It is a kind of generalist identity, making explicit, as Capra puts it in the title of his most recent book, the "hidden connections" between different fields of knowledge.[27] Ecological philosophers, such as the Norwegian Arne Næss, who coined the term deep ecology, is another example of the interpreter, bringing a way of thinking— philosophical, reflective, "deep"—into other life-worlds and other contexts than it is usually found. In the 1970s, Næss left his university post to become a "movement intellectual" and took part in some of the direct actions of civil disobedience that were carried out in Norway in relation to the exploitation of the northern rivers for hydroelectric power. Like the generalists, Næss has continually performed his expertise or displayed his competence in public.

Throughout Europe, we find the mediators and facilitators at the new arenas that have been established at the boundaries or interfaces of the different policy cultures. A good example of a consensus builder is the Dane Lars Klüver, long-time director of the Board of Technology, which has become well known for its regularly organized consensus conferences that bring lay people together to discuss political issues with relevant experts. Such participatory technology assessment, as it is sometimes called, requires a kind of hybrid between an engineer or natural scientist (biologist in Klüver's case), on the one hand, and a politician (Klüver, like many of his counterparts in other European countries, was an active member of environmental organizations before moving to the Board of Technology), on the other hand.

Facilitation can also be carried out by hybrids within already established institutions—at universities, public agencies, environmental organizations, and consulting firms. The strengthening of what the American political scientist Robert Putnam has termed "bridging social capital" has been particularly important in such contexts as local Agenda 21 activities, where local governmental authorities throughout Europe have often established temporary offices for mediating purposes. Like the forms of networking mentioned earlier, social innovation requires organizational skills and social competence, along with a range of experiences from working in different settings. In many of the local Agenda 21 projects that we investigated in the PESTO project we found social innovators, and we also found them at many a university where new programs in environmental management or environmental ethics are being established. The career trajectory of Robin Grove-White, who in the 1970s and 1980s worked within a large environmental organization (the Council for the Protection of Rural England), established the Centre for Environmental Change at Lancaster University, and now serves as chairman of British Greenpeace and a member of the British Forestry Commission, is a good example of this kind of hybrid identity: a jack of all trades, as it used to be said, but master of none.

The final categories of our typology are more specialized; these are, we might say, the promoters, or even the salesmen, of sustainable development, managing the projects and marketing the products, and generally taking the economic and personal risks that have long characterized the entrepreneur. Karl-Henrik Robert, the Swedish medical doctor turned environmental management consultant, who created the organizational and business concept The Natural Step, illustrates one kind of entrepreneurial hybrid. As in the case of scientific popularizers, Robert's particular skills are in the arts of simplifying and operationalizing complicated ideas. The hybridization in his case refers to the combination of the popularizing sensibility with a commercial or business mindset. One finds something similar in the promoters of the key concepts of environmental management or green business. In Donald Huisingh, the entrepreneur of pollution prevention and cleaner production, who established the Cleaner Production Roundtable and serves as consultant to many companies and university programs in environmental management, one finds the engineer and the ideologue in a kind of symbiosis; the hybrid identity recombines the technical interest of the engineer with the passion and enthusiasm of the politician.

CONCLUSIONS

Certainly not all people see the making of these and other hybrid identities in relation to green knowledge as something intrinsically positive or progressive. What has become especially significant over the past few years, in North America and Europe alike, is a kind of anti-environmental backlash, a mobilization of reaction against environmental politics in general and some of the specific forms of green knowledge making in particular. In Europe, the process has been most painfully visible in Denmark, where a neo-liberal government took office in 2001 and immediately began to eliminate opportunities for environmental scientists and politicians. Many people were fired from the public environmental administrative authorities, and many of the innovative programs of the previous, Social Democratic-led government were disbanded, perhaps most dramatically the support to wind energy and the so-called Green Fund, which had sponsored a large number of locally based projects in sustainable development. To replace the green experts, the Danish government established a new institute of environmental assessment, headed by the self-proclaimed environmental skeptic Bjørn Lomborg, who has achieved fame and fortune by challenging the claims of green knowledge by making use of the traditional technique of cost-accounting, so that the Danish people, as he often puts it, can get "more environment for their money."[28]

This backlash, similar in many ways to the behavior of the George W. Bush administration in the United States, alerts us to the fragility of green knowledge and the difficulties in retaining and consolidating the hybrid identities that have been formed. To borrow terminology used by Raymond Williams in the 1970s, we can characterize the making of green knowledge as involving a cultural political struggle on two fronts: on the one hand, against a dominant cultural formation that seeks to incorporate the new ideas and practices into its own scientific and professional modes of operation—into green business—and, on the other hand, against residual cultural formations, such as the reactionary forms of populism that have become so influential in America and Denmark, which seek to reject green knowledge in the name of traditional belief systems and ways of life.[29]

While the dominant culture operates on a transnational, global scale with commercialization and professional scientific knowledge as the main ingredients of its cognitive praxis, residual cultures resist green knowledge by reinventing traditional ideologies and techniques: in Denmark, the ideology of rural populism and the techniques of the tight-fisted accountant. It is between these poles of opposition that one finds an emerging ecological culture of green knowledge making, where hybrid identities and exemplary learning are the main cognitive components. It remains to be seen if this emerging culture can survive, and indeed reproduce and sustain itself, or whether the processes of incorporation and reaction that have been so prevalent during the past few years will succeed in appropriating or rejecting the ideas and practices of green knowledge. By clarifying some of the aspects of human agency that are involved in environmental politics, and by specifying, as I have tried to do here, something of the cultural dynamics of green knowledge making, it might be hoped that the emerging ecological culture will at least gain a somewhat clearer sense of what it is all about.

NOTES

1　This paper is based on presentations made, in June 2003, to the workshop on public participation organized by the Linked University Consortia in Environment and Development (LUCED) at the Royal Danish Academy of Architecture in Copenhagen, and in August 2003, to a session at the American Political Science Association's annual meeting in Philadelphia. I would like to thank Gustavo Ribiero and Frank Fischer for inviting me to those events, and to all of those who listened to and commented on my presentations.

2　A. Jamison, *The Making of Green Knowledge: Environmental Politics and Cultural Transformation* (Cambridge: Cambridge University Press, 2001).

3　M. Hajer, *The Politics of Environmental Discourse* (Oxford: Oxford University Press, 1995).

4　N. Carter, *The Politics of the Environment* (Cambridge: Cambridge University Press, 2001).

5　World Commission on Environment and Development (WCED), *Our Common Future* (Oxford: Oxford University Press, 1987).

6　K. Mannheim, *Ideology and Utopia* (New York: Routledge and Kegan Paul, 1948 [1936]).

7　Mannheim, *Ideology and Utopia*, p. 176.

8　R. Everman and A. Jamison, *Social Movements: A Cognitive Approach* (Cambridge: Polity, 1991).

9　See, e.g., A. Dobson, *Green Political Thought* (London: Routledge, 2000).

10　A. Giddens, *Beyond Left and Right: The Future of Radical Politics* (Cambridge: Polity, 1994).

11　A. Jamison, R Eyerman, J Cramer and J Laessoe, *The Making of the New Environmental Consciousness* (Edinburgh: Edinburgh University Press, 1990).

12　M. Hård and A. Jamison, "The Story-lines of Technological Change: Innovation, Construction and Appropriation," *Technology Analysis and Strategic Management* 1(2003): 81–91.

13   See, e.g., H. Bhabha, *The Location of Culture* (New York: Routledge, 1994).

14   B. Latour, *We Have Never Been Modern* (Cambridge, MA: Harvard University Press, 1993).

15   D. Haraway, *Simians, Cyborgs and Women: The Reinvention of Nature* (London: Chapman and Hall, 1991).

16   PESTO included research teams in Denmark, Italy, Lithuania, the Netherlands, Norway, Sweden, and the United Kingdom; TEA included teams in France, Germany, Greece, Italy, Spain, Sweden, and the United Kingdom.

17   This conceptualization was developed in earlier research with Erik Baark and Aant Elzinga. The findings of the PESTO project have been presented in the final report published by the Department of Development Planning, Aalborg University in 1999.

18   A. Jamison and P. Østby, eds., *Public Participation and Sustainable Development: European experiences: PESTO Papers 1* (Aalborg: Aalborg University Press, 1997).

19   In the analytical model that we used in the PESTO project, we referred to a fourth culture, or domain, the academic, which is not relevant for the discussion in this paper.

20   See Jamison *et al.*, *The Making of the New Environmental Consciousness*, for details on the emergence of environmentalism in Denmark, Sweden, and the Netherlands.

21   A. Jamison, ed., *Technology Policy Meets the Public: PESTO Papers 2* (Aalborg: Aalborg University Press, 1998).

22   M. Diani and P. Donati, "Organizational Change in Western European Environmental Groups: A framework for analysis," in C. Rootes, ed., *Environmental Movements, Local, National and Global* (London: Frank Cass, 1999).

23   F. Fischer, *Citizens, Experts and the Environment* (Durham, NC: Duke University Press, 2000).

24   M. Gibbons, C Limoges, H Nowotny, S Schwartzman, P Scott, M Trow, *The New Production of Knowledge* (London: Sage, 1994).

25   T. Kuhn, *The Structure of Scientific Revolutions* (Chicago: University of Chicago Press, 1962).

26   R. Merton, *The Sociology of Science* (Chicago: University of Chicago Press, 1973 [1942]).

27   F. Capra, *The Hidden Connections* (New York: Doubleday, 2002).

28   A. Jamison, "Learning from Lomborg, or Where Do Anti-Environmentalists Come From?," in *Science as Culture* 13.2(June 2004): 173–95.

29   R. Williams, *Marxism and Literature* (Oxford: Oxford University Press, 1977).

15

Responses
to Environmental Threats
in an Age of Globalization

Jennifer Clapp

As globalization continues apace, environmental problems have become increasingly complex, in some cases threatening the sustainability of human livelihoods in both rich and poor countries. Political responses to these threats have not to date been sufficient. The global political system, structured around sovereign states, forces us to rely on inter-state cooperation to address those environmental problems that transcend borders. But the track record over the past 30 years has shown that states, even working together, have proven weak in the face of global environmental threats. Over this same period, it has become increasingly clear that the emergence of many of today's environmental problems is intricately linked with economic relationships. Rapid economic globalization in particular has been largely beyond effective state control, such that environmental problems linked to that process have been difficult for states acting alone to prevent. And once environmental problems manifest themselves, states are finding that, for a variety of reasons, they lack the capacity to manage them effectively, either individually or collectively.

The weakness on the part of states in an era of economic globalization has given rise to new responses from both states themselves as well as non-state actors. The past decade has seen an increased integration of economic and environmental measures at the international level, in both economic and environmental agreements. There has also been increased recognition and participation of non-state actors such as non-governmental organizations, industry actors, and scientific experts in negotiating and implementing international environmental agreements. While these recent trends in global environmental governance represent an attempt to improve states' capacity to prevent and to manage environmental problems, serious doubts remain over whether they go far enough to make much difference in the quality of the environment.

The Global Economy and the Emergence of Environmental Threats

The emergence of environmental problems around the globe is inextricably linked with multi-level and highly complex economic relationships over which states are finding that they have less and less influence. Some argue that economic globalization has the potential to improve the quality of the environment. Their reasoning is that globalization promotes economic growth, which provides both the resources to implement cleaner technologies and the political will to improve environmental regulations.[1] It is no surprise that this argument is widely contested. The increasingly vocal challenge to this view is at the heart of the anti-globalization debate. Critics argue that the relationship between globalization and economic growth on the one hand, and environmental quality on the other, is highly complex, and rarely positive.[2] Regardless of which side of this debate one sides with, most analysts agree that a number of aspects of global economic relationships are linked to environmental problems in complex ways.

The potential environmental impact of global trade has perhaps received the most attention in academic and policy circles. The fact that there is little in the rules of the World Trade Organization (WTO) that can be interpreted as specifically geared toward environmental protection has indeed left the question open. Though the debate over the overall impact of trade on the environment has by no means been resolved, in recent years there has been a growing consensus that certain aspects of global trade have direct negative environmental consequences. These include the export of hazardous wastes to countries unable to cope with them, trade in ivory from African elephants, and the illegal trade in chlorofluorocarbons (CFCs).[3] The environmental impact of transportation from trade is also a consideration. The OECD has estimated that international transportation would rise by 4-5 per cent as a result of the Uruguay Round of trade negotiations that were completed in 1994, and this would mean more energy use and more pollution.[4] Critics are also worried about a decline in environmental standards resulting from trade. This occurs, they argue, because countries, in a bid to reduce costs to become more competitive in international markets, may lower, or at least may fail to strengthen, environmental regulations and their enforcement.[5] This is referred to by some as the "race toward the bottom," or a "political drag" on environmental policy making. Of course there is much debate over whether this actually occurs in practice, but the perceived threat that it will is widely agreed to be real, which affects state policies.[6]

There is also a great deal of concern over global corporate activities and the environment.[7] There are ongoing debates over whether global firms relocate in order to take advantage of lower environmental standards in poor countries.[8] But at the same time, there is wide acknowledgment of a connection between global investment in certain industries and the occurrence of environmental harm. It is well known that the most environmentally damaging industries tend to have a high concentration of transnational corporations (TNCs) as the main investors and operators.[9] Global corporations operating in hazardous manufacturing industries such as chemicals, electronics, and textiles, as well as extractive industries such as mining, oil drilling, and logging, are particularly notable for their negative environmental impact. While many accept that environmental damage from these industries occurred in the past, there is a great deal of debate today over whether global firms have left such practices behind them. Some see TNCs as spreading good environmental practices, while others argue that globalization has made it much easier for global firms to exploit the developing world's lower environmental standards.[10] But recent cases of toxic mine spills in Guyana and the Philippines, pollution from oil extraction in Ecuador and Nigeria, toxic waste from *maquiladora* plants in Mexico, to name but a few examples, demonstrate that some of the problems do continue with modern-day TNCs operating in these industries within developing countries.[11]

Similarly, links have been established between global financial relationships and the environment. It is widely recognized that, in the past, international financial institutions have funded large-scale infrastructure projects in developing countries that have resulted in environmental harm. The cases of forest destruction caused by the Polonoreste Project in Brazil in the 1980s and the displacement of hundreds of thousands of people for the Narmada Valley dams in India in the 1990s are but two prominent examples among many.[12] Lending agencies such as the World Bank claim that such practices are now behind them, though critics still have their doubts, as will be discussed below. In addition, there is wide acknowledgement that private sources of international finance pose environmental problems as well. This is because private finance promotes a short-term mentality among borrowing firms and this in turn runs counter to the long-term outlook necessary to tackle environmental problems effectively.[13]

Globalization can affect the environment in less direct ways as well, and these are equally controversial. Some argue that globalization exacerbates global inequality, which in turn has implications for the environment.[14] According to the UNDP, income inequalities have become more pronounced over the past 30 years.[15] This income difference is reflected in skewed consumption as well. Per-capita private consumption in industrialized countries in 1995 stood at US $16,000 while it was only US $300 in much of the developing world. Africa's consumption has actually declined over the past 20 years, while it has risen just about everywhere else. Industrial countries, though they only account for 15 per cent of global population, are responsible for 76 per cent of global consumption expenditure.[16]

Extremes of both poverty and wealth have been identified as major sources of environmental problems in both rich and poor countries. The widespread existence of poverty and its cyclical relationship to environmental degradation currently threaten the livelihoods of the bulk of the human race. Some three-quarters of the world's population live in the lesser developed countries. The pursuit of daily survival by the poor often means a direct and immediate reliance on their natural surroundings. Environmental quality often suffers from this heavy burden of poverty because the impoverished, particularly in the poor countries, often have no choice but to degrade the very environment from which they gain their livelihoods.[17] They lack access to enough land and money to enable them to gain their living in a more sustainable manner. The poor in many parts of the developing world, for example, find that they have little choice but to rely on local trees, even when scarce, for fuel-wood; to over-cultivate the often already marginal lands to which they have access; and to use environmentally unsound technologies in local manufacturing processes. The poor undertake these activities not out of ignorance or a lack of concern for the natural environment, but because of inadequate access to more environmentally positive alternatives. The inequitable distribution of natural and monetary resources, both locally and globally, leaves the poor in this cycle from which it is very difficult to break loose.

At the same time that poverty has harmful environmental impacts, wealth and overconsumption also threaten human livelihoods and well-being. The industrialization process that has been associated with wealth throughout the global economy has contributed to many environmental problems worldwide, as is well known.[18] Industrial processes have caused some of the worst pollutants known to humans. Some of these have not only local effects, but also regional and global consequences. As parts of the rich world are now entering a "post-industrial" age, the presence and environmental consequences of industrialization are reappearing in parts of the developing world, where the same environmentally harmful technologies now abandoned in many of the rich countries are often used.

In this era of economic globalization, international market transactions are now largely outside of state control. The deliberate move of states to disengage from even attempting to regulate global economic processes, as seen by the liberalization of international trade, production, and finance has led to what Robert Cox calls an "internationalization of the state."[19] States in both the rich and poor countries find themselves heavily influenced by some combination of global financial markets and global financial institutions because of high levels of external debt, global markets because of the perceived need to sell ever more products, or TNCs because of the constant need for new investment. This internationalization of the state means that states have surrendered effective control over activities that directly and indirectly affect not only their economies, but also their environments.[20] States are also finding it difficult to meet obligations toward the global environment and to their own domestic environments. Some states have been more able than others to control economic activities related to environmental damage and to meet environmental obligations. For example, advanced industrialized countries have on average been much more able to control economic flows and to impose environmental regulations within their borders than developing countries. But the ability of all states to control the global economy has decayed, compromising their capacity to prevent the emergence of environmental problems that are connected, both directly and indirectly, with globalization.

STATE INCAPACITY IN THE MANAGEMENT OF GLOBAL ENVIRONMENTAL PROBLEMS

A second key characteristic of environmental problems in this era of globalization is the patterned way in which states attempt to address them. Over the past 30 years states have relied almost exclusively on "after-the-fact" management, rather than prevention. Individual states, as well as states actively cooperating with one another, are finding themselves increasingly incapable of effectively addressing environmental threats using this approach. The degree to which states are able to muddle through depends very much on their ability and willingness to pay for it, with many rich countries being somewhat more "successful" in cleaning up problems than many poorer countries.

Part of the reason why many environmental problems are so intractable once they occur is that they do not respect national boundaries. Environmental harm that originates in one state can affect other states as well as the global commons. The emergence of transboundary and global environmental problems has meant that no one state can single-handedly put a halt to them. Nor can any one state ensure that it is not affected by environmental problems emanating from other states. Global problems such as ozone depletion, biodiversity loss, and global warming, as well as transboundary problems such as the hazardous waste trade, acid rain, and international river pollution, are vivid and well-known examples of this. Garnering the agreement of all the parties involved in these transborder environmental issues has been time-consuming and difficult.

The slow-moving nature of global environmental problems makes it extremely difficult for states to reach agreement on how to address them. Though many of the more important global environmental problems have been identified, they have not yet reached what states might consider to be a "crisis" point. Global warming, biodiversity loss, and ozone depletion have been evident for decades, but many states, particularly those lacking financial capacity, have thus far felt that the situation is not yet sufficiently critical to warrant drastic action. Support and funding for such long-range planning is often very difficult for state politicians to win, as they usually operate on very short time horizons set by election cycles and short-term "economic imperatives."[21] Stalling by countries such as the US and Canada over ratifying and implementing the 1997 Kyoto Protocol is a case in point. Though these states do have the resources to put toward such a commitment, their politicians calculate that the political benefits are not yet equal to the costs. States also find it difficult to address such problems with the same urgency as security threats when there is no immediate and widely agreed-upon "enemy" to blame.[22]

Adding to the complexity of global environmental problems is the scientific uncertainty that typically surrounds them. Without scientific research we would not be aware of the severity and in some cases even the existence of these problems, but much is still unknown. Scientific experts have played a crucial role in identifying many environmental problems, such as ozone depletion, global warming, biodiversity loss, persistent organic pollutants, and acid rain.[23] And new information on the condition of these problems and on the attempts to address them is constantly emerging as part of the ongoing process of scientific research, and is often fraught with controversy. It is only once a broad consensus is reached that change in strategies to mitigate environmental harm is embraced, as occurred in the late 1980s and early 1990s when phase-outs of CFCs and other ozone-depleting substances were sped up under the Montreal Protocol once scientists agreed that the ozone hole was indeed real. Action on other issues is slow, however, because debates rage over whose science "counts," and the extent of scientific proof required to warrant precautionary initiatives.

A further aspect of their complexity is that these problems are very dynamic and unpredictable. For example, substitutes for environmentally harmful chemicals may also be dangerous. We just do not know, as environmental and environmental-health problems often take years to discover and document. The complexity of the issues is compounded because it is difficult to separate cause and effect. For this reason, environmental problems and their politics tend to be circular in nature, rather than linear like more traditional problems in international politics.[24] In other words, it is simply not possible to declare environmental problems to be "solved," as protection of the environment is an ongoing process. This complexity and uncertainty render states weak in the face of these issues.

Their weakness in both preventing and managing environmental problems has prompted states to increase cooperation with one another, as they recognize the difficulties inherent in these issues, particularly those with global consequences or transboundary implications. Over the past three decades there has been a proliferation of environmental agreements among states in an attempt to create new and more effective "regimes," defined as "norms, rules, principles and decision-making procedures"[25] for environmental protection. There are now over 200 international environmental agreements in place. A growing literature has sought to explain state behavior in such regimes as well as their outcomes in terms of environmental quality.[26] It has become clear that not all states have the same goals toward the environment, which makes unanimous agreement on protective measures elusive. Because of the difficulties in building effective agreements that are acceptable to all states, those treaties that are agreed upon by a number of states often have no firm sanctions to ensure compliance or enforcement, and they do not result in significant change in the behavior of states. Moreover, global agreements are binding only on those states that ratify them, and some states, such as the US, routinely choose not to do so.

RECENT TRENDS
IN GLOBAL ENVIRONMENTAL GOVERNANCE

The growing realization that states are weak both in preventing and addressing environmental problems in this era of globalization has led to a number of new trends in global environmental governance. There have been two general trends in the past decade with respect to the norms, rules, and institutions of global environmental governance that take account of the state weaknesses discussed above. First, there has been a growing recognition that there is a need to explicitly link global cooperation on economic issues with global cooperation on environmental issues. Second, there is growing participation and institutionalization of non-state actors in the process of negotiating and implementing environmental agreements to help improve the capacity of states to manage global environmental problems. These trends are changing the face of global environmental governance and the role of states within it. But while these changes may be a step in the right direction, important questions remain over whether they go far enough to be fully effective.

Integration of Economic and Environmental Measures

With the rising awareness over the past decade that the global economy is inextricably linked to the global environment, there has been a distinct move toward integrating environmental and economic elements within international agreements. Efforts are now routinely made in both old and new economic regimes to incorporate environmental provisions, and environmental regimes have begun in many cases to incorporate economic provisions. The result is a system of global environmental governance that relies increasingly on the melding of economic and environmental measures in an attempt to avoid environmental problems by curtailing the types of economic activity most directly linked to their occurrence.

The incorporation of environmental provisions into economic regimes has been clearly evident in recent years in international trade agreements. Despite much debate over the linkages between free trade and the environment in general, for those certain types of trade that have clear links to environmental harm, measures have been adopted in trade agreements to mitigate this harm. The North American Free Trade Agreement (NAFTA), for example, stipulates that three specific environmental treaties dealing with trade issues—the Basel Convention, the Montreal Protocol, and the Convention on International Trade in Endangered Species (CITES)—are to be respected despite any restrictions they may place on free trade. The agreement also requests parties to avoid seeking to attract investment by lowering environmental standards. In addition, there is a separate environmental side agreement to NAFTA which includes provisions that are intended to ensure the enforcement of environmental standards in Mexico, the US, and Canada and is overseen by the North American Commission on the Environment.[27]

In 1995 the WTO reconstituted its Committee on Trade and Environment that has produced studies on key areas where environment and trade meet.[28] There has been much discussion on issues such as eco-labeling, dispute resolution on trade and environment conflicts, the link between trade agreements and multi-lateral environmental agreements (MEAs), and whether to make exceptions for environmental goals more explicit at the WTO. But while studies have been produced, there has been little concrete change in the WTO with respect to the environment thus far, and the issue of MEAs and the WTO rules has not been resolved. Dispute panel decisions on trade and environment issues in the early 1990s, such as those on the tuna-dolphin issue, led many to question the environmental credentials of the WTO. Dispute panels twice ruled that unilateral trade sanctions imposed by the US that were geared to protecting dolphins outside of its own territory were WTO illegal.[29] There was movement to incorporate environmental discussions into the next WTO trade round, but this seems to have been suspended following the Seattle protests. However, recent dispute-panel decisions such as those on shrimp-sea turtles are seen by some to show remarkable acceptance on the part of the WTO of the need to allow countries considerable scope to use trade measures for environmental protection, provided they meet trade goals as well.[30]

In the area of global investment rules, recent years have seen the emergence of several international initiatives to establish voluntary codes of environmental conduct for industry. This has been partly in response to the public perception of industry's role in poor site practices in the most environmentally damaging industries. Voluntary codes for industry include, for example, the Coalition for Environmentally Responsible Economies' (CERES) Principles, the International Chamber of Commerce's Business Charter for Sustainable Development, the International Organization for Standardization's ISO 14000 environmental management standards, and the Chemical Manufacturers Association's Responsible Care.[31] "Best practices" codes for specific industries have also been developed, including those for forestry, mining, and oil extraction. The idea behind these codes and standards is that firms set their own environmental goals, and they establish their own procedures to enable them to work toward meeting those goals. But while such voluntary measures on the part of firms represent an awareness of the importance of environmental issues in investment, critics are wary of voluntary measures and claim that these are weak.[32]

Multilateral development banks are also beginning to incorporate environmental concerns into their lending policies after having admitted that much of their lending in the past had harmful consequences for the environment.[33] After much criticism from environmental groups for not taking environmental concerns into consideration in its lending, the World Bank has made efforts to improve its environmental record through the adoption of a number of measures. It created a separate environment department in 1988 and by 1993 employed over 100 environmental experts, up from only 5 in the mid-1980s.[34] The Bank also began to require environmental impact assessments on all project lending in

1991, and between 1990 and 1995 it increased thirty-fold its lending for projects which were deemed to have positive environmental impact. Other multilateral lending agencies, such as the Inter-American Development Bank, the Asian Development Bank, and the African Development Bank, have all begun to follow the World Bank in improving the environmental record of their lending. But while great effort has been made to give the appearance that these institutions are environmentally friendly, environmental groups are still highly skeptical that these changes have not yet gone far enough or that they do not necessarily represent permanent change.[35] For example, the World Bank's support for environmental projects fell in subsequent years, from 3.6 per cent of its lending in 1994 to only 1.02 per cent in 1998.[36]

At the same time that global economic governance has begun to incorporate environmental measures, international environmental agreements have tended to include economic provisions such as trade restrictions. There are now some 20 international environmental agreements with trade restrictions built into them. The Basel Convention, for example, places strict regulations on the international trade in hazardous wastes. In 1994 the parties to the Basel Convention decided to prohibit the export of waste from OECD to non-OECD countries for waste that was destined both for disposal and for recycling on the grounds that non-OECD countries were highly unlikely to be able to offer environmentally sound disposal sites.[37] This decision was reconfirmed in 1995 when the parties decided to amend the convention to include this ban. The CITES agreement has also placed trade restrictions on certain animals and animal products listed in its annexes, such as the trade in African elephant ivory.[38] The Stockholm Convention on Persistent Organic Pollutants has banned the production, use, and trade of twelve industrial chemicals,[39] and the Biosafety Protocol gives states the right to refuse the import of living modified organisms based on risk assessment.[40] The Montreal Protocol establishes the use of economic sanctions against those states not complying with the convention's provisions to protect the ozone layer, effectively banning the trade in CFCs that are not covered by the convention.[41]

A further aspect of this coupling of international economic and environmental governance is the increased use of compensatory mechanisms to help facilitate environmental protection. The Kyoto Protocol, for example, incorporates provisions for joint implementation via the Clean Development Mechanism (CDM). The CDM allows Northern countries to count the reductions in CO2 levels attained through projects that they fund in developing countries as reductions of their *own* emissions. A mechanism such as this in theory enables developing countries to attain cleaner technology at a lower cost than they could have otherwise. The Montreal Protocol Multilateral Fund also establishes an aid mechanism to enable the South to purchase technology aimed at reducing emissions of ozone-depleting CFCs.[42] In the early 1990s the creation of the Global Environment Facility (GEF) aimed to specifically provide funding to poorer countries to enable them to invest in activities that would benefit the global environment—

namely climate change, biodiversity loss, ocean pollution, and ozone depletion. The GEF was earmarked at UNCED to be the official funding mechanism for the implementation of the global treaties on climate change and biodiversity.[43] It is also the official funding mechanism for the Stockholm Convention on Persistent Organic Pollutants, having recently added POPs elimination activities as a further category eligible for funding. These various mechanisms for economic compensation offered to poorer countries to enable them to protect their environments have brought benefits to some developing countries, but many argue that they are still far too little given the vast amounts of money required on the environmental front.[44]

A melding of economic and environmental governance has also taken place in the area of private finance. The UN Environment Programme (UNEP) organized a Statement by Banks on the Environment and Sustainable Development in the mid-1990s, which has been signed by over 260 financial institutions.[45] This statement is very market friendly but supports the precautionary approach to environmental management. It is not a binding agreement, but rather is "soft" law in that it only requests signatories to abide by its principles. This has led some to ask whether it is a genuinely green move, or just a risk-minimization strategy on the part of banks.

The growing number of environmentally based restrictions on trade and environmental improvements incorporated into the design of aid programs and projects indicates that states have accepted a degree of global environmental governance that relies on economic measures to prevent problems from arising, rather than relying solely on after-the-fact damage control. But the criticisms raised of these initiatives thus far indicate that there is a need to continually reassess these measures to ensure that they are achieving the goals that they aim for. Ongoing evaluation of global environmental governance structures is necessary because environmental problems are constantly evolving as globalization continues apace, creating new outlets for environmental problems that are not as yet regulated.

The Rise of Non-State Actors

A second trend that has emerged in global environmental governance is the growing participation and importance of non-state actors in global environmental politics. The number of non-state actors attending international environmental and economic conferences and treaty negotiations has been growing steadily over the past decade. Non-state actors such as intergovernmental organizations (IGOs), non-governmental environmental organizations (NGOs), business advocacy groups, and scientific and environmental expert groups have all become vital players in the process of international environmental regime formation. Since their overwhelming presence and participation in the Rio Earth Summit process, the roles of these non-state actors have become more institutionalized in the formation and maintenance of international environmental regimes.

Though much of the thinking on regime formation has in the past focused primarily on the role of states in international cooperation, there has been a growing recognition of the important role played by intergovernmental organizations in regime formation.[46] For example, UNEP has taken a key role in the coordination and negotiation of international environmental accords such as the Basel Convention, the Convention on Biodiversity, and the Stockholm Convention. Other organizations have also taken this role, such as the International Maritime Organization's coordination of discussions on the London Dumping Convention. The international secretariats that are created along with the implementation of many new environmental treaties also represent a new political role for IGOs. These organizations have important roles in collecting and disseminating information, and could potentially play a part in monitoring states' implementation of, and compliance with, international agreements if they were given the power to do so.[47] These organizations in effect create the framework around which states can rally to do something about a specific environmental problem. While these organizations do not have absolute power to force states into measures they do not wish to adopt because they are ultimately made up of and financed by member states, they do have their own distinct agendas and can wield some influence over states.

In reaction to the slow pace at which states attempt to deal politically with these issues, we have seen an important and dramatic rise in the visibility and activity of environmental NGOs in recent years, especially at the global level.[48] These groups often are key critics of states and act to push states into action by lobbying governments, participating in negotiations of environmental agreements, and launching public education campaigns. This growth in the activity of NGOs has been seen as a major force behind the rise of "global civil society."[49] Networks of non-state organizations have expanded their presence and activities particularly around environmental issues in response to the inaction and inadequacy of states to identify and counter such problems. NGOs have indeed enjoyed an enhanced role in educating the public on issues, lobbying governments to take action, and participating as observers in international environmental treaty negotiation.[50] This latter role has been especially effective when NGOs form alliances with certain states at the bargaining table. This was the case at the 1994 and 1995 conferences of the parties to the Basel Convention, at which an alliance between Greenpeace and developing countries was seen to be the main force behind the decision to impose a ban on the rich-to-poor-country waste trade.[51] NGOs have been a vital force at the negotiations of a number of other environmental treaties and are also now taking on roles to ensure states' compliance with agreements. They do this by disseminating information to the public and mass media with the implicit threat to embarrass delinquent governments.[52] Local and grassroots NGOs have also grown in numbers in recent years, in rich and poor countries alike. The aims of these groups are varied, from promoting local resource management to forming linkages with international environmental NGOs on both local and global issues.

Riding on the coat-tails of the environmental NGOs, business advocacy groups are also increasingly present at international environmental negotiations.

Because of their influential position in an ever more globalized economy, business players are increasingly seen as crucial in terms of protection of the environment.[53] Industry and business advocacy groups and representatives are also keenly interested in knowing what deals are being struck that might affect them, and they also attempt to lobby governments in their favor. For example, groups such as the International Chamber of Commerce were in full force at the Rio Earth Summit and have attended negotiations and meetings of various international environmental agreements, for example the Basel Convention, the Montreal Protocol, the Biosafety Protocol, and the Climate Change Convention. These groups are now attempting to portray themselves as "green" players through their environmental reports and magazines. Critics argue that such reports cannot be taken at face value, and that much of their attempt to satisfy the public is merely "greenwash."[54] Nonetheless, industry groups often have more money and a more singly focused agenda than other non-state actors and thus are able to exert an important influence on the regime-formation process.[55]

The complexity of environmental issues has led to an increased role for scientists and environmental experts in helping policy makers and the public to understand environmental issues and to strategize on how to mitigate or manage them. They have specialized knowledge that is vital to understanding environmental problems, and this helps to explain the enhanced power of these experts groups in the international arena.[56] With regard to environmental issues, such scientific experts have been indispensable in identifying and laying out the problems in laypersons' language for policy makers and the public. They have also taken on roles as negotiators of international agreements. For example, scientists were important in these respects in formulating state policy and in negotiating the Montreal Protocol, and in the Mediterranean Action Plan associated with the Barcelona Convention.[57] While some argue that these players hold shared beliefs and bodies of knowledge that are not inherently political, there is growing recognition that they are very political actors and their research can be used by other groups to promote their own position.[58] Though scientific uncertainty abounds with respect to environmental issues that can weaken the influence these actors have on the policy process, their input is still very important.[59]

All of these groups of non-state actors are key to informing states and the public, influencing states at negotiations, and ensuring the implementation of and compliance with environmental agreements. The presence of non-state actors is now standard at such meetings, and any attempts to exclude them would no doubt elicit widespread protest. The rise of these groups and the institutionalization of their presence at negotiations show that states are not the only legitimate actors promoting environmental cooperation in the international system. But while each of these non-state actors plays an important role, their influence relies to a great extent on the cooperation of states. The entire process of incorporation of non-state actors is still centered on helping to improve the state-based system with respect to the environment, by critiquing and prodding states to take action. Yet this system is still firmly in place, with states still holding enormous influence in the global political arena. The presence of non-state actors may in fact act to reinforce the state system and bolster states' power in this realm simply by operating within the state-based system. This has led some to argue that many non-state actors are being "co-opted" through the institutionalization of their presence in the global environmental policy-making process.[60]

CONCLUSION

In an era of economic globalization, environmental problems are increasingly tied to global economic relationships. Despite a growing number of agreements designed to encourage states to protect the natural environment over the past three decades, these agreements have not made a large enough impact on the quality of the natural environment thus far. The highly complex nature of environmental problems has made it extremely difficult for states to take effective action, even when they work together through the process of forming environmental regimes on specific issues. Though some states have been more successful than others in the pursuit of environmental protection, the capacity of the state system as a whole has been distinctly lacking on this front. Changes in global environmental governance have begun to take place as a response to state weakness in the face of environmental threats in an era of globalization, but although they mark a step in a positive direction—in the sense that they recognize the interconnected nature of global economic and environmental issues and the need for wider participation in global environmental policy making—thus far there is little indication that these measures are sufficient to halt global environmental harm. More radical measures are necessary. Below I outline some of the key measures that need to be taken.

With respect to global trade, the relationship between multilateral environmental agreements and the rules of the WTO must be clarified. The lack of clear rules delineating which treaties take priority for states that are party both to MEAs with trade restrictions as well as to the WTO has left MEAs open to being officially challenged as WTO-inconsistent.[61] While to date no MEA has been formally challenged at the WTO, numerous studies are being undertaken by those who would like to see such a challenge filed, and this has been very worrying for many concerned with environmental issues. WTO members did agree at their 2001 ministerial meeting in Doha, Qatar, that this issue must be clarified, and the WTO's committee on trade and environment has the item on its agenda.[62] Whether other groups will be allowed in on this discussion remains to be seen, however, and it is important that the process be open and participatory to ensure that the decision is not simply to make WTO rules a priority over global environmental rules.

On global investment, global rules of some kind are needed to ensure that transnational corporations do not take advantage of less strict or less strictly enforced environmental regulations in developing countries. Because of the weak and voluntary nature of the ISO 14000 environmental management standards, there is growing recognition that further global rules are necessary to ensure that global corporations fully embrace environmental principles. The

OECD guidelines for Multinational Enterprises, revised in 2000, mention the need for multinational corporations to be environmentally minded, but these are not binding on states.[63] Some environmental groups are now calling for a binding international agreement on investment and environmental practices. Such rules should include obligations for corporations to meet certain environmental performance standards as well as provisions for corporate liability in cases of environmental harm.[64] This sort of binding agreement would go some way toward ensuring that global corporations pursue sound environmental practices.

There is also a need for further reform of global financial institutions such as the World Bank. Though the World Bank has undertaken some reforms for environmental improvement over the past 15 years, environmental groups would like to see further reforms that incorporate environmental principles more firmly in that institution. Proposed reforms include adherence to a "do more good" and "do no harm" set of lending guidelines. Doing more good would entail increased funding for environmentally sound projects that promote, for example, alternative forms of energy and conservation of natural resources. Doing no harm would mean a radical reduction in lending for large-scale natural resource extraction projects.[65]

More open and participatory processes for the formation and implementation of global economic and environmental governance are also needed to ensure that such reforms are not only undertaken, but are the result of a wide consultation and negotiation. Environmental groups, scientific experts, and industry groups should all be able to have a say in the design and implementation of reforms. But there also need to be checks on the process to ensure that the "non-state actor" participants in such fora are not dominated by those actors, such as industry groups, with access to more funding.

These are just some of the key measures that the global community should consider seriously to improve global environmental governance. In global fora on these issues, many states—the US, Canada, and Japan in particular—are aligning themselves with industry groups in seeking to promote the globalization agenda as a panacea for environmental problems; the EU and most developing countries, along with many environmental NGOs, are seeking to promote radical changes in global environmental governance that rein in global economic actors and make them more accountable. The perspective on these issues that will ultimately prevail remains to be seen.

NOTES

1   Gene Grossman and Alan Krueger, "Economic Growth and the Environment," *Quarterly Journal of Economics* 40(1995): 353–77; World Bank, *World Development Report 1992: Development and Environment* (Oxford: Oxford University Press, 1992).

2   Wolfgang Sachs, *Planet Dialectics: Explorations in Environment and Development* (London: Zed Press, 1999); Herman Daly, *Beyond Growth: The Economics of Sustainable Development* (Boston: Beacon, 1996).

3   Thomas Princen, "The Zero Option and Ecological Rationality in International Environmental Politics," *International Environmental Affairs* 18.1(1997): 147–76; Jennifer Clapp, "The Illicit Trade in Hazardous Wastes and CFCs: International Responses to Environmental 'Bads,'" in R. Friman and P. Andreas, eds., *The Illicit Global Economy and State Power* (Lanham, MD: Rowman and Littlefield, 1999).

4   Eric Neumayer, *Greening Trade and Investment: Environmental Protection without Protectionism* (London: Earthscan, 2001), p. 108.

5   Herman Daly, "The Perils of Free Trade," *Scientific American* Nov. 1993: 50–57.

6   Gareth Porter, "Trade Competition and Pollution Standards: 'Race to the Bottom' or 'Stuck at the Bottom,'" *Journal of Environment and Development* 8.2(1999): 136.

7   See, for example, Nazli Choucri, "Multinational Corporations and the Global Environment," in N. Choucri, ed., *Global Accord* (Cambridge, MA: MIT Press, 1993), pp. 205–209; David Levy and Peter Newell, eds., *Business in International Environmental Governance: A Political Economy Approach* (Cambridge, MA: MIT Press, forthcoming); Joshua Karliner, *The Corporate Planet: Ecology and Politics in an Age of Globalization* (San Francisco: Sierra Club, 1997).

8   For an excellent overview of the debate, see Peter Thompson and Laura A. Strohm, "Trade and Environmental Quality: A Review of the Evidence," *Journal of Environment and Development* 5.4(1996): 365–90, and Eric Neumayer, "Pollution Havens: An Analysis of Policy Options for Dealing With an Elusive Phenomenon," *Journal of Environment and Development* 10.2(2001): 147–77.

9   U.N. Transnational Corporations and Management Division, Department of Economic and Social Development, *World Investment Report 1992* (New York: UN, 1992), p. 226.

10 See, for example, Ronie Garcia-Johnson, *Exporting Environmentalism* (Cambridge, MA: MIT Press, 2000), and, for the opposing view, Karliner, *The Corporate Planet*.

11 On mine spills, see Moira Hutchinson, "Beyond Best Practice: The Mining Sector," in North-South Institute, *Canadian Corporations and Social Responsibility* (Ottawa: North South Institute, 1998), pp. 74–90; on oil extraction, see Judith Kimerling, "Corporate Ethics in the Era of Globalization: The Promise and Peril of International Environmental Standards," *Journal of Agricultural and Environmental Ethics* 14.4(2001): 425–55; on hazardous waste in Mexico, see Cyrus Reed, "Hazardous Waste Management on the Border: Problems with Practices and Oversight Continue," *Borderlines* 46 6.5 (July 1998): 1–4; 14–15.

12 Bruce Rich, *Mortgaging the Earth* (London: Earthscan, 1994); Robert Wade, "Greening the Bank: The Struggle Over the Environment, 1970–1995," in *The World Bank: Its First Half Century*, vol. 2 (Washington, DC: Brookings Institute, 1997).

13 Stephan Schmidheiny and Federico Zorraquin, *Financing Change: The Financial Community, Eco-Efficiency and Sustainable Development* (Cambridge, MA: MIT Press, 1998).

14 Wolfgang Sachs, "Global Ecology and the Shadow of 'Development,'" in W. Sachs, ed., *Global Ecology* (London: Zed, 1993), pp. 4–6; Tim Lang and Colin Hines, *The New Protectionism* (London: Earthscan, 1993); Robert Wade, "Global Inequality: Winners and Losers," *The Economist* 28 April 2001: 72–74.

15 UNDP, "Consumption in a Global Village—Unequal and Unbalanced," *Human Development Report 1998* (Oxford: Oxford University Press, 1998), pp. 46–65.

16 UNDP, "Consumption in a Global Village," p.50.

17 Akin Mabogunje, "Poverty and Environmental Degradation: Challenges Within the Global Economy," *Environment* 44.1(2002): 9–18.

18 Nick Robbins and Alex Trisoglio, "Restructuring Industry for Sustainable Development," in J. Holmberg, ed., *Policies for a Small Planet* (London: Earthscan, 1992); K.A. Gourlay, *World of Waste: Dilemmas of Industrial Development* (London: Zed, 1992).

19 Robert Cox, "Global Restructuring: Making Sense of the Changing International Political Economy," in R. Stubbs and G. Underhill, eds., *Political Economy and the Changing Global Order* (Toronto: McClelland and Stewart, 1994), p. 49.

20 Cox, "Global Restructuring," p. 52.

21 Ken Booth, ed., *New Thinking About Strategy and International Security* (London: Harper Collins Academic, 1991), p. 348; Karen Litfin, "Eco-Regimes: Playing Tug of War with the Nation-State," in R. Lipschutz and K. Conca, eds., *The State and Social Power in Global Environmental Politics* (New York: Columbia University Press, 1993), p. 100.

22 Gwyn Prins, ed., *Threats Without Enemies* (London: Earthscan, 1993).

23 Lawrence Susskind, *Environmental Diplomacy* (Oxford: Oxford University Press, 1994), p. 63.

24 Gwyn Prins, "Politics and the Environment," *International Affairs* 66.4(1990): 717-18.

25 Stephen Krasner, "Structural Causes and Regime Consequences: Regimes as Intervening Variables," in Stephen Krasner, ed., *International Regimes* (Ithaca, NY: Cornell University Press, 1983), p. 2.

26 See for example, Oran Young, *International Cooperation: Building Regimes for Natural Resources and the Environment* (Ithaca, NY: Cornell University Press, 1989), and *International Governance: Protecting the Environment in a Stateless Society* (Ithaca, NY: Cornell University Press, 1994).

27 Gilbert Winham, "Enforcement of Environmental Measures: Negotiating the NAFTA Environmental Side Agreement," *Journal of Environment and Development* 3.1(1994): 29–41.

28 Daniel Esty, *Greening the GATT: Trade, Environment and the Future* (Washington, DC: Institute for International Economics, 1994), pp. 205–206; Scott Vaughn, "The Environment and Trade," *Our Planet* 5.6(1993): 11.

29 Neumayer, *Greening Trade and Investment*, p. 134.

30 Elizabeth DeSombre and J. Samual Barkin, "Turtles and Trade: The WTO's Acceptance of Environmental Trade Restrictions," *Global Environmental Politics* 2.1(2002): 12–18.

31 Jennifer Nash and John Ehrenfeld, "Code Green," *Environment* 37.1(1996): 16–45; UNCTAD, Division on Transnational Corporations and Investment, *Self-Regulation of Environmental Management: An Analysis of Guidelines Set by World Industry Associations for Their Member Firms* (Geneva: United Nations, 1996).

32 Riva Krut and Harris Gleckman, *ISO 14001: A Missed Opportunity for Global Sustainable Industrial Development* (London: Earthscan, 1998).

33 Wade, "Greening the Bank."

34 Mohammed El Ashry, "Development Assistance Institutions and Sustainable Development," *The Washington Quarterly* 16.2(1993): 86–87.

35 Rich, *Mortgaging the Earth.*

36 Friends of the Earth, *Not in the Public Interest: The World Bank's Environmental Record*, <http://www.foe.org/international/worldbank/wb.pdf>.

37 Jennifer Clapp, "The Toxic Waste Trade With Less Industrialised Countries: Economic Linkages and Political Alliances," *Third World Quarterly* 15.3(1994): 505–18.

38 Thomas Princen, "The Ivory Trade Ban: NGOs and International Conservation," in Thomas Princen and Matthias Finger, *Environmental NGOs in World Politics* (London: Routledge, 1994).

39 See Michael Buenker, "The Signing of the Stockholm Convention," *Environmental Policy and Law* 31.4/5(2001): 200–05.

40 See Robert Falkner, "Regulating Biotech Trade: The Cartagena Protocol on Biosafety," *International Affairs* 76.2(2000): 299–313.

41 See Rosalind Twum-Barima and Laura Campbell, "Protecting the Ozone Layer through Trade Measures," *UNEP Environment and Trade Series* (Geneva: UNEP, 1994).

42 Elizabeth DeSombre and Joanne Kauffman, "Montreal Protocol Multilateral Fund: Partial Success Story," in Robert Keohane and Marc Levy, eds., *Institutions for Environmental Aid: Pitfalls and Promise* (Cambridge, MA: MIT Press, 1996).

43 El Ashry "Development Assistance Institutions," pp. 91–93.

44 Pratap Chatterjee and Matthias Finger, *The Earth Brokers* (London: Routledge, 1994), pp. 53–57.

45 See UNEP initiative on banking at <http://www.unep.ch/finance/bank1.html>.

46 Patricia Birnie and Allen Boyle, *International Law and the Environment* (Oxford: Clarendon Press, 1992), pp. 35–44.

47 Hilary French, "Strengthening International Environmental Governance," *Journal of Environment and Development* 3.1(1994): 62.

48 Princen and Finger, *Environmental NGOs in World Politics*, pp. 1–9.

49 Ronnie Lipschutz, "Reconstructing World Politics: The Emergence of Global Civil Society," *Millennium* 21.3(1992): 389–420. See also Paul Wapner, "Politics Beyond the State: Environmental Activism and World Civic Politics," *World Politics* 47(April 1995): 311–340.

50 Peter Spiro, "New Global Communities: Nongovernmental Organizations in International Decision-Making Institutions," *The Washington Quarterly* 18.1(1994): 45–56.

51 Jennifer Clapp, "The Toxic Waste Trade."

52 Kevin Stairs and Peter Taylor, "Non-Governmental Organizations and the Legal Protection of the Oceans: A Case Study," in Andrew Hurrell and Benedict Kingsbury, eds., *The International Politics of the Environment* (Oxford: Clarendon Press, 1992), pp. 112–17.

53 See for example, Stephan Schmidheiny, *Changing Course: A Global Business Perspective on Development and the Environment* (Cambridge, MA: MIT Press, 1992).

54 Chatterjee and Finger, *The Earth Brokers*.

55 David Levy and Peter Newell, "Business Strategy and International Environmental Governance: Toward a Neo-Gramscian Synthesis," *Global Environmental Politics* 2.4(2002): 84–101.

56 Peter Haas, "Epistemic Communities in International Policy Coordination," *International Organization* 46.2(1992): 1–35.

57 Peter Haas, "Do Regimes Matter? Epistemic Communities and Mediterranean Pollution Control," *International Organization* 43.3(1992): 377–403; Karen Litfin, *Ozone Discourses* (New York: Columbia University Press, 1994).

58 Litfin, *Ozone Discourses*.

59 Susskind, *Environmental Diplomacy*, pp. 64–68.

60 Chatterjee and Finger, *The Earth Brokers*, pp. 89–91.

61 For more information, see William Krist, "The WTO and MEAs: Time for a Good Neighbor Policy," Woodrow Wilson Center (2001), <http://wwics.si.edu/tef/paper.pdf>.

62 See WTO website on Doha <http://www.wto.org/english/tratop_e/dda_e/doha-explained_e.htm>.

63 These are posted on the OECD website: <http://www.oecd.org>.

64 See Friends of the Earth, Corporate Responsibility website <http://www.foe.org/earth-summit/rightsforpeople.html>. See also Greenpeace International, *Corporate Crimes: The Need for an International Instrument on Corporate Accountability and Liability*, June 2002.

65 Andrea Durban and Carol Welch, *Greening the Bretton Woods Institutions* (Friends of the Earth, December 1998) <http://www.foe.org>.

16

Green Governance and
the Green State:
Capacity Building as a Political Project

Peter Christoff

Optimism about the state has diminished as policy makers, activists, and academics have responded to what some have termed state failure—the state's apparently endemic inability to deal with complex problems and deliver intended outcomes. This fading optimism is evident in the environmental domain where, despite some thirty years of institutional innovation, there is a feeling that the pace of reform has stalled, early gains in environmental quality are being eroded, and critical problems such as climate change are being addressed ineffectively. The overall result has been a reassessment of the ability of the state to deliver positive social and environmental outcomes, and a shift in emphasis from government to governance.

These changes are central concerns of this chapter, in which I first summarize trends and pressures moving us away from government and toward governance. I argue that the current shift to governance presents us with a problem insofar as it involves downgrading the environmental role and capacities of the state, which are diminished in stature at a time when state intervention—of a certain sort—is most urgently required. In response, I outline a range of capacities—for the state, but also for civil society and the economic sphere—required for effective green governance.

Which of these capacities is developed, and how, will largely determine the extent to which we are able to move toward stronger forms of ecological modernization. In particular, I argue that neglecting the state is not an option: the state remains vital to creating the possibilities for strong ecological modernization, and therefore contests to shape and control the state's substantial and necessary resources and capacities remain inevitable and essential.

BATHWATER GONE, BABY GONE?
TRENDS IN GREEN GOVERNANCE

Over thirty years ago, *The Ecologist* published *A Blueprint for Survival*, with its piercing commentary on the barriers to what would later be called paths to sustainability. Its analyses still offer insights into some of the impediments to meeting the environmental challenge: "Unfortunately, government has an increasingly powerful incentive for continued expansion in the tendency for economic growth to create the need for more economic growth."[1] This incentive was seen as the product of certain political and economic imperatives. The political imperative requires governments wishing to be re-elected to provide employment via the stimulation of economic growth (judged by increases in GNP), for without economic growth, given the technological replacement of labour, there will be social unrest and crisis. The economic imperative demands that businesses make surpluses for future investment. These imperatives remain largely unaltered.

A Blueprint for Survival focused on the national state at a time when critical concern about processes of globalization was still mainly limited to Marxist critiques of imperialism. In the intervening period, the state has been reshaped by various trends—some positive, some overwhelmingly negative.

First, environmental problems have become an established feature of popular consciousness, political agendas, and policy landscapes, sometimes accompanied by an underlying sense of crisis that has encouraged fitful technological and institutional innovation. In addition, over the past two decades, we have seen an evolving recognition that "the environment" and "sustainability" are not partial or additive policy concerns but ones that are systemic and require holistic responses, and that the environment has features relating to space and time which, if not entirely unique to this policy domain, nevertheless come together with particular and peculiar force, requiring anticipatory and transboundary action.

The environmental policy domain is now also understood to mobilize a set of values and concerns that *are* uniquely its own—in the irresolvable tension between anthropocentric and ecocentric values and views, reflecting different paradigms of concern for other species and ecosystems. Herein lies the root of the difference between "strong" and "weak" ecological modernization. Strong ecological modernization is characterized by its ecocentric aim to reclaim the life-world from its wholesale conversion into a resource and commodity for human benefit, and its belief in the need for new institutions and reflexive practices in order to achieve this goal. Weak ecological modernization is more narrowly anthropocentric in its aims concerning the impacts of industrial production on human health, species, and ecosystems, and it accepts that existing institutions and practices are sufficient to "harmonize" relations between the environment and (capitalist) economy for human benefit.[2]

Second, numerous state-related institutional failings have been identified as sources of policy failure in the environmental domain. These have included the administrative confinement and marginalization of specific interests (such as environmental concerns) within the state, and "companion" difficulties of problem decomposition and failures of policy coordination and integration. In response, these inadequacies of administrative process and logic have been partly addressed by the rise of new forms of cross-sectoral communication and decision making and a growing focus on developing actor- and action-centred networks, network governance, and "joined up government."[3] Experiments have included increased public participation in policy formulation and implementation, the establishment of mega-ministries that incorporate a diversity of portfolios and are intended to facilitate policy integration across these portfolios, inter-ministerial councils, and the implanting of "green ministers" in departments that do not have the environment as their primary objective—all intended, where environmental representation is concerned, to inject green considerations into other portfolios. However, the larger impediments to ecologically coherent, integrated decision making and policy implementation largely remain unresolved. Attempts to eliminate or minimize the conflicts among departments and agencies established to protect the environment or, conversely, to promote resource exploitation and consumption have generally been rare or superficial in their implementation. The opening of administrative processes to public scrutiny and involvement remains, on the whole, cosmetic.

Third, as suggested earlier, there is widespread recognition that the state has failed to achieve the goals set for it and that the manner of policy development and implementation has often been perversely constituted in the face of complex problems (especially environmental ones). Indeed, the term "state failure," which Martin Janicke once used to refer to the state's economic inability to supply high-quality, low-priced public goods and its political inability to take decisions widely agreed to be necessary,[4] has now come to represent the state's apparently endemic inability to deliver sought-after outcomes. This interpretation neatly distracts from some of the political sources of this failure, namely ascendant neo-liberalism's concerted political campaign against the welfare state itself.

In any case, this perception of state failure has led to experimentation with new forms and styles of state action, including some of the ones mentioned above. Specifically, it has shifted attention away from a "state-centric" view of how policy can be developed and delivered and from an exclusive reliance on the formal institutions of the state to do so. Rather, policy makers and analysts have sought greater reliance on policy networks, advocacy coalitions, and policy communities that extend beyond the state to define and implement public policy, and have looked to the greater use of the market and market-based or market-related instruments as supplements or alternatives for delivering environmental and other social welfare outcomes. This change has generally been termed the shift from government to governance.[5]

As Helmut Weidner comments, "intensifying in the 1990s, the globalization debate and hasty adoption of neo-liberal economic principles by many governments raised doubts about whether ecological modernization is realistic in economies that are increasingly competitive and driven by shareholder value. This debate comes at a time when national governments are weakening and industry is gaining far greater scope for eluding the demands and norms of government and society."[6] The retreat both by and from the state, under the influence of neo-liberalism, from certain forms of interventionism—the shift from rowing to steering (or merely feathering the oars), which has been most pronounced in such English-speaking states as the US, the UK, Canada, New Zealand, and Australia—has led to the privatization or corporatization of public services, increased reliance on the private sector to deliver previously "public" services, and the loss—or deliberate dismantling—of what were once regarded as key capacities for planning, policy implementation, and "service" delivery.

Diminished interest in national planning and centralized policy intervention in most Western industrialized countries has also affected the environmental domain. This trend has sometimes included devolution of policy making and implementation to "lower" levels of government and to smaller and more autonomous administrative units, occasionally leading to greater community participation and the effective realization of the principle of subsidiarity. However, incremental devolution of environmental policy responsibility from national to sub-national levels of government in federated states such as Canada and Australia has not necessarily been undertaken with good environmental governance in mind. More generally, the use of overarching strategic means to direct state activity and to influence economic activity (broadly defined) appears to have stalled. Few of the meta-strategies for sustainability that were announced in the period immediately following the Brundtland Report have proved substantial or durable. Instead, there is evidence of increased reliance on voluntary agreements and market-based mechanisms to facilitate *ad hoc* progress toward weak ecological modernization.[7]

Fourth, the state has been transformed and made more porous by the processes, tensions, and challenges of economic, cultural, and environmental globalization. It is more open to and likely to be influenced by policy experiments occurring elsewhere, and its policy development positively informed through formal and informal transnational networks, and the agencies and institutions of the OECD, the EU, or the UN. But it is also more vulnerable, through the effects of economic globalization, to fluctuations in investment and currency value that then serve to discipline and restrain courageous domestic policy shifts. The size, diversity, and economic robustness of individual national economies, and the degree and nature of their integration into global markets, greatly influence the extent to which individual states are susceptible to pressure on domestic policies, environmental or otherwise—contrast the United States, Germany, and Australia, for instance.

Worries that globalization will lead to an erosion of environmental standards within European countries via a "race to the bottom," and the creation of pollution havens elsewhere, appear to have been exaggerated. Indeed, Weidner argues that, empirically, there appears to be "no correlation between progressive environmental policy and economic decline,"[8] and that "if globalization is in fact weakening national environmental policies, then environmental capacity building should be slowing down or reversing, and countries strongly integrated in world markets would likely not be front-runners in environmental policy."[9]

However, claims that national and multilateral environmental policies remain unconstrained by the forces of economic globalization must be treated with care. For instance, Ken Conca and Robyn Eckersley have pointed to the chilling effect on environmental regulations of the WTO's rules supporting trade liberalization.[10] Similarly, intensifying trade interdependency, and the growing volume and rapidity of international capital flows, have increased the volatility of economic conditions for most nations and reduced the space for national and subnational policy formation and regulatory control in most policy domains. In addition, the continuing globalization and integration of chains of production and consumption have made nation-level regulation of product quality more difficult to achieve in all but the largest internal markets (e.g., EU, China, India, etc.). The substantial relocation of manufacturing to newly industrializing countries (especially China, India, and Brazil, but also the former Eastern Bloc as well as other parts of Asia and Latin America) and the increase in the total volume of global material flows mean that the planetary volume of resource use and global levels of environmental degradation and pollution continue to increase. New forms of international cooperation are required to deal with the spatial displacement of previously domestic environmental impacts, but these have barely been considered under the nation-focused institutional arrangements currently driving weak ecological modernization.

Fifth, most states have failed to deal with environmental concerns and issues in ways commensurate with those perceived problems. This has meant an increase, during the past decade, in the severity of those problems and an accentuation of major negative environmental trends. For instance, in Australia, salinity has been recognized as a critical form of land degradation since the 1940s and has been identified as a national policy problem since the mid-1970s. Yet inadequate action over the past three decades has meant that the problem has grown tremendously in the area of land affected and the costs associated with its treatment.[11] The "big" issues of global warming, land degradation, and biodiversity loss are beginning to compound each other, even within Europe.[12]

Do these admitted problems of state underperformance amount to a case against the state as such? Certainly the trend toward shedding state capacity and placing strong emphasis on non-state action or green governance with minimal state involvement would suggest so, reinforced as it is by endemic interpretations of state failure and by neo-liberal fantasies about market compensation for such failure. Or are these collective action problems that require *greater* state involvement? Before we throw the baby out with the bathwater, perhaps we need to consider one of the uncertainties of green governance: as we move away from government to governance, we are unsure what or how much "state" we now want or need.

Building Capacity for Green Governance

The shift from government to governance has been accompanied by a retreat from analyzing the state and its trajectories, and exaggerated hopes—mainly among academic environmental analysts rather than policy practitioners[13]—that the invisible hand of the market will provide a solution to environmental problems that the state was unable to resolve.[14] However, there are some things only a state can do; therefore I now want to argue for strengthening a range of (in particular, state) environmental capacities to ameliorate or help overcome acknowledged areas of state failure and reinforce areas of state strength.

Love it or hate it, we can't do without the state. This is evident when we look beyond the state's administrative and regulatory roles to its substantial material involvement in the reproduction of capital, its direct participation in domestic economic activity and, depending on its size and wealth, its international economic activity. We can add the state's role in social reproduction in general (through provision of social welfare, broadly defined, and its formal monopoly over violence), in cultural reproduction (through its involvement in education, the media, etc.), and in facilitating or effecting the redistribution of wealth and power.[15]

The systemic realization of strong ecological modernization requires a proactive, interventionist state, to help undo the ecological ravages of two centuries of industrialization and to facilitate more ecologically rational modes of production and activity. This requires improved relations between the state and industry on the one hand, and between the state and civil society on the other. Indeed, the sort of green state contemplated here cannot occur without strong political interventions from civil society to overcome resistance to green governance by established forces in the state and industry.

At the same time, as Albert Weale argued over a decade ago, key changes in the relationship between the state, industry, and the public would require strong state involvement in policy development and implementation, including a proactive and interventionist role in environmental management, a well-developed culture of policy innovation guided by a set of principles relating to ecological sustainability (prominently including the precautionary principle), general acceptance of the utility of significant public investment and subsidy as a means of achieving economic advantage and environmental outcomes, support for an integrated regulatory environment and strong structural and process cross-linkages between different parts of the state, the development of a synoptic and reflexive use of environmental information in policy formation and implementation, and the fostering of a "green market" through both regulatory and educational assistance.[16]

To be clear, given the issues and trends noted above regarding state limitations and the requirements of effective governance, strong ecological modernization requires interdependent, mutually supportive capacities in the state, in the economic sphere, and in civil society, which will import and reinforce "ecological rationality" in each "realm."[17]

Policy depends on the interaction of actors, institutions, and context, and the extent and quality of their interaction can be altered deliberately through a careful process of capacity building. Janicke argues that "it is not primarily the institutional set-up of representative democracies which is advantageous for positive policy outcomes, but rather the constitutional civil rights of western democracies—the participatory, legal and informational opportunity structures available to proponents of environmental interests—which appear to be most decisive."[18] His emphasis is on resourceful actors and entrepreneurs. But one can mount an equally powerful case for focusing on institutions—political, legal, and so on— that constrain or enable those actors and entrepreneurs. If we recognize that the state (and other realms, such as the economy, or civil society) are complex amalgams and interplays of institutions and actors, capacity building cannot merely pay attention to one rather than the other: it needs to enhance the capacities of actors and institutions equally.[19]

Leaving aside the issue of agency for a moment (in other words, the question of who will *initiate* or *do* the capacity-building process), I now want to turn to consider those capacities that the trends and experiences just discussed seem to highlight as deficient in the past yet necessary for strong ecological modernization. Perhaps the most succinct summary of different facets of *society-wide* environmental capacity is provided by Janicke, who suggests that the capacities for actively pursuing environmental policy outcomes are composed of "the strength, competence and configuration of governmental and non-governmental proponents of environmental protection," and "framework conditions" such as "the cognitive–informational, political–institutional and economic–technical context." The actual utilization of existing capacity depends on "the strategy, will and skill of proponents, and their situative opportunities" in relation to the "the kind of environmental problem being confronted—its urgency as well as the power, resources and options" of those involved in its resolution.[20]

Bringing the state back in, again—building state environmental capacity

Several themes are evident in the literature on environmental policy and policy failure. In response to such failure, the state is often called on to better coordinate planning and resource allocation in national or sub-national projects for sustainable development and environmental remediation. This call is accompanied by an emphasis on the need to develop cross-sectoral and interdisciplinary approaches to managing resources and environmental problems, approaches that are integrative across the state as well as between the state, the private sector, and civil society. Emphasis is also placed on the state's ability to link environmental and economic planning, and its involvement in institutional development and fostering technical capacity. The state is also called on to establish inter-organizational networks—organizational alliances and partnerships—to create links between the increasing number of institutions. At the same time, the full breadth of policy instruments (regulatory, economic, market-based, educational, and strategic planning) is often sought to meet the needs of different domains. As well, there is a concern to facilitate input from scientific communities and non-governmental organizations (NGOs), and to create the forums in which communicative interactions might lead to greater cross-sectional understanding of, and support for, policy as a whole.

Even when naive liberal pluralist views of the state are set aside and the state is recognized as a site of bitter contest between opposing forces rather than a benign, unified and neutral umpire, the state is often considered to be society's (and the environment's) best bet—or last hope—as a necessary and partial judge, overseer, guarantor, or provider of resources. The green state is needed as a coordinator and planner of social activity and ecological outcomes. Crudely put, if not the state, then what (or who) will play this role?

Drawing these themes together,[21] I would suggest that the ability to foster strong ecological modernization critically depends on four tightly interrelated aspects of *state* environmental capacity—its communicative, strategic, integrative, and implementation capacities—that would enable the state's potential involvement in fostering strong, reflexive ecological modernization.

Communicative capacity

Green theorists have long argued that open and informed participatory processes, forums and other deliberative and discursive designs may serve as communicative measures more likely to promote public acceptance of ecologically beneficial programs and the resolution of complex environmental problems than closed, secretive, "bounded" decision-making stratagems from which policies emerge to be implemented by force, by stealth, or not at all.[22]

As Douglas Torgerson and Robert Paehlke note, conventional approaches to administration presuppose centralized planning and control, and assume that the state enacts a unified will privileged by superior knowledge. The tendency is to enclose and depoliticize decision making accordingly, "collapsing a diversity of interests into a single, homogeneous interest." [23] These approaches and assumptions are one source of failure for such administrative modes.

Public participatory processes and deliberative forums to shape and consider potential policy directions are essential antidotes to these failings and delusions. They are necessary measures in a context where the state itself is internally divided over environmental issues and policy directions and decisions, where problem decomposition leads to the exacerbation of the problems to be solved,[24] and where uncritical popular belief in the authority, the legitimacy, the selflessness, and the effectiveness of autonomous, technocratic policy professionalism has been severely eroded. It is also clear that public involvement in policy and administrative processes is needed, not just to generate or secure the democratic legitimacy of public decision making, but also to provide both popular and scientific/technical informational input not available to the state, thereby making possible the effective management of highly complex problems that reach beyond the state and are also sometimes beyond the state's reach.

Ideally, such participation and deliberation also lead to enhanced and mutualistic policy learning and deeply embedded cultural change within government, industry, NGOs, and communities at large. They may produce cooperative associations—policy communities and networks—that enable ideas for positive environmental change to pass between "practitioners." They also clarify and limit disagreement to those grounds where profound value differences exist.

In other words, this capacity (re)defines the state's ability to facilitate and participate in meaningful discursive democratization, and to weld effective and legitimate policy through the exchange. The extent to which this communicative capacity is realized will determine the extent to which the state will foster ecological modernization that is open and reflexive rather than closed and narrowly technocratic.

Strategic capacity

It is possible, without succumbing to naïve liberal pluralism, to acknowledge that the state potentially serves as a unique and privileged site from which to represent the interests of a society as a whole. It potentially offers a vantage point—which, by definition, vested interests cannot reflect—from which to recognize environmental problems, develop policy, and make strategic decisions that would lead to ecologically sustainable outcomes for the "whole of society" and the "whole of nature" if implemented effectively.[25] In addition, it is most likely that only the state can be "moved" to manage, protect or restore environmental public goods in the public interest. These factors can serve to distinguish state as opposed to sectoral strategic interests.

The state's strategic or steering capacity incorporates and depends on the existence of internal and exogenous ("open" and "external") networks and communities that link the state to critical public spheres and, in turn, alert it to emergent issues. In this sense, the notion of state involvement in strategic development is very different from that conventionally ascribed to state administration. The notion, rather, is one of a negotiated and alternative pattern of development that is constantly tested "in the outside world." Such strategic capacity depends on the availability of adequate information and data, a skill base enabling timely interpretations of such information and consequent coherent policy development, an institutionalized memory of previous environmental successes and failures, and a policy-learning capacity sufficient for it to benefit from its own and others' policy experiments and experiences.

Integrative capacity

The state depends on its ability to engage in two related forms of integrative activity—one focused externally and one focused internally—if it seeks to insert ecological principles and goals into (whole-of-government) public policy formation and implementation and into private sector activity.

The externally focused form of integration involves the state in generating, participating in, and perhaps managing policy coalitions and networks that reach beyond itself—connecting government, industry, and community, both sectorally and cross-sectorally. These networks are critical to both effective environmental policy formation and implementation, particularly when problems are complex.

Consider induced climate change, the most challenging environmental problem we face at present. Global warming requires a complex response that integrates most aspects of government decision making within and between nation states. It encompasses all forms of economic activity and requires an integrated response within and across administrative and industrial sectors. It has radical implications for personal behaviour and material consumption in industrialized societies. It demands new paths for international development. It requires rapid and complex technological innovation and diffusion. It requires the integration of sophisticated scientific interpretations into future policy work and planning. It demands radical policy and planning initiatives—for instance, closing down coal-fired power stations, closing coal mines, transforming the basis of energy and transport systems, and weaning whole economies off their dependency on trade in fossil fuels—that in turn require public participation for legitimacy and support. Substantial proportions of national budgets will be required if adaptation to climate change is to be timely and effective. And all this must occur in a very short period of time—one or two decades—if we are to cut global greenhouse emissions by over 60 per cent from 1990 levels by 2050 and move rapidly to a post-carbon economy, and if the international response is to minimize the worst consequences of global warming.

The internally focused form of integration occurs predominantly within government and involves policy integration that leads to the comprehensive, consistent, and effective incorporation of ecological principles into policy work "horizontally" across departments and agencies (especially incorporating previously "non-environmental" areas of government), "vertically" within particular areas of sectoral responsibility (for instance, among units in a department of energy), and "up" and "down" between levels of government.[26]

"Participation without integration is," as Janicke observes, "ineffective": "integration relates to the reduction of contradictions within governments. The modern state is able to institutionalize quite different, even contradictory policy goals…. Environmental policy generally starts with the establishment of a new special agency or bureaucracy. The institutional differentiation has little effect, however, if the capacity for intra- and inter-policy integration remains low. Overcoming the incremental and isolated role of environmental administrations within government then becomes an indispensable next step. The establishment of a well-functioning network of 'green' interest organizations, industry and environmental administrations is a further step in the process of capacity building."[27]

The extent to which ecological principles and considerations are given equal status or even priority among other concerns addressed in the integration process—rather than being relegated, gesturally, to the periphery—will influence the extent to which the state promotes strong over weak ecological modernization.

Implementation capacity

Strategic planning, communicative and integrative capacities are useless without the capacity for implementation. To do these things, the state is dependent on the availability of adequate economic, intellectual, and physical resources appropriate for effectively implementing its policy initiatives or for supporting private sector initiatives to meet its ecological requirements. Consequently, the state needs to provide, facilitate, or ensure a parcel of "subsidiary" capacities or resources to support the implementation of green policies. This capacity may therefore be seen to have five constituent components, relating to the state's bureaucratic/administrative, economic, legal, regulatory/enforcement, and cognitive/informational activities.

Principally, in terms of its *bureaucratic/administrative* ability, the state must have sufficient human resources (staffing levels and skill base) to be able to recognize and react effectively to environmental and other challenges. It must nurture policy cultures and networks that extend beyond the state itself, are capable of policy learning and adaptation over time, and are sufficiently skilled to be able to sustain and benefit from research, monitoring, public reporting, and reflexive review. It must have the capacity to ensure that welfare and other adjustments necessary for transitions toward ecological modernization are delivered effectively and equitably.

The state must also have the material or *economic* capability (including the capacity to ensure sufficient revenue and resources) to provide for social welfare, environmental management and remediation, research and development, and public infrastructure investment, and to assist or ameliorate the impacts of significant social and economic adjustments. Only the state has the potential authority and legitimacy to raise revenue sufficient to enable the range of activities encompassed by the green agenda, and the capacity to do so equitably and efficiently.[28]

The state's *legal* powers must be sufficient to enable and protect environmentally appropriate decisions; enable democratic representation and protect a diversity of views in the administrative apparatus itself; require transparent and effective review, reporting, and participatory processes; and, more broadly, protect human rights and ecological values. The state requires the power to regulate for ecologically appropriate production and consumption, to prevent, limit, or eliminate environmental impacts, and to ensure compliance with its regulations. It also needs to be able to establish and maintain a framework of market-based measures (for instance, through the creation of resource pricing/trading schemes, eco-taxes, product levies, and so on) that reach beyond and compensate for the limitations and deficiencies of direct regulation. As well, the state needs to be able to establish the bases of reflexive policy and behaviour through public and private sector monitoring and reporting requirements.

Finally, green governance requires a state that can create or materially support the *cognitive/informational* (to use Janicke's term) underpinnings of strong ecological modernization through its investment in research and development, public reporting, and cultural/educational programs (very broadly defined), including by non-state (community-based and economic sector) organizations.

The four capacities—for communication, steering, integration, and implementation—are interrelated and mutually informing. Successfully creating and using capacity in each of these areas should translate into significant improvements in environmental trends and conditions in ways that also protect the full range of ecological values. Conversely, the absence or weakening of any of these capacities is likely to lead to worsening ecological outcomes and threats to, or the destruction of, those values.

However, the existence of such capacities does not guarantee their use in practice. They are politically contested by vested interests opposed to the extension of ecological democracy implied in many of these capacities. Contextual factors or variables will also lead to their development, mobilization, or neglect: for example, the emergence of effective political and policy entrepreneurs or opponents, the nurturing or stifling influence of political institutions, the vitality of civil society, and changes in public opinion.

Weakness in some capacities may serve to undermine others. For instance, in Australia widespread public concern over climate change has, since 1997, led to consistently high levels of public support for the ratification of the Kyoto Protocol—but successive conservative Australian governments have refused such ratification. In this case, weaknesses in Australia's legal/political institutions—which permit governments to ignore majority public views on specific issues—undermine strengths in other capacity areas.[29]

These capacities are also subject to the impact of "external" influences and events—but how these interact and affect individual states is not always predictable.[30] For instance, the floods, fires, and days of soaring temperatures that have beset Europe since 2000 have played a major part in elevating climate change policy on the political agenda—particularly in Germany—but similar events have had no commensurate impact in Australia. The creation of the European Union and the influence of the EU's Fifth Action Programme in 1992 have played a major role in fostering certain environmental capacities within the EU's member states,[31] while also entrenching certain pathologies of policy compartmentalization rather than integration.[32] Economic recession in the 1990s reinforced or "supported" the policies of budgetary austerity adopted by neo-liberal governments during that decade. The subsequent programmatic "hollowing out" of the state[33] often meant the shedding of staff, loss of internal research capacity, and limitations on environmental monitoring and reporting. These developments undermined all of the capacities and hampered longer-term reflexivity and policy learning.

Environmental capacity in civil society and the economic sphere

Recent literature on neo-corporatism, on trends toward governance, and separately, on the role of policy coalitions and networks, has emphasized the state's functional dependency on resources beyond itself for the articulation and implementation of policies. The literature has underscored the importance of reciprocal capacities in civil society and among actors in the economic sphere, capacities that are compatible with and comparable, in some places, to those of the state.

For example, to be able to engage meaningfully—rather than cosmetically—in participatory forums, NGOs depend on their capacities for reviewing and interpreting data, consulting among their members and with related groups, generating input into public debate, and ensuring that a multiplicity of voices is projected into the public domain. These elements of effective everyday green activism, accompanied as they are by the dangers of policy professionalization, depend on NGOs having capacities that parallel, but do not mimic exactly, those of the state—capacities for consensus formation, strategy development, and implementation (requiring adequate intellectual capital, funding, and staffing to succeed in these tasks).

Such groups are also critically dependent on an institutional context that enables actors in civil society to engage in public discursive contests over competing practical and policy options—a context that includes, for example, the existence of free, open, and diverse media (increasing public awareness and also reinforcing and compelling political action), and the freedom to mobilize politically and seek to shape public opinion "autonomously," to contest the practices of discourses of its "opponents," and to both dissent from the state and pressure it from "outside."

The state can serve to facilitate such capacities by providing material resources and creating discursive spaces—including, in the latter instance, by regulating to safeguard media diversity. Access to policy forums and instances of direct material support, particularly among those nations with neo-corporatist political traditions and policy cultures, has fostered the growth of the environment movement and its organizations, including green parties. But these developments have been accompanied by problems of institutionalization, ossification, internal bureaucratization, and deradicalization, and the degrees of incorporation into and dependency on the state.[34] To facilitate the development of capacities in civil society, the state thus also needs to *vacate* certain terrains of engagement.

The economic sphere also exhibits serious capacity deficiencies that are problematic for green governance. To the extent that they are governed by the logic of capital accumulation, economic actors need to shelter—or be sheltered—from the driving imperatives of this domain. These imperatives—toward profit maximization, growth of the firm, and a narrowly defined accountability to owners or shareholders—work against the requirements of even weak ecological modernization for longer-term planning and investment horizons (including research and innovation), for cooperative development and diffusion of socially and environmentally beneficial technologies and practices, and for investment practices that accept the limits set by ecological parameters.

The flexibility of corporations to resist or even break with short-term commercial imperatives has long been understood to depend, to some degree, on the size—the material capacity—of individual enterprises, as well as on the nature of the specific industry sector, the prevailing investment culture, and finally—of particular importance—the cultural context that shapes the social and ecological awareness and sense of responsibility which leading entrepreneurs and actors bring to specific sectors.

The economic sphere, like civil society and the state, has been subject to shifting contextual influences, not the least of which have been environmental ones (such as climate change), which have encouraged individual entrepreneurs and enterprises to identify market advantage amid environmental crisis. Among insurance companies there is a growing need to assess risk and to predict and respond to the increasing severity of "natural" disasters. Energy companies need to plan for changes in regulatory environment and for changes in consumer demand that arise from a sense of green responsibility as well as price changes. Finally, the interpenetration of civil society and "commercial life"—with a new generation of environmentally aware managers, entrepreneurs, and investors—is forcing the pace of "virtuous" production and ethical investment.

A green state depends on its potential to establish regulatory and policy settings that guide, facilitate, and "protect" the development of these capacities in the economic sphere. Such a state needs to regulate for industry accountability against social and environmental parameters. The state must facilitate and support ecologically important industrial research and innovation, using financial incentives and even venture capital. Finally, the green state has to encourage or even require industry involvement in policy development.

WHERE ARE WE HEADING?

As recent reviews of national environmental policy and performance have indicated, over the past three decades industrialized states have developed and strengthened their environmental capacities, predominantly with respect to the state, to varying degrees.[35] However, assessments of environmental capacity focusing on the state have shown these developments to be uneven across states, highly dependent on specific national cultural, political, and economic circumstances. The tendency has been to confirm rather than disrupt existing institutional settings.

States such as Sweden and the Netherlands have well developed communicative capacities, while Austria and Germany remain strong regulatory states with powerful legal/political and implementation capacities. Over the past two decades the Netherlands has shown strong strategic capacity through the development, institutionalization, and iterative refinement of its national environment policy plan.[36] On the other hand, although Australia has experienced a decade of institutional innovations to combat climate change and land degradation, and has greatly increased state environmental funding, its legal/political and policy implementation capacities have weakened and been shown to be deficient given the magnitude of continental problems.[37]

However, while there have been undoubted advances in institutional innovation and capacity building along the lines described by Janicke and Weidner[38] and Lafferty and Meadowcroft,[39] it can be difficult to distinguish between real innovation and cosmetic institutional adjustment. Indeed, the several waves of institutional innovation have also been followed by a backlash of reaction and institutional ossification, and the empirical evidence is more ambiguous than is suggested by lists of dates when various lead environmental agencies were established[40] or sustainability strategies announced.[41] The fact of organizational and institutional innovation is deceptive and can serve to mask superficial political attempts to accommodate and deflect popular pressure for substantial action. As in the Australian instance, rhetoric and spectacle too often disguise inaction. Actual performance is better sought in environmental data, which indicate that—in Europe, as elsewhere—total greenhouse gas emissions continue to rise and total material throughput, waste production, and domestic pollutants continue to increase.[42]

This brings us to a critical problem with capacity building. Who, exactly, is to undertake this task? It is, in a sense, a "chicken or egg" problem: capacity creates the capacity for more capacity. If the will and capacity to create capacity are present, then half the problem is solved. Weidner rightly comments that the development of capacity may be described as a multifactorial process determined by conflicting organized actor groups and their resources, abilities, and opportunities; cultural, political, and economic conditions; the environmental situation; and the nature and extent of the problem.[43]

Countries with strongly embedded neo-corporatist institutions—such as Austria, Germany, the Netherlands, and the Scandinavian bloc—seem not only to bring in the state but also to reach out to the full range of actors affected by and with an interest in environmental outcomes. With well-developed environmental organizations and/or with effective green political parties, these countries have established and maintained their lead in terms of environmental performance and are stronger across the range of capacities discussed above than other industrialized nations.

ONE GREEN STATE OR MORE?

Some of these recent trends and developments suggest the possible emergence of not one style of green governance and one type of green state but of several very different sorts. These are described here in shorthand as ideal types, of which the neo-liberal environmental state and the environmental welfare state are at present the most likely and prominent candidates.[44]

The neo-liberal state is broadly characterized by reductions in the state's welfare functions and budget, together with the privatization of public resources and state services—a retreat to the "nightwatchman" state. These trends may extend to the environmental domain through the privatization of ownership of, or control over, public natural resources and the diminution of public environmental regulatory oversight.

Because of actual environmental issues and pressures, however, these neo-liberal trends may *not* be duplicated in the environmental domain. Instead, growth may be evident in environment-related state funding and activity, and/or in state environmental administration designed to deal with emergent environmental problems and thus maintain the productivity of natural resources. The result at best is a "split" state, in which social welfare functions and related capacities are being reduced while, selectively, some environmental functions and capacities are being maintained or even increased. These trends would characterize the *environmental* neo-liberal state, which would likely foster a very weak form of ecological modernization, primarily concerned with environmental management to maintain national industrial capacity and economic productivity. Australia is an example of the trend toward such a state.

By contrast, the environmental welfare state describes a further extension of the social welfare state into areas of environmental concern, predominantly as the state leads attempts to ameliorate or repair the environmental impacts of industrialization and to manage and minimize public anxiety about the loss of critical "non-productive" environmental values. Again, the outcome is, at best, a stronger version of weak ecological modernization, but one with greater regard for aspects of what Eckersley has called human welfare environmentalism[45]—attention to environmental sources of human health and amenity, including the protection of parts of the environment for non-utilitarian reasons. Sweden, Germany, and the Netherlands are exemplars of the trend toward such a type of state.

However, beyond these two variants lies another "truly" green state, in which ecological values and considerations are fully integrated into the heart of the state and are protected and promulgated by that state both domestically, including throughout civil society and in the economic sphere, and internationally—encouraging the emergence of a strong form of ecological modernization. However this seems a distant prospect at present.[46]

CHOOSING THE STATE WE'RE IN

Despite the turn towards green governance—or perhaps because of it—the state remains vital to the possibilities for strong ecological modernization. As this chapter suggests, there is nothing automatic about this trajectory. Contests over control of the state's substantial resources and capacities will continue as "green champions" seek to extend capacities in each of the areas mentioned above—

only to be resisted by those protecting the administrative state as a site for the exercise of conventional bureaucratic power and by those benefiting from the state as an enabler of environmentally destructive industrial development and resource exploitation. The environment movement and green parties are critical actors in constructing the terms and sites of such engagement.

The importance of these contests has been perhaps misunderstood by those theorists[47] and activists who warn of the threats to deliberative democratic designs and "autonomous" public spheres that accompany engagement with the state. Their warning about the threat of cooption and the consequent deradicalization of environmentalist and citizen participants, while important, is nevertheless theoretically and practically inadequate.

Part of the problem here may be the manner in which the state is being conceptualized—as an entity that is organizationally and administratively "solid," if not monolithic, rather than as a set of contested relationships enlivened by struggles to gain or secure control over significant public resources and regulatory powers (including those powers to permit and legitimize violence against nature). In the 1970s, such contests—which involved groups and interests both inside and outside the state and therefore ran "through" the state—were well theorized by Marxist and neo-Marxist theorists, albeit in terms of class struggle that focused mainly on state involvement in the reproduction of capital and on issues of power, wealth, and social welfare.[48] This debate, now veiled by the amnesia that has settled over anything to do with Marxism, contained nuances that need to be recovered in green thinking.[49]

The consequence for the environmental movement has been either *too great* a concentration on state power and diminished attention to the construction of public spheres, or the reverse: *too little*. The latter tendency has led to a "wishing away of the state" based on the assumption that the state is too problematic or, on the other hand, now increasingly marginal in social, economic, and environmental life. The environment movement and some green theorists have failed to adequately conceptualize the interrelationship between the state and public spheres.[50] Insofar as modern public spheres and the modern state (and those who inhabit them) are mutually constituted, a degree of engagement is inevitable. Cooption is always possible during dynamic, discursive engagement with the state, but influence over state policy and its outcomes is radically diminished in the absence or refusal of contact.[51] Some environmentalists have thus sought to capture public imagination merely in order to exert instrumental influence on policy but with little regard for the inadequacies of the administrative state itself. Engagement with industry (broadly defined) has been a little more vigorous, especially subsequent to the impact of neo-liberal strategies for state minimization, but this has also been inadequately conceived.

Neglecting the state—analytically and practically—is not an option if we are seeking effective green goverance. Central to the political project of enabling good green governance must be the aim of creating a green state with capacities that complement a greening of civil society and the economic sphere. This task is pressing if we are to create momentum for strong ecological modernization and deal with a looming environmental crisis.

Notes

1   *The Ecologist, A Blueprint for Survival* (London: Penguin Books, 1972), p. 27.

2   For discussion of strong and weak ecological modernization, see Peter Christoff, "Ecological modernization, Ecological modernities," *Environmental Politics* 5.3(1996): 476–500. Also see John S. Dryzek, *Politics of the Earth: Environmental Discourse* (Oxford and New York: Oxford University Press, 1997); Maarten Hajer, *The Politics of Environmental Discourse: Ecological Modernization and the Policy Process* (Oxford and New York: Oxford University Press, 1995); Arthur P.J. Mol, *The Refinement of Production: Ecological Modernization Theory and the Chemical Industry* (Den Haag: CIP-Data Koninklijke Bibliotheek, 1995); Arthur P.J. Mol, "Ecological Modernization and Institutional Reflexivity: Environmental Reform in the Late Modern Age," *Environmental Politics* 5.2(1996): 302-23; Arthur P.J. Mol and David A. Sonnenfeld, eds., *Ecological Modernization around the World: Perspectives and Critical Debates*, special issue of *Environmental Politics* 9.1(2000).

3   See, for instance, Rod Rhodes, *Understanding Governance: Policy Networks, Governance, Reflexivity, and Accountability* (Buckingham: Open University Press, 1997); Michael Carley and Ian Christie, *Managing Sustainable Development* (London: Earthscan, 2000); Christopher Hood, *The Art of the State: Culture, Rhetoric, and Public Management* (Oxford: Clarendon, 1998).

4   Martin Janicke, *State Failure* (London: Polity Press, 1990), p. 1.

5   See also Rhodes, *Understanding Governance*; Jon Pierre, ed., *Debating Governance* (Oxford: Oxford University Press, 2000); Maarten Hajer and Hendrik Wagenaar, eds., *Deliberative Policy Analysis: Understanding Governance in the Network Society* (Cambridge: Cambridge University Press, 2003).

6   Helmut Weidner, "Capacity Building for Ecological Modernization," *American Behavioral Scientist* 45.9(2002): 1341.

7   See Andrew Jordan, Rudiger K.W. Wurzel, and Anthony R. Zito, *"New" Instruments of Environmental Governance? National Experiences and Prospects*, special issue of *Environmental Politics* 12.1(2003).

8   Weidner, "Capacity Building for Ecological Modernization," p. 1361.

9   Weidner, "Capacity Building for Ecological Modernization," p. 1341. Alternatively, this may be because the aims and impacts of environment policy have been too meek to pose a serious economic threat.

10   See for instance, Ken Conca, "The WTO and the Undermining of Global Environmental Governance," *Review of International Political Economy* 7.3(2000): 484–94, and Robyn Eckersley, "The Big Chill: The WTO and Multilateral Environmental Agreements," *Global Environmental Politics* 4.1(2004): 24–50.

11   For instance, Woods's 1975 national assessment indicated that some 970,000 hectares of land required treatment for dryland salinity (L.E. Woods, *Land Degradation in Australia*, [Canberra: Australian Government Publishing Service, 1983]). Presently 2.5 million hectares of Australian farmland are salt-affected to some degree. The National Land and Water Resources Audit's *Australian Dryland Salinity Assessment 2000* (Canberra, 2002), suggests that approximately 5.7 million hectares are at risk or affected by dryland salin-

ity and that in 50 years the area of high risk may almost triple, to 17 million hectares, with major impacts on biodiversity and agricultural output.

12 EEA (European Environment Agency), *EEA Signals 2004: A European Environment Agency Update on Selected Issues*, EEA Report 2/2004 (Copenhagen: EEA, 2004).

13 The special edition of *Environmental Politics* on "new" instruments of environmental governance, edited by Jordan et al. (2003), seems to indicate caution among European states against moving strongly toward voluntary and market-based environmental policy measures, and a calculated—as well as inertial—reliance on direct regulation to provide the basis for environmental policy achievements.

14 See Jordan et al., "'New' Instruments of Environmental Governance."

15 Though not necessarily from rich to poor, or powerful to powerless.

16 See Albert Weale, *The New Politics of Pollution* (Manchester and New York: Manchester University Press, 1992).

17 Mine is therefore not a "statist" position in any conventional sense of the term, contrary to claims made by John S. Dryzek, David Downes, Christian Hunold, David Schlosberg, with Hans-Kristian Hernes, in *Green States and Social Movements: Environmentalism in the United States, United Kingdom, Germany and Norway* (Oxford and New York: Oxford University Press, 2003), p. 165.

18 Martin Janicke, "Democracy as a precondition for environmental policy success: the importance of non-institutional factors," in William Lafferty and James Meadowcroft, eds., *Democracy and the Environment: Problems and Prospects* (Cheltenham: Edward Elgar, 1996), p. 82.

19 Weidner, "Capacity Building for Ecological Modernization," pp. 1340–68.

20 Janicke, "The Political System's Capacity for Environmental Policy," p. 8.

21 See Peter Christoff, "Degreening Government in the Garden State: Environment Policy under the Kennett Government," *Environmental and Planning Law Journal* 15.1(1998): 10–32, and Peter Christoff, *Ecological Modernization, Ecologically Sustainable Development, and Australia's National ESD Strategy*, Doctoral dissertation (University of Melbourne, 2002). I also build on the work of Mikael S. Anderson, *Ecological Modernization: Between Policy Styles and Policy Instruments—The Case of Water Pollution Control*, Centre for Social Science Environmental Research, University of Aarhus, Denmark, paper delivered at ECPR Conference, Leiden, 1993; Mikael S. Anderson, "Ecological Modernization Capacity: Finding Patterns in the Mosaic of Studies," in Stephen Young, ed., *The Emergence of Ecological Modernization: Integrating the environment and the economy?* (London and New York: Routledge, 2000), pp. 107–32; Janicke, "Democracy as a Precondition for Environmental Policy Success"; Janicke, "The Political System's Capacity for Environmental Policy"; Weidner, "Capacity Building for Ecological Modernization."

22 On the benefits of deliberative democratic processes and communicative politics for environmental policy outcomes and the workings of green public spheres, see, for instance, John S. Dryzek, *Discursive Democracy: Politics, Policy and Political Science* (Cambridge: Cambridge University Press, 1990); Frank Fischer, "Citizen Participation and the Democratization of Policy Expertise: From Political Theory to Practical Cases," *Policy Sciences* 26(1993): 165–87; Frank Fischer and John Forester, eds., *The Argumentative Turn in Policy Analysis and Planning* (London, University College London, 1993); Lafferty and Meadowcroft, eds., *Democracy and the Environment*; John Forester, *The Deliberative Practitioner: Encouraging Participatory Planning Processes* (Cambridge, MA, and London: MIT Press, 1999); and Douglas Torgerson, *The Promise of Green*

Politics: Environmentalism and the Green Public Sphere (Durham, NC, and London: Duke University Press, 1999).

23   Douglas Torgerson and Robert Paehlke, "Environmental Administration: Revising the Agenda of Inquiry and Practice," this volume.

24   To the extent that, as Doug Torgerson comments in "Obsolescent Leviathan: Problems of Order in Administrative Thought," this volume, "the organizational environment has become so troublesome that the bureaucratic form itself has been thrown into question."

25   This is not to ignore the claims of Marxists and others that the state has been constituted by and around vested interests, including those of capital and the destruction of nature, "in the final instance." However, a more nuanced interpretation of the state suggests that it is composed of and reflects contradictory social concerns, including those of (subordinate) ecocentric and welfare interests that are at play in trying to determine state actions and agendas, which may make such an outcome possible in specific instances, even in the short term.

26   This rendering of vertical environmental policy integration extends the definition used by William M. Lafferty and James Meadowcroft, "Patterns of Governmental Engagement," in William M. Lafferty and James Meadowcroft, eds., *Implementing Sustainable Development: Strategic Initiatives in High Consumption Societies* (Oxford and New York: Oxford University Press, 2000), p. 433; and William M. Lafferty and Eivind Hovden, "Environmental Policy Integration: Towards an Analytical Framework," *Environmental Politics* 12.3(2003): 12, by taking into account integration between different spheres of government.

27   Janicke, "Democracy as a precondition for environmental policy success," p. 79.

28   It is also at this point that ecological modernization strategies undertaken by liberal-democratic capitalist states are most vulnerable to the downward pressures on state revenue raising present in an increasingly competitive, neo-liberal, globalized economic environment.

29   Peter Christoff, "Policy Autism or Double-edged Dismissiveness? Australia's Climate Policy under the Howard Government," *Global Change, Peace and Security* 17.1(2005): 29–44.

30   See also Anderson, "Ecological modernization capacity."

31   Andrew Jordan, ed., *Environmental Policy in the European Union: Actors, Institutions and Processes* (London: Earthscan Books, 2002).

32   Albert Weale, "European Environmental Policy by Stealth: the Dysfunctionality of Functionalism?" in Andrew Jordan, ed., *Environmental Policy in the European Union: Actors, Institutions and Processes* (London: Earthscan Books, 2002), pp. 329–47.

33   Rod Rhodes, "The Hollowing Out of the State: The Changing Nature of the Public Service in Britain," *Political Quarterly* 65.2(1994): 138–51.

34   For instance, Hanspeter Kreisi, R. Koopmans, J.W. Dyvendak, and M.G. Guigni, *New Social Movements in Western Europe: a Comparative Study* (Minneapolis: University of Minneapolis Press, 1995) and Dryzek et al., *Green States and Social Movements*.

35   Consider the various OECD Environmental Performance Reports for member states, and also Mikael Skou Anderson and Duncan Liefferink, *European Environmental Policy: The Pioneers* (Manchester and New York: Manchester University Press, 1997); Kenneth Hanf and Alf-Inge Jansen, eds., *Governance and Environmental Quality: Environmental Politics, Policy and Administration in Western Europe* (New York: Addison Wesley Longman, 1998); Martin Janicke and Helmut Weidner, eds., *National Environmental*

Policies: A Comparative Study of Capacity-Building (Berlin: Springer Verlag, 1997); Jordan, ed., *Environmental Policy in the European Union;* Jordan et al., "'New' Instruments of Environmental Governance?"; Lafferty and Meadowcroft, eds., *Implementing Sustainable Development*; and Albert Weale, Geoffrey Pridham, Michelle Cini, Dimitrios Konstadakopulos, Martin Porter, and Brenda Flynn, *Environmental Governance in Europe: An Ever Closer Ecological Union?* (Oxford and New York: Oxford University Press, 2000).

36 E.g., Rudiger K.W. Wurzel, Lars Bruckner, Andrew Jordan, and Anthony R. Zito, "Struggling to Leave Behind a Highly Regulated Past? 'New' Environmental Policy Instruments in Austria," *Environmental Politics* 12.1(2003): 51–72; Rudiger K.W. Wurzel, Andrew Jordan, Anthony R. Zito, and Lars Bruckner, "From High Regulatory State to Social and Ecological Market Economy? 'New' Environmental Policy Instruments in Germany," *Environmental Politics* 12.1(2003): 115–37; Anthony R. Zito, Lars Bruckner, Andrew Jordan, and Rudiger K.W. Wurzel, "Instrument Innovation in an Environmental Lead State: 'New' Environmental Policy Instruments in the Netherlands," *Environmental Politics* 12.1(2003): 157–78.

37 Peter Christoff, *In Reverse: Australian Environmental Performance 1992–2002* (Melbourne: Australian Conservation Foundation, 2002). By contrast, Elim Papadakis and Richard Grant, "The Politics of 'Light-Handed Regulation': 'New' Environmental Policy Instruments in Australia," *Environmental Politics* 12.1(2003): 27–50, provides an uncritical recitation of Australian developments.

38 Janicke and Weidner, eds., *National Environmental Policies.*

39 Lafferty and Meadowcroft, eds., *Implementing Sustainable Development.*

40 As per Janicke and Weidner, eds., *National Environmental Policies.*

41 As per William M. Lafferty and James Meadowcroft, "Patterns of Governmental Engagement," in William M. Lafferty and James Meadowcroft, eds., *Implementing Sustainable Development: Strategic Initiatives in High Consumption Societies* (Oxford and New York: Oxford University Press, 2000), pp. 337–421. See also, *passim,* the same volume.

42 EEA, *EEA Signals 2004*; EEA, *Impacts of Europe's changing climate: and indicator-based assessment,* EEA Report 2/2004 (Copenhagen: EEA, 2004).

43 Weidner, "Capacity Building for Ecological Modernization," p. 1342.

44 This argument is developed further in Peter Christoff, "Out of Chaos a Shining Star? Towards a Typology of Green States," in John Barry and Robyn Eckersley, eds., *The State and the Global Ecological Crisis* (Cambridge, MA, and London: MIT Press, 2005), pp. 25–52.

45 Robyn Eckersley, *Environmentalism and Political Theory: Toward an Ecocentric Approach* (New York: SUNY Press, 1992).

46 See also Robyn Eckersley, *The Green State: Rethinking Democracy and Sovereignty,* (Cambridge, MA, and London: MIT Press, 2004).

47 For instance, as in Dryzek et al., *Green States and Social Movements.*

48 See, for example, John Holloway and Sol Picciotto, *State and Capital: A Marxist Debate* (London: Edward Arnold, 1978); London Edinburgh Weekend Return Group, *In and against the State* (London: Pluto Press, 1979); Nicos Poulantzas, *State, Power, Socialism* (London: Verso Press, 1980); and Boris Frankel, *Beyond the State?* (London: Macmillan, 1983).

49 See also Jim O'Connor, *Natural Causes: Essays in Ecological Marxism* (New York: Guildford Press, 1998).

50 The works of Dryzek, Eckersley, and Torgerson are prominent exceptions.

51 On contextually contingent opportunities that such discursive openings might provide, and on the issue of cooption, also see Douglas Torgerson, "The Ambivalence of Discourse: Beyond the Administrative Mind?," this volume; Robert Bartlett, "Ecological Reason in Administration: Environmental Impact Assessment and Administrative Theory," this volume; and Robert Paehlke "Environmental Challenges to Democratic Practice," in William M. Lafferty and James Meadowcroft, eds., *Democracy and the Environment* (Brookfield: Edward Elgar, 1996).

Conclusion

17

Environmental Politics and the Administrative State

Robert Paehlke and Douglas Torgerson

In the context of advancing industrialization, the fiction of apolitical administration readily appears plausible. Made in the image of the machine, the administrative apparatus becomes both an achievement and an instrument of rationalization—of technological progress in an increasingly mechanized universe. Indeed, Thorstein Veblen went so far as to claim, "mechanical technology is impersonal and dispassionate, and its end is very simply to serve human needs, without fear or favor or respect of persons, prerogatives, or politics."[1] In this context, bureaucratic organization in both the public and private sectors emerges as a mechanism especially well suited to promoting a natural and necessary course of development. The administrative state, in particular, can thus appear as a form of governance beyond politics.

The advent of environmental politics has not completely dispelled this technocratic illusion, but has challenged it. The conventional agenda—including the continued promotion of economic growth despite obvious costs—no longer appears simply as natural and necessary, but stands out clearly as a matter of choice, as something potentially subject to revision. As this agenda comes under scrutiny, attention also turns to the process in which it is formulated and in which concrete policy decisions are made. Here the divide between politics and administration collapses: the two intermingle in a way that violates rationalistic expectations and prevailing canons of administrative legitimacy. The technocratic imagery now appears as a veil, obscuring the normal interplay of forces in the administrative sphere of state and economy. What is drawn into question is not only the historical direction created and maintained by the convergence of these forces, but also the institutional form that they collectively constitute.

ENVIRONMENTAL POLITICS

Environmental politics disturbs the composure of the administrative state. Even though Leviathan endeavors to force environmental problems onto the procrustean bed of conventional administrative thought and practice, the goal proves to be elusive. With the dramatic outburst of environmental concern in the late 1960s, officials were generally quick to align their statements with the prevailing sentiment. Just as quickly, however, there emerged among them a sense that environmental problems had either been solved by modest reforms or displaced by more serious and pressing economic difficulties. Environmentalism, many hopefully believed, was going out of style and would not hold public attention for long. It seemed safe for officials to slight environmental concerns, and eventually neo-conservative forces were able to mount a determined assault upon environmentalism and the reforms it had initiated in the administrative state. Nonetheless, environmental politics had been animated by a particular perception of environmental problems—a perception that was strong and pervasive enough to sustain environmental concern in a substantial network of environmental organizations and among a significant proportion of environmental professionals and citizens. It remains difficult for public officials to ignore environmental concerns or simply to repeat the clichéd promises of progress.[2]

To say that environmental politics is animated by a particular perception of environmental problems is not to say that all actors in this arena share this perception. Indeed, it is a perception that has often been ridiculed by forces committed to the conventional vision of order and progress. Nonetheless, environmental politics has emerged as an identifiable arena of contemporary politics and administration through the impetus of actors sharing a view that challenges the complacent notion that there is nothing new in environmental problems—that these are really just problems like any others and can be handled in the ordinary way.[3]

In a manner necessarily irritating to the administrative mind, environmental problems are deemed both enormously complex and serious—as raising in a dramatic fashion moral issues that once seemed settled and technical questions that few had even imagined. Against the expectations of the administrative mind, this view focuses on problems that may be entirely unmanageable and, at the very least, call for a thorough revision of administrative inquiry and practice. In its view of the complexity and seriousness of environmental problems, this perception contains a paradox. The problems seem virtually beyond comprehension, yet enough is known to demand urgent action.

Environmental problems are perceived as being multidimensional, interconnected, interactive, and dynamic. They point beyond the controlled setting of the laboratory or the production process to an ambiguous world where innumerable variables elude identification, much less measurement. The very scope of the unknown seems to expand dramatically with each little bit learned. Yet the problems appear not only extraordinarily complex, but also extremely threatening to particular concerns and, indeed, to the general interests of humanity.

A sense of crisis demands action and innovative directions in problem solving. No single fact or model demonstrates an emerging crisis, but a litany of difficulties becomes increasingly impressive. Environmental impacts appear largely cumulative, moreover, and it becomes increasingly hard to deny that the maximum sustainable level of imposition of economy on environment has been reached or exceeded. Human populations and activities are encroaching in some way on the habitats of other species on nearly every hectare of land on the planet. Virtually all the best agricultural land now carries human-imposed (and even now human-created) eco-systems, maintained in many cases through the use of toxic chemicals. Ground water, river water, lake water, and the oceans are laced with chemicals; polar bears carry toxic chemicals in their livers. Precipitation around the world appears altered in both quantity and quality, the ozone layer has been disrupted, and the climate of the planet is changing. Tropical rainforests continue to shrink and unacceptable—and "acceptable"—levels of pollution are still killing people.

The perception alternates, then, between a sense of human limits and a confidence that human action has at least a chance of solving environmental problems. This ambivalence allows for differing approaches, including the reflex response of looking to established authority, as some environmentalists have done. What that approach fails to recognize, however, is that established authority is itself seldom bothered by a sense of human limits and instead typically exudes unshakable confidence in prevailing institutions and their capacity to resolve problems. Of course, this capacity cannot, in principle, be disproven. Problems that seem to be insoluble in the context of established institutions could—however dim the possibility—conceivably be resolved through some unanticipated innovation, or through some unforeseen way of defining the problems. What remains striking, nonetheless, is the unshakable character of this confidence, for its foundation is as suspect as the rationalistic imagery that adorns it: "The achievements of modern science and technology, however impressive, do not of themselves provide solid evidence that the problems which they confront and, in fact, create, can actually be overcome."[4] There is, indeed, reason for doubt. The administrative sphere, while singularly successful in promoting the established pattern of development, has not shown itself to be effective in either restraining or qualitatively redirecting industrialization. The administrative sphere, moreover, craves that which is definite, precise, and calculable—tolerating little in the way of ambivalence. Ambivalent perception, nonetheless, may well be in accord with an organizational form oriented toward a balance between the humility of recognizing limits and the confidence needed for effective action.

Environmental politics arises out of a particular view of environmental problems and is a dimension of political life that is different from the politics of left, right, and center. While the center has typically endorsed environmental concern—even at times reducing the environment to a so-called "motherhood" issue—environmentalism has also been portrayed as a mere extension of socialism, liberalism, or the conservation movement. Despite the frequently unabashed hostility of neo-conservatism to the environmental movement and its goals, there is also an ambiguous relationship between environmentalism and the appeals of traditional conservatism and even neo-conservatism.[5] Environmental politics, moreover, stands apart from conventional interest-group politics and thus bears a distinctive relationship to the state and the administrative world generally.[6]

The intriguing ambiguity in the relationship between environmentalism and neo-conservatism turns largely on how the two view the administrative state. Both exhibit a notable hostility. For neo-conservatives the goal has been economic expansion and re-distribution upwards through disproportionate tax reductions, deregulation, entrepreneurship, and the "magic of the market." Environmentalists, in turn, have often emphasized alternative patterns of development, comprising grass-roots citizen participation and empowerment, responsible individual action, and both public and private decentralized initiatives. For environmentalism, this emphasis in part represents a reaction against the administrative orientation of the earlier conservation movement. Neo-conservatives react against the expansion of the "positive state" or even its very existence.

In terms of concrete policy thrusts, neo-conservatism from Ronald Reagan through George W. Bush has—despite its rhetoric—ironically pursued a course promoting both the continued growth and presence of the administrative state in economy and society. This course has included direct and indirect subsidies to private corporations, a megaproject approach to energy production and the exploration of space, bailouts for companies and industries "too big to fail," and—especially in the American context—mammoth and seemingly perpetual military expenditures.

Nor was such a course really avoidable, because neo-conservatism has by no means replaced the prevailing consensus that attributes to the administrative state ultimate responsibility for the economic management of advanced industrial society. A further irony is that neo-conservatives must, from time to time, restrain their visceral hostility to environmentalism in order to project at least an appearance of environmental concern. A remarkable Canadian case provides an object lesson in what can happen when this hostility is not restrained. That lesson is the fate of Mike Harris, the hyper-conservative premier of Ontario. In the face of increasing unpopularity, he declined to stand for re-election and his party was nonetheless still crushingly defeated, having never recovered politically from the tragic Walkerton water-poisoning scandal in 2000 that followed several years of open hostility to environmental protection expenditures.[7]

A real struggle is underway for that segment of political opinion that wants to restrain the bureaucratic dominance of contemporary society. Liberals and the traditional left share a heritage which looked hopefully upon the administrative state as potentially an impartial mechanism that could serve the general interests of society. It remains an open question whether they can come to terms with an environmentalist view that focuses upon the limitations of conventional administration. It remains an open question, as well, whether neo-conservatives can adapt to environmentalist doubts regarding economic growth, corporate bureaucracies, or the supposed magic of the autonomous market. Finally, it remains an open question how environmentalists will come to locate themselves in terms of the left-right continuum—whether distributing along it or somehow realigning and redefining it, perhaps through the establishment of viable green parties.

Besides its unique orientation to the prevailing ideological map, environmental politics also departs from the conventional framework of interest-group politics. The focus of environmental groups, that is, is concerned more with a broad public interest than with a narrow, particular interest. This point is implicit in the literature on "post-materialist" values and the new popularity of doubts regarding excessive consumption.[8] Environmentalists often see themselves as defending a general human interest (including future generations) or as speaking for other species and especially threatened parts of non-human nature—indeed, more comprehensively, as working in the interests of the planet and its inhabitants as a whole. At the same time, environmental politics now does exhibit a wide range of particularly focused concerns. Many perspectives on environmentalism, such as ecofeminism and environmental justice, highlight connections between environmental problems and the inequities of human societies.[9] Those who are devoted to environmental politics are, in any case, not typically seeking the narrow advantages that typically animate those engaged in conventional politics.

The distinctive orientation of environmentalism is significant in the politics of the administrative state. This realm works smoothly only if those seeking favors are uniformly professional and responsible—if they speak the proper language of precision and instrumentality while standing ready to make the trade-offs necessary for compromise solutions. With their particular perspective and interests, environmentalists often do not measure up to these standards. Yet as they seek concrete results in the policy process, they are bound to interact over time with the administrative state and the corporate world. Then environmentalists do—often in a dramatic and deliberate fashion—become increasingly professional and "responsible." Indeed, participation in public hearings and other administrative procedures often requires time and expertise. Since environmentalists are hardly less likely than others to need a means of livelihood, they may well become reliant on the continuing success and stability of an environmental organization or network—even if remuneration tends to be meager. Moreover, with the frankly moral character of its demands, environmentalism can appear overbearing and untrustworthy in a world where one gets along by going along. Environmentalists are pressed to compromise simply in order not to appear uncompromising.

Yet this is not the entire story, for professionalized environmentalists are frequently eclipsed by events and "out-greened" by others. This tension runs through existing groups and is increased with the entry of new groups and individuals into environmental politics. A significant impetus in this regard arises with local land-use decisions and the so-called NIMBY syndrome. Here local residents may oppose development that would degrade the amenities of the area or decrease the sale value of their property. Clearly, these motives are common to interest-group politics, and there is an arsenal of compensatory devices available in conventional politics and administration. Yet, typically in such situations, there are two elements that resist ready compromise and a smooth resolution to disputes. One is the attachment that people may feel to a place with which they identify. The other is the fact that some who object to a landfill, a toxic waste depository, or an oil refinery do so not only with their particular interests in view, but also with concern for a broader, interrelated context of environmental problems. Indeed, when such opposition resists conventional compromises, there is more than an immediate difficulty for the administrative state. For these situations also direct the attention of a broader citizenry to environmental concerns: face-to-face with particular consequences of industrialization, some are led to perceive broader questions and perhaps to inject a vigorous and uncompromising attitude into environmental politics.

ENVIRONMENTAL ADMINISTRATION

In its collision with the administrative state, as we have seen, environmental politics is influenced by an historically unique perception that takes environmental problems not to be ordinary problems, easily remedied or administered in the conventional manner. Environmental politics thereby clearly departs from the earlier politics of conservation and its tendency to align itself with the administrative apparatus of an emerging industrialism. Indeed, at times environmental politics seems moved by an impulse to have done with administration altogether.[10] Yet this impulse would appear to be based in a recognition of the inadequacies of conventional administration in grappling with environmental problems. What the impulse obscures is that administration cannot simply be abolished: the historical possibility is for a form of administration more adequate to the environmental problems that are emerging as we move into the aftermath of industrialization. The at least implicit logic of environmentalism, of environmental politics, is to realize this new kind of administration.

Environmental administration possesses no completed form or systematic program but is an emerging orientation of inquiry and practice distinctly at odds with the conventional agenda. Exposing the hidden political nature of that agenda, environmental administration is itself constituted as a political goal that, implicitly or explicitly, serves as a common focus of effort for the diverse environmental movement. As a political goal, environmental administration remains somewhat fluid and indefinite, with the precise content of the goal shifting with differing perspectives. Nonetheless, it is possible to briefly characterize an emerging agenda.

As a departure from the conventional approach to administration, environmental administration is not simply administration that deals with environmental matters. Of course, it begins by taking a focus on the environment, thus distinguishing itself from an earlier administrative tendency to focus on the internal operations of a single organization and to take the external environment for granted. By now, however, both the social and natural environments of organizations have increasingly been added on as categories to the conventional administrative form. Environmental administration differs, however, in that its way of seeing the environment promotes a distinctive mode of defining and grappling with environmental problems. Moreover, environmental administration is not in principle restricted to dealing with environmental problems directly; that is to say, it offers an orientation that can deal with a range of economic processes—e.g., manufacturing, agriculture, resource extraction, urban design, transportation—in a manner that anticipates environmental problems in both planning and implementation.

Environmental administration, in other words, departs both from conventional administration and from the pattern of development that it has served. In order to grasp the idea of environmental administration more fully, we can provisionally characterize it with an interrelated and incomplete list of adjectives: (1) non-compartmentalized, (2) open, (3) decentralized, (4) anti-technocratic, and (5) flexible. Here we will focus, in turn, on each of these characteristics.

(1) *Non-compartmentalized.* Environmental administration resists the typical bureaucratic tendency toward compartmentalization. Because it recognizes a pervasive complex of problems, environmental administration has indefinite boundaries and has, indeed, challenged early efforts to confine environmental concerns to a single, often marginal, sub-division of government. The institutionalization of environmental impact assessment, for example, has—despite its limitations—prompted a broad range of government departments and agencies to think environmentally. Even the military now includes environmental factors in its decision-making processes. Government printing offices procure paper from recycled sources and US farm policies and some state land registration and taxation procedures promote the creation of ecological land trusts. During the course of electricity shortages, California administrative agencies took up or promoted extensive energy efficiency improvements. In some jurisdictions, revenue policies have come to have environmental protection as a secondary objective. This is the case even in Texas, where wind power is booming as a result of revenue and other policies. The fact that nongovernmental organizations (NGOs) are going much further serves to reinforce the point that environmental administration is not easily confined or isolated.[11]

(2) *Open.* While the hallmark of conventional administration is secrecy in a cloistered decision-making process, the hallmark of environmental administration is openness. The relatively unbounded character of environmental concerns

creates perplexities for any effort to neatly mark the boundary lines of the administrative process and to definitively circumscribe the range of legitimate participants. This problem in principle is compounded by the political reality that educated citizens are increasingly reluctant to accept the secrecy of the administrative sphere. Public administrators, and even private decision makers, may find themselves at public hearings or in a courtroom, rather than closeted in the offices of a confidential world. And, should they escape that fate, they may still need to operate in more public business settings such as conferences or the media with groups of aware and socially conscious investors. The conventional framework of administration is challenged by such openings for discourse and deliberation.

In recent years, however, closure has re-entered the world of environmental decision making through the mechanism of trade treaty enforcement panels. Legislative and administrative progress in environmental matters achieved openly at the domestic level has become subject to international bodies such as the World Trade Organization that are utterly closed to citizen or NGO influence, insight or participation. This world of trade lawyers and panels with a vested interest in turning back existing domestic environmental rules (in order to attain additional lucrative clients seeking further gains) is closed to politics that involves actors without large-scale economic interests. Democracy and openness hard won on the domestic level can be lost in this new and deliberately created "higher" realm. The only recourse may be also to take environmental politics to the global level.[12]

(3) *Decentralized.* The slogan "think globally, act locally" reflects a significant ambivalence in environmental administration. For the impetus toward decentralization provides a reorientation, but by no means entirely replaces centralization. Environmental administration is concerned with problems that at once entail pressures toward decentralized, even local, decision making and, as noted, toward centralized, even international, decision making.

Global problems in some cases require common, cooperative global solutions, with little room for wide variations in approach: diverse initiatives here need coordination to be effective. Prompt efforts to stem the depletion of ozone in the upper atmosphere, or to deal with climate change, to take obvious examples, could well be pointless if China and India fail to take environmental factors into account as they continue their remarkable economic expansion and provide transportation and appliances to their vast populations. Some central administration, or environmentally conscious trade rules, are necessary, moreover, to prevent havens for pollution in areas where authorities are inclined to trade environmental quality for economic opportunities: the air of much of a continent can be fouled from within a single, neglectful political jurisdiction.

Yet the pressures for centralization, seen from the conventional administrative viewpoint, can easily obscure a key distinctive feature of environmental administration, which itself has arisen in significant part from pressures brought to bear by a diverse, mobilizing citizenry. Environmental administration must also deal with the local and the particular, with widely varying geographical and cultural contexts. Here necessary knowledge and initiative cannot be the preserve of a centralized administrative structure, staffed by remote and anonymous personnel. Knowledge and initiative, indeed, arise from intimate involvement in the context.

Established patterns of centralized power in advanced industrial society, moreover, retain an orientation that typically leaves them unsympathetic to rapid, vigorous, large-scale action for environmental protection. So the political and historical context by itself clearly sets limits to reliance upon centralization; implicit, though not always recognized, in such reliance is a challenge to established centralized hierarchies, which would effectively replace them with new ones. Yet political support for such a change would, paradoxically, itself require decentralized initiative and action.

Obviously, environmental administration anticipates some kind of new balance, integration, or alignment of centralization and decentralization. While some provisional guidelines to approach this relationship could no doubt be developed, especially in the context of specific problems, any comprehensive formula is likely to remain elusive not only because of the obvious complexities involved, but also because of a reason which those wanting such a formula might not recognize: the present relationship between centralization and decentralization has emerged as part of a pattern of historical development, and any proffered formula would be inadequate if it failed to take this context into account. Yet to take this context into account would be to expect the unexpected, to anticipate contingencies which are not repetitive and predictable, but new and surprising. At the very least, one would have to recognize that those who manage and confront Leviathan also find themselves perhaps in a transitional phase—and that the relationship between centralization and decentralization in environmental administration may emerge as something qualitatively different should that time pass: should, that is, the pattern of social and economic life change into one in which massive environmental problems are no longer generated routinely by an enormous complex of centralized hierarchies.

(4) *Anti-technocratic.* As a goal arising from environmental politics, environmental administration emerges in part as an alternative to conventional administration and, by contrast, as a mirror that exposes the surreptitious political dimensions of prevailing practices. What is exposed is the at least implicit commitment to a form of life and historical vision that anticipates a smoothly functioning social system, guided by experts in the administrative sphere. Environmental administration departs from this technocratic commitment and advances, moreover, with a more or less clear recognition of the interest-group machinations and class forces that actually infuse the administrative state despite its technocratic imagery. Obviously, this frankly political orientation raises questions of administrative legitimacy. The cloistered politics of conventional administration are

rejected in favor of the more open patterns of communication deemed appropriate to democratic government and society.[13]

This appeal to democracy, however, is only partly effective. While it may be possible to parody and ridicule the technocratic style and idiom by drawing upon popular sentiment, technocracy is still potent in projecting a mystique suggesting it holds a monopoly on relevant knowledge. A key challenge to environmental administration is to counter this claim by placing expertise in context.

Environmental administration necessarily draws heavily on the findings and opinions of experts. Indeed, sciences such as ecology, epidemiology, and toxicology provide important foundations for environmentalism, a perspective that supports environmental administration in its challenge to technocracy. But expertise, almost by definition, is specialized and thus insufficient by itself for handling environmental problems. With its features of non-compartmentalization and openness, environmental administration clearly draws attention to the importance of the generalist capable of viewing problems in a broader configuration, of perceiving and judging collectivities, interactions, and relationships across systems. The importance of the generalist suggests, moreover, that the boundary between relevant expertise and common sense is often fluid and indistinct. The door is thus open to citizen participation in a process that could educate *both* citizens and experts.

The insufficiency of specialized expertise means that the administrative process needs to remain open to a range of influences and experiences that are typically excluded in conventional practice. This point reinforces the importance of the knowledge and initiative to be gained through a relatively decentralized pattern of interaction involving both citizens and experts. Such a pattern could no doubt prove annoying to those accustomed to a more closed process, and resistance to such innovation is often evident. Yet environmental administration points to the limited effectiveness of a cloistered administrative domain, protected from the trouble of dealing with external concerns. In William J. Woodhouse's words, "weak outside scrutiny insulates the regulatory system from substantive criticism that could lead to improved effectiveness."[14]

No doubt there is often a rationale to exclude such influences. For example, there is often concern about the supposedly unwarranted delays occasioned by the NIMBY Syndrome. Yet this concern is based upon the assumption that administrative officials have both the competence and commitment to handle environmental problems effectively without external influences, including citizen influences, exerted in open settings. In more closed settings, forces that are relatively better organized or more likely to have an influence come to bear on administrative decisions. The Newfoundland cod fishery collapsed when the political and administrative influence of large economic interests overwhelmed both technical expertise within the bureaucracy and the externally based insights of small-scale inland fishers.

The technocratic orientation distributes benefits of doubt and burdens of proof in a way that promotes the prevailing pattern of socio-economic development—

and does so by appealing to an imagery of expertise, precision, and knowledge while conjuring up a "number" to support any decision. This practice obscures the actual process and its bias. As William Leiss has said, "The 'number' selected for an environmental standard only appears to be derived directly from the pure disinterested inquiries of the laboratory; in fact, it usually represents a rough compromise among vested interests, balancing science, politics, and economy on the knife-edge of potential catastrophe."[15]

The challenge to technocracy does not propose, of course, to miraculously abolish the uncertainties and perplexities of decision making. Environmental administration, indeed, is oriented toward a process that would make the problems more visible—dispelling the mystique that supports unbounded confidence that problems generated by the prevailing pattern of development can be overcome. Informed by a different view of environmental problems, the processes of environmental administration tend toward a reallocation of the benefits of doubt and the burdens of proof.[16]

(5) *Flexible.* Conventional problem solving focuses on a form of analysis that proceeds from a fairly fixed conceptual framework, seeking impatiently to reduce ambiguity and diversity in the subject-matter to something manageable and familiar. What is lost is sensitivity to those changes and differences that resist ready recognition, much less classification. Following from its non-compartmentalized, open, decentralized, and anti-technocratic characteristics, environmental administration remains flexible in its orientation to problems. There is a change in orientation, but no fixed formula. Environmental goals can be served at the local level by new municipal planning and zoning or by national-level governmental energy programs, by market-based initiatives regarding renewable energy, by industrial re-design or green buildings with or without public incentives. Neither the appropriate scale nor the location of effective action can be easily predetermined. What matters is the development of an institutional capacity to respond effectively to administrative challenges.

Indeed, environmental administration is even flexible in another—perhaps perplexing—sense: it resists precisely the type of characterization we are trying to give it, for it is an emergent phenomenon. Environmental administration is taking shape, and it remains to be shaped further. But no one is in a position to offer a comprehensive description or prescription. The very vocabulary now available is inadequate, distorting environmental administration even while describing, prescribing, and emerging along with it. For it would be ridiculous to say, taking the opposites of the terms employed here, that environmental administration possesses no features that could be considered somehow compartmentalized, closed, centralized, technocratic, or fixed. Such a notion of environmental administration would itself be absurdly rigid, yet such a distortion is certainly possible given the prevailing political and administrative context. Obviously, to speak of environmental administration is a task more complex than coming down on one side or another of a polar opposition. Yet the words to grasp and convey the right balance, integration, or realignment are not yet part of the available vocabulary. To create such a vocabulary is part of an intellectual—indeed political—task that would change the prevailing agenda of inquiry and practice.

ENVIRONMENTAL ADMINISTRATION
AND THE ADMINISTRATIVE STATE

To emphasize the interpenetration of politics and administration—in particular, to portray environmental administration as intrinsically political and a goal of environmental politics—is not to deny a distinction. Political and administrative life both contain, in varying degrees, contrary elements of innovation and routine, disagreement and consensus, chaos and order. In politics, the tendency is toward innovation, disagreement, and chaos while, in administration, it is toward routine, consensus, and order. The overlapping of the two domains is fluid, so that any conceptual boundary necessarily remains imprecise and provisional. There is nonetheless a difference between politics and administration, and this difference holds in the case of environmental administration.

The carnival atmosphere that accompanied the rise of environmental politics was bound both to create a political backlash and to establish a more orderly administrative approach to more manageable concerns. The response of conventional administration was to absorb opposition and smooth over conflict with modest reforms prone to be eroded as public attention lapsed and political dynamics shifted. Still, with these reforms, with a continuing and widespread recognition of environmental problems, and with a self-organizing environmental movement, a significant institutionalization of environmental concern was achieved: the emergence of environmental administration became perceptible and could be deliberately promoted through inquiry and practice. To be sure, there is no central direction and control of this effort. Indeed, environmentalism betrays differences and tensions as some groups tend toward professionalism, compromise, and workable solutions while other groups accentuate an oppositional posture accompanied by direct action and sensational stunts. Both these elements are necessary, though perhaps not sufficient, in the emergence of environmental administration.[17]

Impatience with Leviathan should not obscure what is both obvious and paradoxical: moving beyond Leviathan would also mean initially helping to manage it. This is not to deny that the process could be long, even interminable—that opposition could significantly be absorbed through accommodation. Yet institutionalization has a memory that is more than momentary. Once established and set in motion, an administrative process gains a dynamism of its own and may see something through, especially if there are pressures that will not allow it to forget what it might prefer to forget. Institutional changes that make the administrative process more open and participatory introduce an element of unpredictability that can be denied only through the illusion that the administrative mind fosters of its unbounded capacity to control events. Innovation of this kind, moreover, raises the prospect not only of citizens interacting with experts, but also of citizens *as* experts and experts *as* citizens. The strengthening of this already-present tendency would be a key event in the emergence of environmental administration: Leviathan might then become manageable.

NOTES

1 Thorstein Veblen, *The Engineers and the Price System* (New York: Viking Press, 1933 [1921]), pp. 135–36. This book inspired the technocracy movement of the 1930s; the term *technocracy* has since, of course, come to have a broader application.

2 Still worth reading in this regard is Anthony Downs, "Up and Down with Ecology: The 'Issue-Attention Cycle,'" *The Public Interest* 38(1972): 38–50.

3 The distinctive character of the environmental perspective is emphasized in Robert Paehlke, *Environmentalism and the Future of Progressive Politics* (New Haven, CT: Yale University Press, 1989; 1991).

4 Douglas Torgerson, *Industrialization and Assessment: Social Impact Assessment as a Social Phenomenon* (Toronto: York University, 1980), p. 72. Also see ch. 2 generally and pp. 186–89.

5 On the relationship of environmentalism to the major political ideologies, see Paehlke, *Environmentalism and the Future of Progressive Politics*, ch. 7.

6 Some argue that European green parties are part of a process that could bring environmental politics into the fold (with both positive and negative implications). See, for example, Christopher Rootes, ed., *Environmental Protest in Western Europe* (New York: Oxford University Press, 2003).

7 See Anita Kranjc, "Whither Ontario's Environment? Neo-conservatism and the Decline of the Environment Ministry," *Canadian Public Policy* 26(March 2000): 111–27.

8 See Ronald Inglehart, "Post-Materialism in an Environment of Insecurity," *American Political Science Review* 75(1981): 880–900, and Thomas Princen, Michael Maniates, and Ken Conca, eds., *Confronting Consumption* (Cambridge: MIT Press, 2002).

9 See Douglas Torgerson, "Environmentalism," in Shepard Krech III, John McNeill, and Carolyn Merchant, eds., *Encyclopedia of World Environmental History*, vol. 1 (New York: Routledge, 2003), pp. 121–28.

10 For a response to the view that the state is unimportant to, and necessarily ineffective in, the resolution of environmental problems, see Robyn Eckersley, *The Green State* (Cambridge: MIT Press, 2004).

11 See, for example, Alan Thein Durning and Yoram Bauman, *Tax Shift* (Seattle: Northwest Environment Watch, 1998), and the recent federal platform of the Green Party of Canada at <http://www.greenparty.ca>.

12 For a full discussion on this point see Robert Paehlke, *Democracy's Dilemma: Environment, Social Equity and the Global Economy* (Cambridge: MIT Press, 2003).

13 See Robert Paehlke, "Cycles of Closure in Environmental Politics and Policy," in Ben A. Minteer and Bob Papperman Taylor, eds., *Democracy and the Claims of Nature* (Lanham, MD: Rowman & Littlefield, 2002), pp. 279–99.

14 Edward J. Woodhouse, "External Influences on Productivity: EPA's Implementation of TSCA," *Policy Studies Review* 4.3(1985): 501.

15 William Leiss, "Political Aspects of Environmental Issues," in William Leiss, ed., *Ecology versus Politics in Canada* (Toronto: University of Toronto Press, 1979), p. 264.

16 See T.J. Schrecker, *Political Economy of Environmental Hazards* (Ottawa: Law Reform Commission of Canada, 1984).

17 See Ulf Hjelmar, *The Political Practice of Environmental Organizations* (Aldershot, UK: Averbury, 1996).

Index

Aarhus Convention, 221
abatement, 93, 154–56
Aboriginal people (Australia), 241, 243–44, 247
absolute authority, 12, 20–21
absolutism, 102
academic-industrial interaction, 164, 262
acceptable risk. *See* risk-benefit analysis
access to information. *See* Aarhus Convention; information
"accord-style" of politics, 237
accountability, 221
acid rain, 154, 275–76
  Canada-US abatement initiatives, 156
  international action on, 153, 155
  media attention, 155
  political choices, 157–58
Ackerman, B.A., 86, 157
"action-oriented" research, 263
ad hoc projects and networks, 32, 263–65
Adelaide Advertiser, The, 246
administered systems. *See* administrative state
administrative decisions
  political and value-laden, 6, 18
administrative form, 20
"administrative man," 18
administrative mind, 101, 103–5, 108, 110, 112–15
  challenges to, 97, 111
  limits of, 214

technocratic version of, 99
traditional version of, 98–99
Administrative Procedures Act, 29
administrative process
  inadequacies, 291
administrative sphere, 98–108, 110, 112–15
administrative state, 3, 92, 99–102, 165, 173, 305, 313–18
  biases, 8
  epistemology, 84–85, 87
  green political theory on, 82
  J. Dryzek's criticism of, 83–86
  links with environmental degradation, 47–48
  participation in, 30
  priorities, 84
  public cynicism, 145, 149
  rationality, 8, 98, 180
  reforms, 81
  rise of, 14, 16
  as separate from politics, 6
  subverting, 53, 56
advanced industrial society, 103, 172, 177, 185
advocacy coalitions, 291
Africa, 133
African Development Bank, 279
agency, 263, 295
  in cultural transformation, 260
  in environmental politics, 258
Agenda 21, 192, 198, 221, 259, 267
  integration of environmental and development concerns, 201

local, 194, 197, 262–63
Norway's approach to, 193–96
agenda setting, 171–74, 179, 184
agricultural policy monopoly, 215
agriculture, 129
  ecological, 259
  organic agricultural networks,
    264
  organic farming, 161
Agriculture and Environment
  Biotechnology Commission
  (AEBC), 225–26
Agriculture Canada, 31
air pollution, 132, 174
Alaska, 32
Alaska Berger inquiry, 88–89, 91
Alaska Native Claims Settlement Act,
  88
Alberta, 34, 129
alternative dispute resolution, 52, 89
alternative pattern of development,
  107, 109
"amenity-driven growth," 132
American exceptionalism, xi, xii. *See
  also* U.S.
Amy, Douglas, 90
analytic-deliberative process, 77–78.
  See also deliberative democracy
Andrews, Richard, 28–29, 60
Annan, Kofi, 221
anthropocentric values, 20, 69, 180,
  290
anti-environmental backlash, 235,
  268
anti-globalization, 91, 272
anti-nuclear organizations, 88, 241
anti-toxics movement, 175, 178, 184
apocalypse, 106
Arabunna peoples, 244
Asian Development Bank, 279
assurances of safety, 164
Atlantic Canada, 129
attitudes, 195, 203

Australia, 32–33, 292
  anti-environmentalist stance, 235
  environmental policy, 225
  environmentalism, 237–38
  government-nuclear industry
    alliance, 245
  Howard, John, 238–39
  Kyoto Protocol, 235, 300
  land degradation, 293
  large-scale special inquiries, 33
  South Australia, 239, 249
Australian Conservation Foundation
  (ACF), 250
Australian Policy Handbook (Bridgeman), 253
Australian Workers Union, 243
Austria, 33, 303
authority, 14, 85
  absolute, 12, 20–21
  authoritarian state, 26
  "illusion of final authority," 110
  monarchical, 102
automobile use, 127
automotive industry, 128

Bacillus thuringienses, 161
Bangladesh, 133
Barcelona Convention, 282
bargaining, 51
Barnet, Richard J., 38–39
Bartlett, Robert V., ix
Basel Convention, 277, 279, 281–
  82
Baskerville, Gordon, 151
Beamish, Richard, 154
Beck, Ulrich, 93
  "risk society," 62
Beckett, Margaret, 226
Beierle, T., 247
Berger, Thomas R., 185
  Alaskan inquiry, 88–89, 91
  creation of public sphere, 32,
    88–89, 91–92

Mackenzie Valley Pipeline Inquiry,
    32, 88–89, 92
"best practices" codes, 278
Better Quality of Life, A, 219
biodiversity loss, 153, 275–76, 280,
    293
biological systems, 175
bioregionalists, 48
Biosafety Protocol, 279, 282
biotechnology, 158–59, 224
    ethical issues, 161–62
    genetic engineering, 61, 69, 224
    GM foods or organisms, 34,
        158–61, 163–64, 218, 225–27
    regulatory intervention, 162–63
    risks, 160–61
Blair Labour government, 213–14
Blueprint for Survival, 259, 290
Blundell, Tom, 226
bottom-up engagement, 263
Brazil, 273, 293
Bregnballe, Anne, 195–97
Brent Spar, 218
Bridgeman, P., 253
Britain. *See* United Kingdom
British Columbia, 34, 129, 131,
    134
    Campbell government, 127, 131
    conflicts between conservationists
        and resource industries, 127
    environmental protection policy
        shifts, 126–27
broad-based community coalitions,
    253
Brundtland Commission, 192, 194,
    198, 258, 292
budworm
    chemical pesticide spraying,
        149–50
    lessons about uncertainty, 151
    public controversy, 149–50
burden of proof, 179, 184, 322–
    23

bureaucracy, 7, 15, 101. *See also*
    administrative state; centralized
    hierarchy
    limitations, 85
    managed participation, 30
    positivist mode of thinking, 70
    rationality, 16, 49
bureaucratic/administrative ability
    (state), 299
"bureaucratic symbiosis," 17
bureaucratization, 8, 14, 16, 20, 84
    agenda of historical development,
        7
    of political parties, 36
Bush, George W., 268, 316
Bush administration, 135
    elite-driven economic growth,
        38
    implications for Canadian environ-
        mental policy, 129
business advocacy, 280–82
business as usual, 82, 200, 237. *See
    also* status quo
business management, 258

Cabinet Committee on the Environ-
    ment, 215
Cabinet-Sub-Committee of Green
    Ministers, 215
calculability, 17–19
Caldwell, Lynton, 28–29
California, 35
Campbell government. *See under*
    British Columbia
Canada, 125, 160, 277, 284, 292
    acid rain, 154, 156
    decision-making on nuclear safety,
        33
    deficit reduction, 126
    devolution of environmental
        responsibilities, 126
    environment assessment process,
        31, 33

on genetically modified food products, 159, 163
Green Plan, 126
growth of suburban municipalities,
135
Kyoto Protocol, 275
market-oriented policies, 130
multi-stakeholder sustainable
development committees, 36
public inquiries, 34
reliance on resource industries, 129
spatial segregation, 134
use of Royal Commissions, 32
Canada Metals plant, 147
Canada-US abatement initiatives on
acid rain, 156
Canada-US Air Quality Agreement,
156
Canada-US Free Trade Agreement
(FTA), 128
Canadian Biotechnology Advisory
Committee (CBAC), 160, 162, 164
Canadian Centre for Policy Alternatives, 131
Canadian Coalition on Acid Rain,
156
*Canadian Environmental Protection
Act*, 126
capacity building, 295, 303
Cape Breton, 149
capitalism, 92, 198
Capra, Fritiof, 266
Carson, Rachel, 175
on right-to-know, 34
Silent Spring, 29, 150
Castells, Manuel, 133
cause-effect relations, 148, 155
unintended consequences, 19
centralization and decentralization,
12, 321
need for new balance, 110
centralized authority, 14, 100–101,
320

centralized hierarchy, 15, 17, 20, 48.
See also administrative state;
bureaucracy
closed process of decision making,
7
conventionial bias favouring, 4–7,
12, 19
"necessity" of, 21
reducing, 52
Centre for Environmental Change at
Lancaster University, 267
Chain Reaction, 247
chaos. *See* disorder
Chemical Manufacturers Association's Responsible Care, 278
chemical pesticide spraying, 34, 110,
149, 151
cosmetic use, 31
human health threats, 150
non-target species, 150
chemicals and chemical manufacturing, 61, 242, 273
organic chemical pollutants, 132
Chernobyl, 33
China, 128, 293
chlorofluorocarbons(CFCs)
illegal trade in, 272, 279
phase-out, 276
choices, 162–64
Christoff, Peter, ix
citizen activism at municipal level,
31. *See also* direct action
citizen/consumer distinction, 136
citizen deliberation, 236. *See also*
deliberative decision making
citizen engagement, 136, 220, 225
institutionalization, 227
international promotion of, 221
citizens, 200, 203
and experts, 76–77, 195, 322,
325
informed, 8, 89
participation, 30, 332

"participatory expertise," 185
"strong citizens," 183
Citizens' Advisory Panels (CAPs), 242
citizens' forums, 246
citizens' juries, 89–90, 222–25, 246–49
citizenship
    association with deliberative democracy, 211
    instrumental conception of, 197
civil society, 103, 112, 259, 289, 294, 300
    environmental capacity, 301
    "global civil society," 281
    greening of, 306
clamshell packaging, 36
Clapp, Jennifer, ix
class differences, 127. See also poverty
    in exposure to environmental hazards, 132
    physical barriers, 134
Clean Air Act, 85
Clean Development Mechanism (CDM), 279
Clean Water Act, 85
Cleaner Production Roundtable, 268
climate action networks, 264
climate change, 153, 200, 280, 298, 303
Climate Change Convention, 282
    co-optation, 82, 115, 172, 228, 283, 305
    in mediation, 90
Coalition for Environmentally Responsible Economies' (CERES) Principles, 278
coercion, 27
collective decision making, 52
Commissioner for the Environment and Sustainable Development, 126

commodification, 131
    of animals, 161
common sense, 203
    in scientific practice, 178
"Common Sense Revolution," 126
Commoner, Barry, 85
Commonwealth Science Industry Research Organization (CSIRO), 239
communicative capacity (state), 296–97, 300
communicative rationality, 87–88
Community Consultative Forum (CCF), 243–44
community cooperation, 107
community-generated information, 249
community planning, 15
community right-to-know legislation, 34
compartmentalization, 109, 212, 214
complex interdependence, 181
complex system realities, 151–52
complexity, 164
    complex interdependence, 181
comprehensive systems, 177
Conca, Ken, 293
concensus, 116, 242, 267, 301
    by limiting stakeholders, 243
consensus conferences, 89, 222–25, 267
    genetic modification (GM) debate, 226-27
conservation, 28, 182, 318
Conservation Council of South Australia, 240, 242, 244, 247
Conservative government (Britain), 215
Construction Forestry Mining and Energy Union, 243
consultation process, 196
consumer/citizen distinction, 136, 196, 199

consumption, 195–96, 198, 203, 274,
   317
   both promoted and blamed, 204
   consumer culture, 200–201, 203
   two-vehicle households, 135
context, 105, 108, 110, 263
   of power, 113–15
continental economic integration,
   128–29
   effect on Canadian environmental
      protection, 130
contingencies, 18, 263
"contingency" approach to administration, 7
Convention on Biodiversity, 281
Convention on International Trade in
   Endangered Species (CITES), 277,
   279
coordination, 51
core executive, 213, 216, 219, 227
   steering environmental governance,
      215
corporate management, 62, 259
corporations
   partnerships with, 81
   rising power of, 36
   transnational (TNCs), 98, 101, 273,
      283
corporatist models of power, 237–
   38
corporatization of public services,
   292
cosmetic use of pesticides, 31
cosmos as mechanism, 100
Cossman, Brenda, 131
cost-benefit analysis, 59, 66, 86
Council for the Protection of Rural
   England, 267
"counter-publics," 98
Cox, Robert, 274
Cramer, Jacqueline, 266
"creative third alternatives," 48
crisis. See environmental crisis

critical public spheres, 98, 103,
   112–13
critical theorists, 84, 87–88
Crosby, Ned, 224
cross-sectoral and interdisciplinary
   approaches, 291, 294–95. See also
   hybrid identities
   social interfaces, 263
cultural/educational programs, 300
cultural rationality, 70–71
cultural tensions, 261–62
cultural transformation, 260
"cyborgs," 261

Daimler-Chrysler Corporation, 128
Damman, Erik, 201–2
David Suzuki Foundation, 136
Davis, G., 253
DDT, 132, 150
decentralization, 3, 5, 15, 19–20, 107,
   110
deep ecology, 48, 267
deliberation vs. representation, 225
deliberative decision making, 73,
   165, 235–36
deliberative democracy, 52–53,
   76–78, 82, 87, 246, 296, 305
   definitions, 209
   deliberative ideal, 216, 218
   educative power of, 223
   Environmental Audit Committee
      (EAC), 216–17
   epistemological defence, 210
   ethical defence, 210
   financial issues, 228
   in green political theory, 209–11
   institutional barriers, 216
   institutionalization, 53, 209–11
   public-spiritedness, 211
   stakeholder arrangements as,
      219
deliberative opinion polls, 89,
   222–23, 225

democracy, 3–4, 19–20, 28, 38, 56, 322. *See also* deliberative democracy
in age of environmental limits, 25
assumptions, 202–3
attack on, 201–2
blame for environmental problems, 198
as educational and mobilizing tool, 38
green, 82
impact of environmental movement, 26–37
indeterminacy, 92
liberal democracy, 37
participatory democracy, 78
R. Barnet on, 38
state-associated democratization, 53
supposed conflict with effective administration, 5
demos, 197, 202–3
Denmark, 226
anti-environmental backlash, 268–69
consensus conferences, 89, 224
"green guides" program, 264
public participation, 261–62
Department of Environment, Food, and Rural Affairs (DEFRA), 215
Department of Environment, Housing, and Aboriginal Affairs (DEHAA), 239
Department of Environment, Transport, and the Regions (DETR), 214
Department of Primary Industry (PIRSA), 239
Department of Transport (Britain), 213
depoliticization of environmental politics, 191–93, 197–98, 201–2, 204
deradicalization, 82
deregulation, 129–30

Descartes, René, 180
developing countries, 279–81
environmental standards, 273, 283
devolution, 126–27, 292
Dienel, Peter, 224
Diesing, Paul, 49
differentiation in government, 212, 298
direct action, 218, 324
discursive democracy, 52, 82–83, 87–88, 297
discursive designs, 53, 90, 93, 185, 296
challenge to dominant institutional forms, 92
in context, 91
need for distance from state, 90
discursive innovations, 97
institutionalization of, 111–12
discursive openings, 111–14, 116
legitimacy, 115
disorder, 5–6
dissident evironmentalism, 171, 173
dissident professionalism, 179, 184–85
domestic policies. *See* nation-level regulation
Doyle, Timothy, ix
Dryzek, John S., ix, 50–53, 55, 185, 228
Dubos, Rene, 259

Earth Day, 172–74, 182
Earth First!, 91
Eastern coal producers, 86, 90
Eckersley, Robyn, 211, 293, 304
eco-labeling, 278
ecocentric values, 290
"ecoefficiency," 199
ecofeminists, 48, 317
ecological consciousness, 181–82
ecological design networks, 264

ecological modernization, 84, 93–94,
    197, 258, 289, 291, 293
  strong ecological modernization,
    290, 294–96, 299–300, 304
  weak ecological modernization,
    290, 292–93, 304
ecological rationality, 48–51, 53–54,
    56, 182–83
ecological science, 236
ecological sensitivity, 107
ecological solutions, 252
Ecologist, The, 259, 290
ecology, 322
ecology and systems theory, 105, 181
economic capacity (state), 299
economic globalization. *See* global-
    ization
economic growth, 38, 290. *See also*
    progress
  at expense of environment, 27, 37
economic imperative, 93–94, 290
economic integration, 126. *See also*
    continental economic integration;
    globalization
economic rationality, 49
economic recession, 300
economic sphere, 289
environmental capacity, 301–2
  greening of, 306
Economist, The, 128
Ecuador, 273
efficiency, 49, 182
electronics, 273
employer-employee relations, 35
"end of the pipe," 174
energy
  conservation, 223
  crisis (1970s), 27
  efficiency, 259
  fossil fuels, 200, 298
  nuclear fuel, 33, 245, 254
  renewable, 223, 264
  wind, 268

Enlightenment *philosophes*, 102
environmental activism. *See* environ-
    mentalism
environmental administration, 64,
    157, 318–19, 321–24
  anti-technocratic, 321–23
  decentralized, 320–21
  early practices, 29
  flexible, 323
  isolation of, 298
  market punishment, 85–86
  open, 319–20
  troubling questions, 47
environmental appraisals (Britain),
    216
Environmental Audit Committee
    (EAC), 216–17, 227
environmental concerns
  compartmentalized, 214
  global, 153
  institutionalization, 173–74
environmental crisis, 14, 105–8,
    181–82, 202, 275, 315
  energy crisis (1970s), 27
  perception of, 15
Environmental Defense Fund, 36
environmental degradation, 27, 293
  causes, 59
  links to administrative state, 47–48
  poverty and, 273–74
  self-interest and, 211
environmental governance, 215
environmental hazards, 61–62. *See
    also* toxic waste
  cause-effect relations, 148, 155
  delayed effects, 157
  inadequate knowledge of, 65
  related to poverty, 132
  synergistic effect of, 61
environmental humility, 183
environmental impact assessment
    (EIA), 4, 31, 33, 49, 53–56, 59,
    108, 174, 185, 278

mandatory, 48
with mandatory public comment,
  82
significance and potential, 55
environmental issues of the 1970s,
  28
environmental justice, 133, 317
  movement, 94, 132
  networks, 264
environmental justice movement, 94,
  132
environmental justice networks, 264
environmental limits, 26
environmental management, 109,
  111, 280, 294
  technical language of, 59
environmental mediation, 52, 89, 111
  co-optation, 90
environmental movement. *See* environmentalism
environmental NGOs. *See* non-governmental organizations (NGOs)
environmental politics, 8, 78, 164,
  171, 258–59, 265, 313–18
  Australia, 235
  democratic participation, 39
  depoliticization of, 198
  global level, 320
  human agency, 269
  Norway, 191
  politics of expertise, 63, 65, 71, 75,
    184
  redefinition, 257
  transition, 260
environmental problematique, 48
environmental problems, 315
  administrative definition of, 108–9
  aftermath of industrialization, 5
  challenges to conventional admin-
    istration, 102
  complexity of, 314
  defined in isolation, 214
  generated by central hierarchies, 15

link with economic relationships,
  271–72
  redefinition, 110
environmental product policies, 266
environmental professionalism, 172
environmental protection, 125
  low priority, 7
  as public good, 131–32
  public participation, 30
  purchase of, 131–32, 137
  role of scientists and expertise,
    280, 282 (*See also* expertise; sci-
    ence)
  rolling back, 125, 127, 129–30
  standards, 107, 128, 272 (*See also*
    developing countries; pollution
    havens)
Environmental Protection Agency
  (EPA), 60, 66, 85–86, 174
environmental risk. *See* environmental hazards
environmental values/economic goals
  conflict, 84, 199
environmentalism, 4, 62, 103, 172,
  182, 257, 305. *See also* non-governmental organizations (NGOs)
  broad public interest, 317
  bypassing state, 238
  democratic opportunities, 28–29,
    37–38
  dissident, 171, 173
  end of democracy theory, 25–28
  environmental lobbies, 156
  grounding in social critique or
    political ideology, 72
  hostility to the state, 316
  institutionalization, 262
  left-right continuum, 317
  traditional political tactics, 59
epidemiology, 178–79, 184, 322
epistemology, 171–72, 178–79, 181,
  184
  challenge to scientism, 183

ethical issues, 165
  aesthetic and moral judgments, 181
  applied ethics, 152
  biotechnology, 161–62
  and investment, 302
European Commission, 258, 261
European Union, 261, 284, 292–93, 300
  public concern about GM crops, 34
Expert Panel on the Future of Food Biotechnology, 160, 162–64
expertise, 59, 103, 152, 176, 179
  barrier to popular participation, 68
expert administration as protector of public interest, 28
"expert" and "lay" knowledge divisions, 210
expert bias, 184–85
expert judgments, 64, 69
expert witnesses, 247
experts, 3, 16, 19, 145, 172–73, 180, 236, 271, 280, 282, 322
  conflicts among, 157, 249
  decision making, 64, 68–69
  facilitator role, 77
  supposed neutrality, 67
  insufficiency, 322
  politics of, 65, 71, 75
  uncertainty and unreliability, 149
extra-parliamentary dissent, 33
extractive industries, 235, 273, 278. See also resource industries

Fairfax, Sally, 30
"feedforward" mechanisms, 48, 55
feminists, 84, 88
  ecofeminists, 48, 317
Ferge, Zsuzsa, 137
Fifth Action Programme, 300
Fischer, Frank, x, 185, 253
Fishkin, James, 89, 223
"folk devils," 237
food biotechnology. See biotechnology

foot-and-mouth policy disaster, 215
foreign investment. See investment
forest industry, 127, 129, 278. See also budworm
  Australia, 235
  logging, 273
  management, 150–52
fossil fuels, 298. See also greenhouse gas emissions
  gasoline costs, 135
  Norway, 200
fragmentation. See differentiation in government
France, 33
franchise, 102
free marketeers, 84
free-riding, 210
free trade. See continental economic integration; globalization; international trade agreements
Friends of the Earth, 217, 242, 251–52
Fudge, Judy, 131
Future in Our Hands (grassroots movement), 201

"Gaia hypothesis," 181
gas masks, 131, 133
gated communities, 134
GEF. See Global Environment Facility
genetic engineering, 61, 69, 224
genetically modified (GM) foods and organisms, 158–64, 218
  British debate on, 225–27
  evaluative criteria, 164
  labelling, 34
  public concern, 159
  public concern in Europe, 34
  regulatory response, 162–63
geographical districts. See place
Germany, 94, 258, 292, 300, 303–4

Green Party, 36–37
  planning cells, 89, 224, 247
Gibbons, Michael, 265
Gibson, Robert B., x, 183
global corporations. *See* transnational
  corporations (TNCs)
global economic governance, 279
global economy, 133–34, 277
Global Environment Facility (GEF),
  279–80
global environmental concerns, 153,
  275
global environmental governance
  non-state actors, 280–83
  recent trends, 271
  role of states in, 277
  state capacity changes, 283
global warming, 275–76, 293, 298
globalization, 35, 37, 127–29, 271,
  273, 291–92
  effect on working class, 133
  effects on domestic class struc-
    tures, 137
  negative environmental conse-
    quences, 272, 277
  pollution havens, 292, 320
  relocation of manufacturing, 293
Goldrich, Daniel, 39
good life, 69
Goodin, Robert E., 82, 211
Gore, Al, 174
governance, 215, 289, 291, 293–94,
  301
  global environmental governance,
    271, 277, 280–83
  green governance, 289, 293, 300,
    303–4
  network governance, 291
  "new governance," 81
Governing Under Pressure (Richardson), 212
government to governance shift, 289,
  291, 293–94

Graham, Gary, 242
Great Artesian Basin, 241, 250–51
Great Lakes, 126
green anarchists, 48
green business, 268
green democracy, 82
Green Fund, 268
green governance. *See under* governance
"green guides" program, 264
green knowledge. *See under* knowledge
"green market," 294
Green Ministers, 215–16, 290–91
green parties, 36–37, 301, 303, 305,
  317
Green Plan (Mulroney government),
  126
green political theory
  deliberative democracy in, 209–11
"green product" innovations, 258–59
green public sphere, 82, 93–94, 98,
  103, 112
"green stamp," 243
green state, 296, 303, 306
"greenfield" manufacturing, 128
greenhouse gas emissions, 153, 298,
  303
  costs of limiting, 86
Greening of Industry Network (GIN),
  266
Greenpeace, 91, 217, 264
  alliance with developing countries,
    281
  direct action (Brent Spar), 218
greens, 69, 72. *See also* environmentalism
Grove-White, Robin, 267
GST (Goods and Services Tax), 130
guerilla theatre, 91
Guyana, 273

Habermas, Jürgen, 82, 87

Haraway, Donna
  "cyborgs," 261
Harris, Mike, 34, 127, 130, 316
  "Common Sense Revolution," 126
Harvey, Harold, 154
Hassler, W. T., 86, 157
Hawke, Bob, 237
Hays, Samuel, 172
hazardous wastes. *See* toxic waste
health care, 15
health effects, 32, 34, 134, 146, 148,
  150, 157, 200
Heilbroner, Robert, 25–27, 37
Hendriks, C., 246–47, 249
Hill, Robert, 241
Hobbes, Thomas, 3, 12–14, 17, 20–21
  Leviathan, 12
Holling, C.S., 152
"hollowing out of the state," 213, 300
Holmstrom, Nancy, 131, 133
House of Commons Select Commit-
  tee on Public Administration, 222
House of Lords Select Committee on
  Sustainable Development, 214
Howard, John, 238–39
Hughes, Vera, 252
Huisingh, Donald, 268
"human capital," 137
human limits, 315
human/nature relationship, 8, 69–70,
  180–81, 290
human rights, 299
hybrid identities, 258, 260–61,
  264–69
  consensus builders, 267
  interpreters, 267

implementation capacity (state),
  299–300
inclusion and exclusion, 137
Inco Ltd., 154–55, 157
independent and multi-stakeholder
  review bodies, 162

independent science, 238–40
  need for, 249–50, 252, 254
  state abandonment, 235–36, 240,
    242
India, 273, 293
individual, 14, 191–93, 195, 203
  blame for environmental problems,
    198, 200–202, 204
individualization, 131, 191–92, 204n2
industrial ecology, 259
industrial lobbies, 156
industrial society, 48, 191
  advanced, 103, 114, 171–72, 177,
    185
  transformed to risk society, 93
industrialization, 5, 8, 14, 16–17, 20,
  315
  environmental problems, 173, 183,
    274, 294
  fundamental flaw in, 105–6
  harmful effects, 60
  need for administrative state,
    99–101
industry, 128, 292
industry actors, 271
information, 147, 210, 297. *See also*
  knowledge
  access to, 115, 147, 221
  alternative, 249
  delivery of, 195
  as key resource, 114
  popular *vs.* scientific/technical,
    296–97
informed citizenry, 8, 89
Infralab (Netherlands), 264
insider politics, 237
institutional differentiation, 212,
  298
institutional innovation, 52, 303
institutionalization
  of discursive innovations, 111–12
  of discursive openings, 115
  environmental activism, 173

of environmental concerns,
173–74, 324
of substantive and procedural rationality, 53
instrumental rationality, 49, 84, 90
integrated adaptive management, 151
integration across policy issues, 215
integrative capacity (state), 297–98,
300
Inter-American Development Bank,
279
inter-ministerial councils, 291. *See
also* cross-sectoral and interdisciplinary approaches
interdependencies, 177, 180–81
intergovernmental organizations
(IGOs), 280–81
intergovernmental programs, 264
internal responsibility system, 34–
35
International Chamber of Commerce,
282
Business Charter for Sustainable
Development, 278
international environmental agreements, 271, 276–78, 281–82
trade restrictions, 279
International Organization for Standardization
ISO 14000 environmental management standards, 278, 283
international trade agreements, 128,
272, 320
environmental provisions, 130,
277–78, 283, 293
Inuit Circumpolar Conference, 91
investment
ecological parameters, 302
environmental standards and, 130,
273, 277, 283–84
ethical, 302
investor confidence, 82
NAFTA and, 302

issue attention cycle, 31, 214–15
"issue network," 212

Jamison, Andrew, x, 34
Janicke, Martin, 291, 295, 298, 300,
303
Japan, 284
Jasanoff, Sheila, 64–65
"joined up government," 291
Joint Waste Reduction Task Force
(1990-91), 36
Jordan, Grant, 212
judicial review, 64
justice, 158, 221
environmental, 94, 132–33, 317

Kakadu uranium mine, 243
Kann, Mark E., 37
Killarney Park, 154
Klüver, Lars, 267
knowledge, 5, 16, 85, 103, 321. *See
also* expertise; information
alignment with power, 3
alternative forms of knowing, 254
as consensually "accepted belief,"
74
green knowledge, 258, 261,
265–66, 268–69
inadequate, 254
local and traditional, 181
new forms of, 264
socio-cultural, 70–73, 178
Kokotha peoples, 244
Konisky, D., 247
Kuhn, Thomas, 265
Kyoto Protocol, 86, 235, 259, 275,
279, 300
Canadian \ratification of, 129

La Cloche mountain lakes, 154
labor, 101
labor unions, 238
Lafferty, William M., 303

laissez-faire, 100–101
land, 101
land degradation, 293, 303
Latin America, 128
Latour, Bruno, 260
Lauber, Volkmar, 37
lead poisoning, 146–49
legal powers (state), 299
legal rationality, 49
legitimacy, 84, 114–15, 200–201,
    209–10, 220, 298, 321
legitimation, 31
    of business as usual, 82
    crisis of the state, 93
Leiss, William, 182, 323
Leviathan, 3, 13, 15, 20, 314, 321,
    324
    as absolute authority, 12
    modern-day, 38
    obsolescence of, 21
    recourse to, 20
    resurrecting, 14
Leviathan (Hobbes), 12
"Leviathan or Oblivion?", 12
liberal democracy, 37, 81
Liberal government (Canada)
    deficit reduction, 126
Liberal view of the state, 316
"life-support value of ecosystems,"
    182
Limits to Growth, 259
Lindblom, Charles, 84, 128
Local *Agenda 21*, 194, 197, 262–63
local and grassroots NGOs, 281
local and traditional knowledge,
    181
local autonomy, 52
Lomborg, Bjorn, 268
London Dumping Convention, 281
Los Angeles, 132
Love Canal, 175, 178
Lovins, Amory, 175, 185, 266
low-wage regions, 128

Mackenzie Valley Pipeline Inquiry,
    32, 88–89, 92
    media coverage, 32
magus, 99
Majone, Giandomenico, 184–85
Malthusian dilemma, 26
managed participation, 30
management by objectives, 197
Mannheim, Karl, 258, 266
manufacturing. *See* industry
maquiladora plants, Mexico, 273
Marcuse, Herbert, 257
Maritime provinces
    acid rain, 155
market-based instruments, 101,
    291–92, 299
market economy, 92, 109, 127, 131,
    133, 236
    constraints, 90
    "discipline of the market," 129
market liberalism, 82
market or monopoly capitalism, 92
market-oriented environmental poli-
    cies, 258
market-oriented social policy, 130
market punishment, 85–86
market society, 200–201, 203
market solutions, 238, 294
marketization, 81
Marsh, David, 212–13
Marxism, 305
Matheny, Albert, 183
matrix organization, 85
McCloskey, Michael, 243
McConnell, Grant, 28–29
McDonald's Corporation, 36
Meacher, Michael, 224
Meadowcroft, James, 303
mechanistic world order, 180–81
media and media attention, 102, 200,
    281, 301
    acid rain, 155
    consensus conferences, 224

Mackenzie Valley Pipeline Inquiry, 32
Public Inquiry into Uranium, 254
Toronto lead smelters case, 146, 148
United Kingdom Round Table on Sustainable Development, 219
mediation, 260–61, 263
mega-ministries, 291
Merton, Robert, 265
meta-design and meta-policy, 51
Mexico, 128, 130, 273, 277
Mexico City's *colonias populares*, 133
Mildara Blass, 240
Miller, David, 210
Milne, K., 247
mining, 129, 235, 273, 278
Ministry of Agriculture, Fisheries and Food (MAFF), 213
"mobilization of bias," 114
mobilizing populations, 38
  as consumers not as citizens, 196
  educated and prosperous populations, 28
  techniques, 237, 243
"modern movement," 237
modern state. *See* state
money, 66, 101. *See also* poverty
Montreal Protocol, 276–77, 279, 282
moral persuasion, 51
"movement scientists," 59
Mulroney, Brian, 125, 130
Mulroney Green Plan, 126
multi-lateral environmental agreements (MEAs), 278
  WTO and, 283, 293
multi-methodical approach, 74–75
multi-stakeholder review bodies, 162
multi-stakeholder sustainable development committees, 36
multifactorial process, 303
multilateral development banks, 278

multiple use models, 242
municipalities
  fiscal squeeze, 127

NAFTA. *See* North American Free Trade Agreement
Narmada Valley dams, 273
Næss, Arne, 267
nation-level regulation, 292–93, 320
National Action Plan for Sustainable Development (Norway), 192, 196
National Biotechnology Strategy (Canada), 159
National Environmental Policy Act (NEPA), 4, 29–30
National Farmers' Union (NFU), 213
National Pollutant Release Inventory, 126
National Research Council (U.S.), 76–77
Native lands claims, 89
native vegetation, 239–40
Native Vegetation Assessment Branch of DEHAA, 239
natural laws, 102
natural order, 12, 100–101
The Natural Step, 267
nature, 19
  as free market, 238, 253
  as harmonious, 106
  human domination of, 8, 20, 69–70, 180, 290
  nature's interest, 211
  negative feedback, 51, 55
Nelkin, Dorothy, 33
neo-conservatism, 314, 316–17
neo-corporatism, 301, 303
Neo-Hobbesian conclusions, 38
neo-liberalism, 239, 291–93, 300, 304
neo-Malthusian, 38
"neo-Weberian model," 17–18

Netherlands, 33, 94, 224, 226, 258,
    263, 303–4
  public participation, 261–62
network governance, 291
"network society," 133
networks of environmental manage-
    ment, 262
New Brunswick forest industry,
    149–52
"new governance," 81
New Jersey
  right-to-know legislation, 34
New Perspectives Quarterly, 133
new social movements, 88, 91, 103
  public sphere created by, 92
New York, 134
New Zealand, 224, 292
Newfoundland, 149, 322
Nigeria, 273
"nightwatchman" state, 304
NIMBY syndrome, 4, 8, 61, 71,
    176–77, 318, 322
Noble, Charles, 35
non-expert opinion, 184
non-governmental organizations
    (NGOs), 201, 262, 271, 280, 284,
    296, 301, 303
  alliances with states, 281
  bureaucratization, 36
  incorporated into government's
    policy-making, 238
  local and grassroots, 281
  mainstream green, 237–38
  public education campaigns, 281
  public participation through, 36
  transformation, 262
non-state actors, 282, 293, 300
  co-optation, 283
  in global environmental gover-
    nance, 280–83
Noonan, David, 251
Nordskag, Morten, 193
"normal science," 265

normative indeterminacy, 75
norms of fairness and openness in
    communication, 115–16
North American Commission on the
    Environment, 277
North American Free Trade Agree-
    ment (NAFTA), 128
  environmental provisions, 130, 277
North Atlantic cod fishery, 129, 322
North Carolina, 128
Northwest Power Act (1980), 39
Norway, 267
  discrepancy between action and
    words, 193
  environmental policy programs,
    200
  environmental politics, 191, 193
  "environmentalist" nation, 192
  fossil fuels, 200
  Ministry of the Environment,
    192–93, 196–97, 200–201
  mobilizing the population, 194–95
  National Strategy for Sustainable
    Development, 192, 196,
    198–200
  non-governmental organizations,
    201
not-in-my-back-yard. *See* NIMBY
  syndrome
Nova Scotia, 149
nuclear fuel, 33, 245, 254
Nuclear Issues Coalition, 241, 245,
    247
nuclear power, 59, 61, 69, 185
  government subsidy of, 87
nuclear power plants, 33, 88
nuclear testing, 153

obedience, 13–14, 21
occupational health and safety, 15, 34
ocean pollution, 280
O'Connor, Dennis, 34
OECD, 193, 284, 292

Office of the Supervising Scientist (Environment Australia), 248
"official secrets," 16
oil extraction, 273, 278
Olympic Dam Community Consultative Forum, 243
Olympic Dam site, 242, 250
one-way "communication," 195
Only One Earth (Ward), 259
Ontario, 126, 130, 149, 316
  acid rain, 155
  effects of continental integration, 128
  environmental protection policy shifts, 126
  Harris government, 34, 126–27, 130, 316
  response to acid rain, 154–56
  rollback of environmental protection, 127
  Royal Commissions, 32
  voter orientations on environment, 135
Ontario Environment Ministry, 147–48
Ontario Ministry of the Environment, 155
Ontario Supreme Court, 147
Open Channels: Public Dialogue in Science and Technology, 222
Ophuls, William, 12, 25–27, 37
opinion polling, 221
order, 13–14, 20, 105–10
  faith in, 99
  generating disorder, 17, 19
organic agricultural networks, 264
organic chemical pollutants, 132
organic farming, 161
organicism, 181
Organization for Economic Co-operation and Development. *See* OECD
Our Common Future, 258
outsider politics, 237

ownership, 196–97
ozone depletion, 132, 153, 176, 275–76, 280

Paehlke, Robert, x, 53, 82, 296
Parliamentary Office of Science and Technology (Britain), 222, 226–27
participation, 15, 28, 196–97, 261
  citizen, 30, 322
  managed, 30
  necessary conditions for, 263
  popular, 68
  as voluntary acitivity, 260
participatory democracy, 78
"participatory expertise," 185
partnerships, 81, 194
Passmore, John, 26–27
peace groups, 88
peer review, 164
people's inquiries, 246–47, 249
persistent organic pollutants, 276
pesticides, 34, 110, 149–52
  budworm, 149–51
  DDT, 34, 150
  decision-making in Canada, 31
PESTO, 261–63, 267
Philippines, 273
Philips
  environmental product policy, 266
place and space, 137
  class inequalities, 134
  spatial segregation, 133–34
planning cells, 89, 224, 247. *See also* citizens' juries
pluralism, 7, 109, 218, 237–38
plurality, 114
policy communities, 212, 214, 291, 297
"policy cultures" or policy domains, 261, 299
"policy dialogue," 183

policy issues, 213
  cross-departmental relevance,
    212–13
  integration and dialogue across,
    215
policy making
  compartmentalization, 212
  cultural tensions, 261–62
  domination by business forces, 236
policy monopolies, 213, 215
policy networks, 212–14, 291,
    298–99, 301
  exclusionary character, 218
policy professionalism, 171–72,
    176–77, 179–84
  "objectivist ideal," 173
  supposed rationality, 182
political choice, 157
political conflict, 63
political dialogue, 196
political imperative, 290
political parties
  bureaucratization, 36
  green parties, 36–37, 301, 303,
    305, 317
political pressure, 65
political rationality, 49
politics/administration divide, 313
politics of expertise, 65, 71, 75, 184
politics of risk, 61
Pollack, Michael, 33
pollution, 107, 128, 272–73, 293
  ocean, 280
  smog, 157
  water, 174
pollution havens, 292, 320
Polonoreste Project, 273
polyarchy, 51
popular empowerment, 27
popular sovereignty, 3, 14, 21
popular vote, 134–35
population growth, 27
populism, 268

Porrit, Jonathan, 219
Port Hawkesbury pulp mill, 149
positivism, 70, 74
post-colonialism, 260
post-empiricist constructionism,
    74–75
"post-materialist" values, 317
poverty, 125, 131–32, 134. See also
    developing countries
  biotechnology and, 161
  environmental hazards related to,
    132
  relationship to environmental
    degradation, 273–74
power, 3, 133, 248
  balance between authorities and
    their subjects, 192
  context of, 113–15
  by hiding knowledge, 16
  and powerlessness within global
    economy, 134
pre-environmentalist assumptions,
    180
precautionary principle, 162, 165,
    276, 280, 294
  in face of uncertainty, 163
pressure groups, 212, 214, 216–17,
    220, 224
  internal democracy, 219
private bureaucracy, 17
private consultancy, 240
private investment, 127
privatization, 130–31, 133–35, 137,
    213, 292, 304
  discursive shift toward, 127
  of water testing, 34
problem definition, 104, 109–10, 112,
    171, 175–77, 179, 182, 184
problem redefinition, 113, 172, 175,
    179
procedural ecological rationality, 51,
    55
procedural rationality, 50

professionalism, 317, 324
progress, 7, 14, 20, 69, 93, 99,
    105–10, 171. *See also* economic
    growth
progressive environmental
    policy/economic decline correla-
    tion, 292–93
Progressive era (U.S.), 182
proof
    burden of, 179, 184, 322–23
    of harm, 147, 155
propaganda techniques, 102
ProSus (research group), 196–97
public choice, 152
    denial of, 161
public choice theory, 81–82, 85
public discourse, 185, 301
public good, 131–32, 211
public inquiries, 32, 52, 82, 88, 111,
    247
    Canada, 34
    Royal Commissions, 32, 221, 226–27
    Public Inquiry into Uranium, 235–37,
        239–40, 245–51, 253
    media coverage, 254
public interest, 28, 146
public opinion, 13–14, 102, 300
    informed, 8, 89
public participation, 3–5, 173,
    220–21, 261–62, 291, 296, 298.
    See also citizen engagement
    built into legislation, 31
    control by big companies, 242
    environmental protection, 30
    German Green Party, 37
    innovation in, 222–25
    instrumental terms, 196
Public Participation and Environmen-
    tal Science and Technology Policy
    Options. *See* PESTO
public policy, 75, 173
    conventional approaches to, 235
    whole-of-government, 298

public service, 238, 240
    attack on, 239
public spaces, 263
public sphere, 91–92, 102, 259, 297,
    305
public transportation, 39, 127, 134
purchase of environmental quality,
    131–32
Putnam, Robert, 267

Quebec, 34, 126, 149
    acid rain, 155
Quebec referendum (1995), 126
Quincy Library Group Forest Recov-
    ery and Economic Stability Act,
    242

"race to the bottom," 272, 292
radical environmentalists, 88
radioactive waste management, 224
rational management, 180
rationality, 14, 21, 49–50, 182
    communicative, 87–88
    ecological, 48–51, 53–54, 56,
        182–83
    economic, 49
    functional, 50
    functional ecological, 51, 53
rationality project, 235–36, 253
rationalization, 8, 14, 20, 101
    Weber on, 16
Reagan, Ronald, 316
Reagan administration
    on acid rain, 156
    effect on environmental concerns,
        31, 125
    treatment of EPA, 66, 86
recombinant DNA techniques,
    158–59
referenda, 33–35
reflexive modernity, 93
regulatory negotiation, 52, 89–90, 111
regulatory rollbacks, 135

Reich, Robert, 135
reification, 257
"relevant uncertainty", 181
renewable energy, 223
renewable energy networks, 264
research and development, 300
    "action-oriented" research, 263
resilience, 51
Resource Conservation and Recovery Act, 85
resource industries, 198
    lumber/environmental interest disputes, 127, 242
    scarcity, 126
    vulnerability to global competition, 129
resource management, 182, 253. *See also* forest industry
    U.S. style, 238
Resource Monitoring and Planning Pty Ltd., 252
Rhodes, Rod, 212–13
rich-to-poor-country waste trade, 281
Richardson, Jeremy, 212
right-to-know, 29, 34, 82, 183
right to refuse unsafe work, 35
Rio Earth Summit (1992), 193, 214, 221, 280, 282
risk assessment, 33, 59, 164
    blocking community interests, 68
    public distrust, 76
risk-benefit analysis, 60–63, 75, 78
    alternatives to, 73
    disputes between scientific camps, 66
    environmentalist criticisms of, 67–70
    normative dimensions, 77
    politicization of, 63
    value judgments, 162
"risk communication," 62
"risk society," 62, 93–94
Robert, Karl-Henrik, 267

robustness, 51
Rootes, Christopher, 261
round-table, 218–19, 253, 263
    community-based group participation, 244
    corporate controlled, 242–43
    U.S. model, 242
Roxby Action Collective (RAC), 251–52
Roxby Downs, 242, 245, 249
Roxby Downs Indenture Ratification Act, 241
Royal Commission on Electric Power Planning (Ontario), 32
Royal Commission on Environmental Pollution (Britain), 221, 226–27
Royal Commission on Matters of Health and Safety Arising from the Use of Asbestos (Ontario), 32
Royal Commission on the Northern Environment (Ontario), 32
Royal Society of Canada, 160, 162
Royal Society's Expert Panel. *See* Expert Panel on the Future of Food Biotechnology
Ruckelshaus, William, 60, 66

Sagoff, Mark, 136
San Francisco
    Green electoral breakthrough, 37
Saskatchewan, 34, 129
Scandinavia, 94, 258, 303
    acid rain, 153, 155
Schot, Johan, 266
Schrecker, Ted, x
science, 59, 72, 249, 315. *See also* expertise
    conflicts, 276
    as disinterested and objective, 63, 66
    ecological science, 236
    funding and political support, 239

independent, 235–36, 238–40, 242, 249–50, 252, 254
and power, 65
social construction, 178
Science, 30
"science policy paradigm," 64–65
scientific analysis, 60–61
scientific communities, 296
scientific expertise/politics conflicts, 59, 61. *See also* expertise
scientific indeterminacy, 63–65, 73–75, 78, 176, 276, 282
scientific proof, 276
scientific research
financial backers and, 66
as value-neutral, 69, 71
scientism, 180–81, 183–85
"search for safety," 61
"the secession of the successful," 135
Secrett, Charles, 225
Select Committee on Public Administration, 227–28
Select Senate Committee into Uranium Mining and Milling, 241, 245, 247–49
self-interest, 89, 200
self-sufficiency, 52
September 11, 2001, 203
Sequoia National Park, 136
service delivery, 5, 15, 81, 85
Setting Environmental Standards, 221
Shiva, Vandana, 266
shrimp-sea turtle decision, 278
Sierra Club, 243
Sierra Legal Defence Fund, 136
Silent Spring (Carson), 29, 150
Simon, Herbert, 18
Simpson Desert Regional Reserve Ten Year Review, 252
Sizewell Public Inquiry, 247
small farmers, 161
small-scale projects, 107
Smith, Graham, x

smog, 157
social capital, 267
human capital, 137
social choice mechanisms, 51–52, 54–56
experimentation with, 53
social impact assessments, 48, 108, 185
social movements, 259
influence from a distance, 88
new, 88, 91–92, 103
social rationality, 49
socio-cultural knowledge, 70–73
South Africa, 128
South Asia, 128
South Australia, 239
water depletion, 249
spruce budworm. *See* budworm
St. Lawrence River, 126
stakeholders, 243, 248
"stakeholder" dialogue, 263
stakeholder philosophy, 218–19
state, 13–14, 100, 102, 295
bypassing, 238, 243
effect of transnational networks, 292
as essential, 289
greater involvement, 293
"hollowing out of the state," 213, 300
internationalization, 274
Liberal view of, 316
resource management role, 253
retreat from responsibilities, 239
role of government, 131
transformation, 92–93
"wishing away of the state," 305
state capacity, 289, 296–300, 303–5
"state-centric" view, 291
state failure, 289, 291, 293–94, 296
state incapacity
global environmental problems, 271–72, 274–76

state/industry relations, 294
state/society relations, 294
statistical analysis, 67, 75
status quo, 53, 67, 90, 92, 193, 199,
    203
steering. *See* strategic capacity (state)
Stockholm Convention on Persistent
    Organic Pollutants, 279–81
Stoker, Gerry, 213
Stone, Deborah, 235
strategic capacity (state), 297, 300
Straume, Ingerid S., x
"strong citizens," 183
strong ecological modernization, 290,
    294–96, 299, 304
    cognitive/informational underpin-
        nings, 300
structural change, 202–3
structural individualization, 191–92
subpolitics, 93
substantive ecological rationality, 51,
    55–56
"substantive equivalence," 164
substantive rationality, 50
suburban sprawl, 127, 135–36
"subversive" science of ecology (eco-
    logical science), 237
Sudbury, Ont., 153
sustainable development, 36, 84,
    192–95, 197, 201, 214–15, 217–18,
    257–64, 267–68
    agriculture, 215
    cultural significance, 265
    and multiple use, 237–38
    retreat from, 125, 292
    strategies, 126
    of technology, 259
    as win-win ecomodernist reform,
        198
Sustainable Development Commis-
    sion (SDC), 219–20, 227
Sustainable Development Unit
    (SDU), 216

Sustainable Local Communities (pilot
    project), 194–96
Sustainable Technology Program
    (Netherlands), 263
Sweden, 33, 303–4
    acid rain, 153
    public participation, 261–62
    referendum on nuclear power, 36
Swinton, Katherine, 35
Switzerland, 33
systems approach, 17, 19, 105, 181

tax cuts, 126–27, 135
Taylor, Serge, 55
TEA, 261–63
technical rationality, 49
techno-industrial world, 62, 69
    bias favouring, 67
    challenge to, 70
    value assumptions, 69
technocracy, 72, 323
technocratic approach, 17–18, 59, 78
technocratic management, 105–6
technological assessments, 59
technological risk, 59, 61–62
technology, 59, 61, 101, 105, 133,
    315
    "appropriate," 107
    "cleaner," 258
    post-industrial, 5
technology assessments, 48, 108, 185
    participatory, 267
Tensions of Europe (network), 266
Tesh, Sylvia, 178–79, 184
Texaco, 242
Texas, 90
    deliberative opinion polls, 223
Thatcher, Margaret, 128, 236
thinking in another direction, 109–12
"third space," 260
Three Mile Island, 33
Time, 125
top-down initiative, 263

Torgerson, Douglas, x, 56, 82, 296
Toronto
  cosmetic use of pesticides, 31
  lead smelters case, 146–49
Toronto Board of Health, 148
toxic waste, 61, 171, 174–75,
  182–83, 273
  costs borne by producers, 178
  export, 272
  fixation on disposal, 175–77
  managing of, 126
  past mistakes, 176
  public policy agenda, 176
  radioactive waste, 224
  reduce, reuse, recycle, 175–77
  trade in, 275, 279
toxicology, 322
trade in ivory, 272, 279
Trans-Alaska Pipeline, 4
"trans-scientific" issues, 183
Transformation of Environmental
  Activism. See TEA
"transgovernmentalism," 81
transnational corporations (TNCs),
  98, 101, 283
  investment in environmentally
    damaging industries, 273
transnational political economy, 81
transparency, 164, 183, 221
transportation, 104, 110, 258, 264,
  319–20
  automoblie use, 127
  public, 39, 127, 134
  trade related, 200, 272
Tribe, Laurence, 173
Trist, Eric, 18–19
tuna-dolphin decision, 278
"twin-track" strategy
  environmental pressure groups,
    217
two-vehicle households, 135

UK. See United Kingdom

UN Conference on Environment and
  Development, 259, 292
UN Conference on the Human Environment, 153, 259
UN Environment Programme
  (UNEP), 280–81
uncertainty, 70, 145–46, 148, 154,
  161–62, 164. See also scientific
  indeterminacy
  about ecological and human health
    effects, 157
  about governments as defenders of
    public health, 146
  necessary link with choice, 163
  pervasive, 165
  "relevant uncertainty", 181
Unilever, 266
United Kingdom, 32, 147, 224, 258,
  292
  acid rain, 153–55
  agricultural policy monopoly, 215
  British Road Federation, 213
  citizens' juries, 89–90, 224–25,
    247
  deliberative democracy, 209–28
  Department of Transport, 213
  environmental policy process,
    211
  environmental pressure groups,
    217–20
  House of Commons Select Com-
    mittee on Public Administration,
    222
  House of Lords Select Committee
    on Sustainable Development,
    214
  Labour Government, 216
  large-scale special inquiries, 33
  policy process, 212–13
  public participation, 261–62
  stakeholder philosophy, 218
  sustainable development strategies,
    213–14, 218–19

United Kingdom National Concensus
    Conference (UKNCC), 224
United Kingdom Round Table on
    Sustainable Development, 218–19
United Nations Economic Commis-
    sion for Europe (UNECE), 221
uranium industry, 32–33, 235,
    240–45, 254
    water use, 249
urban sprawl, 127, 135–36
Uruguay Round, 272
U.S., 31, 60, 125, 130, 243, 276–77,
    284, 292
    acid rain, 155, 157
    Administrative Procedures Act, 29
    American exceptionalism, xi, xii,
        94, 129
    anti-environmental backlash, 268
    Bush administration, 38, 129, 135,
        268, 316
    citizens' juries, 223–24
    decision-making on nuclear safety,
        33
    decline of employment in manufac-
        turing, 133
    deliberative opinion polls, 89
    deregulation, 129
    environmental justice movement,
        94, 132
    environmental mediation, 89
    Environmental Protection Agency,
        85–86
    Kyoto Protocol, 275
    legislation on toxic waste manage-
        ment, 174
    National Environmental Policy Act
        (NEPA), 4, 29–30
    Progressive era, 182
    Reagan administration, 31, 66, 86,
        125, 156, 316
    rejection of Kyoto protocol, 129
    voter orientation on environment,
        135

U.S. Industrial Biotest (IBT) scan-
    dals, 31
U.S. review of advances in under-
    standing acid rain (2001), 154
US *Clean Air Act*, 156–57

Veblen, Thorstein, 313
"virtuous" production, 302
voluntary agreements, 278, 292
voter orientations on environment,
    135. *See also* popular vote
voting with their feet, 133

Walkerton, Ont., 32, 34, 316
Walsh, Stephen, 244
Wandesforde-Smith, Geoffrey, 54
Ward, Barbara, 259
Warner, Stuart, 154
Warren, Mark, 220
waste management, 110, 196. *See
    also* toxic waste
water
    Great Lakes Basin, 126
    pollution issues, 174
    uranium mining, 241, 249–51
water and sewage treatment plants
    devolution to municipalities, 127
weak ecological modernization, 290,
    292–93, 304
Weale, Albert, 294
Weber, Max, 7, 14–18, 20, 30, 36, 49,
    84, 180
Weidner, Helmut, 291–92, 303
welfare state, 91, 291
welfare state, environmental, 304
West Germany, 33
Western Mining Corporation (WMC),
    241–46, 249–50, 254
Whitlam Labor government, 237
Williams, Bruce, 183
Williams, Raymond, 268
win-win principle, 198–99, 242, 253
wind energy, 268

Winner, Langdon, 67–69
wise use, 238, 242–43, 253
"wishing away of the state," 305
Woodhouse, William J., 322
working class. *See also* class differ-
    ences
    impact of trade liberalization, 133
    low-wage insecure jobs, 133
    low-wage regions, 128
    public sphere, 91
World Bank, 273, 279, 284
    environmental impact assessments,
    278
World Business Council for Sustain-
    able Development, 264
World Commission on Environment
    and Development. *See* Brundtland
    Commission

World Health Organization, 146
World Resources Institute, 36
World Summit for Sustainable Devel-
    opment in Johannesburg, 198
World Trade Organization (WTO),
    272, 320
    Committee on Trade and Environ-
    ment, 278, 283, 293
World Wide Fund for Nature, 243
World Wildlife Fund, 264
"worm in the brain" strategies, 48,
    54, 174, 185
Wuppertal Institute, Germany, 260
Wyller, T.C., 202

Yearley, Stephen, 193–94
Y2Y (wildland corridor from Yellow-
    stone to Yukon), 132